UNDERSTANDING ECONOMIC BEHAVIOUR

THEORY AND DECISION LIBRARY

General Editors: W. Leinfellner and G. Eberlein

Series A: Philosophy and Methodology of the Social Sciences
Editors: W. Leinfellner (Technical University of Vienna)
G. Eberlein (Technical University of Munich)

Series B: Mathematical and Statistical Methods
Editor: H. Skala (University of Paderborn)

Series C: Game Theory, Mathematical Programming and
Operations Research
Editor: S. H. Tijs (University of Nijmegen)

Series D: System Theory, Knowledge Engineering and Problem
Solving
Editor: W. Janko (University of Economics, Vienna)

SERIES A: PHILOSOPHY AND METHODOLOGY OF THE SOCIAL SCIENCES

Volume 11

Editors: W. Leinfellner (Technical University of Vienna)
G. Eberlein (Technical University of Munich)

Scope

This series deals with the foundations, the general methodology and the criteria, goals and purpose of the social sciences. The emphasis in the new Series A will be on well-argued, thoroughly analytical rather than advanced mathematical treatments. In this context, particular attention will be paid to game and decision theory and general philosophical topics from mathematics, psychology and economics, such as game theory, voting and welfare theory, with applications to political science, sociology, law and ethics.

For a list of titles published in this series, see final page.

UNDERSTANDING ECONOMIC BEHAVIOUR

edited by

KLAUS G. GRUNERT and **FOLKE ÖLANDER**

The Aarhus School of Business, Denmark

KLUWER ACADEMIC PUBLISHERS

DORDRECHT / BOSTON / LONDON

Library of Congress Cataloging in Publication Data

Understanding economic behaviour / edited by Klaus G. Grunert and
  Folke Ölander.
        p.   cm. -- (Theory and decision library. Series A, Philosophy
  and methodology of the social sciences)
     A selection of rev. papers originally presented at a conference
  which was held by the International Association for Research in
  Economic Psychology in Ebeltoft, Denmark in 1987.
     Includes bibliographical references.
     ISBN 0-7923-0482-9 (U.S.)
     1. Economics--Psychological aspects--Congresses.. 2. Decision
  -making--Congresses. 3. Consumer behavior--Congresses.
  I. Grunert, Klaus G., 1953-   . II. Ölander, Folke, 1935-   .
  III. International Association for Research in Economic Psychology.
  IV. Title: Understanding economic behavior. V. Series.
  HB74.P8U53   1989
  330'.01'9--dc20   89-38684

ISBN 0-7923-0482-9

Published by Kluwer Academic Publishers,
P.O. Box 17, 3300 AA Dordrecht, The Netherlands.

Kluwer Academic Publishers incorporates
the publishing programmes of
D. Reidel, Martinus Nijhoff, Dr W. Junk and MTP Press.

Sold and distributed in the U.S.A. and Canada
by Kluwer Academic Publishers,
101 Philip Drive, Norwell, MA 02061, U.S.A.

In all other countries, sold and distributed
by Kluwer Academic Publishers Group,
P.O. Box 322, 3300 AH Dordrecht, The Netherlands.

Printed on acid-free paper

Printed in The Netherlands

Table of Contents

Klaus G. Grunert and Folke Ölander

Introduction to the Volume

Contrary to what a layman might think, economics is not the only scientific discipline concerned with "understanding economic behaviour" – other disciplines like psychology, business administration, sociology, or anthropology are likewise concerned with this type of human behaviour. While the object of inquiry is, at least at a sufficiently abstract level, the same, the disciplines differ in the research paradigm that they use in studying it, and hence each can make its unique contribution.

This volume contains research from *economic psychology*. The psychological view of the study of economic behaviour is distinct from the other views, notably that of economics, with regard to the basic kinds of research questions that are investigated, with regard to basic theoretical assumptions, and with regard to the research methods used.

The *research questions* investigated are always concerned with *individual behaviour*. After all, psychology *is* the science of individual human behaviour. Economic behaviour is thus always viewed from the standpoint of individual actors. Macroeconomic phenomena are analysed, of course, but only to the extent that they influence individual behaviour, or that individual behaviour impacts macroeconomic phenomena. While there is thus some structural similarity between economic psychology and microeconomics, there is nothing like an economic macropsychology.

The basic *theoretical assumption* in economic psychology is that human behaviour is governed by how the world is *perceived*, and not by how it actually stands. To illustrate this distinction it is not necessary to go into the involved question of whether there is any objective world at all. The distinction is more simple: it is not the actual, but the perceived rate of inflation, rate of economic growth, etc., that determines people's economic behaviour. This allows for the fact that the data generated in one's environment becomes distorted under perception, which in turn

1

may be related to another basic assumption in economic psychology: that the human capacity to process information from the environment is limited, and that the kind of optimal use of that information postulated in many economic theories is therefore not possible.

The *research methods* used are mainly geared towards *empirical research*, and there mostly towards survey research and experimentation. Experimentation involves most often simulated behaviour in a laboratory, which allows the experimental manipulation of possible causes of behaviour which would not be possible in real life. Survey research is the most widely used instrument for investigating real-world behaviour, with all its caveats about establishing causal explanations.

Several introductory books (e.g., Furnham & Lewis, 1986; Lea, Tarpy, & Webley, 1987; van Raaij, van Veldhoven, & Wärneryd, 1988) and articles (e.g., van Raaij, 1979; Wiswede, 1988) have appeared recently, which try to give an overview of the field of economic psychology, and which, in varying degrees, demonstrate the three foundations of economic psychology just mentioned. Others have concentrated on certain subtopics, such as the psychology of the labour market (e.g., Baxter, 1988; Pelzmann, 1986). There is, however, in our opinion, a need for a volume that draws together some of the newest and best research in all areas of economic psychology, such that the reader sees both the common foundations of that research, as mentioned above, some current trends in that research, and also the fascinating diversity of topics investigated. This is what this volume intends to accomplish.

The three basic characteristics of economic psychology are apparent in the collection of 22 papers that follows. All of them are concerned with *individual behaviour*, also those concerned with what would generally be termed macroeconomic phenomena. Economic growth (Veenhoven), unemployment (Lunt), and inflation (Hudson; Batchelor & Jonung) are, for example, all analysed from the individual actor's viewpoint. Likewise, the *perception* of economic phenomena is at the centre of many articles. Especially good examples for this are Wahlund's paper on the perception of tax rate changes, showing that such changes may in fact not be perceived at all, or the paper by Lassarre and Roland-Levy, looking at the way children form opinions on how economic phenomena are related. Witt, in the final paper of the volume, gives a general treatment on the problem of subjectivism in economics. Finally, the great majority of the papers in this volume are *empirical,* and two of them are experimental:

Robben et al. present an innovative approach to the study of tax evasion, which presents formidable methodological problems when done in a field setting, and Hursh et al. show in which ingenious ways psychological experimentation can be brought to bear on economic behaviour: they show that animal experimentation can be a useful tool for studying basic economic phenomena like the price elasticity of demand.

But in addition to demonstrating these basic characteristics of economic psychology, this collection of papers also shows the main trends occurring in that area right now. The grouping of the papers mirrors these trends.

The first group of papers (Veenhoven, Gärling et al., Davidsson, and Helman et al.), on *Economic Factors and Individual Satisfaction,* are all concerned with the relationship between economic factors and personal well-being. In economics, the question of personal well-being has been (and still is) well-hidden behind the notion of *utility,* but psychology too has only recently begun to address the question of overall life satisfaction. The papers in this section give an indication of how research on the economic determinants of life satisfaction has progressed.

The second group of papers (Hudson, Batchelor & Jonung, Lunt, Robben et al., and Wahlund) is on *Inflation, Unemployment, and Taxation* and demonstrate the increasing concern of economic psychologists with macroeconomic phenomena. The special virtue of these papers in demonstrating the importance of perception as a process intervening between economic phenomena and human behaviour has already been mentioned.

The notion of *utility,* which was relevant in the first group of papers, is taken up again in the third section on *Utility and Decision Theory* (papers by Madsen, Bolle, K.G. Grunert, Sokolowska, Munera, and Uusitalo), albeit from a different perspective: not general welfare, but the individual welfare or satisfaction associated with some specific behaviour, which can be interpreted as a choice between alternatives, is in question. Decision-making is obviously a core economic activity, and its analysis is of long standing in economic psychology. The papers in this section show a major trend in that area, namely away from decision-models oriented only towards narrowly defined and well-structured problems, and towards the integration of such small-scale theories into higher-order theories which cover a broader range of economic decision-making.

3

Just like decision-making, *Consumer Behaviour* (papers by Wikström et al., S.C. Grunert, Lassnigg, Lassarre & Roland-Levy, and Wosinski) has been a traditional topic in economic psychology. One might even argue that consumer buying decisions have constituted a major part of the decisions that have been studied by economic psychologists, and hence the two groups are not really distinct. The trend here is, however, an increased interest in those aspects of consumer behaviour which are not concerned with the choice between brands - a trend clearly mirrored in this selection.

In the final section, *New Views on Economic Analysis*, two papers already mentioned (Hursh et al., Witt) come back to some of the basic characteristics of research in economic psychology: a subjectivist approach, and rigorous experimental research.

This volume developed out of a conference which the *International Association for Research in Economic Psychology (IAREP)* held in Ebeltoft, Denmark, in 1987. The papers in this volume were hand-picked from the presentations at that conference, and many of them have been substantially revised. We would like to thank all authors for their patient collaboration. Thanks are also due to Werner Leinfellner, series editor of the *Theory and Decision Library,* who suggested the publication of this volume and endorsed its inclusion in this series. The Danish Social Science Research Council and the Aarhus School of Business provided financial support for the preparation of this volume. Margaret E. Clark scrutinized the authors' English in a very painstaking fashion. Finally, Mariann Holmslykke did a superb job in handling all the technical matters involved in the production of the volume.

References

Baxter, J.L. (1988). *Social and psychological foundations of economic analysis*. Hemel Hempstead: Harvester-Wheatsheaf.

Furnham, A., & Lewis, A. (1986). *The economic mind: The social psychology of economic behaviour*. Brighton: Wheatsheaf.

Lea, S. E.G., Tarpy, R. N., & Webley, P. (1987). *The individual in the economy: A textbook of economic psychology*. Cambridge: Cambridge University Press.

Pelzmann, L. (1985). *Wirtschaftspsychologie*. Vienna: Springer.

van Raaij, W. F. (1981). Economic psychology. *Journal of Economic Psychology, 1*, 1-24.

van Raaij, W. F., van Veldhoven, G. M., & Wärneryd, K.-E. (Eds.) (1988). *Handbook of economic psychology*. Amsterdam: Dordrecht: Kluwer.

Wiswede, G. (1988). Ökonomische Psychologie - Psychologische Ökonomie. *Zeitschrift für Wirtschafts- und Sozialwissenschaften, 108*, 503-592.

Part I

Economic Factors and Individual Satisfaction

Ruut Veenhoven
National Wealth and Individual Happiness

Tommy Gärling et al.
Beliefs about Attainment of Life Satisfaction as
Determinants of Preferences for Everyday Activities

Per Davidsson
Need for Achievement and Entrepreneurial Activity in
Small Firms

Amir Helman et al.
The Kibbutz and Private Property

Ruut Veenhoven

National Wealth and Individual Happiness

Abstract

Easterlin has argued that national economic prosperity is of no consequence for the individual's appreciation of life. He contends that people in poor countries are as happy as those of rich welfare states, and that decades of economic growth have left people no happier than before. This paper attacks these empirical claims, as well as the underlying theory that happiness depends largely on social comparison.

Cross-national comparison shows that people in the poorest countries of the world are actually the least happy. This appears both in a re-analysis of Easterlin's own data and also in a new, more representative sample of countries. In fact, a curvilinear pattern emerges, indicating that wealth is subject to the law of diminishing utility.

Comparison over time in Western Europe shows that the post-war economic recovery was paralleled by an increase in happiness. The slower rate of growth during the last decade has not been accompanied by a definite rise in happiness, though fluctuations in happiness have tended to follow economic ups and downs with a year's delay.

It is argued that social comparison theory cannot explain these results.

This paper was prepared during a stay at Mannheim University, SFB 3, West Germany, in June 1987.

Author's address: Ruut Veenhoven, Erasmus University Rotterdam, Faculty of the Social Sciences, P.O. Box 1738, NL-3000 DR Rotterdam, The Netherlands.

Introduction

This paper asks whether the economic prosperity of a nation contributes to the happiness of its citizens. Happiness or life satisfaction is the degree to which an individual evaluates the overall quality of his life-as-a-whole positively (Veenhoven, 1984, Ch.1). The question about the relationship between prosperity and happiness is the subject of a long-standing debate. Arguments in favour of an affirmative answer are, among others, that wealth reduces suffering from hunger and illness to a great extent, softens inequalities, and opens the way to new satisfactions, not only in the sphere of leisure and consumption, but also in the realm of arts, science, and spiritual life. Arguments to the contrary claim that affluence undermines moral consciousness and social networks, and that material comforts do not provide real satisfaction, while their production involves considerable alienation.

This discussion is not merely academic. It is of considerable consequence for economic policy making, in particular for the priority awarded to economic growth. Economic growth is a main goal of modern nations. Rational policy making requires not only finding the best means for reaching major goals, but also a systematic surveillance of these goals themselves, in order to detect inherent incompatibilities.

In spite of its long duration and its political relevance, the debate about the happiness revenues of economic growth has remained inconclusive. Plausible speculations have been advanced on both sides, and there is empirical proof of some costs as well as of various benefits. Yet the relative weights of these costs and benefits are unclear. Consequently, the net effect on happiness is unclear as well. Lacking anchorage in solid facts, the dominant opinion has drifted with the tide of ideology.

Hence a reconsideration of the matter is due. To that end I will first review current research on the matter and then report new data derived from a secondary analysis of two cross-cultural studies.

Current Views

The favourable view of economic expansion dominated during the nineteen-fifties. The scars of the Great Depression and World War II were still being felt at that time, and it was widely believed that improvement of the material standard of living would open the way to a better life. Hence nobody was surprised when, in the early sixties, an American psychologist reported that inhabitants of rich countries found more pleasure in life than people in poor countries. This psychologist was Headly Cantril.

Cantril's View of Positive Effects

In his famous *Patterns of Human Concern,* Cantril reported on a first worldwide survey study. This study involved interviews with representative samples of the population in 14 countries selected to represent differences in economic development. Interviews took place in 1960. In all countries happiness was assessed by means of an ingenious interview technique.[1] He found reported life satisfaction to be higher in the economically most developed countries: The rank correlation between average life satisfaction and his index of economic development was +.67 (Cantril, 1965, pp. 193-195).

Cantril suggested two reasons for this statistical relationship. Firstly, citizens in the poor countries would be "objectively deprived," their economic system failing to provide minimal necessities. Secondly, inhabitants of the poor countries would also be the victim of "subjective deprivation": the awareness that life is better in the rich world, lowering the appreciation of their own.

Easterlin's Claim That Wealth Does Not Buy Happiness

In the late sixties the ideological tide changed. The newly emerged Consumption Society came under fire. The satisfactions of mass consumption were discounted as "false happiness." "Real" satisfactions were projected in inner self-actualization and social utopias. In this climate of opinion an article by Ronald Easterlin with the title: "Does money buy happiness?" (Easterlin, 1973; expanded in Easterlin, 1974) received much attention .

Easterlin had re-examined Cantril's data. Instead of Cantril's multiple index of economic development he considered GNP per head only. He found the differences in life satisfaction between rich and poor countries rather small and not quite consistent (1974, p. 106). In a different set of nine countries he failed to find any strong relationship either (p. 107). Easterlin also made comparisons over time. He examined whether the post-war economic upsurge in the USA had resulted in a greater satisfaction with life. He found no effect at all. In spite of a doubling of the national income between 1945 and 1970, Americans had remained equally happy (p. 109). Yet people appeared not insensitive to the riches, surveys in various countries showing more life satisfaction in the high income brackets than in the low ones (pp. 99-104).

On the basis of these observations Easterlin concluded that happiness is essentially relative. The enjoyment of life does not depend on the actual quality of living conditions, but rather on the degree to which one considers oneself better off than others, one's compatriots in particular. Easterlin illustrated this point with the analogy of "height." A European of one and a half meters will currently consider himself to be "short," even though this size was quite respectable in the Middle Ages and is considered tall among the Pygmies (pp. 116-118). This view has been corroborated in various studies in related fields. Experiments by van Praag and Kapteyn (1973) showed, for instance, that salary increases tend to inflate aspirations and therefore do not have a lasting effect on income satisfaction, while Brickman, Coates, and Janoff-Bulman (1978) demonstrated that lottery winners are no happier than average, and permanently injured accident victims not noticeably unhappier.

Zolatas' View of Declining Welfare Effects

The "Limits to Growth" movement that emerged in the early seventies called attention to various "costs" of affluence. The **costs of mass consumption** were vividly sketched by Hirsch (1976), in particular the negative effects of increased car-ownership. In his opinion individuals gain little because they must pay high road taxes but still get stuck during rush hours, yet they cannot revert to a deteriorated public transport system. At the collective level mass ownership of cars has devastating consequences in terms of traffic accidents, pollution, and loss of scenery. Scitovsky (1976) emphasized the **costs of mass production.** Not only is the required assembly-line work alienating for the workers, but its products do not provide consumers with much pleasure either. Consumption goods produced in our economy provide sullen "comfort" rather than "stimulation." The development of mass persuasion techniques will nevertheless make people buy and will, in fact, create unappeasable "false" wants. More recently, the **costs of collective welfare** came to be recognized. State-provided health care and social security tend to dissolve informal social networks, the family in particular. This leads us into loneliness and makes us vulnerable to the cuts in social security that are inevitable when the system renders itself unpayable.

In his book *Economic Growth and Declining Social Welfare*, Xenophon Zolatas (1981) reviewed these arguments and considered their implications for societies at different stages of economic development. He believes that the richer the country, the more likely it is that the costs of economic growth outweigh its benefits. Thus he comes to suggest a curvilinear pattern, depicting a declining yield of economic growth which may even turn to the negative.

Zolatas does not focus on life satisfaction, but speaks more broadly about "quality of life" and "social welfare." Nor does he provide empirical data on the relationship between individual happiness and national economic prosperity. Yet his view is obviously of interest for the – more focussed – discussion at hand here.

Predicted Effects of National Economic Wealth and Growth on Individual Happiness

The three views just outlined predict different configurations of happiness and wealth which are shown in Figure 1.

Cantril's view implies that a comparison of average happiness between countries that differ in affluence must produce a positive linear pattern (Figure 1a). Comparisons over time should reveal parallel variation in economic growth/decline and average happiness in the separate countries (Figure 1b) .

Easterlin's view also predicts that the plotting of national wealth against happiness produces a linear relationship, but this time a zero one, as symbolized by the horizontal line in Figure 1c. Comparison over time would show a similar horizontal line, happiness being insensitive to economic growth and decline (Figure 1d).

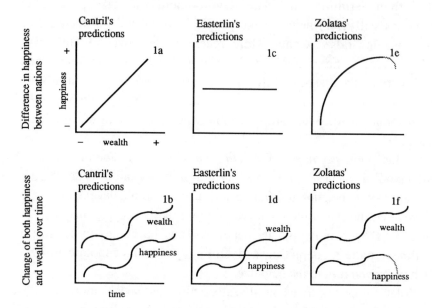

Figure 1: Predicted configuration of average happiness and economic wealth.

Zolatas' view predicts that happiness follows a curvilinear pattern in both cases. The higher the levels of affluence, the less its happiness returns, and at some point the effects may even become negative (Figures 1e and 1f).

Below I will examine which of these predictions comes closest to the facts. To that end I will first reconsider earlier empirical claims, in particular those of Easterlin. Next I will introduce some new information based on a secondary analysis of two large-scale cross-national surveys. I will consider the patterns that emerge from comparisons among nations of different economic development as well as the variation of happiness over time along with economic growth and decline.

Happiness in Rich and Poor Countries

As noted above, current findings have been interpreted differently. I will try to resolve the issue by considering the disputed data in detail and by presenting a replication.

Easterlin's Analysis Is Misleading

The dispute is primarily about the interpretation of Cantril's data. Cantril claimed that his results show there is more happiness in the rich countries, while Easterlin held that there is hardly any difference.

Easterlin supported his claim by presenting Cantril's data graphically; see Figure 2a. He argues that most countries are at the medium level (indicated by horizontal lines) in spite of great differences in GNP. Yet this presentation is misleading, Easterlin playing the classic trick of manipulating scales.

In Easterlin's presentation the GNP variable is depicted on a scale 2.5 times larger than the happiness scale. Thus the pattern is flattened. When both variables are awarded equal scales, a different picture emerges.

Table 1: Second Set of Nations Compared by Easterlin

Country	Very happy	Fairly happy	Not very happy	Other	N	Real GNP per head 1961
	Percent Distribution of Population by Happiness, Nine Countries, 1965					
Great Britain	52	42	4	1	1179	$1777
United States	49	42	4	2	3531	$2790
West Germany	20	66	11	3	1255	$1860
Thailand	13	74	12	1	500	$202
Japan (a)	81.0		13	5	920	$613
Philippines	13.5	73	13.5	0	500	$282
Malaysia	17	64	15	4	502	$552
France	12	64	18	5	1228	$1663
Italy	11	52	33	4	1166	$1077

(a) Question read "not happy" rather than "not very happy."

Source: Easterlin (1974, p. 107, Table 7).

2a: Easterlin's presentation (Easterlin, 1974, p. 106)

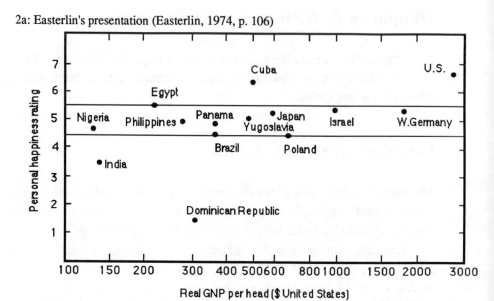

2b: My presentation (based on the same data)

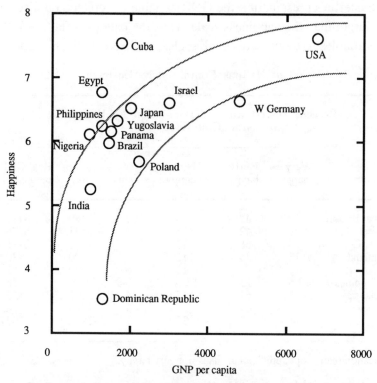

Figure 2: Presentations of Cantril's data on average happiness in countries of different wealth in 1960.

Rather than a horizontal line the plot produces an ascending curve; see Figure 2b.

Beside Cantril's 14 countries, Easterlin compared another set of nations as well. These are the nine nations enumerated in Table 1, in which Gallup polls in 1965 had included identical questions on how happy one felt. Easterlin stated that these data leave one "uncertain" whether there is a positive association between GNP and happiness (p. 118). That contention is dubious as well. At first glance one can see a clear – though not perfect – relationship. To make sure, I computed the product moment correlation on the basis of the data Easterlin presented in Table 7 of his article: $r = +.59$. Taking into account that correlations based on aggregate data tend to be high, this is still a relationship one can hardly characterize as "uncertain."

New World Survey Shows a Positive Curvilinear Relationship As Well

It is likely that even the two sets of data shown above do not depict the relationship to its full extent. In both sets of nations the very poor countries are underrepresented. Therefore, I examined the same relationship in the data of a large scale "World Survey" from 1975 (Gallup, 1976/77). This study sampled parts of the world rather than nations. It covered the poor regions of the Southern Sahara region of Africa and South East Asia. Unfortunately, the communist world, North Africa, and the Middle East could not be included. For the purpose of this paper it suffices that the poorest parts of the world are represented.

The Gallup World Survey assessed life satisfaction in essentially the same way as Cantril's earlier study (instead of a ladder, a mountain-like rating scale was used), and presented average scores for seven parts of the world and some well-represented nations. Like Easterlin, I cross-tabulated the averages[2] with GNP.[3] A clear relationship emerged; see Figure 3. The correlation between happiness and GNP in this world sample is +.85.

As can be seen in Figure 3, the relationship is again curvilinear. The difference in happiness between the "very poor" and "rather poor" regions is far greater than the difference between the "rather poor" and

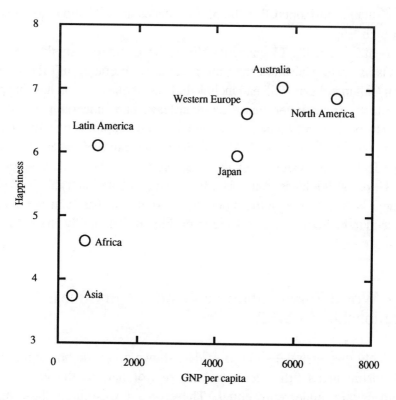

Figure 3: Happiness in seven parts of the world by GNP per head in 1975. Source: Veenhoven (1984, p. 149).

the "rich" regions. When we omit Africa and Asia, hardly any relationship is left. This is, in fact, what happened to Easterlin. It also happened to Inglehart, who found no difference between rich and very rich countries in his analysis of happiness in the EC countries in 1975 (Inglehart, 1977, p. 150).

Happiness During Economic Rise and Decline

Easterlin's main piece of evidence was that Americans did not become happier between 1946 and 1975, in spite of a doubling of the GNP during that period. Does this example prove his general claim that happiness depends on social comparison and is therefore insensitive to collective movements towards better or worse? I will show that it does not.

In Post-War Europe Wealth and Happiness Rose Together

Americans were already quite happy in 1946: 40% claiming to be "very happy" and 50% "fairly happy." At this level room for improvement is obviously small, not least because there is always a margin of inevitable unhappiness due to illness and mental disturbances. Increases in wealth may affect happiness more in countries where dissatisfaction prevails.

Likewise, we should not forget that the USA was already fairly affluent at the end of World War II. If wealth is subject to the law of diminishing returns, it is thus quite comprehensible that further increase did not add much to happiness. Yet matters are likely to be different in countries that start with a lower standard of living.

These points are neatly illustrated by the case of Western Europe. At the end of World War II happiness was low in England, France, the Netherlands, and West Germany. The level of living was low as well, housing shortage and food rationing being the rule. Between 1948 and 1975 these countries witnessed both a startling economic recovery and a general rise in happiness. The percentage of unhappy persons in the population was halved during that period (Veenhoven, 1984, p. 171).

Table 2: Average Happiness in the EC Countries in the Years 1975-1986

Year	Happiness	Life satisfaction
1975	2.33	2.90
1976	2.30	2.90
1977	2.55	2.97
1978	2.39	2.97
1979	2.59	2.94
1980	–	2.95
1981	–	2.92
1982	2.45	2.95
1983	2.42	2.90
1984	2.48	2.95
1985	2.48	2.87
1986	2.52	2.97

Derived from Eurobarometer Report No. 24.

In the 1970's Western Europe had become about as happy and affluent as the USA earlier. Hence it is not unlikely that the continued –

though slower – economic growth in the later decades did not add that much to the enjoyment of life. Inspection of the Eurobarometer surveys data[4] shows that this is indeed the case; see Table 2. Responses to the questions about "life satisfaction" remained largely at the same level, while favourable responses to the "happiness" item increased by some 15%.

The Last Few Decades' Economic Fluctuations Affected Happiness in Europe With Some Delay

Easterlin's conclusion is too easy for another reason: The fact that American happiness did not rise during the post-war decades does not mean that it remained static all the time. In fact, happiness fluctuated somewhat over the years. It is possible that economic ups and downs affected at least these surface ripples. If so, that would not fit Easterlin's social comparison theory. If everybody is affected similarly, comparisons should not turn out differently.

The following reports on an empirical check of this possibility undertaken by myself and Piet Ouweneel (more details in Ouweneel, 1987). It is also based upon the Eurobarometer surveys, covering the period between 1975 and 1986, during which considerable economic fluctuations took place.

Data

The Eurobarometer survey involves bi-annual polls in each of the EC countries. The standard questionnaire involves two items on happiness.[5] On the basis of frequency tables in the Eurobarometer Report No. 24, yearly happiness averages were computed for each of the EC countries and the EC as a whole. Next, the year-to-year changes in happiness were transformed into a percentage of the earlier year's average. This procedure was followed for both happiness items. Changes varied from +12% to –8%. Fluctuations in average happiness were greatest in the years 1976 to 1979.

Fluctuations in the standard of living in the EC countries were measured by growth rates in real GNP per head at market prices (OECD,

1986). To avoid scale problems, the growth rates were also expressed as a percentage of the earlier years' rate. These fluctuations varied from +5% to –1% and were also relatively great in the late seventies.

Analysis

We first considered whether happiness varies simultaneously with the economic tide, i.e., whether changes in the same direction tend to occur in the same year. For that purpose we plotted the change scores of both happiness and GNP and inspected the graphs. We also computed product-moment correlations. We did so for all ten EC countries and for the EC as a whole. These analyses were performed for the two happiness items separately.

In addition to this analysis of simultaneous covariation, we considered the possibility that economic changes have a delayed effect on happiness. It is not unlikely that macro-economic growth and decline affect most citizens only at a later point in time. In a study in Kansas City, USA, Calatano, Dooley, and Jackson (1981) found the number of admissions to mental health facilities increased during the two to four months following the onset of a recession. Since our data provide yearly averages only, we assessed correlations at time lags of one and two years.

Lastly, we also checked whether changes in happiness precede economic change. Similar to more specific economic attitudes such as "economic optimism" and "consumer trust," life satisfaction could indeed affect economic behaviour. There is, for instance, evidence that a positive appreciation of life fosters an optimistic view of the world and stimulates activity (Veenhoven, 1984, pp. 285-287, 293). Therefore, we looked at the correspondence between economic fluctuations and variation in happiness one and two years earlier.

Results

At first sight the data confirm Easterlin's contention that fluctuations in national wealth are irrelevant for the individual's appreciation of life.

The analysis of simultaneous correlations reveals no consistent correspondence. Yet, when the time perspective is changed, a clear

21

pattern emerges. Happiness appears to follow fluctuations in the economy; see Figure 4.

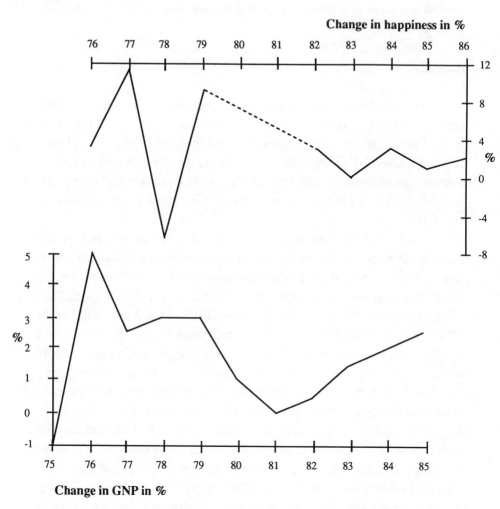

Figure 4: Year-to-year changes in happiness and changes in GNP per head between 1976 and 1986 in ten EC countries.

Figure 4 shows that the 6% economic upsurge in 1975-76 was followed by a 12% rise in happiness in the years 1976-77. Likewise the 3% economic decline that occurred between 1976 and 1977 manifested itself only between 1977 and 1978 in a 8% drop in happiness. The more gradual pattern of declining economic growth between 1977 and 1981 is followed by an equally gradual diminishing of yearly happiness gains in 1982 and 1983. The zero growth in 1981 corresponds to a slight drop in happiness in 1983. The quite limited economic recovery after 1981 is followed by an equally minimal rise in happiness from 1983 onward. The correspondence is highest at a one-year interval. For the EC as a whole r = +.56.

Similar correlations appear in the individual countries, with the exception of Germany and Luxemburg (zero correlation) and Eire (negative correlation); see Table 3.

Table 3: Correlations[1] of Yearly[2] Fluctuations[3] in GNP[4] With Fluctuations in Happiness[5] in the EC Countries Between 1976 and 1986

Country	Same time[6]	One year lag[7]
Belgium	−.29	+.88
Denmark	−.31	+.52
Germany	+.28	−.04
Great Britain	−.73	+.42
France	−.13	+.47
Ireland	−.06	−.34
Italy	−.28	+.70
Luxemburg	−.18	−.12
Netherlands	+.12	+.40
EC as a whole	−.12	+.56

[1]Product-moment correlation.
[2]Changes in both happiness and GNP from one year to another. Ten changes were observed.
[3]Amount of yearly change expressed in percentage of the level of the foregoing year.
[4]BNP per head, in each year. Source: OECD (1986).
[5]Average happiness in the country in each year. Assessed on the basis of Eurobarometer Report nr. 24.
[6]Covariation of change in happiness in a year with change in GNP in the same year. (Ten year pairs compared for each country.)
[7]Covariation of change in happiness in a year to rise or decline of GNP a year earlier. (Ten year pairs compared for each country.)

The two individual happiness items produce similar patterns, though the question of how "happy" one feels appears to be more sensitive to economic fluctuations than the question about "satisfaction with one's way of life." The difference may be due to two things: Firstly, the "happiness" item focusses more on current feelings ("these days," see Note 5) and is therefore more likely to reflect short-term economic fluctuations than the "satisfaction" item that, in fact, covers one's whole life. Secondly, the somewhat distant judgement elicited by the latter question may be leveled off somewhat by cognitive adjustments, while the happiness item could more pronouncedly reflect the "raw" experiences of hope and despair.

The hypothesis that economic rise or decline is **caused** by an earlier change in happiness was not supported by these data.

Diminishing Happiness Returns of Economic Wealth and Growth

The Empirical Pattern

Figure 5a represents the pattern of diminishing utility of macro-economic welfare that appeared both in the cross-national comparison and in the comparison over time in post-war western Europe.

Figure 5b represents the effects of short-term economic fluctuations. The solid part of that line represents the pattern of oscillations around the same level of happiness observed in Western Europe during the last decade. The intermittent extension of the thin line to the left reflects a hypothesis held by the author. I expect economic fluctuations to affect happiness in less affluent countries even more pronouncedly. There are at least two reasons for this expectation. Firstly, consequences in terms of need gratification are greater at the poorest end of the curve. Secondly, costs of growth are likely to be greater at the affluent end and are therefore likely to neutralize the effects of growth and decline to a greater extent. Figure 5 provides a schematic representation of the findings.

Predictions Checked

Which of the predictions presented in Figure 1 meets this observed pattern best? Clearly not Easterlin's. His claim that individual happiness is insensitive to the economic condition of the nation holds only in the stratum of affluent societies, and even there does not predict the observed short-term variation of happiness with the economic tide. Cantril's is more adequate. It fits both the observed greater happiness in rich countries and the fluctuations in happiness following economic rise and decline. Zolatas' does even better. The curvilinear pattern he predicted did in fact emerge, though there is no evidence for the drop to the negative he held to be possible at the greatest level of affluence.

5a: The declining happiness revenue of national wealth

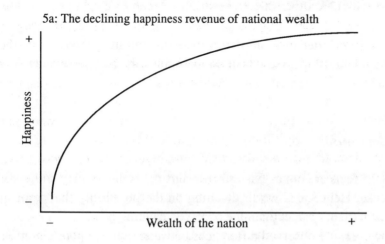

5b: Declining susceptibility of happiness to economic fluctuations

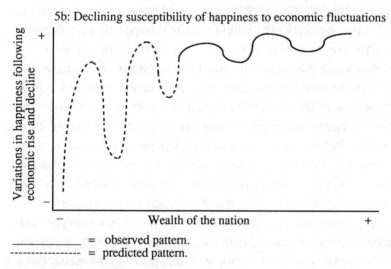

```
_____   =  observed pattern.
----------------   =  predicted pattern.
```

Figure 5: Schematic summary.

Of the three views presented in the beginning of this paper Easterlin's is the best known. It figures in many textbooks. Easterlin's theory is, in fact, accepted as one of those remarkable research results that seems counter-intuitive at first sight, but marks the superiority of scientific understanding. Yet it is simply wrong. Empirically it depicts an exception rather than a rule and theoretically it is very one-sided (to be argued below). I wonder whether the "world" will ever discard this theory, or whether its celebrity will keep the misunderstanding alive.

Explanations Checked

Let us now consider in more detail the explanations proposed for the predicted relationships. How well do these meet the pattern that actually emerged?

Social Comparison

Though the facts are not as Easterlin presumed, his theory may still make some sense. Hence it is worth dwelling on the possibility that a social comparison theory can explain the observed pattern.

However, the observed differences between rich and poor countries can hardly be explained by social comparison theory. Explaining the fact that any difference at all exists would require that people compare their situation with foreigners rather than with compatriots. This is not probable. Reference groups tend to be close, and most people have only dim ideas of the standard of living in other parts of the world. Moreover, the curvilinear pattern can be accounted for only if we assume that Indians and Africans compare themselves with the rich world more frequently than do Latin Americans and the Japanese. The reverse seems to be the case.

Nor can social comparison theory account for the fact that oscillations in happiness were found to follow economic fluctuations. As noted earlier, economic ups and downs tend to affect everybody to approximately the same degree. Hence, social comparison theory can apply only in special cases, for example, where people notice changes in their own finances more clearly than fluctuations in the general level of living, or when economic fluctuations cause a redistribution of income. I

26

will not discuss all the possibilities here. Let it suffice to note that extra assumptions are required to make social comparison theory fit these data.

If comparison is involved at all, comparisons of one's own situations over time are more likely to be involved. Happiness could decrease somewhat when people notice that they can no longer afford the things they were used to, whereas it might be boosted slightly when one perceives progress and expectations are surpassed. Cognitive mechanisms are likely to neutralize these changes to a great extent. Habituation and inflation of expectations may soon reduce the joys of economic growth, while people adjust in similar ways to decline, as long as no basic needs are frustrated.

At a more basic level, it is not very plausible to assume that human happiness depends entirely on comparison. Why would nature have left us with a tendency to orient ourselves towards such arbitrary standards of the good life?

Need Theory

The theory Cantril hints at rather assumes that happiness depends on the gratification of universal "basic needs." Such needs are presumed to have evolved in the human species because their pursuit has survival value. Various attempts have been made to grasp what these needs involve. The best known of these is Maslow's (1968) theory which proposes a hierarchically ordered set of needs for physiological "subsistence," "safety," "belonging," "esteem," and "actualization." This theory fits the observed pattern of differences in happiness between poor and rich nations better. Basic needs for food, shelter, and safety are clearly less well met in the poor countries, as is demonstrated in the relatively short average life-expectancy of their citizens. Need theory also explains the curvilinear pattern more easily. Maslow's theory holds that so-called "deficiency needs" tend to lose salience once reasonably satisfied. Diminishing satisfaction from extra gratification is the result. This view would imply that economic wealth is less relevant for the higher "being needs" which Maslow presumes to be infinite.

Need gratification theory can less easily explain the short-term effects of economic rise and decline on happiness in the rich EC countries. Not only did the recession not involve any threat of subsistence, but the effects were also short-lived. Still, need theory can account for this phenomenon if one assumes that the deprivations caused by economic recession are largely symbolical. Feelings of safety are likely to have been shattered in many persons and mass unemployment has certainly frustrated "esteem" needs, and in many cases, also the need for "belongingness." The recuperation that appears can then be explained by a reorientation, both at the individual level (e.g., seeking other meaningful tasks) and at the societal level (e.g., boosted optimism, changed attitudes to unemployment). This reorientation is a more active way of coping than the comparison theory explanation of this phenomenon in terms of resignation. Though economic growth, too, may involve similar disruptive effects, these are likely to be less frequent: growth leaving the individual more room for self-determination than decline. Hence, economic prosperity can allow people better opportunities to follow a way of life that meets their needs and can thereby result in more enjoyment of life. As "freedom of choice" is the critical variable here, the effects depend more on **turns** in the economic tide than on the **level** of affluence. This can also explain the short-livedness of the effect. Obviously, the surplus of freedom allowed by economic prosperity depends on the socio-political context. National variations are therefore likely.

Costs of Affluence

Though Zolatas' prediction was closest to the observed pattern, not all of his reasoning is equally convincing. Part of his argument follows the above line of basic need theory, but he also points out the drawbacks of affluent society (false wants, dull products, commuting, pollution, undermining of family). These latter effects could bend the curve towards the negative, while the satiation of needs can at best reduce the effect of wealth to zero. It may be true that the negative side-effects of affluence tend to counterbalance the positive effects. Yet it is difficult to establish whether the costs of affluence are really disproportionally high in the rich countries. One could make a good case for the contrary as well, for example by arguing that production conditions in the poor countries are even more alienating than they are in the rich world, that consumer goods produced by subsistence economies are even more dull, and that material dependence on intimates burdens interpersonal relations. Anyway, since there is no sign of the curve bending towards the negative, there is no independent evidence for Zolata's explanation.

The pattern of short-lived oscillations in happiness following the economic tide with some delay cannot be explained in terms of costs of affluence. In fact, the theory would predict a lowering rather than a rise in happiness one or two years after an upsurge of the economy because of a "suffocation" through newly purchased goods and services, while economic decline should raise happiness after some time. Moreover, this explanation does not account for the short-livedness of the effects on happiness. It would, in fact, predict enduring change.

Challenges for Further Research

As the above discussion indicates, our understanding of the mechanisms underlying the observed pattern of diminishing happiness returns by increasing affluence is still rather limited and speculative. It would be worth giving the matter more thought. One way of finding clues might be to look for differences in the bending of the curve. In other words, trying to identify conditions in which growth of affluence sooner or later catches up with the rise in happiness. It could be, for example, that the happiness returns of affluence are lower when economic development is paralleled by individualization. If so, patterns should differ between Western Europe and South-East Asia.

Another issue worth investigating is whether the delayed sequel of economic rise and decline we observed in "subjective" indicators of well-being also appears in "objective" ones. We could, for example, check whether the economic recession of 1980-1982 was followed by a rise in physical illness and mental afflictions. If not, the observed drop in happiness is apparently a surface phenomenon, to be attributed to comparison. In the other case "real" deprivations are more likely to be involved, as predicted by need theory.

Conclusion

The economic prosperity of the country **does** affect the degree to which its citizens enjoy life. In the poor countries people are clearly less happy than in the rich countries. However, the returns of wealth are subject to the law of diminishing utility. In the Western affluent societies the last few decades' economic growth hardly raised the average level of happiness. Still, in the rich countries, economic ups and downs result in fluctuations in happiness around an otherwise stable average level of high satisfaction.

These results contradict Easterlin's (1973, 1974) theory that happiness is socially relative and therefore essentially insensitive to collective economic conditions. The results can be fairly well explained in terms of Maslow's need theory.

Notes

1. Respondents were first asked to describe the "best possible" life they could imagine and next the "worst possible" life. Then a picture of a ten-step ladder was presented and they were asked: "Suppose the top of the ladder represents the best possible life for you, and the bottom the worst possible life for you, where on the ladder do you feel you personally stand at this time?" (Cantril, 1965, pp. 22-23).

2. Japan was taken separately because its economic development differs too much from the other countries in the Asia sample. The remaining sample is heavily dominated by India.

3. Data from World Bank Atlas (1971).

4. The Eurobarometer surveys have been held twice a year since 1975 in each of the EC countries. The standard questionnaire involves two items on happiness (see Note 5). Spain, Portugal, and Greece were not included in the analysis, because these countries joined the EEC later and are therefore not represented in all the surveys. In the years 1980 and 1981 item 1 was not included.

5. The standard questionnaire of the Eurobarometer survey involves the following two happiness items:
　1. Taking all things together, how would you say you are these days – would you say you are very happy, fairly happy, or not too happy these days?

2. On the whole, are you very satisfied, fairly satisfied, not very satisfied, or not at all satisfied with the life you lead?

References

Brickman, R., Coates, D., & Janoff-Bulman, R. (1978). Lottery winners and accident victims: Is happiness relative? *Journal of Personality and Social Psychology, 36*, 917-927.

Cantril, H. (1965). *The pattern of human concern*. New Brunswick, NJ: Rutgers University Press.

Calatano, R., Dooley, D., & Jackson, R. (1981). Economic predictors of admissions to mental health facilities in a non-metropolitan community. *Journal of Health and Social Behavior, 22*, 284-297.

Easterlin, R.A. (1973). Does money buy happiness? *Public Interest, 30*(30), 3-10.

Easterlin, R.A. (1974). Does economic growth improve the human lot? In: P.A. David & W.E. Melvin (Eds.), *Nations and households in economic growth*, pp. 98-125. Palo Alto, CA: Stanford University Press.

Eurobarometer Report 24 (1985). Brussels: Commission of the European Community.

Gallup, G.H. (1976/77). Human needs and satisfactions: A global survey. *Public Opinion Quarterly, 41*, 459-467.

Hirsch, F. (1976). *The social limits of growth*. Cambridge, MA: Harvard University Press.

Inglehart, R. (1977). *The silent revolution: Changing values and political values among Western publics*. Princeton, NJ: Princeton University Press.

Maslow, A.H. (1970). *Motivation and personality*. New York: Harper & Row.

OECD (1986). *OECD Economic Outlook*, No. 39.

Ouweneel, P. (1987). Geluk volgt welvaart (Happiness follows prosperity). *Economisch Statistische Berichten*, 1987, pp. 840-842.

Scitovsky, T. (1976). *The joyless economy*. London: Oxford University Press.

van Praag, B.M.S., & Kapteyn, A. (1973). Wat is ons inkomen ons waard (How do we value our income)? *Economisch Statistische Berichten*, 1973, pp. 360-361, 380-382.

Veenhoven, R. (1984). *Conditions of happiness.* Dordrecht: Reidel.

World Bank Atlas. Population, product, and growth rates in 1969 (1971). Washington, DC: International Bank for Reconstruction and Development.

Zolatas, X. (1981). *Economic growth and declining social welfare.* New York: New York University Press.

Tommy Gärling, Erik Lindberg, and Henry Montgomery

Beliefs about Attainment of Life Satisfaction as Determinants of Preferences for Everyday Activities

Abstract

The assumption has been made that life satisfaction depends on the attainment of psychological values such as, for instance, feelings of security, freedom, and accomplishment. A related question investigated in the present study is whether the type of everyday activities in which people engage, and which are related to their patterns of consumption, are seen as means by which such psychological values are attained.

A questionnaire was distributed to a heterogeneous group of 112 subjects who first rated how important for life satisfaction they believed the performance of a sample of everyday activities and the attainment of a number of psychological values to be, then indicated for each activity whether or not it facilitated (or hindered) the attainment of each value. In support of the hypothesis, positive correlations were found for individual subjects between the rated importance of the activities, on the one hand, and the importance predicted on the basis of the values believed to be attained by the activities, on the other.

The reported research was financially supported by grants from the Swedish Council for Building Research and the Swedish Council for Research in the Humanities and Social Sciences. The authors thank Håkan Alm and Jörgen Garvill for valuable suggestions on earlier drafts, and Ann Thors for assistance in collecting the data.

Authors' addresses: Tommy Gärling and Erik Lindberg, Department of Psychology, University of Umeå, S-90187 Umeå, Sweden; Henry Montgomery, Department of Psychology, University of Göteborg, S-40020 Göteborg, Sweden.

Background

When, where, and for how long people engage in various everyday activities have been investigated in studies of time allocation (Chapin, 1974; Michelson & Reed, 1975; Szalai, Converse, Feldheim, Scheuch, & Stone, 1972). Such studies are of immediate interest to society because what people do with their time is an indicator of the objective quality of life (Campbell, Converse, & Rodgers, 1976). However, as interest broadens to include a desire to know how satisfied people are subjectively (cf. Diener, 1984), time use data are less useful unless a psychological theory exists which specifies how time allocation is related to satisfaction (Robinson, 1977; Stone, 1972).

Kuhl (1986), taking as his point of departure the motivational theory of Atkinson and Birch (1986), assumes that the amount of time devoted to an activity is proportional to its perceived attractiveness. Kuhl found support for this assumption in an experimental setting, but it seems questionable whether it holds true under most ordinary, everyday circumstances. People probably try to maximize their utility in allocating time to activities (Becker, 1976; Winston, 1987), without however necessarily succeeding because they lack some of the needed resources, such as physical and mental abilities, social and environmental support, money, and time (Frey & Foppa, 1986; Triandis, 1977). Furthermore, for different reasons, everyday activities are usually not independent of one another. Thus choice of one activity implies that one or several other activities must also be chosen. In an empirical study by the present authors (Lindberg, Gärling, Montgomery, & Waara, 1987) all these circumstances might have contributed to the modest correlation found between subjects' stated preferences for a set of everyday activities and their self-reports of how often they engaged in those activities.

Fishbein and Ajzen (1975; Ajzen & Fishbein, 1980) propose in their theory of reasoned action that intentions to perform an action or activity mediate between preference and performance of the action. Because of constraining factors such intentions can usually not be implemented directly but form parts of plans (Ajzen, 1985; Warshaw & Dröge, 1986). It may thus be assumed that in everyday life, intentions are formed in connection with a planning process (Hayes-Roth & Hayes-Roth, 1979; Miller, Galanter, & Pribram, 1960; Sacerdoti, 1977; Wilenski, 1981) of which time allocation is the observed end result. In a similar vein, script theory (Abelson, 1981; Schank, 1982; Schank & Abelson, 1977) emphasizes the role of scripts or already executed plans as building blocks of plans under formation. This is certainly true of actions which are components of activities (Galambos & Rips, 1982; Nottenburg & Schoben, 1980; Reiser, Black, & Abelson, 1985) but may also to some extent be true of most everyday activities and their temporal organization.

Even though several, rather complex factors, in addition to preferences, determine how much time people devote to everyday activities, it may still be asked what factors determine preferences for everyday activities. According to expectancy-value models in psychology (Feather, 1982; Fishbein & Ajzen, 1975), preferences for actions are determined by beliefs about their consequences and the value assigned to these consequences. To what extent this holds true for everyday activities, and what the likely consequences of such activities are perceived to be, were the primary questions which the present study tried to answer.

Rokeach (1970, 1973) assumes that people while seeking life satisfaction strive to attain **values,** defined as psychological end-states, such as feelings of, for instance, security, freedom, and accomplishment. Although Rokeach may still be right in this basic assumption about the role of values, it appears as if he were partly wrong in his choice of values. This has been shown empirically by Montgomery (1984) and Montgomery, Drottz, Gärling, Persson, and Waara (1985). A system for classifying psychological values was recently proposed by Montgomery and Johansson (1988).

In addition to end-states or "terminal values," different desirable modes of conduct were identified by Rokeach (1973) as "instrumental values." These instrumental values, which actually consist of a number of personality traits (e.g., ambitious, helpful, independent), were assumed to be the means whereby the terminal values are attained. No further attempt was, however, made to elucidate the beliefs people may have about how the values are attained, although such beliefs are likely to underlie many decisions people make. Examples are decisions leading to consumption of goods, services, and energy. Conversely, one may ask what values people believe they will attain when making such decisions (Keeney & Raiffa, 1976).

The hypothesis in the present study was that the attainment of values which are believed to lead to life satisfaction is perceived as an important consequence of many everyday activities. If this is true, it should be possible to predict the preferences for everyday activities from knowledge about the important values that a person believes are attained by performing the activities. Analogous with the model proposed by Fishbein and Ajzen (1975), the following equation was proposed to relate preference for an activity i (P_i) to the evaluations (E_j) of the values j to which the activity is believed to lead (p_{ij}, the instrumentality of an activity for attaining a given value, different from zero):

(1) $$P_i = \sum_j p_{ij} \, E_j \, / \sum_j E_j$$

The validity of Equation 1 was investigated by means of a questionnaire distributed to a heterogeneous group of subjects. In this questionnaire, ratings expressed how important a number of everyday activities and values were believed to be for the attainment of life satisfaction as well as whether or not each activity contributed to the attainment of each value.

Method

Questionnaire and Procedure

Forty-seven everyday activities and 18 hypothesized perceived consequences, in the form of values, were presented in the questionnaire. The choice of everyday activities was based on classifications of activities employed in studies of time use (Chapin, 1974; Robinson, 1977; Szalai et al., 1972). Hence, as Table 1 indicates, those activities included in the questionnaire related to work, education, housekeeping, personal needs, family, social interaction, community, culture, and leisure. In constructing these items, the aim was to be as specific as possible without overlooking any important activities. Furthermore, the intention was that the activities should represent meaningful cognitive units (Reiser et al., 1985).

Of the values, also shown in Table 1, 13 were direct translations of items used by Rokeach (1973). The remaining five were adapted after Montgomery (1984).

Table 1: The Everyday Activities and Their Hypothesized Perceived Value Consequences

Everyday activities		
Work	**Personal needs**	**Community**
Regular *work*[1]	Personal *hygiene*	Going to *church*
Working *overtime*	Keep *healthy*	*Club* activities
	Keep *neat*	
Education	Physical *exercise*	**Culture**
Attend *school*	Make *love*	*Sports* events
Attend *courses*	*Alcohol* consumption	*Cultural* events
	Tobacco consumption	*Museums*/exhibitions
Domestic work	Personal *shopping*	
House *cleaning*		**Leisure**
Food preparation	**Family activities**	News *media*
Repair/upkeep	*Child* care	Home-based *hobbies*
Pet care	Be with *family*	Practising *sports*
Gardening	Be with *spouse*	Be in weekend *cottage*
Home *decoration*	Be with *child*	Be in *countryside*
Domestic *economy*	*Meals* at home	*Outings*
Shopping *groceries*		*Vacation*
Purchase of *durables*	**Social interaction**	*Gambling*
	Be with *relatives*	*Pastimes*
	Be with *friends*	*Relaxing*
	Party-organizing	
	Attend *parties*	
	Meals at *restaurants*	
	Dancing	

Values	
Recognition	Being respected, liked, or admired
Freedom	Independence and freedom of choice
Togetherness	A feeling of belonging
Morals	Living a moral life. Being honest
Excitement	A life full of variety. Satisfying curiosity
Influence	Being able to influence other people
Inner harmony	To feel relieved from inner conflicts
Comfort	A comfortable life
Love	To love someone
Happiness	Contentedness and joy
Pleasure	All kinds of pleasure. Enjoyment
Self-respect	A feeling of self-esteem
Beauty	Enjoying beautiful things
Believing	All kinds of belief in a just cause
Security	Not feeling worried or threatened
Accomplishment	A sense of having accomplished something
Wisdom	Understanding important things. Life experience
Survival	Not having to die young. Survival of the human species

[1]Italicized words are used as abbreviations in the following tables.

The questionnaire was distributed to groups of subjects seated in a classroom. The questionnaire, which was more extensive than reported here (Gärling, Lindberg, Montgomery, & Waara, 1985), was completed by the subjects while being supervised by an experimenter. Each such session took about 2 hours. In addition to the questionnaire, the subjects had access to a list of all items. This list included explanations of the meanings of the values (see Table 1). Some of the activities were also exemplified by referring to more specific activities.

Ratings were required in two parts of the questionnaire. After a one-page general description of the purpose of the study and some background questions, the first part requested the subjects to rate, on 13-point scales, how important for life satisfaction they perceived the different values and activities to be (E_j and p_i, respectively). The order in which the items appeared on the pages of the questionnaire was random.

In the following part of the questionnaire, p_{ij} was measured. For each activity subjects indicated a plus sign for all those values which they believed to be attained by performing the particular activity. If an activity was believed to have the opposite consequence (i.e., to hinder the attainment of the value), a minus sign was indicated. The activities were presented on separate pages appearing in a random order.

Subjects

The questionnaire was distributed to 120 students attending a college for adults located in Umeå which is an average-siz·d Swedish city with about 100,000 residents. The data from 8 subjects had to be discarded due to incompleteness and/or misinterpretations of the instructions. Of the 112 remaining subjects, 48 were women, 64 men. Their ages varied from 18 to 49 years ($M = 28.3$, $s = 8.2$); in the subsequent analysis subjects were divided into three categories, 18 to 24, 25 to 35, and 36 to 49. Sixty subjects were single, 52 had a family.

Results

As shown in Table 2, the values were all given high importance ratings ($M = 9.5$), whereas the importance of the activities showed considerably larger variation ($M = 6.7$).

Table 2: Mean Ratings of Importance for Life Satisfaction

Everyday activities				Values	
Hygiene	10. 6	Food	6. 4	Happiness	11. 2
Healthy	10. 0	Cultural events	6. 4	Love	10. 8
Spouse	9. 7	Relatives	6. 4	Security	10. 7
Family	9. 3	Parties	6. 2	Freedom	10. 5
Meals	9. 3	Restaurants	5. 9	Inner harmony	10. 5
School	9. 2	Shopping	5. 9	Accomplishment	10. 1
Love	9. 1	Dancing	5. 8	Togetherness	10. 0
Work	9. 1	Party-organizing	5. 8	Survival	9. 8
Friends	9. 0	Pet care	5. 5	Pleasure	9. 7
Child	8. 9	Clubs	5. 4	Self-respect	9. 7
Media	8. 9	Courses	5. 3	Wisdom	9. 6
Vacation	8. 6	Gardening	5. 2	Excitement	9. 4
Economy	8. 5	Museums	5. 1	Morals	9. 2
Countryside	8. 5	Cottage	4. 9	Recognition	9. 1
Neat	7. 9	Sports events	4. 8	Beauty	8. 4
Child care	7. 8	Durables	4. 4	Comfort	7. 9
Repair	7. 7	Overtime	4. 2	Believing	7. 3
Groceries	7. 6	Relaxing	4. 1	Influence	7. 1
Exercise	7. 4	Sports	3. 9		
Hobbies	7. 4	Alcohol	3. 7		
Outings	7. 4	Tobacco	3. 3		
Pastimes	6. 9	Gambling	3. 1		
Decoration	6. 8	Church	2. 4		
Cleaning	6. 5				

Analyses of variance (ANOVAs) were carried out separately for the activities and values (age x sex x marital status x items, with repeated measures on the last factor). No main effects confined to the between-subject factors reached significance, but the means for individual items varied slightly across the different groups of subjects. Because of the small and unequal cell sizes resulting from the different combinations of the between-subject factors, only their two-way interactions with items were analyzed. For the values, the interactions of sex and of marital status with items were significant, $F(17,1700) = 2.77$ and 2.07, respectively, $p<.01$, and for the activities all three between-subject factors showed significant interactions with items, $F(92,4600) = 2.28$, $F(46,4600) =$ 1.76, and 2.63 for age, sex, and marital status, respectively, $p<.01$. The items which differentiated most clearly between different groups of subjects are presented in Table 3. This table lists for each group all items with a mean rating of at least one point above that of the other group(s).

Table 3: Activities and Values Rated as More Important for Life Satisfaction by Subjects Differing in Age, Sex, and Marital Status

	Age (years)			Sex		Marital status	
	18-24	25-35	36-49	Women	Men	Single	Family
Activities	Friends	Friends	Family	Course	Repair	Friends	Spouse
	Exercise	Cultural	Work	Gardening	Sports	Party	Family
	Cultural	events	Child		events	Restaurant	Meals
	events	Party	Media		Durables	Shopping	Child
	Party	Restaurant	Economy		Sports	Dancing	Child care
	Restaurant	Dancing	Child care		Alcohol	Overtime	Repair
	Dancing	Relaxing	Repair				Hobbies
	Party-		Pastimes				Pastimes
	organizing		Cleaning				
	Sports		Relatives				
	events		Gardening				
	Overtime		Church				
	Sports						
	Tobacco						
Values	Togetherness	Pleasure	Wisdom	Togetherness	Comfort	Influence	Survival
	Pleasure	Morals	Morals	Self-respect			
	Recognition	Believing		Recognition			
	Influence	Influence					

Activities were in general reported to facilitate rather than to hinder the fulfilment of the values. At most 40% of the subjects reported a negative relationship in any particular case, and in the large majority of cases less than 5% reported negative relationships. The positive relationships which were perceived to exist by at least 50% of all subjects are presented in Table 4. Although not reported here, there were group differences as large as .47 in the percentage to which group members perceived a particular relationship. The largest differences were found between the age groups.

Table 5 shows the mean product moment correlations between individual subjects' ratings of how important for life satisfaction they perceived the activities to be, on the one hand, and importance predicted by means of Equation 1, on the other. As can be seen, all the correlations were statistically reliable but modestly large. Despite the group differences reported above, the correlations did not differ markedly with

Table 4: Values Perceived as Consequences by at Least 50% of Subjects

Everyday activities	Values
Hygiene	--------------------
Healthy	Inner harmony
Spouse	Happiness, Love, Security, Inner harmony, Togetherness, Pleasure
Family	Happiness, Love, Togetherness
Meals	Survival, Pleasure
School	Accomplishment, Excitement
Love	Happiness, Love, Inner harmony, Togetherness, Pleasure
Work	Accomplishment, Togetherness
Friends	Togetherness
Child	Happiness, Love, Togetherness
Media	Wisdom
Vacation	Freedom, Excitement
Economy	--------------------
Countryside	Freedom, Inner harmony, Pleasure
Neat	--------------------
Child care	Love, Togetherness
Repair	Accomplishment
Groceries	--------------------
Exercise	Inner harmony
Hobbies	Excitement
Outings	Freedom, Togetherness
Pastimes	--------------------
Decoration	--------------------
Cleaning	Accomplishment
Food	Accomplishment
Cultural events	Excitement
Relatives	Togetherness
Parties	Togetherness
Restaurants	Togetherness
Shopping	--------------------
Dancing	Togetherness
Party-organizing	Togetherness, Recognition
Pet care	--------------------
Clubs	Togetherness
Courses	Togetherness, Excitement
Gardening	--------------------
Museums	Excitement
Cottage	Freedom
Sports events	--------------------
Durables	--------------------
Overtime	--------------------
Relaxing	--------------------
Sports	--------------------
Alcohol	--------------------
Tobacco	--------------------
Gambling	--------------------
Church	--------------------

age, sex, or marital status. An ANOVA on the correlations yielded for $p<.05$ no significant main effects of any of the between-subject factors.

Table 5: Correlations Between Rated Importance and Importance Predicted from Equation 1

Age (years)			Sex		Marital status		
18-24	25-35	36-49	Women	Men	Single	Family	All subjects
.440[1]	.549	.501	.509	.470	.452	.527	.490

[1]All the correlations are significant for $p <.001$.

Discussion

The present study set out to investigate the hypothesis that preferences for everyday activities are determined by beliefs about the extent to which performance of the activities facilitates the attainment of psychological values which are important for life satisfaction. In support of the hypothesis, positive correlations, modestly large but statistically reliable in all subject groups, were obtained between the observed ratings of how important the activities were and importance predicted, by means of Equation 1, from the ratings of how important those values were which performance of the activities was believed to facilitate. It should in this connection be mentioned that in previous research (Lindberg, Gärling, & Montgomery, 1988) a subset of the values was shown to be sufficient to achieve the same degree of correlation. This may also be true in this study although the binary judgments obtained with regard to the beliefs precluded analyses of this issue with multiple regression methods. Even though such a finding would not invalidate the hypothesis under study, it would illustrate the fact that a set of valid values as yet needs to be found (Montgomery et al., 1985).

More of a problem for the hypothesis is posed by the modest sizes of the observed correlations. If one or several important values were not included among the values designated as possible consequences of the activities, this would lead to lower correlations. However, the careful selection of a rather large number of values, based on the results of previous studies (e.g., Montgomery, 1984; Rokeach, 1973), should rule out this possibility. A related possibility is that the ratings of the importance of the values were invalid, but, because the values did not differ much in rated importance, only whether or not a value was perceived to be a consequence was of any importance for predicting the preferences.

It seems unavoidable to conclude from the present results that preferences for everyday activities have some other major determinants in addition to those hypothesized. Two such possibilities come to mind. First, activities are possibly not only perceived to facilitate the attainment of values but also the attainment of resources, for instance material resources such as money, and personal resources such as competence and health. Some activities are furthermore perhaps perceived to facilitate the performance of other activities which in turn facilitate the attainment of values and/or resources. In support Gärling et al. (1985) found that other valued consequences such as the contribution of resources and the facilitation of other activities somewhat increased the correlations between the observed and predicted importance ratings.

Secondly, it is possible that other factors than consequences are important. Triandis (1977), among others, assumes that the thought of an action or activity gives rise to an affect, for instance pleasure (if previous experiences of performing the activity have been pleasurable). Such an affect may also determine the preference for the activity. However, although it appears reasonable to make a distinction between the affective outcome of performing an activity and its value consequences, it is not clear to what extent affective outcomes of the activities were in fact captured by some of the values used in this study (e.g., excitement, pleasure). Such "confounding" was not intended but might have taken place if that was how subjects interpreted these values.

This discussion may be summarized by stating that, despite clear support for the hypothesis under study, it was evident that other, additional determinants of preferences for everyday activities need to be investigated in future studies. The most promising focus of such studies appears to be the probably rather intricate **systems** of beliefs about how activities, in addition to how they are related to values, depend on each other and on personal and material resources. In future studies it would furthermore be valuable if the distinction between affective outcomes and consequences could be made operationally clearer. It should also be pointed out that, as indicated by way of introduction, much further research is needed before the relationship between preferences for and the actual allocation of time to everyday activities is begun to be understood.

References

Abelson, R.P. (1981). Psychological status of the script concept. *American Psychologist, 36*, 715-729.

Ajzen, I. (1985). From intentions to actions: A theory of planned behavior. In: J. Kuhl & J. Beckman (Eds.), *Action control: From cognition to behavior,* pp. 11-39. Berlin: Springer.

Ajzen, I., & Fishbein, M. (1980). *Understanding attitudes and predicting social behavior*. Englewood Cliffs, NJ: Prentice-Hall.

Atkinson, J.W., & Birch, D. (1986). Fundamentals of the dynamics of action. In: J. Kuhl & J.W. Atkinson (Eds.), *Motivation, thought and action*, pp. 3-48. New York: Praeger.

Becker, G. (1976). *The economic approach to human behavior*. Chicago, IL: University of Chicago Press.

Campbell, A., Converse. P.E., & Rodgers, W.L. (1976). *The quality of American life*. New York: Sage.

Chapin, F.S. (1974). *Human activity patterns in the city*. New York: Wiley.

Diener, E. (1984). Subjective well-being. *Psychological Bulletin, 95*, 542-575.

Feather, N.T. (Ed.) (1982). *Expectations and actions: Expectancy-value models in psychology*. Hillsdale, NJ: Erlbaum.

Fishbein, M., & Ajzen, I. (1975). *Belief, attitude, intention, and behavior: An introduction to theory and research*. Reading, MA: Addison-Wesley.

Frey, B.S., & Foppa, K. (1986). Human behavior: Possibilities explain action. *Journal of Economic Psychology, 7*, 137-160.

Galambos, J.A., & Rips, L.J. (1952). Memory for routines. *Journal of Verbal Learning and Verbal Memory, 21*, 260-251.

Gärling, T., Lindberg, E., Montgomery, H., & Waara, R. (1985). Beliefs about the attainment of life values. *Umeå Psychological Reports No. 181*. Umeå: University of Umeå, Department of Psychology.

Hayes-Roth, B., & Hayes-Roth, F. (1979). A cognitive model of planning. *Cognitive Science, 3*, 275-310.

Keeney, R.L., & Raiffa, H. (1976). *Decisions with multiple objectives: Preferences and value tradeoffs.* New York: Wiley.

Kuhl, J. (1986). The dynamic theory of the anxiety-behavior relationship: A study of resistance and time allocation. In: J. Kuhl & J.W. Atkinson (Eds.), *Motivation, thought and action,* pp. 76-93. New York: Praeger.

Lindberg, E., Gärling, T., & Montgomery, H. (1988). People's beliefs and values as determinants of housing preferences and simulated choices. *Scandinavian Housing and Planning Research, 5,* 81-103.

Lindberg, E., Gärling, T., Montgomery, H., & Waara, R. (1987). People's evaluations of housing attributes: A study of underlying beliefs and values. *Scandinavian Housing and Planning Research, 4,* 81-103.

Michelson, W., & Reed, P. (1975). The time budget. In: W. Michelson (Ed.), *Behavioral research methods in environmental design,* pp. 180-234. Stroudsberg, PA: Dowden, Hutchinson & Ross.

Miller, G.A., Galanter, E., & Pribram, K.H. (1960). *Plans and the structure of behavior.* New York: Holt, Rinehart & Winston.

Montgomery, H. (1984). Cognitive and affective aspects of life values as determinants of well-being: A pilot study. *Göteborg Psychological Reports No. 14:3.* Göteborg: University of Göteborg, Department of Psychology.

Montgomery, H., Drottz, B.M., Gärling, T., Persson, A.-L., & Waara, R. (1985). Conceptions of material and immaterial values in a sample of Swedish subjects. In: H. Brandstätter & E. Kirchler (Eds.), *Economic psychology,* pp. 427-437. Linz: Rudolf Trauner Verlag.

Montgomery, H., & Johansson, U.-S. (1988). Life values: Their structure and relation to life conditions. In: S. Maital (Ed.), *Applied behavioral economics,* Vol. 1, pp. 420-437. Brighton: Wheatsheaf.

Nottenburg, G., & Schoben, E.J. (1980). Scripts as linear orders. *Journal of Experimental Social Psychology, 16,* 329-347.

Reiser, B.J., Black, J.B., & Abelson, R.P. (1985). Knowledge structures in the organization and retrieval of autobiographical memories. *Cognitive Psychology, 17,* 89-137.

Robinson, J.P. (1977). *How Americans use time: A social-psychological analysis of everyday behavior.* New York: Praeger.

Rokeach, M. (1970). *Beliefs, attitudes, and values*. San Francisco: Jossey-Bass.

Rokeach, M. (1973). *The nature of human values*. New York: Free Press.

Sacerdoti, E.D. (1977). *A structure for plans and behavior*. Amsterdam: Elsevier.

Schank, R.C. (1982). *Dynamic memory*. Cambridge: Cambridge University Press.

Schank, R.C., & Abelson, H.P. (1977). *Scripts, plans, goals, and understanding*. Hillsdale, NJ: Erlbaum.

Stone, P.J. (1972). Models of everyday time allocations. In: A. Szalai, P.E. Converse, P. Feldheim, E.K. Scheuch, & P.J. Stone (Eds.), *The use of time*, pp. 179-189. The Hague: Mouton.

Szalai, A., Converse, P.E., Feldheim, P., Scheuch, E.K., & Stone, P.J. (1972). *The use of time*. The Hague: Mouton.

Triandis, H.C. (1977). *Interpersonal behavior*. Belmont, CA: Wadsworth.

Warshaw, P.R., & Dröge, C. (1986). Economic utility versus the attitudinal perspective of consumer choice. *Journal of Economic Psychology, 7*, 37-60.

Wilenski, R. (1981). Meta-planning: Representing and using knowledge about planning in problem solving and natural language understanding. *Cognitive Science, 5*, 197-233.

Winston, G.C. (1987). Activity choice: A new approach to economic behavior. *Journal of Economic Behavior and Organization, 8*, 567-585.

Per Davidsson

Need for Achievement and Entrepreneurial Activity in Small Firms

Abstract

Since the publishing of David McClelland's book "The Achieving Society" in 1961, the need for achievement (nAch) has been one of the most discussed psychological concepts in research on entrepreneurship. In the book as well as in continued research, McClelland presents empirical support for his hypothesis that the level of nAch in a society is a major determinant of its rate of economic development.

However, research on nAch has also been criticized for a number of reasons. Establishing strong evidence for the relation between nAch and entrepreneurial behaviour at the individual level seems to be especially troublesome. Nevertheless, nAch has been used also at this level, e.g., to investigate how it relates to small firm start-up and survival.

In a fairly large survey of small firms in Sweden, nAch was included as one factor potentially explaining differences in entrepreneurial activity. As expected, the results show positive relationships between nAch and various forms of entrepreneurial activity in the firms, although differences in nAch do not account for a lion's share of the variation.

It is argued that although the nAch concept has problems with definition and measurement, and although more recent developments within an attribution theory framework promises more sophisticated explanations, nAch might still have a role to play in cases where very simple generalizations are sought.

Author's address: Per Davidsson, The Economic Research Institute at the Stockholm School of Economics, P.O. Box 6501, S-113 83 Stockholm, Sweden.

Introduction

The world has seen few attempts to explain social phenomena at the macro level by means of empirically supported psychological theory. The appearance of David McClelland's book "The Achieving Society" in 1961 was therefore quite sensational, since it suggested that economic development was to a large extent determined by the level of achievement motivation (*n*Ach) in the society and especially among its business people. The research effort presented in the book is really an enormous one, and considering the complexity of the problem studied the empirical support for the importance of this single psychological dimension is impressive. Accordingly, its author was not exactly modest when attacking economic theory. An example:

Here, at least, is evidence for what economists and others have so long and so inaccurately called the "profit motive." If we can assume, as all our evidence indicates, that western capitalists were actually motivated primarily by the achievement motive, we can now understand why they were so interested in money and profit, although, paradoxically, not for its own sake. Money, to them, was a measure of success. ... What gallons of ink and acres of paper might have been saved if economic and political theorists had understood this distinction sooner! (McClelland, 1961, p. 236)

McClelland probably grossly overestimated the importance economic theorists would attribute to such a distinction, but he was apparently right in assuming that his contribution would attract much attention. Since then, *n*Ach has been one of the most used and discussed psychological concepts in research on entrepreneurship, and it is used also by economists (Casson, 1982; Leibenstein, 1968).

Although McClelland and his associates regularly seem to find support for their hypotheses also in their continued work (McClelland 1965, 1966; McClelland & Winter, 1969; Miron & McClelland, 1979), the *n*Ach findings have also been questioned and sometimes heavily criticized, both as regards measurement (e.g., Gasse, 1982), the effectiveness of *n*Ach training (Brockhaus, 1982; Gibb, 1986), the results concerning entrepreneurial success (Deeks, 1976), and the relation to macroeconomic development (Finison, 1976).

The problems, as I see it, are largely due to the lack of a stringent definition of *n*Ach. McClelland defines *n*Ach very loosely as "a competition with some standard of excellence" or some variation on that theme (Wärneryd, 1988). The lack of a definition has led to a rather sloppy use of the concept, where anything measured in any way, be it single-item scales, multiple-item scales, factors extracted in a factor analysis, or interpretations of in-depth interviews, has been called "need for achievement." While adding another measure of *n*Ach in this paper, I will at the same time try to evaluate the appropriateness of the *n*Ach-label.

Purpose

The purpose of this paper is to investigate the relationship between *n*Ach and the degree of entrepreneurial activity in small, owner-managed firms. Entrepreneurial activity is understood as innovative and growth-oriented behaviour and attitudes.

Method

A sample of 540 small business managers was drawn from Statistics Sweden's register of all Swedish firms. Attempts were made to restrict the frame to independent, owner-managed, commercial firms with 2-19 employees. The sample was stratified into three size classes and four industries (Manufacturing, High-Tech, Repair Services, and Retailing), giving 12 cells from each of which a simple random sample of 45 companies was drawn.

Of the 540 managers, 439 (81%) were interviewed by telephone. In addition, 335 returned a postal follow-up, in which the *n*Ach-indicators were contained. Additional non-response on one or more of the *n*Ach-indicators reduced the effective sample to a maximum of 325 subjects or 60% of the original sample.

The main problem with *n*Ach is, of course, how to operationalize it. McClelland favours projective techniques, such as the TAT or content analysis of symbolic behaviour. In fact, he suggests quite strongly that *n*Ach **cannot** be measured directly and states explicitly that individuals (American males) with high *n*Ach cannot give accurate reports on what their "inner concern" with achievement is (McClelland, 1961, p. 44).

However, the projective techniques have been shown to entail problems such as sensitivity to instructions, situational pressures, and various cues in the environment (Atkinson, 1964) as well as with the interpretation of data (Gasse, 1982). Aside from this, projective techniques are very impractical when nAch is but one among many independent variables to study. Therefore, a more objective and "easy-to-administer" measure is needed. Although attempts have been made (see, e.g., Hornaday & Aboud, 1971; Lynn, 1969) no agreement on an alternative to the projective techniques has been reached.

In this study, a four-item Likert scale was used. The items included were:

1. I have always wanted to succeed and to accomplish something in my lifetime. (high nAch)

2. I find it hard to understand people who always keep on striving for new goals although they have already achieved all the success they could possibly have imagined. (low nAch)

3. To face new challenges and to manage to cope with them is important to me. (high nAch)

4. I am so satisfied with what I have achieved in my life that I think now I can confine myself to keeping what I already have. (low nAch)

Degree of agreement was measured on five-point balanced scales. The negatively loaded items (2 and 4) were recoded so that a higher score means more achievement motivation. The intercorrelations range from 0.13 to 0.38 and are thus not very high. The combined measure yields a Cronbach Alpha of 0.55, which is only moderately good. The distribution and some statistics are given in Figure 1.

Apparently, the index differentiates among the respondents. But does it measure "need for achievement according to McClelland?" Of course, there is no direct way to settle that matter, since TAT scores have not been collected. If the relationships between the measure used and other variables, for which there are empirically established relationships with nAch, are the predicted ones, one could at least say that this index

```
Count   Value

  2      9  ==
  7     10  =====
  6     11  ====
 24     12  ===================
 36     13  ===============================
 37     14  ================================
 56     15  ==================================================
 52     16  ============================================
 40     17  ----------------------=======================
 24     18  ===================
 19     19  ================
 22     20  =================
```

```
      I..............I..............I..............I..............I..............I
      0            12            24            36            48            60
```

Mean = 15.4, Median = 15.0, s.d. = 2.46, *n* = 325.

Figure 1: Distribution of *n*Ach scores.

is a reasonable approximation of *n*Ach. From various parts of the "The Achieving Society" the following characteristics of individuals high in need for achievement have been assembled:

1. They are moderate risk takers. They like to take some objective risks but are not attracted to games of chance.

2. Profit is important to them as a measure of success and not for its own sake.

3. Ownership control is not critical to them.

4. They prefer experts rather than friends as workmates/ business partners.

These relationships have been checked against data in the study, and in each case at least a tendency in the expected direction was found. When those above the median in *n*Ach are contrasted with those below the median it turns out that the importance attributed to profitability is significantly ($p < 0.05$) higher in the "high" group, whereas the difference in importance rating for "high private financial standard," although in the same direction, is far from significant. No difference in ratings of importance of ownership control appears, but the average actual ownership is significantly lower in the "high" group. Rankings of importance of different personal sources of advice show a close to significant lower rating for spouse/family for the "high" group. Consultants and non-family-board members get higher ratings in the "high" group, although the differences are not significant. The pattern for risk preferences is especially interesting. Two "risk attitude" measures were included in this survey. More or less by chance, their wordings happen to be nearly perfect for the present purpose. They read:

1. I take a chance and face a loss now and then, rather than withdraw and afterwards realize that I missed a good business deal.

2. I am always careful and do not take any great risks when I do business.

The first item stresses chance and should therefore not be approved of by high *n*Ach individuals. The other item suggests a passivity which would not go with high *n*Ach. The responses reflect this: The degree of approval is lower in both cases in the "high" group in spite of the fact that the first item is pro risk and the second against. For the second item, the difference is significant.

In all then, it seems that the *n*Ach-index measures a psychological difference between subjects and that labeling this difference "need for achievement" is reasonably well justified.

Hypotheses

Need for Achievement and the Entrepreneurial Decision

According to McClelland, individuals high in *n*Ach can be found, and can themselves find an arena to exploit their entrepreneurial talents, within any kind of organization as well as outside business. Since owning and managing a firm provide great opportunities for concrete feedback about success leading to achievement satisfaction, the proportion of high *n*Ach individuals should be high among small business managers. Other researchers also find support for a relationship between *n*Ach and the decision to become an entrepreneur, but they often do not seem convinced that *n*Ach is a very important dimension (Borland, 1975; Hull, Bosley, & Udell, 1980). Brockhaus (1982) concluded that the causal link between ownership of a small business and *n*Ach had not been proved.

In this study, all respondents were small business owners and thus no comparison with other populations are possible. However, founding or buying a firm may be considered more entrepreneurial than merely inheriting an existing firm. If there is a relationship between *n*Ach and entrepreneurial activity, the following should hold:

> **Hypothesis 1**: Managers who have founded (or bought) their own businesses have higher *n*Ach than those who have inherited existing firms.

If this hypothesis is supported, it would at the same time uphold the idea that *n*Ach is to some degree a stable personality characteristic, since reversed causality is somewhat harder to imagine here than in the case of growth or success.

Need for Achievement and Expansion

A very general hypothesis would be that small business managers with high *n*Ach are more inclined to pursue some kind of development in their firms, since they need concrete feedback of success to obtain achievement satisfaction. Status quo would normally provide little feedback of this kind. Growth is one possible way of getting achievement feedback, since it is easily measured and in a small firm very much attributable to its manager. However, a relationship between *n*Ach and growth is not self-evident.

Firstly, existing empirical evidence is inconclusive. McClelland and Winter (1969) found that firms whose managers had taken part in *n*Ach training grew faster than other, comparable firms in the same area. Miron and McClelland (1979) found the picture not so clear but arrived at essentially the same conclusion. Deeks (1976), however, claimed that no satisfactory evidence for a connection between high *n*Ach and "success" had been presented and Khan (1986) found that *n*Ach was not a very reliable selection criterion for venture capitalists to use when choosing among investment objects.

Secondly, from a theoretical perspective it is doubtful whether the pursuit of growth is in the long run compatible with the need for concrete success feedback. The transition from a "purely" entrepreneurial role to a more administrative one is often a problem in growing firms (cf. Maidique, 1980), and to keep the close link between his/her own actions and the outcomes, the small business owner-manager might instead be better off striving for success in terms of percentage profitability and qualitative development. However, in firms as small as in the present sample, growth is still likely to be one of the success criteria used by the high *n*Ach managers, since it would probably not severely disconnect the manager from direct responsibility for the outcomes. Therefore, the next hypothesis is:

Hypothesis 2: There is a positive relationship between *n*Ach and growth aspirations.

Yet, aspirations are not all it takes to create growth. If Hypothesis 2 holds true, it might indicate nothing more than a difference in response styles. Therefore, a measure of real growth is preferable. Since the present study is cross-sectional, previous growth is the only available measure of real growth. Accordingly:

Hypothesis 3: There is a positive relationship between *n*Ach and previous growth.

A problem with this hypothesis is the nature of the sample. The firms were selected with present size as a criterion. Comparable firms with higher growth rates are therefore underrepresented, since it is more likely that they had already passed the size limit. Secondly, if the hypothesis is not rejected, the causal direction still cannot be determined. Although a positive relationship between *n*Ach and previous growth as well as growth aspirations would be supportive, there is no way to prove that high *n*Ach leads to growth rather than the reverse. Most likely there is a subtle interrelationship between past success, locus-of-control, need for achievement, and growth aspirations (cf. Weiner et al., 1972).

Another measure of expansion is the geographic market served by the firm. Irrespective of whether they aim for higher total growth or not, more entrepreneurial managers should be inclined to look for business opportunities also outside the local market. If high nAch-individuals are more entrepreneurial, the following hypothesis emerges:

Hypothesis 4: There is a negative relationship between nAch and the proportion of annual turnover obtained in the local market.

Even if the manager is interested in expansion, this expansion does not necessarily have to be manifested through growth within a firm; it could also lead to the starting and managing of additional business activities. If high nAch individuals are more entrepreneurial, this hypothesis follows:

Hypothesis 5: Managers with high nAch are more likely to operate more than one firm than are those low in nAch.

Need for Achievement and Innovativeness

As mentioned above, a need for development and concrete feedback about success does not have growth as the "single outlet." If growth is perceived as threatening the possibility to attribute success to one's own ability and effort, qualitative achievements would be safer. Also for those striving for growth, the successful development and marketing of new products would provide an extra source of achievement satisfaction. Accordingly:

Hypothesis 6: Firms with managers high in nAch devote more effort to the development of new products.

If the hypothesis holds true it could of course also be interpreted as showing that new product development is one of the means used to create quantitative growth.

Results

Hypothesis 1

Table 1 displays the mean difference between inheritors and buyers/founders. Eighteen subjects, who gave answers in the category "other," have been excluded from this analysis.

Table 1: *n*Ach Scores for Inheritors and Founders/Buyers

	n	Mean	S.d.	*t*-value	Sign.level
Inheritors	45	14.3	2.6	−2.88	0.005
Founders/buyers	259	15.5	2.4		

The mean difference is highly significant and Hypothesis 1 cannot be rejected. This result confirms earlier empirical findings indicating that inheritors are less entrepreneurial (e.g., Boswell, 1972). However, it cannot be ruled out that the difference is due to a tendency for unsuccessful inheritors to stay in business longer than unsuccessful founders. If such is the case, the difference implies a relationship between *n*Ach and success, but not necessarily between *n*Ach and the decision to start or buy a business firm.

Hypothesis 2

The computed percentage difference between present size and an "ideal state" five years ahead, both as stated by the respondent, was used as the dependent variable for testing Hypothesis 2. Measures were collected for turnover and for number of employees. The measures have been logarithmized and combined, forming a "growth aspiration index" (Cronbach's Alpha = 0.79). Here and in later analyses, the respondents have been split up into two groups, viz., those having *n*Ach scores above the median and all others. A *t*-test yielded the results displayed in Table 2.

Table 2: Growth Aspirations Among High and Low *n*Ach Respondents

Growth aspirations (log percent)					
	n	Mean	S.d.	*t*-value	Sign.level
High *n*Ach group	149	21.65	18.10	3.93	0.001
Low *n*Ach group	157	14.39	13.85		

The mean difference is large and highly significant. Thus, Hypothesis 2 gets some support. In an earlier paper (Davidsson, 1987) the relationship between expected outcomes of growth (how an increase in size would affect workload, income, employee well-being, stability, independence, control, quality and work satisfaction) and growth aspiration was investigated. It was shown that in individual regressions all these expected outcome variables had significant coefficients in the expected directions and that together they and two subgroup dummies (high-tech and smallest size group) accounted for around 25 percent of the variation in growth aspirations.

To check whether *n*Ach contributes significantly to explanatory power when these relationships are controlled for, the regression displayed in Table 3 was run. For simplicity, the expected outcome variables have been summarized in a single index (Cronbach's Alpha = 0.72) which could be interpreted as "Attitude towards growth." *n*Ach is here used as a continuous variable, i.e., the original *n*Ach scores of the subjects were used. Since the independent variables were measured on different scales, only the standardized scores are displayed. The magnitude of these may be interpreted as indicators of the relative importance of the variables.

Table 3: Factors Explaining Growth Aspirations

Independent variables	Stand. coeff.	Sign. level
*n*Ach	.147	.01
Attitude	.403	.0001
Small (dummy)	.120	.01
Hitech (dummy)	.208	.0001

$R^2 = 0.29$, $n = 306$, $F = 32.51$, sign. $F = 0.0001$.

57

As can be seen, the influence of nAch is highly significant also in the multivariate case. Thus, Hypothesis 2 cannot be rejected. However, the unique contribution of the nAch index to the explanatory power is modest both in absolute terms (increase in R^2 is less than 3 percentage points) and compared to the expected outcomes index.

Interestingly, the positive relationship between nAch and growth aspiration does **not** appear in a separate analysis of the 40% of the respondents who do not expect financial gains from growth. This result is in line with McClelland's suggestion that for individuals high in nAch, money serves as a measure of success. Accordingly, in the absence of financial reward, growth does not provide achievement satisfaction, and the positive relationship between nAch and growth disappears.

Hypothesis 3

The respondents were also asked about the size of the firm three years previously, or, in the event of the firm being less than 3 years old, what the size was during the first year of operation. The differences between these sizes and present size, expressed as annual growth rates, are the variables used to test the third hypothesis. Both distributions are highly skewed due to the fact that most firms had grown very little or not at all. The t-tests in Table 4 are therefore accompanied by a non-parametric test of significance, the Mann-Whitney U-test.

The relationship between nAch and previous growth is quite firmly established. The highly significant result of the M-W test shows that the mean difference is not due to a few extreme cases in the high nAch group. Hypothesis 3 cannot be rejected.

Hypothesis 4

In the postal follow-up, the respondents were asked to estimate the distribution of their annual turnover according to four categories: the home county, the rest of Sweden, Scandinavia excluding Sweden, and the rest of the world. Since very few of the firms engage in export, only the proportion of the annual turnover falling within the home county was used to test Hypothesis 4. Here too, the distribution is highly skewed and a

Table 4: Previous Annual Growth Rates in High and Low *n*Ach Groups

Annual growth rate as regards number of employees (percent)					
	n	Mean	S.d. *t*-value	Sign. level	M-W sign.
High *n*Ach group	143	14.4	22.9		
			2.65	0.01	0.001
Low *n*Ach group	159	7.5	21.6		

Annual growth rate as regards turnover (percent)					
	n	Mean	S.d. *t*-value	Sign. level	M-W sign.
High *n*Ach group	141	27.9	31.9		
			2.65	0.01	0.001
Low *n*Ach group	154	18.7	27.2		

Mann-Whitney test has therefore been performed alongside the ordinary *t*-test (Table 5).

Table 5: Proportion of Turnover Within Home County in High and Low *n*Ach Groups

Proportion of turnover within home county (percent)					
	n	Mean	S.d. *t*-value	Sign. level	M-W sign.
High *n*Ach group	154	59.9	37.9		
			−2.55	0.05	0.05
Low *n*Ach group	166	70.2	33.7		

Again, data are in line with expectation, supporting the hypothesis. However, when the sample is broken down into four industries, it turns out that the difference is entirely due to a very large difference within the manufacturing industry. In the other industries, there is no tendency whatsoever in the direction suggested by the hypothesis. In all, Hypothesis 4 cannot be rejected, but it is only partly supported by the data. Apparently, within certain industries market characteristics are so important for determining a firm's geographic market that any effect of nAch on geographic expansion is barred.

Hypothesis 5

The respondents were asked whether they owned/managed only the selected firm, a second, or more business operations. The contingency table shows that the pattern suggested by the hypothesis appears, but the difference does not reach statistical significance ($\chi^2 = 3.92$; $p<0.15$). A Mann-Whitney test does, however, give a significant result (M-W $z = -1.69$; $p<0.05$ single-tailed). Hypothesis 5 thus cannot be rejected. Operating more than one business appears to be slightly more common among the high nAch managers.

Hypothesis 6

The managers who stated that the main activity of their firms was production (as opposed to service or trade) were asked to what degree they were subcontractors or produced their own products, and whether they were at present developing any new products. These questions were used to test Hypothesis 6.

Four categories were used to code the proportion of annual turnover yielded by the company's own products. Of course, this is a very indirect way of measuring new product development effort. A contingency table test reveals that the pattern looks as expected, but the differences are not very large and do not reach satisfactory statistical significance ($\chi^2 = 6.91$; $p<0.08$). If the proportion of own product turnover is collapsed into two categories (i.e., no own products vs. at least some turnover from own products), the result reaches statistical significance ($\chi^2 = 5.33$; $p<0.05$). Moreover, the Pearson correlation coefficient between nAch scores and the proportion of own product turnover (coded in four categories) is as high as 0.24 and highly significant ($p<0.005$). Apparently the extreme ends of the nAch distributions differ substantially in this respect. This can also be seen in Table 6, where the respondents have been regrouped into three levels of nAch.

Table 6: Production of Own Products in Manufacturing Firms with Low, Intermediate, and High *n*Ach Managers

| | *n*Ach | | | |
	Low	Inter-mediate	High	Row total
No own products	19	12	8	39 32.0%
Own products	15	31	37	83 68.0%
Column total	34 27.9%	43 35.2%	45 36.9%	122 100.0%

χ^2 = 13.43, Sign.level = 0.001.

Here, the relationship between *n*Ach and the propensity to produce one's own products stands out quite clearly. Thus, Hypothesis 6 gets some support.

A more direct test of the hypothesis is given by a contingency table test of the answers to a question in which the managers were asked whether the firm was at present developing any new product which was not as yet launched but which they assumed would be on the market within two years. Although the difference found is still in the expected direction, here the relationship is much weaker and close to non-existent (χ^2 = 0.15; $p<0.71$). Recoding into three *n*Ach groups does not help here.

In all, Hypothesis 6 gets only indirect support. It might appear, then, as if high *n*Ach is more closely related to quantitative growth than to qualitative development. There is a logic to such a finding, since quantitative growth is easily measured and thus provides the manager with the concrete feedback he is supposed to need, whereas the development of new products often is an undertaking with a considerable risk to it, and feedback appears only after a long period. Therefore to the high *n*Ach mind it might not be as well suited as a criterion of success. Such a conclusion would perhaps be a bit premature if based on these data alone, since Hypothesis 6 was tested on a small subgroup of the sample.

Discussion

The results presented in this paper generally indicate that at the individual level there is a positive relationship between need for achievement – as measured here – and entrepreneurial activity in small firms. Some of the relationships are weak and the hypotheses only partly supported, but the relationship between *n*Ach and quantitative growth appears to be quite strong. Causality has not been proven, of course. Irrespective of whether the relationships between *n*Ach and both previous growth **and** present growth aspirations is interpreted as *n*Ach causing growth or as success causing both achievement motivation and growth aspirations, the results are still interesting. It should be remembered, though, that although significant results are obtained in most of the analyses above, *n*Ach does not account for a very large share of the variation.

According to a number of authors referred to in Wärneryd (1988), there is a decreasing interest in McClelland's notion of achievement, but a growing interest in a more differentiated theory of motivation dealing with causal attributions. I find this very understandable and in many respects a sound development. Need for achievement is an ill-defined (and sometimes abused) concept, and the work of Weiner et al. (1972) and others provide a much more detailed understanding of what really goes on in our minds.

However, detailed knowledge is not always needed – sometimes simplicity is a must. **If** *n*Ach can be measured by questionnaires, **if** the results presented here are for real, i.e., if *n*Ach is a variable which causes development efforts, and **if** *n*Ach can be taught or affected in other ways, e.g., by the contents of media, then despite its flaws the concept certainly should not be abandoned. Of course, measurement techniques could be improved. Of the indicators in the index used here, it appears that the two items dealing with "not settling down despite success" (2 and 4) are the ones that account for most of the differences presented in this paper. Adding more statements of this kind, i.e., statements for which it is not clear whether an answer in one direction is more socially desirable than an answer in the other direction, may result in a useful scale. The other two items (1 and 2) are so generally stated that anybody could – or feel they should – agree. These items, therefore, have little discriminatory power.

References

Atkinson, J.W. (1964). *An introduction to motivation.* New York: American Book-Van Nostrand-Reinhold.

Borland, C. (1975). *Locus of control, need for achievement, and entrepreneurship.* Austin: University of Texas. Unpublished doctoral dissertation.

Boswell, J. (1972). *The rise and decline of small firms.* London: Allen & Unwin.

Brockhaus, R.H. (1982). The psychology of the entrepreneur. In: C.A. Kent, D.L. Sexton, & K.H. Vesper (Eds.), *Encyclopedia of entrepreneurship*, pp. 39-57. Englewood Cliffs, NJ: Prentice-Hall.

Casson, M. (1982). *The entrepreneur: An economic theory.* Oxford: Martin Robertson.

Davidsson, P. (1987). *Small business managers' willingness to pursue growth – The role of beliefs about outcomes of growth for attitudes towards growth and growth aspirations.* Paper presented at Workshop on Recent Research on Entrepreneurship in Europe, European Institute for Advanced Studies in Management, Brussels, May 14-15.

Deeks, J. (1976). *The small firm owner-manager: Entrepreneurial behavior and management practice.* New York: Praeger.

Finison, L.J. (1976). The application of McClelland's national development to recent data. *Journal of Social Psychology, 52*, 55-59.

Gasse, Y. (1982). Elaborations on the psychology of the entrepreneur. In: C.A. Kent, D.L. Sexton, & K.H. Vesper (Eds.), *Encyclopedia of entrepreneurship*, pp. 57-61. Englewood Cliffs, NJ: Prentice-Hall.

Gibb, A. (1986). *Entrepreneurship – State of the art?* Paper presented at the 4th Nordic Research Conference on Small Business, Umeå/Vasa, June.

Hornaday, J.A., & Aboud, J. (1971). Characteristics of successful entrepreneurs. *Personnal Psychology, 24*, 141-153.

Hull, D.L., Bosley, J.J., & Udell, G.G. (1980). Renewing the hunt for the Heffalump: Identifying potential entrepreneurs by personality characteristics. *Journal of Small Business Management, 18*, 11-18.

Khan, A.M. (1986). Entrepreneur characteristics and the prediction of new venture success. *Omega, 14*, 365-372.

Leibenstein, H. (1968). Entrepreneurship and development. *American Economic Review, 63*, 72-83.

Lynn, R. (1969). An achievement motivation questionnaire. *British Journal of Psychology, 60*, 529-534.

Maidique, M.A. (1980). Entrepreneurs, champions, and technological innovation. *Sloan Management Review, 21*, 59-76.

McClelland, D.C. (1961). *The achieveing society.* Princeton, NJ: Van Nostrand.

McClelland, D.C. (1965). nAchievement and entrepreneurship: A longitudinal study. *Journal of Personality and Social Psychology, 1*, 389-392.

McClelland, D.C. (1966). That urge to achieve. *Think Magazine*, November-December, pp. 19-23.

McClelland, D.C., & Winter, D.G. (1969). *Motivating economic achievement.* New York: Free Press.

Miron, D., & McClelland, D.C. (1979). The impact of achievement motivation training on small business. *California Management Review, 21*, 13-28.

Weiner, B., Frieze, I., Kukla, A., Reed, L., Rest, S., & Rosenbaum, R.M. (1972). Perceiving the causes of success and failure. In: E. Jones, D. Kanouse, H. Kelley, R. Nisbett, S. Valins, & B. Weiner (Eds.), *Attribution: Perceiving the causes of behavior*, pp. 95-120. Morristown, NJ: General Learning Press.

Wärneryd, K.-E. (1988). The psychology of innovative entrepreneurship. In: W.F. van Raaij, G.M. van Veldhoven, & K.-E. Wärneryd (Eds.), *Handbook of economic psychology*, pp. 404-447. Dordrecht: Kluwer.

Amir Helman, Yoram Kroll, and Ada Lampert

The Kibbutz and Private Property

Abstract

The Kibbutz is a free and voluntary experiment towards accomplishing Marx's "full Communism" and the ideal of satisfying each member of the community according to his/her needs.

The founders of the Kibbutzim (in 1909) strove to build a new society based on freedom, equality, mutual help, tolerance, and brotherhood, excluding any sort of private property.

Second and third generations in the Kibbutz admire their parents' revolution but are seeking now to increase their privacy.

In this research, the attitude of 350 Kibbutz members towards the central question of Private Property was explored. Only 25% of the sample still believe in the Pure Principle of avoiding any private property. Sixty per cent have some private money and/or property, and more than 80% predict that the Kibbutz will become a less and less egalitarian society in the future. All of them realize that in the present situation, many are living a white lie, but feel that the basic desire to possess is stronger than any ideological value. It is interesting to note that people still feel annoyed by the knowledge of other people's private means, suggesting that ideology is stronger when others violate it, rather than oneself. The amount of money people own privately is small, and cannot change their basic standard of living, which is still dependent on the Kibbutz income. Perhaps it is the desire to have something of one's own that matters, more than one's real economic need.

Authors' address: Ruppin Institute, College for Managers in Kibbutzim, 60960 Emek-Hefer, Israel.

65

The Principles of the Kibbutz

Some people claim that the most original invention of the Jewish people is the creation of the Kibbutz in Israel. The specific contribution of the Kibbutz to the human experience is its attempt to translate socialist principles into every day practice within a community based on voluntary membership and direct democracy.

In Israel there are 300 Kibbutzim, with a total population of 120,000 people, which is less than three percent of the Israeli population. The Kibbutz is a communal village with a total population ranging approximately from 100 to 1500 persons, with an average of 400 to 500. Usually all the permanent adult residents know each other personally. This enables the Kibbutz to rely heavily on informal social control, a feature of great importance to the running of the community.

The Kibbutz is a voluntary society in its nature: Members may leave whenever they wish, and non-members may join at any time (provided their candidacy is approved by a stated proportion of the existing membership). The means of production are owned communally and production is carried out collectively. No wages are paid: The Kibbutz supplies the basic needs (education, health, food, clothing, social services, and so on), and in addition a personal allowance to all members on an agreed, equitable basis.

The Kibbutz' main ideal is derived from Marx's communistic ideas "from each according to his ability, to each according to his needs."

The Israeli Kibbutz has a unique method of distributing goods and services among its members (which is completely different from that found in the surrounding population). The Kibbutz uses the criterion of needs as the leading principle. It completely rejects all types of inequality, and even simple equality is against its principles. It opposes the idea that a person highly gifted by nature should be treated better than others. Moreover, the Kibbutz even rejects any connection between one's efforts and what one receives: It completely separates consumption from production.

In order to keep its ideal of equality, a Kibbutz member is not allowed to have any private property or any outside sources of income. For all his personal needs the member should use only the means provided by the Kibbutz (directly or by a personal allowance). The

66

abolishment of private property has always been one of the main principles of the Kibbutz:

Common ownership of property, self-labour, communal control of manpower, and the principle of (distributive) equality ... are the sine qua non of the collective (Barkai, 1977, p. VII).

Barzel dealt with the basic Kibbutz principles and wrote:

All the property of the entire community belongs to all its members. ... The individual who undertakes to join the communal society ceases to function as an individual in the economy, be it in the area of production or consumption. All types of income that he may receive are (ipso facto) the property of the commune. All consumer needs are funded exclusively by the society. The community alone is permitted to hold funds, derived from long-term sureties, such as pension funds, child-support monies, inheritances, and reparations (Barzel, 1986, pp. 9-10).

The exclusion of individual income accounts is the key which allows the Kibbutzim to translate the socialist maxim "to each according to his needs" into everyday practice.

The Development of Private Property in the Kibbutz

The Kibbutz is not a remote island which can keep its unique rules and values isolated from the surrounding society. The founders of the Kibbutzim (in 1909) strove to build a new society based on freedom, equality, mutual help, tolerance, and the abolition of any sort of private property. They hoped that a communal environment would gradually create a new kind of man. Quite early, however, they found that they still could not eradicate all typical characteristics of Economic Man.

The problem of outside sources had existed in the Kibbutz from the earliest days, and there are stories about a member who brought the first private Lux oil lamp to his leaking tent. After World War II there were two different reasons for the penetration of use of private property.

Talmon (1970) claimed that with the beginning of a rise in the standard of living, when the Kibbutz began to allocate items of affluence (housing, furniture, radio, electric kettle, etc.), temporary inequality appeared. The allocation of expensive items takes a long time, which causes a discontinuity between the standard of living of those members who receive first and those members who have to wait, sometimes for many years. "The bitterness and sense of discrimination caused some members to seek outside sources to supplement Kibbutz sources. The use of outside sources fills a need caused by the Kibbutz in order to maintain equality" (Talmon, 1970, pp. 226-227). But the main problem was the use of outside sources to obtain luxury items not yet provided for the Kibbutz.

The Kibbutz as a communal society is based on ordinary human beings, and exists in the spiritual milieu prevailing in its time and circumstance. Thus, the realization of its principles is necessarily a process of struggle and experimentation, attended by doubt and difficulty.

The first important test came after World War II, when veteran soldiers returned to their Kibbutzim, bringing luxury items with them. The Kibbutzim tried to tackle the problem with new guidelines and procedures. But the real ideological test took place in the fifties when hundreds of Kibbutz members received German restitution payments. It was taken for granted that the same rules applied to restitution monies as to all other outside sources, namely that they were the sole property of the Kibbutz and that the individual had no part in them. There was an unanimous stand on the member's duty to hand over all restitution monies to his Kibbutz. In some of the Kibbutzim the decision was to regard this sum as a deposit which would be returned to the member in the event of his leaving the Kibbutz within a certain period of time. In some other Kibbutzim the decision was that a maximum amount would be allowed to each restitution receiver for his personal benefit.

In spite of the success in these early test cases, dissatisfaction grew during the seventies and eighties. The ideal did not seem so strong any more, the power to withstand the influence of alien values was weakened, and the young generation of the Kibbutz was not so keen to avoid private property.

In 1985 the Centre of the Kibbutz Movement arranged a conference in Kibbutz Revivim to deal with the problem of private property in the Kibbutz. The decisions, which all Kibbutzim were obligated to accept, were similar to those of the restitution days: "The member should give all his property, income, and money to the Kibbutz." And "Any private ownership or keeping of money is in contradiction with Kibbutz principles. It is impossible to remain as a Kibbutz member with private property," etc.

The authors of this paper decided to check whether these decisions really reflect the members' will, wishes, and attitudes.

The Study

A questionnaire of 97 different items was prepared. These questionnaires were handed to students in nine of our courses during 1986, after the decision of Revivim's conference, enforcing members to transfer their private property to the Kibbutz. Each student was handed the questionnaire in a sealed envelope, was asked to fill it in, and to put it into a box in the class entrance. Of the students who had received the questionnaire, 98% returned it, so that we had 350 participants. The students belonged to the following courses: Treasurership, Foundation of Economics and Management, Business Administration, Branch Management, Advanced Financing Management, Store-Keeping, and three stages of an Academic Course in Economics and Management.

Most participants were young: None were older than 61, and only 5% older than 51. 95% were between 21 and 50, and 45% were between 31 and 40 years old.

Most participants were born in Israel (72.5%), whereas 19% were from the USA or Europe. While 40% were born in the Kibbutz, 60% arrived from outside the Kibbutz.

Most participants (84%) were married, 14% were single, 2% were divorced, and one participant was widowed.

The Need for Private Property

Members were asked whether they would "refrain from holding private property because of ideological reasons." Two-thirds of them declared that this ideal was not relevant for them, and only one-third gave a positive answer.

The assumption in the Kibbutz is that it is perfectly clear, and completely agreed, that non-ownership of any private property is one of the main principles of Kibbutz life. The only problem, according to conventional wisdom, is the evil inclination of human beings who, in spite of their belief in socialism and equality, tend to acquire money and other assets. We found that members' attitudes towards this principle are completely different – a majority of 66% claimed that the "ideology would not prevent them from holding money."

Another question was: "There are different reasons for which I would like to have private property (money)." An affirmative answer was given by 74% and only 26% gave the "required" Kibbutznik's refusal. We found that the utopian ideal of creating a New Man with no care for money and property has very clearly failed, as three fourths of the members feel a need for and want private property.

The Kibbutz in the Year 2000

Two of our questions dealt with the members' prognosis for the long-run development of the Kibbutz. The statement was: "In the year 2000, the private means of Kibbutz members will have become increased." 84% of the people agreed, and only 16% were optimistic enough to assume a change in this trend. We found a very strong and widespread feeling that the direction is towards more inequality, in spite of the fact that the study took place just after a clear-cut decision by the movement intended to solve the problem. We did not find any correlation between one's ideology and optimism, which means that even the idealists know quite well which way the Kibbutz is going in this respect.

In another question we inquired into the desire for an ideal-utopian Kibbutz: "Assume that we will have two kinds of Kibbutzim in the year 2000: (a) a Kibbutz without any private property, with complete equality, and (b) a Kibbutz with private property as a legitimate attribute. In which one of them would you prefer to live?" 60% of the members were still in favour of the ideal, while 40% would chose a Kibbutz lifestyle which – according to the conventional principles – would not even be a Kibbutz any more. We already saw that the majority of the members recognize the trend towards increasing inequality. Here we found that 40% would be against living in the utopia, even if it was possible. But also many of the 60% "idealists" knew that this desirable Kibbutz is impossible, and that they themselves need, want, and hold private property in spite of their "dream."

We presented a "case" in order to learn about the member's behaviour, were he to acquire a large sum of money. The story was: "Assume that your Kibbutz has significantly increased the assistance to the young generation who decide to leave the Kibbutz, and that one of your children has decided to leave. You have just won 20,000 dollars in the lottery. To whom would you want to devote this money? To your child who is to leave the Kibbutz, to yourself for your own use, or to the Kibbutz?" (The research took place immediately after the conference in Revivim, where the decision was taken that any such money should be given to the Kibbutz, with no other possibility of getting it back other than leaving.) We decided to use this story in order to allow members who may hesitate to declare that they want money for themselves, to use their children as an excuse. Only 21% of the members declared that they would prefer to transfer it to the Kibbutz (according to rules and ideology). Another 12% would prefer to divide the sum between the Kibbutz and their private needs, while 67% admitted that they would use all the money for their private use only (32% for their child, 28% for themselves, 7% for both). Thus, almost 80% revealed that they are ready not only to deviate from one of the main ideas of the Kibbutz, but also to break the clear rule that forbids any private property.

Out of the 21% idealists (those who would choose to give the 20,000 dollars to the Kibbutz), 40% still declared that they want private money. Perhaps we have here a group of members who are trying very hard to keep the formal rules: They would like money but in order to play a fair game, they are ready to transfer their assets to the Kibbutz. It is possible that in other situations, they would react differently. Only a small group of 13% (60% x 21%) seem quite sure – at least in theory – that they would transfer their own capital to the Kibbutz, because they wouldn't wish to have any private property.

Property Declaration

As holding money/property is still against the Kibbutz rules it is unusual to ask a member about his own private property. Members prefer to hide the fact if they have any money. Nevertheless, we asked some very direct questions about private money. We used the fact that the questionnaire was completely anonymous, and through the questionnaire the members were gradually brought to deal with their secret "accounts."

In one question we assumed that for a trip abroad a person needs 1500 dollars, and we asked the following question: "Can you afford such a trip?" 55% admitted that they could. When we asked about the possibility of financing such a trip "for you and your spouse," the percentage of positive answers went down to 44%. We can conclude that 44% of the members had a private property worth more than 3000 dollars. (The yearly personal budget of a Kibbutz member is 500-600 dollars which is hardly enough for his basic expenses: clothing, furniture, household items, etc.) In answer to our direct question ("I have a sum of private money outside of the Kibbutz"), only 30% of the members stated that they had none. Another 25% claimed that they had only very small amounts of less than 1000 dollars. Another 27% had 1000-5000 dollars, 18% more than 5000 dollars, and 9% more than 10,000 dollars. It appears clear that in the main, only small amounts of money (less than 5000 dollars) are privately owned, and yet people are willing to become "out-laws" even for the sake of only insignificant possessions.

Reasons and Justifications

One of the aims of our study was to find the reasons for wanting private property, in spite of the rule against it. We asked the participants to rate the importance of several motives from their point of view (5 = very important..., 1 = irrelevant). The most important justification for holding private property was the need to help children who decide to leave the Kibbutz. 54% thought this factor was important or very important, while 26% put it as not important (or irrelevant), $\bar{x} = 3.5$. It should be noted that the respondents in our sample were mainly young people, not personally afflicted by that problem.

The ideal of the Kibbutz is "to give to each according to his needs," but it does not include helping people who choose to leave. About 50% of the second generation prefer to leave, so that all members ought to assume that only some of their children will stay in the Kibbutz. Parents in the Kibbutz suffer from knowing that everything will be given (flat, job, etc.) to the child who stays with them in the Kibbutz but nothing can be given to the one who leaves.

Another important argument ($\bar{x}$ = 3.3) is "to feel safe in case of some emerging need." The idea of the Kibbutz was to meet one another's needs but in an affluent heterogeneous and multiple-generation society, there is no consensus about the definition of "needs."

A third important motive ($\bar{x}$ = 3.1) is "travelling abroad." Israel is surrounded by hostile countries and there is a lot of inside pressure and stress, so people are very eager to travel abroad. According to the equality principle, every year some 20-30 members enjoy a trip abroad which is paid for by the Kibbutz. In this way, the waiting time is about 20-30 years. But with one's own money, travel is unrestricted, and therefore, 44% of our participants claimed that this is an important or very important reason for holding private money.

Other justifications which were found were: "to keep the possibility to leave the Kibbutz" ($\bar{x}$ = 2.8); "to ensure my future in general" ($\bar{x}$ = 2.7); "to be able to pursue my hobby or special interest" ($\bar{x}$ = 2.6); "to be able to buy desirable goods" ($\bar{x}$ = 2.6). Less important were the arguments: "I like to know I have money" ($\bar{x}$ = 2.3); and "I don't want to be the only sucker, while all the others have money" ($\bar{x}$ = 2.0).

The relative importance of these reasons is further underlined by the answers to another set of items: "I would break the Kibbutz's norm which forbids the use of private money for these reasons." Here followed nine reasons, with the request to state "Yes" and "No." Help for children who left (or intended to leave) is the strongest justification for one's deviation, and 68% of participants were ready to break the rules for that reason. 53% agreed to do it for a feeling of security in case of an emerging need, 47% in favour of traveling abroad. In line with the earlier findings, only 19% were eager to have private property in order "not to be the only sucker." For 29% it is "just nice and pleasant to know they have money."

Conclusion

The Kibbutz can be seen as a laboratory, set up to accomplish the socialist's ideal of "giving each according to his needs." In order to achieve it, the Kibbutz strove to keep its member from private property, and in the past it succeeded in persuading members to give up their assets and money to the benefit of the Kibbutz.

Recently, because of growing dissatisfaction with the increased holding of private property, the Kibbutz Central Institution decided, in a meeting in Revivim, to compel members to deliver their money to the Kibbutz. But it is impossible to force people to give away something they possess. Only their good-will, their identification with the system, and their conscience could lead them to behave according to the ideal. In practice the decision to do so seems to be regarded as unrealistic, as no one appears to declare all of his property, or give it to his Kibbutz.

In our research we found a large gap between the "ideological line" and the members' attitude. Only 25% still believed in the Pure Principle of avoiding any private property. 70% have some private money and/or property, and 84% predict that the Kibbutz will gradually become less equitable in the future. All of them realize that the present situation is characterized by a white lie, but tend to feel that the basic desire to possess is stronger than any ideological value. The amount of money members own privately is quite small, and cannot change their basic standard of living, which is still dependent on the Kibbutz's income. Thus, perhaps it is the desire to have something of one's own that matters, rather than a real economic need.

References

Barkai, H. (1977). *Growth patterns of the Kibbutz economy.* Amsterdam: North-Holland.

Barzel, A. (1986). A reconsideration of Kibbutz thinking. *Shdemot – Education for Kibbutz,* pp. 6-15.

Shur, S. (1984). *Deviance, anomie and structural equality. The problem of private income on the Kibbutz.* Haifa: Haifa University, The Kibbutz University Centre.

Talmon, Y. (1970). *Individual and society in the Kibbutz.* Jerusalem: Magnes Hebrew University Press. (In Hebrew.)

Part II

Inflation, Unemployment, and Taxation

John Hudson
Perceptions of Inflation

Roy Batchelor and Lars Jonung
Cross-Sectional Evidence on the Rationality of the
Mean and Variance of Inflation Expectations

Peter K. Lunt
The Perceived Causal Structure of Unemployment

Henry S.J. Robben et al.
A Cross-National Comparison of Attitudes, Personality,
Behaviour, and Social Comparison in Tax Evasion
Experiments

Richard Wahlund
Perception and Judgment of Marginal Tax Rates After a
Tax Reduction

John Hudson

Perceptions of Inflation

Abstract

This paper compares estimates of different measures of inflationary expectations. Percentage-based expectations and perceptions of inflation appear accurate and reasonable. However, those derived from questions asking individuals how much they expect an £X bundle of goods to cost in a year's time are less so. Moreover, the implied rate of inflation declines as X, the base price of the bundle of goods, increases and appears to converge to some limiting value. It appears reasonable to suggest that from this limiting value we can derive individuals' true shopping basket based expectations. The question as to which of these two measures should be taken as representing the true rate of inflation is then discussed. Differences in the various measures are found to be related to age, sex, and information sources.

The author would like to thank Karl-Erik Wärneryd and an anonymous referee for their comments on the original paper and Leigh Hodges, Susan Smith, and Mark Stowe who helped with the sample survey.

Author's address: John Hudson, School of Humanities & Social Sciences, University of Bath, Claverton Down, Bath, BA2 7AY, England.

Introduction

Considerable work has been done in recent years by economists with respect to how agents form expectations and the subsequent problem of measuring those expectations. Two main theories have developed; adaptive and rational expectations (see Hudson, 1982). The former argues that agents form their expectations of variables from the past behaviour of those variables. The pure adaptive hypothesis sees expectations being corrected in accordance with the most recent forecasting error. Thus if people previously expected a variable to increase by 5% and it actually rose by 7% current expectations would lie somewhere between these two values. Higher order learning schemes are also possible by which individuals respond to more than the last forecasting error. The theory of rational expectations, which can be attributed to Lucas (1972), Sargent (1973), and ultimately Muth (1961), assumes that agents possess full and correct knowledge of the economic model appropriate to explaining the variable in question. If this is so, and if such models are accurate then expectations should differ from actual outcomes only by a random forecasting error.

An enormous amount of effort has gone into both developing these theories and their subsequent testing. There are two main methods of doing the latter. Firstly, one can test between the implications of the two methods where these differ. Although this is somewhat unsatisfactory as it frequently implies that one is also testing the general economic model within which expectations are embedded as well as the particular hypothesis of expectation formation. Alternatively one can attempt to measure expectations themselves and test directly between the competing theories. The problem with this is that it is not clear how one should set about asking individual agents what their expectations are, and because of this many surveys simply ask for a qualitative indication of change rather than a quantitative one. The main problem is whether agents understand questions which ask them to give answers in percentages. If they do, then the problem is simple. If they do not, then how can one formulate questions from which one can elicit specific quantitative data?

One possibility is to ask people how much they expect a specifically priced basket of goods to cost at some time in the future. For example if the basket currently costs £5 and the individual anticipates the future cost to be £6, then it is trivial to work out the implied rate of inflation to be

20%. This is in fact the approach this paper will adopt, presenting results on how comparable these answers are with those based on answers framed in terms of percentages. We will also be examining how the answers vary as the price of the shopping basket increases from £5 to £20 and then £50. Finally, we will examine how inconsistencies between answers and individual forecasting errors are related to individual characteristics.

Theory

This shopping basket approach to calculating annual inflation rates has previously been used by Alt (1979), and Bates and Gabor (1986). Both found that agents tended to greatly overestimate actual inflation rates. Alt, having noted that the distributions had log-normal tendencies, put forward what Bates and Gabor describe as "some highly speculative hypotheses concerning the way in which people might form their estimates of inflation," which they subsequently found little support for in their own research. They did, however, find that as the time span increased from a year the inflation rates declined so that over a sufficiently long period people were underestimating the rate of inflation.

Apart from this work, many aspects of the process by which people form expectations remain singularly unexplored. Most important perhaps is the question of what is the information set agents use in forming expectations. With respect to inflation Wärneryd (1986) has argued that these can be divided into those based on direct exposure to price changes, and indirect experience which emanates from information in the mass media, from policy makers, and from social peers. This latter information set may consist of information about price changes for certain goods or groups of goods like oil or about price index changes like the monthly reports on the changes in the price index.

There has been relatively little work done in economics, more in marketing, on the way people perceive prices and the changes in prices. Behrend (1974) found that people have consistently been most concerned with food price rises, something which Daniel (1975) confirmed. However, whether this implies that they give special emphasis to these in forming expectations is not clear. One possibility is that agents automatically form the appropriate weighted price index for each period on the basis of the prices they actually pay. But this is not the only possibility and it may be that some economic agents exhibit "selective perception" whereby some goods are given more importance than others. These might be goods whose prices are subject to minimal seasonal fluctuation or white noise. Alternatively, in a form of leader-follower model, there might be goods whose prices are thought to be slightly ahead of those of most other goods, thus providing a signal as to more general price movements to follow. Both of these models would lead to a roughly representative index and rate of inflation being formed. But it is also possible that people might be more impressed by polar values, i.e., very large price rises (and falls) and very small ones. If the former is the dominant model then the rate of inflation would be continuously overestimated and vice versa. Whilst a strategy giving an equal weight to both might again lead to a roughly representative index and inflation rate.

Bates and Gabor (1986) noted that respondents to a percentage-based question tended to use numbers such as 5, 10, 20, and 25% for their estimates of the yearly increase. Similarly when people are asked to give answers to a shopping basket question the unit of account tends to be discrete rather than continuous. For example, Alt (1979) found that almost all answers were given in units of 5p or 10p. As Alt was using a base price for his shopping basket of £1, this implies a floor on the inflation rate of either 5% or 10%. Provided that people always give non-zero answers if they expect prices to rise, this will lead to an upward bias in the responses. Answers will also increase in discrete jumps of 5% and 10%, although this is perhaps less likely to impart an upward bias to the answers. By moving the base price of the shopping basket from £1 to £5 or £10 this bias should decline and the resulting measure of inflation become more continuous **provided the unit of account does not also change.**

Results: Summary Statistics Relating to the Sample Survey Data

The sample survey on which this paper is based was carried out in Bath, England in March, 1987, with 149 respondents being stopped at random in the town's major shopping centre. Thus the inflation rate is not meant to be representative of that for the UK as a whole. It is hoped, though, that variations among different answers are representative of variations within this wider population. The mean and standard deviation of the various measures of inflationary expectations, together with perceptions of inflation, are shown in Table 1. For most of the results reported below the sample size was reduced to 140 due to the exclusion of "don't knows."

Table 1: Differing Measures of Inflationary Expectations

	Per%	Exp%	Exp£5	Exp£20	Exp£50	Actual
Mean	5.70	6.81	33.32	21.89	18.30	4.00
Median	4.50	5.00	26.00	20.00	16.00	
Standard deviation	3.77	5.38	30.39	20.00	19.19	

These statistics are based on a sample survey carried out in Bath. Per% and Exp% are percentage based estimates of perceived and expected inflation, respectively. Exp£5, Exp£20, and Exp£50 are also measures of expected inflation derived from shopping basket based questions. Sample size = 140 observations.

The actual inflation rate in the twelve months leading up to the date of the survey was 4.0%, and the latest figure 4.2%. Hence, the percentage figures relating to perceived inflation were quite accurate, and agents were also correct in generally perceiving that inflation was likely to increase, suggesting that people have a good understanding both of percentages and the state of the economy. Interestingly, expectations have a wider variation than perceptions. This is what might be expected, as there is more room for people to differ about what will happen than about what has happened. However, derived expectations tell a different story. The implied rates of inflation from all three questions are wildly improbable and totally incompatible with those from the percentage-based questions. The implied rate does decline, though, at what appears to be a decreasing rate, as the base price of the shopping basket increases. Table 2 shows that this is not just the effect of a few people's answers distorting the average. For when the base price increased from £5 to £20 the implied inflation rate fell for 53.6% of the respondents and either fell or did not change for 77.1%. The corresponding figures as the base price increased from £20 to £50 were even higher. In addition, 39.3% of the answers declined both times and 64.3% either declined or did not change.

Clearly, there is a general, as well as an average, tendency for the implied inflation rate to fall as the base price increases.

Table 2: The Relationship Between the Inflation Rate and Changes in the Base Price

	Exp£5 to Exp£20	Exp£20 to Exp£50	Both Exp£5 to Exp£20 and Exp£20 to Exp£50
Decline	53.6%	61.4%	39.3%
Decline or no change	77.1%	81.4%	64.3%

The variables are defined as in Table 1. The first element of column 1 shows the proportion of the sample whose derived expected inflation rate declined as the base price of the shopping basket increased from £5 to £20. Sample size = 140 observations.

These results suggest that as the base price increases the implied rate of inflation declines towards some limiting value. This can be approximated by something approaching the following non-linear function:

$$(1) \qquad \text{Exp}£X = a + b \, [(1/X)^c]$$

where X is the base price and a the estimate of the limiting value of the inflation rate. Estimating this function using aggregate data is a hazardous business with just three observations, but for what it is worth it was attempted using a grid approach based on values for c of between 0.1 and 1.0. The best estimate was obtained for a value of c equal to 0.7, yielding an estimate for a of 14.7%. This is still in excess of the rate of inflation obtained from the percentage-based question, although not as wildly unreasonable as before. Nonetheless this may still overestimate the "average limiting value." One reason for this is that it appears that the distribution is not normal, it is virtually bounded at the lower end by the fact that nobody expected a fall in the price level, whilst there is no such bound at the upper end. Indeed, some very high implied inflation rates were observed. This may make the mean an unrepresentative measure of expectations for the average economic agent, with the median value possibly being better suited for this. The median values are also shown in Table 1, and they are substantially lower than those for the mean.

There are a number of possible theories which could explain these results. Firstly, it could be that individuals are using two different information sets to derive answers to the two questions. The one for the percentage questions could be based mainly upon information derived from the media, whilst the one for the shopping basket question could be based mainly upon the actual price of goods. In this case, the latter is probably a truer measure of expectations. However, this does not explain the wide differences between the answers obtained for different prices of the shopping basket. To help with this we need to look at what happens to the unit of account as the base price increases. Table 3 gives information on this. Unlike the findings by Alt, who was using a base price of £1, not many of the answers were denominated in units of 5p. For the £5 base price 21.1% of the answers were denominated in units of 10p, but many more used either 50p or £1 as the basic unit of account. As we move from a base of £5 to £20 and then £50 the proportion having a unit of account less than £1 declined sharply and many more people appeared to think in terms of £5 units. This is reflected in the average units of account shown in the final column. Translated into percentages these average figures are 18.2%, 10.15%, and 6.34%, respectively. These give both the floor for the answer and the discrete increment possible from this floor. It is clear that although the unit of account does increase with the base price, this is

Table 3: The Relationship Between the Base Price and the Unit of Account

Base price	Unit of account						Mean
	£0.05	£0.10	£0.25	£0.50	£1	£5	
£5	1.4%	21.1%	5.4%	28.6%	36.0%	7.5%	£0.91
£20	0.0%	11.6%	0.0%	8.2%	51.0%	29.3%	£2.03
£50	0.0%	2.7%	0.0%	9.5%	31.8%	56.1%	£3.17

This table shows the proportion of answers to the shopping basket-based question which was based on various units of account. For example, 36% of the answers to the £5 base price question were multiples of £1 (excluding those which were also multiples of £5). Sample size = 140 observations.

not sufficient to prevent a decline in this unit when translated into percentage terms and in the potential bias resulting from the fact that this is a discrete rather than a continuous measure.

This may be an important factor in explaining both why shopping basket-based expectations tend to be higher than percentage-based ones, and why the gap narrows as the base price increases. But it seems unlikely that this is the whole story. It also appears that in perceptions of proportionate change people exhibit a bias which is dependent upon the base unit used to calculate that change. That is agents tend to underestimate the rate of change when small base numbers are involved. A 6% increase from a base of £5 is just £0.30, whereas a 6% increase from a base of £50 is £3.00. Agents tend to be more ready to identify the latter as being a substantial increase than the former.

Table 4: Correlations Between Expectations

	Per%	Exp%	Exp£5	Exp£20	Exp£50
Per%	1.00	0.58	0.29	0.31	0.26
Exp%		1.00	0.23	0.38	0.45
Exp£5			1.00	0.60	0.55
Exp£20				1.00	0.82
Exp£50					1.00

This table shows the correlations between the variables defined in Table 1. Sample size = 140 observations.

Table 4 gives information upon the degree to which agents were consistent in their rankings of expected inflation across the different measures. This table reinforces the previous conclusions in that there is a relatively small correlation between the percentage-based data and the shopping basket data, implying that there is little or no link between the two sets of expectations. However, it is interesting to note that the correlation tends to increase with the base price, possibly suggesting that the problem lies with the differing ability of economic agents to calculate reasonable price rises when starting from a low base price. The remaining correlations among the shopping basket-based expectations are higher and show that there is some degree of consistency among these answers. It is greatest for adjacently priced baskets.

Results: Regression Analysis of the Individual Responses

Now, an attempt is made to explore differences in perception with the use of regression analysis. I argued earlier that individual differences in expectations would be dependent upon sources of information, together with the ability to process information from these sources. In addition there is the problem that agents face in converting, either implicitly or explicitly, an expected inflation rate into a shopping basket price. This is a technical question and should not differ across agents according to their sources of information but merely according to their ability. Thus the basic equation to be estimated, for each of our measures of expectations together with the single measure of perceived inflation, is:

(2)   Expected/Perceived Inflation = f(Sex, Age, Type of Newspaper)

To an extent, age and sex are included to proxy differences in the composition of individual shopping baskets. However, they also reflect the degree of expertise and experience the individual brings to the task of forming expectations. If there is a learning mechanism, then older people should have more experience than younger ones. However, if the quality of education has been increasing over time, the reverse may be the case. Women, presumably, tend to have more experience and practice in shopping than men, and thus again should bring more expertise to the problem of forming expectations. However, there may be differences in the levels of educational achievement between the sexes, either at school or after leaving school. Newspapers also convey information about the state of the world, although not all do so in equal amounts. Thus I have divided the newspapers, by the use of 0-1 dummy variables, into the quality press, the tabloids, and what I have termed "medium papers" which lie between the two extremes. I have also included a dummy variable indicating whether the individual reads a local paper, as this will contain more information on prices specific to the area in which the questionnaire was carried out. Local papers tend to carry more advertisements on the price structure of local shops than do the national press. These dummy variables may also provide a proxy for intelligence, as the more intelligent may be supposed to read the quality newspapers.

Because one might expect the error terms in the different equations to be correlated across individuals use has been made of the technique of seemingly unrelated regressions (SURE) rather than OLS. The programme used is that found in the RATS econometric package. At first sight it might appear that the dependent variable has a lower bound of zero, which would make SURE and other techniques based on standard OLS unsuitable for the estimation process. However, individuals could have answered that they expected prices to fall and hence this objection is not valid.

Table 5: Regression Results Relating to Different Rates of Inflation

Variable	Per%	Exp%	Exp£5	Exp£20	Exp£50
Constant	5.60(4.64)	2.11(1.35)	20.92(2.05)	12.13(1.83)	12.41(1.97)
Per%		0.73(7.11)	1.51(1.95)	0.65(1.12)	−0.04(0.08)
Exp%			0.27(0.49)	0.97(2.71)	1.50(4.44)
Sex	1.41(2.35)	0.90(1.21)	7.49(1.55)	5.40(1.72)	1.87(0.63)
Age	−0.06(0.32)	−0.12(0.50)	3.13(2.10)	0.88(0.90)	−0.14(0.15)
Quality paper	−1.50(1.30)	−0.14(0.10)	−15.75(1.74)	−8.02(1.36)	−5.98(1.07)
Medium paper	0.49(0.40)	0.47(0.31)	−8.12(0.84)	−3.63(0.57)	−5.48(0.92)
Tabloids	1.71(1.21)	3.31(1.93)	−4.12(0.37)	−3.49(0.48)	−1.93(0.28)
Local paper	−0.71(0.52)	0.41(0.25)	−22.58(2.11)	−7.60(1.09)	−3.60(0.55)
R^2	0.13	0.37	0.18	0.20	0.21

This table shows the regression results estimated using seemingly unrelated regressions. Figures in parentheses are t statistics. Sample size = 140 observations. The 10%, 5%, and 1% significance levels for the t statistics are approximately 1.658, 1.980, and 2.617, respectively.

Turning first to percentage-based perceptions of inflation, Table 5 shows just one significant variable, at the 5% level, and that is sex. Women perceive inflation as having been 1.41% higher than men of similar characteristics. However, it is also interesting to note the steady decrease in the coefficients relating to the quality of newspaper. That is, as we move from the tabloids to the quality press, the coefficient becomes more negative. Thus agents who read quality newspapers tend to have lower perceptions of inflation than agents who read tabloids. In addition the latter have higher perceptions than those who do not read any paper at all.

The second equation shows the relationship between expectations and perceptions of inflation, both measured in percentage terms. As might be expected the latter is a very significant factor, at the 1% level, in determining the former. Of the remaining coefficients only the dummy variable for reading tabloids is significant, at the 5% level. Thus, the effect of reading tabloids is to increase the expected rate of inflation by some 3.31%. Similarly, women tend to have a higher expectation, although this is not significant.

The remaining three columns relate to the shopping basket-based measures of expectations. The one based on £5 shows both age and type of newspaper to be significant. As the age of individuals increases, so does their expectation of the rate of inflation. Readers of quality newspapers have a significantly lower, and more reasonable, expectation at the 10% level, than non-newspaper readers. Again it is interesting to note the steady increase in the coefficient, and therefore the declining accuracy of the expectation, as we move from quality papers to the tabloids. Surprisingly, perhaps, those who read local newspapers have the lowest expectation of all newspaper readers, the coefficient being significant at the 5% level. The remaining two columns tell similar stories, although whereas for the former, percentage-based perceptions are a more important factor than percentage-based expectations, as we move from £20 to £50 so percentage-based expectations become steadily more important. The only other variable which is significant in these latter two columns is sex. Women have significantly higher expectations, at the 10% level, when these are based upon a £20 shopping basket.

The regressions in Table 6, which were again estimated by SURE, provide evidence on the consistency of the individual agent's different expectations. The dependent variable in the first column is the absolute difference between percentage-based expectations and £5 shopping basket-based expectations. The greater this difference is the less is the consistency between the two measures. Both age and the local paper dummy variable are significant at the 5% level, whilst sex and the quality paper dummy are significant at the 10% level. Women and old people tend to have more dispersion between the two answers, and hence less consistency, whilst newspaper readers especially of quality and local papers have less dispersion and more consistency. With respect to women this finding reinforces Jonung's (1986) results, where women appeared less certain than men about percentage-based changes in inflation, although there was no similar effect for age. Other researchers, for example Bates and Gabor (1986) and Kemp (1984), have found no effect for either age or sex. The second and third columns relate percentage-based expectations to those based on £20 and £50 shopping baskets. There is only one significant variable, age in the second column. The final three columns relate to the absolute differences between the shopping basket-based questions. Both sex and age tend to have large positive coefficients, which are significant in several instances. This again suggests that there is less consistency in women's answers and in those of older people. The coefficients on the newspaper dummies are all negative, although significant in only one case. However, the weight of this collective evidence is impressive. It is also interesting to note that there is a general

Table 6: Regression Results Relating to Differences Between the Different Expectations

Variable	Exp% – Exp£5	Exp% – Exp£20	Exp% – Exp£50	Exp£5 – Exp£20	Exp£20 – Exp£50	Exp£5 – Exp£50
Constant	24.28(2.57)	13.90(2.45)	14.71(2.69)	11.99(1.69)	7.73(2.45)	9.76(1.34)
Sex	8.70(1.85)	2.97(1.05)	–0.57(0.21)	4.52(1.28)	4.45(2.83)	4.90(1.35)
Age	3.28(2.20)	2.06(2.30)	1.02(1.19)	2.27(2.02)	0.74(1.49)	3.69(3.20)
Paper:						
Quality	–16.87(1.87)	–5.89(1.09)	–4.30(0.82)	–8.82(1.30)	–7.02(2.33)	–8.80(1.26)
Medium	–7.91(0.82)	–5.26(0.90)	–7.41(1.33)	–3.17(1.33)	–2.92(0.90)	–1.46(0.20)
Tabloids	–5.09(0.46)	–3.54(0.53)	–1.11(0.17)	–0.33(0.04)	–3.57(0.97)	1.08(0.13)
Local	–21.30(2.00)	–8.76(1.36)	–5.18(0.84)	–8.73(1.09)	–5.59(1.57)	–11.48(1.39)
R^2	0.11	0.06	0.03	0.07	0.12	0.13

This table shows the regression results for dependent variables equal to the difference between the various measures of expected inflation. They were estimated using seemingly unrelated regressions. Figures in parentheses are t statistics. Sample size = 140 observations. The 10%, 5%, and 1% significance levels for the T statistics are approximately 1.658, 1.980, and 2.617 respectively.

tendency for these coefficients to increase as we move from the quality press to the tabloids, and that the coefficients on the local press dummy variable are again most similar to those of the quality press.

Conclusions

There are a number of conclusions that one can draw from these results, apart from the obvious one that there is considerable inconsistency among the different measures of expectation. This by itself is an important finding. The answers to the percentage-based questions were both accurate and reasonable, supporting two hypotheses: It is possible to measure inflationary expectations in this way, and individuals are competent in the use of the mathematical technique of calculating percentage changes. This is in contrast to results previously reported by Jonung (1986) where approximately 45% of his sample declined to answer percentage-based questions.

When turning to shopping basket-based expectations, one is led towards opposite conclusions. The derived expectations are wildly improbable. However, they do seem to be converging upon some limiting value as the base price of the shopping basket increases, and it is tempting to regard this limiting value as a valid measure of shopping basket-based expectations. If this is so it would imply firstly that agents have increasing difficulty in perceiving realistic price increases as the base price declines. This does not necessarily mean that they do not understand the mathematical concept of percentages as these answers are likely to be intuitive rather than based on the application of a percentage rate change to the base price. Secondly, this limiting value does appear to be substantially greater than the average percentage-based expectation implying that the two measures are incompatible and leads to the problem as to which to accept as the true one.

Using the terminology defined earlier the shopping basket-based expectations can probably be equated with direct experience, i.e., are formed by direct exposure to actual price changes. It then seems reasonable to suggest that percentage-based expectations can be categorized as being formed by "indirect experience," in particular by exposure to media-provided information regarding the current annual rate of inflation which tends to accompany the monthly announcement of the latest value for the retail price index. Again if this is so it implies that many economic agents have two sets of inflationary expectations, one based on direct experience and one based on indirect experience, and that these are inconsistent with each other. Previously it has been assumed that there is just one set based on an information set derived from both direct and indirect experience. The main problem has then been seen as the choice of a suitable measure for this unique concept. Our results suggest that this is not so and that different approaches to the measurement problem will lead to different sets of expectations. This does not rule out that information provided by both sources (direct and indirect experience) affect both sets of expectations. Rather, the implication is that the weights attached to the different sources of information differ in the two cases. Which of the two should be taken as reflecting the individual's underlying expectations with respect to the rate of inflation? The answer to this probably varies with the context within which the question is asked. However, one is tempted to argue that in most cases it should be the shopping basket-rate of inflation as this clearly reflects the individual's own experience, rather than what he is told by the media. Finally, if one is looking for a measure of average expectations the median is probably a better guide than the mean.

An important factor in explaining the wide variations across individuals in both their expectations and their ability to cope with the shopping basket questions is the different levels of ability and information people bring to the task of forming expectations. Readers of both quality and local newspapers tend to form a more accurate set of expectations as well as ones which are more mutually consistent. In addition, the coefficients on the various newspaper dummies tended to increase steadily as one moved from the quality press to the tabloids. The significance of the quality newspaper dummy could indicate either the influence of information provision or be a proxy for intelligence. However, the importance of local papers can more unambiguously be attributed to the provision of information as to local prices and conditions, which it is almost unique in providing. This is why people who read local papers tend to give more accurate and consistent expectations. Age is more likely to reflect straightforward awareness and intelligence factors. Younger people have on average received more years of schooling than older people, and this would appear to have given them a greater ability to cope with the problem of forming expectations.

References

Alt, J.E. (1979). *The politics of economic decline.* Cambridge: Cambridge University Press.

Bates, J.B., & Gabor, A. (1986). Price perceptions in creeping inflation: Report on an enquiry. *Journal of Economic Psychology, 7,* 291-314.

Behrend, H. (1974). *Attitudes to price increases and pay claims.* London: National Economic Development Office.

Daniel, W.W. (1975). *The PEP survey of inflation.* London: Political and Economic Planning.

Hudson, J. (1982). *Inflation: A theoretical survey and synthesis.* London: George Allen & Unwin.

Jonung, L. (1986). Uncertainty about inflationary perceptions and expectations. *Journal of Economic Psychology, 7,* 315-326.

Kemp, S. (1984). Perceptions of change in the cost of living. *Journal of Economic Psychology, 5,* 313-323.

Lucas, R.E. Jr. (1972). Expectations and the neutrality of money. *Journal of Economic Theory, 4,* 103-124.

Muth, J.F. (1961). Rational expectations and the theory of price movements. *Econometrica, 29,* 315-335.

Sargent, T.J. (1973). Rational expectations, the real rate of interest and the natural rate of unemployment. *Brookings Papers on Economic Activity, 2,* 429-472.

Wärneryd, K.-E. (1986). Introduction: The psychology of inflation. *Journal of Economic Psychology, 7,* 259-268.

Roy Batchelor and Lars Jonung

Cross-Sectional Evidence on the Rationality of the Mean and Variance of Inflation Expectations

Abstract

This paper draws on the results of a specially commissioned survey of consumers in Sweden to test the hypothesis of rational information processing with respect to lay forecasts of inflation. The mean and variance of such forecasts are important inputs to the economic theory of household labour supply, savings, and portfolio choice. Unlike most empirical tests of rational expectations, cross-sectional data on individuals are employed rather than time series data on some group average forecast. This allows testing for the presence of forecasting biases due to socioeconomic factors. "Mean rationality" and "variance rationality" are also examined. That is, we test for the presence of biases both in the mean inflation forecasts and in subjective confidence about the accuracy of the forecasts.

It is found that individuals who face lower information costs, or higher benefits from information collection, do indeed produce the most accurate forecasts, so that the theory of optimal information processing is not rejected. However, there are signs of systematic bias in the mean inflation forecasts of particular socioeconomic groups. Moreover, consumers' subjective ratings of the likely accuracy of their forecasts are systematically in error. Those individuals who consistently produce more accurate forecasts do not express a consistently higher degree of confidence in their forecasts. Hence the hypotheses of mean rationality and variance rationality are both rejected.

This research has been supported by the Economic and Social Research Council, London, the National Institute of Economic Research, Stockholm, and the Jan Wallander Foundation, Stockholm.

Authors' addresses: Roy Batchelor, The City University Business School, Frobisher Cresent, Barbican Centre, London EC2Y 8HB, England; Lars Jonung, Stockholm School of Economics, P.O. Box 6501, S-133 83 Stockholm, Sweden.

Introduction

In economic theory it is almost axiomatic that individuals collect data and use it to make forecasts in an optimising manner. Information is accumulated up to the point where its marginal cost matches its expected marginal benefit. This information is used to form statistically efficient subjective estimates of the parameters of the objective probability distribution for the variable being forecast. The optimising principle is an old one, but its applications to "search theory" and "rational expectations" are due to the work of Stigler (1961), Muth (1961), and more recently Lucas (1972). This paradigm has been strongly challenged by work in experimental psychology, which suggests that in other contexts individuals gather and utilise information in a biased way. Casually acquired data are given too much weight, and too much confidence is placed in ill-founded judgments. The evidence is assembled in Kahneman, Slovic, and Tversky (1982), but doubts about the empirical relevance of "economic man" had been expressed much earlier, notably by Simon (1959).

This paper draws on the results of a specially commissioned survey of consumers in Sweden to test the hypothesis of rational information processing with respect to lay forecasts of inflation. The mean and variance of such forecasts are important inputs to the economic theory of household labour supply, savings, and portfolio choice. Unlike most empirical tests of rational expectations, cross-sectional data on individuals are employed rather than time series data on some group average forecast. This allows testing for the presence of forecasting biases due to socioeconomic factors. "Mean rationality" and "variance rationality" are also examined. That is, we test for the presence of biases both in the mean inflation forecasts and in subjective confidence about the accuracy of the forecasts.

The paper is in three sections. In the first a simple theory of individual differences in information collection and processing is developed, which suggests how empirical tests of rationality might be conducted on cross-sectional data. The second section details the survey data which have been used, and reports the results of rationality tests on these data. The final section discusses possible limitations and extensions of the tests.

Socio-Economic Factors in Expectations Formation

Our first step is to set up a stylised model of expectations formation. This shows how individual differences in expectations arise under rational information collection and processing, and it leads to a number of testable propositions concerning the properties of such differences.

A Theory of Individual Differences

Suppose information on inflation p is available in the form of estimates p_j from a number of equally informative markets j, where $p_i = p + u_i$, $u_j \sim N(O, \sigma^2) \; \forall \; j$. These information sources could be literally the market inflation rates of individual goods within the aggregate price index, in which case σ^2 would be a measure of relative price variability. Alternatively, the p_j could be past inflation rates, the current inflation forecasts of experts, or the future inflation targets of the government. In these cases, σ^2 would reflect the variability of inflation over time, the quality of expert forecasts, or the credibility of policy announcements.

If individual i chooses to sample m_i markets, his rational expectation about the mean rate of inflation p will be

$$(1) \qquad \mu_i = E \{p \mid p_{i\,1}, p_{i\,2},..., p_{im} \} = \sum_j p_{ij} / m_i$$

Similarly, the rational expectation of the variance σ^2 of the market inflation rates around their mean will be

$$(2) \qquad \sigma_i^2 = E \{(p_j - p)^2 \mid p_{i\,1}, p_{i\,2},..., p_{im}\} = \sum (p_{ij} - \mu_i)^2 / m_i$$

The mean estimate μ_i is distributed as $N(p, \tau_i^2)$, where $\tau_i^2 = \sigma^2 / m_i$. The rational individual will therefore form an estimate

$$(3) \qquad \tau_i^2 = \sigma_i^2 / m_i$$

of the sampling variance of his mean estimate of inflation.

In this paper we refer to the subjective mean μ_i as "the expected rate of inflation" of individual i, and to the subjective variance of the mean estimate τ_i^2 as the "inflation uncertainty" experienced by individual i.

As shown by Rothschild and Stiglitz (1971), the equivalence of inflation risk and inflation variance holds only under certain assumptions about the individual's utility function. To satisfy these conditions, and to simplify the algebra below, we assume that all individuals have expected utility functions which exhibit constant absolute risk aversion with respect to real wealth W_i/P. That is

(4) $$E(U_i) = \alpha - \beta \exp\{E(W_i / P) - \tfrac{1}{2}R_i V(W_i / P)\}$$

where R_i is the coefficient of absolute risk aversion $R_i = -U''/U'$. We also assume that future nominal wealth W_i is known with certainty, so that uncertainty about real wealth $V(W_i/P)$ is entirely due to uncertainty about inflation.

Now suppose information is costly in the sense that each market visited reduces the wealth of individual i by c_i, and so reduces expected utility. On the other hand each visit reduces the subjective variance τ_i^2 of inflation, and so increases utility. Indexing the current price level as unity, the utility maximizing number of markets to visit can be found as m_i^*, where

(5) $$\frac{\partial}{\partial m_i}\{W_i(1 - \mu_i) - c_i m_i^* - \tfrac{1}{2}R_i W_i \sigma^2 / m_i^*\} = 0$$

(6) $$\Rightarrow \quad m_i^* = \sqrt{(R_i / 2c_i)} \cdot W_i \sigma$$

(7) $$\Rightarrow \quad \tau_i^2 = \sigma / \{\sqrt{(R_i / 2c_i)} \cdot W_i\}$$

This illustrates the commonsense notions that the optimum amount of information gathered will be larger, and the degree of subjective uncertainty smaller, for individuals with a high degree of risk aversion R_i, individuals who face low information costs c_i, and individuals with high nominal wealth W_i.

In Batchelor and Jonung (1986) we have suggested that these critical differences in risk aversion and information costs might be associated with identifiable socio-economic characteristics of the individuals under scrutiny. Denoting such characteristics as sex, age, location, employment, status, education, and income by the vector x_i, our argument is that

(8) $$m_i^* = m\,(x_i)$$

To be specific, we would argue that individuals with high economic participation rates – the employed, the middle-aged, the wealthy – have strong incentives to be well informed about inflation. These groups also have access, through changes in nominal wage and price offers, to low-cost information on the rate of inflation. Other groups with low-cost information sources include women, who (in Sweden at any rate) spend more time shopping than men, and so involuntarily collect more cross-sectional information on relative prices, city-dwellers, who are similarly exposed to a broader range of individual goods prices, and the old, who have simply through the passage of time collected a relatively large time series of data on inflation.

Tests for Rationality

Since·individuals are certainly aware of their own socioeconomic characteristics, Equation 8 can be substituted into Equations 1 and 2 to yield the following definitions of rational expectations of the mean and forecast variance of inflation

(9) $$\mu_i = E\,\{p\mid p_1,\,p_2,\ldots;x_i\}$$

(10) $$\tau_i^2 = E\,\{(p - \mu_i)^2 \mid p_1,\,p_2,\ldots;x_i\}$$

Denote the actual subjective mean and forecast error variance estimates of individual i by $\hat{\mu}_i$ and $\hat{\tau}_i$. Then Equations 9 and 10 suggest the following tests for rationality in these means and variances.

Mean rationality. From Equation 9, the error in the rational expectation of the mean rate of inflation should be orthogonal to elements of the characteristics vector x. Hence for $\hat{\mu}_i$ to be a rational expectation, we require that in the regression

(11)
$$\hat{\mu}_i - p = a + b' x_i + u_i$$

we find $(a,b) = (0,0)$. That is, the mean rate of inflation forecast by any particular socioeconomic group should not be systematically above or below the actual rate.

Optimal search. Since $\tau_i^2 = \sigma^2 / m_i$ and $m_i^* = m(x_i)$ from Equation 7 above, it follows that

(12)
$$\hat{\tau}_i = \tau(x_i)$$

That is, the variance of the forecast error should be systematically related to the socioeconomic characteristics of the forecaster – lower for the employed, the middle-aged, the wealthy, women, town-dwellers, and the old; higher for the unemployed, the young, the poor, men, and the rural population.

Variance rationality. From Equation 10, $\hat{\tau}_i$ will be a rational expectation of τ_i only if in the regression

(13)
$$(p - \hat{\mu}_i)^2 = a + b\hat{\tau}_i^2 + c'x_i + u_i$$

we find $(a,b,c) = (0,1,0)$. That is, deviations between the objective forecast error variance and the subjective estimate of this variance should not be correlated with identifiable socioeconomic characteristics of the individual making the forecast.

Cross-Sectional Rationality Tests

The data used to perform the three tests of Equations 11 to 13 have been drawn from a specially commissioned survey of consumers in Sweden, conducted as part of a regular consumer omnibus survey by the Stockholm-based Statistiska Centralbyrån (SCB). The survey was carried out on a random sample of some 1200 individuals in April/May 1984.

Respondents were asked the following three questions about their perceptions of past inflation:

Q1. How have prices in general changed during the past twelve months?

(Increased/decreased/remained unchanged/don't know)

Q2. By how many percent have prices increased/decreased?

(percent/don't know)

Q3. How certain are you about your reply concerning price movements during the past twelve months?

(very certain, rather certain, as certain as uncertain, rather uncertain, very uncertain)

A parallel set of three questions was then asked about inflation over the coming twelve months. Satisfactory answers to all six questions were received from 342 of the individuals surveyed. An overview of the main features of these data is given in Jonung (1986).

Figures for the subjective mean expectations of past and future inflation $\hat{\mu}_i$ can be obtained directly from responses to Q2. However, figures for the subjective error variances $\hat{\tau}_i$ surrounding these means can only be inferred indirectly, from responses to Q3. We proxy $\hat{\tau}_i$ by a set of dummy variables $CONF_{i1}$, $CONF_{i2}$,..,$CONF_{i5}$ taking the values 0 or 1 according as individual i professes himself "very uncertain," "rather uncertain,"..., "very certain." This assumes a response function of the form

$$(14) \qquad \text{Prob } \{CONF_{ik} = 1\} = f(\hat{\tau}_i) \qquad k = 1, 2,..., 5$$

where f is monotonically decreasing in $\hat{\tau}_i$.

The vector x_i has been compiled from the answers to a number of additional questions about the socioeconomic characteristics of the respondent. These have been expressed as a set of zero-one dummy variables covering sex (male or female), age (young, mid age, old), location (metro, urban, rural), education (elementary, high school, college), employment (full time, part time, unemployed), and income (low, mid income, rich). Middle age is defined as 35-54 years, middle income as the range SEK 70-150 thousand.

Mean Rationality

The test of Equation 11 for mean rationality involves regressing the individual perceptions (expectations) errors on the vector of socioeconomic characteristics. The results are shown in Table 1. Figures in parentheses after estimated coefficients are t-statistics.

Neither perceptions nor expectations are on average biased ($a = 0$). However, the inflation perceptions of the old are significantly higher than actual inflation, and the perceptions of the unemployed significantly lower. Similarly, the expectations of the best educated group are consistently higher than the actual outturn for inflation. The orthogonality condition for rationality $b = 0$ is therefore technically violated, though not to any major degree.

Table 1: Tests of Mean Rationality[1]

Independent variable	Dependent variable			
	Error in perceptions		Error in expectations	
Constant	−0.57	(0.51)	0.74	(0.88)
Female	−0.60	(0.87)	−0.66	(1.27)
Mid age	−1.12	(1.51)	−0.44	(0.79)
Old	−2.14	(2.49)	−0.80	(1.22)
Urban	1.37	(1.99)	0.06	(0.11)
Rural	0.98	(1.31)	0.03	(0.04)
High school	−0.57	(0.77)	−0.89	(1.58)
College	−1.50	(1.96)	−1.23	(2.11)
Part time	−0.47	(0.52)	0.59	(0.86)
Unemployed	1.67	(2.01)	0.64	(1.03)
Mid income	−0.56	(0.67)	0.07	(0.11)
Rich	1.08	(1.11)	0.87	(1.18)
Statistics				
R^2	0.06		0.02	
F	1.89		0.70	

[1]Estimated parameters of Equation 11 based on sample of 342 individuals. Asymptotic 5% significance levels for t and F are 1.96 and 1.78, respectively.

In a similar test Maital and Maital (1981) found the level of inflation expectations in a cross-section of Israeli consumers to be more strongly correlated with several socioeconomic factors – age, income, and the degree of trust exhibited by the respondent. It is natural to assume that biases result from individuals in these groups placing too much weight on information on inflation which is readily accessible to the group. For example, in other studies we have shown that the inflation expectations of women track food price inflation more closely than the general inflation rate (Batchelor & Jonung, 1986; Jonung, 1981). However, we can offer no convincing rationale along these lines for the particular biases uncovered in Table 1.

Optimal Search

In order to conduct the test of Equation 12 for the dependence of the objective **ex ante** forecast error variance τ_i on the characteristics of the forecaster, some proxy must be found for this unobservable variance. As pointed out by Cukierman and Wachtel (1984), the **ex post** squared forecast error is the maximum likelihood estimator for this parameter. We have therefore used the square root of this figure, the absolute forecast error, computed for perceptions and expectations, as the dependent variables in regressions of the form contained in Equation 12. The results are shown in Table 2.

With regard to perceptions, Table 2 reveals few consistent differences in performance. The rich are perhaps better at tracking the past than other groups. However, with regard to expectations, the rich, the middle-aged, and the old are all significantly more accurate.

While the predictions of the theory of information collection are not precise about what patterns of relative accuracy should be observed, these findings are at least not inconsistent with our prior beliefs about what should be observed if information search is conducted in an optimal fashion.

Variance Rationality

As our empirical counterpart to the variance rationality test of Equation 13 we have regressed the absolute forecast errors, in perceptions and

Table 2: Tests of Optimal Search[1]

Independent variable	Dependent variable			
	Absolute error in perceptions		Absolute error in expectations	
Constant	3.51	(3.83)	3.81	(6.97)
Female	−0.00	(0.01)	0.19	(0.57)
Mid age	0.28	(0.46)	−0.81	(2.23)
Old	1.00	(1.41)	−0.73	(1.74)
Urban	−0.71	(1.26)	−0.18	(0.52)
Rural	−0.95	(1.52)	0.03	(0.07)
High school	0.60	(0.98)	0.32	(0.88)
College	0.79	(1.26)	0.02	(0.04)
Part time	0.61	(0.80)	0.41	(0.90)
Unemployed	−0.40	(0.59)	0.56	(1.38)
Mid income	−0.01	(0.02)	−0.61	(1.49)
Rich	−1.29	(1.63)	−0.86	(1.80)
Statistics				
R^2	0.03		0.06	
F	1.05		0.80	

[1]Estimated parameters of Equation 12 based on sample of 342 individuals. Asymptotic 5% significance levels for t and F are 1.96 and 1.78, respectively.

expectations, on the confidence dummies and the vector of individual characteristics. The results of these regressions are shown in Table 3.

We should expect the coefficients on the confidence dummies to become progressively more negative as we move from the low confidence group $CONF_2$ to the most confident group $CONF_5$. Although all but one of these coefficients are negative, they do not increase as required. That is, the forecast errors of the most confident individuals are not significantly smaller than those expressing less confidence. In this sense, our data suggest that subjective uncertainty about inflation is not unbiased.

In consequence, there are systematic patterns in forecast accuracy which are not picked up by subjective confidence ratings, and which show up in Table 3 as nonzero coefficients on the socioeconomic factors. The rich, for example, are consistently better at tracking the past than they give themselves credit for. Similarly, the middle-aged and the old are better at forecasting than their self-rated confidence would allow, and the unemployed significantly worse. Our subjective uncertainty data therefore also fail the orthogonality test for rationality.

Table 3: Tests of Variance Rationality[1]

Independent variable	Dependent variable			
	Absolute error in perceptions		Absolute error in expectations	
Constant	4.21	(4.01)	4.66	(6.24)
CONF2	−1.01	(1.50)	−0.73	(1.38)
CONF3	−0.77	(0.92)	−0.78	(1.34)
CONF4	0.14	(0.13)	−0.56	(0.83)
CONF5	−0.55	(0.21)	−0.69	(0.48)
Female	−0.12	(0.22)	−0.05	(0.15)
Mid age	0.36	(0.58)	−0.86	(2.28)
Old	1.13	(1.57)	−0.82	(1.86)
Urban	−0.76	(1.33)	−0.10	(0.29)
Rural	−0.91	(1.47)	−0.06	(0.16)
High school	0.67	(1.08)	0.13	(0.34)
College	0.81	(1.26)	−0.19	(0.50)
Part time	0.62	(0.82)	0.56	(1.23)
Unemployed	−0.45	(0.65)	0.85	(2.01)
Mid income	−0.01	(0.02)	−0.49	(1.17)
Rich	−1.34	(1.67)	−0.55	(1.14)
Statistics				
R^2	0.04		0.06	
F	1.98		1.43	

[1]Estimated parameters of Equation 13 based on sample of 342 individuals. Asymptotic 5% significance levels for t and F are 1.96 and 1.78, respectively.

Conclusions

The balance of evidence in this paper favours the psychologist's view of how consumers perceive inflation, over that of the economist. It suggests that individuals will often fail to anticipate changes in inflation and changes in inflation risk, and will in consequence make suboptimal economic decisions.

Our study is, however, subject to several limitations, and it is important to recognize these. With respect to variance rationality it is for example arguable that our proxy for subjective uncertainty is imperfect, and hence the test has been failed not because consumers are poor judges of risk, but because the assumed response function of Equation 14 is incorrect. It would be desirable in the future to obtain a more direct measure of the subjective forecast variance. With respect to our test for optimal information search, it is similarly arguable that our priors about intergroup differences are rather imprecise. This seems unavoidable. However, our conjecture that groups with greater incentives produce more accurate forecasts is borne out by other, more vivid, types of comparison – for example between lay and expert forecasters (Batchelor & Dua, forthcoming).

Finally, it is arguable that our cross-sectional, microeconomic tests of the mean rationality of individuals do not in any case undermine the validity of rational expectations macroeconomics, which requires only that the average expectation in the population of key decision-makers in markets be rational. Most time series studies of average consumer, business, and expert forecasts suggest that these are at least weak-form rational, and our own time series tests of variance rationality do not reject this hypothesis (Batchelor & Jonung, 1987). Clearly there is a conflict between our understanding of individual and aggregate economic behavior, effectively between inferences from cross-sectional and time series data, which remains to be resolved.

References

Batchelor, R.A., & Dua, P. (forthcoming). Household v. economist forecasts of inflation: A reassessment. *Journal of Money, Credit and Banking.*

Batchelor, R.A., & Jonung, L. (1986). *Information theory and group differences in inflation expectations.* London: City University Centre for Banking and International Finance. Discussion Paper 53.

Batchelor, R.A., & Jonung, L. (1987). Confidence about inflation forecasts: Evidence from surveys of Swedish consumers. In: K.N.Oppenlander & G. Poser (Eds.), *Contributions of business cycle surveys to empirical economics.* Aldershot: Gower Press.

Cukierman, A., & Wachtel, P. (1982). Inflationary expectations and further thoughts on inflation uncertainty. *American Economic Review, 72,* 508-512.

Jonung, L. (1981). Perceived and expected rates of inflation in Sweden. *American Economic Review, 71,* 961-968.

Jonung, L.(1986). Uncertainty of inflationary perceptions and expectations. *Journal of Economic Psychology, 7,* 315-325.

Kahnemann, D., Slovic, P., & Tversky, A. (1982). *Judgment under uncertainty: Heuristics and biases.* Cambridge: Cambridge University Press.

Lucas, R.E., Jr. (1972). Expectations and the neutrality of money. *Journal of Economic Theory, 4,* 103-124.

Maital, S., & Maital, S. (1981). Individual-rational and group-rational inflation expectations: Theory and cross-section evidence. *Journal of Economic Behaviour and Organisation, 2,* 179-186.

Muth, J.F. (1961). Rational expectations and the theory of price movements. *Econometrica, 29,* 315-335.

Rothschild, M. & Stiglitz, J.E. (1971). Increasing risk I: A definition. *Journal of Economic Theory, 2,* 225-243.

Simon, H.A. (1959). Theories of decision-making in economics and behavioural science. *American Economic Review, 49,* 253-283.

Stigler, G.J. (1961). The economics of information. *Journal of Political Economy, 69,* 213-225.

Peter K. Lunt

The Perceived Causal Structure of Unemployment

Abstract

There have been a number of studies of divergence in social perception of the causes of various economic phenomena (Furnham, 1984). Differences between supporters of the major British political parties have been found in terms of the salience of causal categories. Conservative supporters emphasize individualistic causes whereas labour supporters focus on societal causes. This research assumes that people across political affiliations basically share the same category system for the causes and differ in terms of which categories are salient.

An alternative approach to social perception has been developed based on **perceived causal structures**. A method based on sociometry has been developed to obtain representations of causes as implicit causal models.

A study of divergence in social perception as difference in perceived causal structure shows that people with different political affiliations have implicit causal structures which vary in complexity and direction of causality. The implications of these results for theories of social perception and attribution are considered.

The author wishes to thank Jos Jaspars, Mansur Lalljee, and Sonia Livingstone for comments and E.S.R.C. U.K. for support.

Author's address: Peter K. Lunt, Rutherford College, The University, Canterbury, Kent CT2 7NX, England.

Introduction

Since the 1950's (Heider, 1958), social psychologists have examined ordinary people's indigenous psychologies. Initially research focussed on people's ability to explain the causes of their own and others' behaviour in social interaction. More recently there has been a growing interest in ordinary people's broader explanatory practices including their understanding of academic achievement, science, and socio-economic phenomena such as poverty and unemployment.

One aspect of research into ordinary explanations has been to examine the way in which people classify the various causes that they perceive to operate in a given domain. Weiner (1986) and his colleagues, in particular, have examined ordinary people's understanding of multiple causes in the form of semantic spaces derived from perceived similarities between causes. These spaces are interpreted in the traditional manner as revealing a few connotative dimensions depicting features of the causes. The basic distinctions that people have been found to make between causes reflect the dimensions of locus (causes with internal or external origins), stability, and controllability. Thus across a variety of explanatory domains people have been shown to have a coherent scheme based on perceived features for classifying causes. Lay causal classification has been used to study differences in social perception. For example, Bar-Tal and Guttman (1981) found that teachers, pupils, and parents emphasized different categories of causes in explaining academic success and failure.

This approach has been applied to economic psychology by Feather (1974) and Furnham (1984). A typical example of this work is a study by Furnham (1982) which examined differences in the perception of the causes of unemployment according to political affiliation. He found that people with different political affiliations attached different levels of importance to various classes of causes. Specifically, Conservatives emphasize individualistic causes and Labour supporters focus upon societal causes. Furnham (1982) interprets these results as an example of different social representations held by different groups (Moscovici, 1984). The method that Furnham uses implies a particular view of the nature of divergence in social perception. It is perhaps a truism that people with different political affiliations will differ in their perceptions of the causes of unemployment. The interesting issue is what kind of difference will be found. Furnham's method is premised on the idea that supporters of all the parties **share** the same taxonomy of causes and **differ** in terms of which categories they perceive as most important.

An alternative approach to group differences in social perception will be pursued in the present paper. The idea will be explored that people represent multiple causes of unemployment not simply as a semantic space but also as a causal system in the form of a network. This follows up suggestions by Kelley (1983) who proposed that "the common person's understanding of a particular event is based on the perceived location of that event within a temporally ordered network of interconnected causes and effects." Lunt (1987, 1988) has developed a method to study implicit causal models or perceived causal structures. Subjects make judgements of the likelihood of interconnection between the causes in a given domain. These judgements are subjected to Network Analysis (Knoke & Kuklinski, 1982) which reveals the structure of interconnection of the causes. It shows the network structure that underlies people's judgement of interconnection. This structure can be examined to see what role the various causes are seen to play in the causal system and has a variety of structural features as a network which can be studied. This technique will be extended in the present study to examine differences in social perception.

In the study to be presented here, people with different political affiliations (supporters of the three political parties) will complete a questionnaire asking for judgements of causal interconnection for causes used by Furnham (1982). The causes are presented in Table 1. It is predicted that the previously reported salience of causal categories (Conservatives prefer individualistic, Labour societal) will be related to direction of causality between the fundamental aspects of causation, the personal and the societal. Specifically that salient causes will be perceived as causal origins, or distal causes. In particular that the direction of causality between personal and societal causes will be opposite for Conservative and Labour voters. Labour voters will see societal causes as causally prior to personal causes, and the Conservatives will perceive personal causes as causally prior.

It is also predicted that the salient causes will be the ones that are perceived as most elaborately interconnected. Salience may be related to perceived complexity, because complexity is one measure of power.

Table 1: Causes of Unemployment From Furnham (1982) With Short Forms

Unemployed people can earn more money on social security	Social security payments
Lack of effort and laziness among unemployed people	Lack of effort
Unwillingness of the unemployed to move to work	Unwilling to move
Lack of intelligence or ability among the unemployed.	Lack of intelligence
Poor education and qualifications among the unemployed	Poor education
Weak trade unions that do not fight to keep jobs	Weak trade unions
Incompetent industrial management with poor planning	Incompetent management
The introduction of widespread automation	Automation
World-wide recession and inflation	Recession
The policies and strategies of the present government	Present government
The policies and strategies of previous governments	Previous government
Bad luck	Bad luck

It is possible to have one all-powerful cause, but when there is a system, the complex causes are the ones that have most interconnections and their influence is therefore more spread over the structure. This may make them more salient, or it may be that people represent the causes they see as more salient in a more complex manner. Tetlock (1983) found that people complexified the attitudes they most wanted to justify. There may be a similar effect in perceived causal structures where people can justify their belief in the power of particular causes by representing them as complexes.

There are no clear predictions to be made about the way that Alliance voters will perceive the causes of unemployment as a system.

The present study will focus on the similarities and differences between the Alliance supporters' views and the extremes of Labour and Conservative voters.

The data collected by Furnham shows which causes people believe to be most important as a function of their political persuasion. The present study attempts to go beyond this to see whether differences in salience are related to the different roles these causes are perceived to play in a causal model.

Method

Subjects

Sixty subjects from the Oxford Department of Experimental Psychology subject panel were paid participants in the study. Twenty subjects were supporters of each of the three major political parties.

The Questionnaire

Subjects each completed a questionnaire after reading the following written instructions:

This questionnaire is concerned with causes of unemployment. The causes you will be asked to rate were given by people as explanations of unemployment. Your task is to rate the likelihood that one factor in unemployment causes another factor in unemployment. Put a ring round the answer that best describes your opinion. There are no right or wrong answers.

Twelve of the causes of unemployment used in Furnham's (1982) study were used (Table 1). They were selected so as to be representative of each of the groups of causes identified by Furnham (1982). All possible pairings of the causes in both directions were presented in the questionnaires. Subjects made their judgements on a five point rating scale (impossible, possible but unlikely, moderately likely, fairly likely, and highly likely).

After completing the questionnaire the subjects handed it to the experimenter who checked it for completion and answered any questions the subjects had about the study.

Results

Each subject's data produced a matrix of likelihood ratings for all possible pairs of the causes of unemployment. For each of the three groups (Alliance, Conservative, and Labour supporters), a matrix of mean likelihood ratings over subjects was produced. The matrices from each of the three groups of subjects were analysed separately using network analysis.

A network is constructed by drawing directional arcs between nodes that are linked. In the present data, nodes will represent the twelve causes, and a link between two nodes will represent a perceived causal relation between a given pair of causes. The link will be represented as an arrow, indicating the direction of perceived causality.

The data from which networks are derived take the form of an asymmetric matrix of binary relations. However, in this study each cell contains a mean likelihood rating, therefore, in order to derive a binary matrix, a criterion has to be found which divides the links into those to be included and those to be excluded from the network.

The task of finding a reasonable criterion for selecting the links to be included in a network has traditionally been solved by finding the "minimum system criterion." This is the smallest value at which all the concepts are included in the network with at least one link. It makes the assumption that the set of entities (in this case causes) form a single system. In the present study, a constraint was used to stop the convergence of the network analysis before the minimum system criterion. In view of the nature of the hypotheses that the interconnection between the internal and external causes would reveal structural differences between the groups, the networks were halted at the point when interconnection was achieved.

The final criteria at which the analysis stopped were: Conservatives 3, Labour 3, and Alliance 3. This is equivalent to the judgement of **moderately** likely on the original questionnaire. At this criterion, eleven of the twelve causes were included in all three networks. In each case, **Bad luck** was excluded from further analysis.

The networks of links included at or above these criteria for each of the three groups are presented in Figures 1 (Alliance), 2 (Conservative), and 3 (Labour).

The three networks are very similar in density as indexed by the number of links each has. The Alliance network has 19 links, Conservative 18, and Labour 17. These links can be broken down over the main division of causes between individualistic and societal causes. Alliance supporters perceived 7 links among the individualistic causes and 9 among the societal causes. The Conservatives perceived 10 links among individualistic and 6 among societal, whereas Labour supporters saw 3 links among individualistic and 12 among societal causes. As to links **between** the two types of causes, the Alliance network has 3 (all from societal to individualistic), the Conservatives 2 (both from individualistic to societal), and Labour 2 (both from societal to individualistic).

These frequencies were submitted to chi-square analysis. There was no significant association between party and number of individualistic or societal causes over all parties ($x^2 = 5.73$, $df = 1$). However, there was a significant difference when the Alliance were removed from the analysis

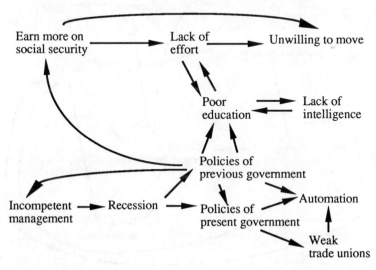

Figure 1: Alliance voters' perceived causal structure of unemployment.

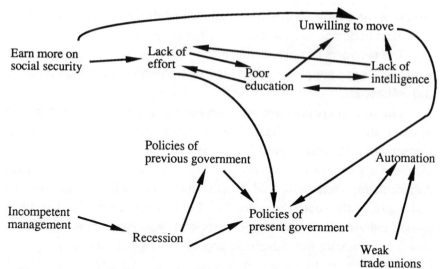

Figure 2: Conservative voters' perceived causal structure of unemployment.

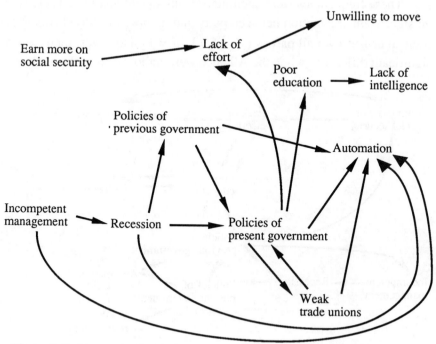

Figure 3: Labour voters' perceived causal structure of unemployment.

($\chi^2 = 5.73$, $df = 2$, $p = 0.025$). There is therefore an association between political extremes (Conservative and Labour) and perceived interconnection of societal and individualistic causes. Conservative supporters put more emphasis on the complex interrelation of individualistic causes, whereas Labour supporters emphasize complex interrelation in societal causes.

Discussion

I will discuss the differences between the networks in relation to the hypotheses of the study before commenting on the commonalty in these representations. The Labour and Conservative structures are most divergent, so most of the discussion of differences between structures will be in terms of the networks derived from the Conservative and Labour supporters.

The hypothesis that the Conservatives would perceive the direction of causality between internal and external causes as going from internal to external and the Labour supporters the opposite was confirmed by the data. The Alliance supporters are in agreement with the Labour voters on this issue.

The second hypothesis, that the causes that are perceived as most important would be the ones most interconnected is also confirmed. The Conservatives perceive complex and multiple interconnections among the internal causes whereas the Labour supporters perceive more complexity among the external causes. The Alliance supporters see a similar degree of complexity in both systems.

In a study of the perceived importance of these causes of unemployment, Furnham (1982) found that Conservatives placed more emphasis on internal causes and Labour supporters placed more emphasis on societal causes. This difference in perceived importance or salience of causes is therefore correlated with a divergence in the perceived causal role of these factors. The causes that are most salient are perceived as more complex in their relations to other causes and as being causally basic. These differences between supporters of the three main political parties in terms of perceived causal structure can be summarized using the concepts of complexity and direction of causality. Conservative supporters perceive internal causes as more complex than external causes

115

and internal causes as influencing external causes. Labour supporters see external causes as more complex than internal causes and external causes as influencing internal causes. Alliance supporters do not differentiate between internal and external causes in terms of complexity and see external causes as influencing internal causes.

These differences reflect different theories about political and social processes. The Conservatives think of the activities of individuals as the basic causes of unemployment. The Labour supporters are committed to the idea that social and political causes are more basic than personal causes of unemployment. The personal motivations and abilities of the unemployed to obtain work are influenced by social and political forces. The Alliance supporters agree with Labour that personal causes are causally dependent on societal causes. However, they do not give weight to one of these clusters in terms of complexity. If we take Labour and Conservative supporters as providing upper and lower bounds for complexity and simplicity for both individualistic and societal causes, then the Alliance supporters are in the middle of the complexity scale for both types of cause.

These beliefs of the supporters of the three major political parties reflect the different parties' policies on reducing unemployment. The Conservative supporters perceive government policy as a reaction to the lack of motivation of the unemployed. The current (Conservative) government policy of **Action for jobs** is an example of government policy organized around a belief that the basic causes of unemployment are various inadequacies in the unemployed. The reasonable response to this is then to give help to individuals in overcoming their problems in obtaining employment. On this issue, the Conservative government's policy complements the beliefs of their supporters about the processes that lead to unemployment. However, there is no indication in the present results that Conservative supporters accept the policy of their party that changes in the economic environment will eventually lead to the creation of jobs.

Labour supporters' beliefs are also in harmony with their party's policies. They see direct government intervention as the result of economic, industrial, and social pressure as a potential power in affecting the motivations of the unemployed. Labour supporters also do not perceive a close interrelation among the individualistic causes. They are less prepared to think of unemployed people as bundles of problems, preferring to see particular aspects of their psychology as the result of government policy.

The Alliance supporters' beliefs reflect "mixed" policy. They believe in some government intervention to create jobs and to mitigate the effects of societal causes. However, they are more committed to the view that unemployed people are likely to have a compound of deficits. This suggests they may be less cynical about training schemes than Labour supporters would.

This discussion is reminiscent of Heider's (1958) thought experiment about sand on his desk. Heider described the situation of sand being on his desk. One option is to wipe away the sand. However, if the sand has blown through a crack in the walls it will simply reappear the next day. The cracks in the wall can be filled, but if they are an indication of weakness in the walls, then the most appropriate solution is to strengthen the walls. The point is that certain causes are more basic and important as a level of intervention. The causes perceived as basic to the system are those that people seek to change. Heider seeks to fix his walls as the result of the causal model he constructed of the causes of sand appearing on his desk. Similarly, the Conservatives seek to change people, Labour seeks to change society, and the Alliance want action in both areas.

This difference in complexity may be related to other judgements. For example, the Conservative's views on the highly interconnected nature of the individualistic causes may be related to stereotyping of the unemployed, since it reflects a belief that once a person has one of the disadvantages that lead them to be unable to get a job, this is likely to lead to them having the other problems. So someone who finds they can earn more money on social security is likely to lose motivation and thereby less likely to gain further educational qualifications and thereby be less likely to become geographically mobile. The Labour supporters do not focus on the interconnectedness of individualistic causes. Therefore they are less inclined to believe that people will inevitably come to have all the disadvantages that can lead to unemployment. Further research is needed into the relation of the beliefs about causal processes and attitudinal and stereotyping processes in group perception.

There are some important similarities in the Alliance, Conservative, and Labour models of the interconnections of causes of unemployment. The most basic similarity is that all three groups agree that there is a basic difference between individualistic and societal causes in terms of the role they play in the causal system. These sets of causes are essentially perceived as two separate systems with few connections between them. This result complements those found in factor analytic studies of the perceived importance of the causes of unemployment where an internal - external dimension was found. Societal and individualistic causes are different because they are perceived to be functionally separated in the role they play in the system of causes of unemployment.

Another similarity is that, in all three networks, the policies of the present government are perceived as the causes that mediate between social/economic causes and individualistic causes. Although the direction of causality was perceived to be in opposite directions, both Conservative and Labour supporters agree that government policy plays a central role in relating individual and social factors.

The network representing the judgements of the Alliance supporters is very similar to the Conservative network in terms of the links that exist within the clusters of individualistic and societal causes. However, it is similar to the Labour network in terms of the direction of causality between these two systems of causes.

These results demonstrate that network analysis of judgements of causal interconnection to reveal perceived causal structures can be used to examine group differences in social perception. These structures show causal models that differ in terms of direction of causality and where complexity occurs in the system. These results complement existing findings describing differences in salience of causes but also allow an examination of the divergence in the perception of the way that these causes operate as a causal system. This is a significant advance, previous studies show **which** causes people regard as important, the present study indicates **why** they are so perceived.

The loci of divergence in social perception, complexity, and direction of causality, are related to the perceived functions of causes within a causal system. Previous approaches to group differences in social perception were based on the idea that difference was due to the variant salience that various categories of cause had for different groups. The traditional approach conceives of lay understanding as a taxonomy based on the perceived features of causes. The present approach treats lay understanding as lay theory which results in a representation of causal processes as a system.

There are a number of potential applications of this method, beyond studying the properties of lay theories. For example, disputes, arguments, and misunderstandings may be the result of groups or individuals having different perceived causal structures. This is not an academic difference because questions of responsibility would depend on who or what was perceived as the basic cause and notions of intervention would be affected by perceived causal structure. There may be differences in what are perceived to be the fundamental causes of a given phenomena and also views about complexity may affect notions of intervention. People may argue that it is better to intervene in the simpler part of the system, or be pessimistic about intervention if they saw the fundamental causes as the most complex.

There are a few points about the limitations of the network method introduced in this paper that need further work. There is no provision in this method for subjects to record their belief that there is a conjunction of causes. That is, they may believe that *A* does not cause *C* and that *B* does not cause *C* but believe that *A* and *B* together may cause *C*. Also, since the networks produced were not linear structures that clearly end in unemployment, it is likely that unemployment itself could be located in the networks. Thus the method could be improved by including an option for conjoining causes and by including the presumed end state in the network.

In summary, two principles for locating divergence in social perception have emerged from this study of different perceived causal structures. There is divergence in the perceived direction of causality between clusters of causes. Also there are differences in the perceived complexity of interconnection of causes within clusters.

References

Bar-Tal, D., & Guttman, J. (1981). A comparison of teachers', pupils', and parents' attributions regarding pupils academic achievements. *British Journal of Educational Psychology, 51*, 301-311.

Feather, N. (1974). Explanations for poverty in Australian and American samples: The person, society, and fate? *Australian Journal of Psychology, 26*, 199-216.

Furnham, A. (1982). Explanations for unemployment in Britain. *European Journal of Social Psychology, 12*, 335-352.

Furnham, A. (1984). Unemployment, attribution theory, and mental health: A review of the British literature. *International Journal of Mental Health, 13*, 51-67.

Heider, F. (1958). *The psychology of interpersonal relations.* New York: Wiley.

Kelley, H.H. (1983). Perceived causal structures. In: J. Jaspars, F.D. Fincham, & M. Hewstone (Eds.), *Attribution theory and research: Conceptual, developmental, & social dimensions,* London: Academic Press.

Knoke, D., & Kuklinski, J.H. (1982). *Network analysis.* Beverly Hills: Sage Publications.

Lunt, P.K. (1987). *Perceived causal structure and attributional reasoning.* Oxford: University of Oxford. Unpublished doctoral dissertation.

Lunt, P.K. (1988). The perceived causal structure of examination failure. *British Journal of Social Psychology, 27*, 171-179.

Moscovici, S. (1984). The phenomenon of social representations. In: R.M. Farr & S. Moscovici (Eds.), *Social representations,* Cambridge: Cambridge University Press.

Tetlock, P.E. (1983). Accountability and complexity of thought. *Journal of Personality and Social Psychology, 45*, 74-83.

Weiner, B. (1986). *An attributional theory of motivation and emotion.* New York: Springer.

Henry S.J. Robben, Paul Webley, Henk Elffers, and
Dick J. Hessing

A Cross-National Comparison of Attitudes, Personality, Behaviour, and Social Comparison in Tax Evasion Experiments

Abstract

This paper reports on an experimental study of tax evasion in which members of the Dutch public participated. Three variables were manipulated: type of social comparison (personal or categorical), nature of comparison (inferior, neutral, or superior), and the period in which the tax return was audited. In addition, participants completed a series of questionnaires based on the work of Hessing and Elffers (1985). No effects of type and nature of social comparison on the propensity to evade taxes and on the magnitude of taxes evaded were found. The frequency of tax evasion was positively correlated with alienation, competitiveness, disinhibition, and attitudes to tax evasion and negatively correlated with age. The magnitude of tax evasion was positively correlated only with alienation and competitiveness. This pattern of correlations is generally similar to findings obtained in research on documented tax evasion behaviour, although in contrast to the latter research, attitudes towards tax evasion were significant correlates of experimental evasion behaviour. These findings were also broadly comparable to a similar British experimental study except that tax evasion was more frequent in the Dutch sample.

The authors want to thank Marion van Engelen for collecting most of the data. Stephen Lea's help in converting the computer programme is greatly appreciated.

Authors' addresses: Henry S.J. Robben, Henk Elffers, and Dick J. Hessing, Erasmus University, Faculty of Law, P.O. Box 1738, 3000 DR Rotterdam, The Netherlands; Paul Webley, Department of Psychology, Washington Singer Laboratories, University of Exeter, Exeter EX4 4QG, England.

121

Introduction

Tax evasion is a serious problem for revenue authorities (estimates of the percentage of gross national product that evades taxation range from 4% to 25%) and one that has both economic and psychological aspects. Economic approaches to evasion have generally assumed that people are rational decision makers and have treated evading income tax as formally equivalent to buying a risky asset with a particular rate of return. Such models usually involve objective variables such as fine rates and the probability of detection (e.g., Allingham & Sandmo, 1972). By way of contrast, psychological and sociological models have usually concentrated on subjective and societal variables, such as perceived risks, attitudes towards evasion, and social norms. Furthermore, instead of regarding motivation as given, they are concerned with individual differences in predispositions to evade (for a review of different approaches, see Hessing, Elffers, Weigel, & Kinsey, 1988).

This, rather caricatured, difference also extends to the investigative methods employed. Surveys and other self-report methods have been extensively used by sociologists and psychologists whereas economists have preferred econometric modelling. Recently, however, a shared interest in laboratory experimentation has developed (Friedland, Maital, & Rutenberg, 1978; Spicer & Becker, 1980; Webley, Morris, & Amstutz, 1985). Furnham and Lewis (1986) discuss some "obvious weaknesses" of the simulation studies reported up to now. They suggest that the relationship between simulation and reality is not perfect, and that usually small samples have been used, more often than not consisting of students instead of "long-standing" taxpayers. However, they conclude that experimental studies could be useful if these weaknesses were rectified and "subjective" variables, i.e. attitudes and perceptions, were studied as well as "objective" variables, such as tax rates and probability of detection. This paper describes such a study, based on that of Webley, Robben, and Morris (1988). They made some important improvements on earlier simulations. A sample of the general public was used, measurements of attitudes and personality variables were obtained, and subjects were presented with an environment in which some economic parameters were present but not manipulated.

The fact that experimental studies of tax evasion do not fully match the real-life situation does not lessen the value of the approach. The aim in tax evasion experiments is not so much to create "mundane realism" (Aronson & Carlsmith, 1968) as a convincing experimental psychological realism. In an experiment one is trying to devise an instrument with which a certain behaviour (or part of it) may be measured more validly and/or reliably than by current questionnaire methodology. The hazards of relying on self-reports when investigating tax evasion behaviour have been demonstrated by Elffers, Weigel, and Hessing (1987). With the quite exceptional help of the Dutch Ministry of Finance and using a very complicated methodology to guarantee confidentiality, they studied two carefully audited groups of individuals; one group who had made accurate returns, the other who had evaded tax. They showed that documented and self-reported tax evasion did not correspond at all; furthermore, personality variables predicted documented evasion whereas attitudes and subjective norms correlated with self-reported evasion. Thus it is not possible to take at face value respondents' answers to the question whether they have evaded taxes when filing a tax return. The method Elffers et al. describe to explore these inconsistencies is, however, difficult to implement and requires cooperation by the tax authorities. Experimental studies may be able to fill part of the gap between the easy administrable surveys and this more difficult approach.

To further develop the experimental approach, information is needed on how well such studies do in comparison to survey and documented-behaviour research. The Webley et al. (1988) study showed that similar personality variables predict evasion within an experiment as predict documented evasion. This cross-validation certainly adds to the credibility of results obtained using an experimental approach.

Social Comparison and Tax Evasion

Tax evasion has been linked to a number of social psychological variables, such as social influence, equity, normative pressures, and social comparison. In the case of inequity, people perceive a difference in fiscal treatment between themselves and others in similar positions. Tax evasion is associated with feelings of inequity (Wärneryd & Walerud, 1982). Other effects of the social environment include the influence of other people on the individual taxpayer's behaviour. Spicer and

Lundstedt (1976), for example, have shown – using surveys – that self-reported tax evasion is positively related to the number of people one knows to have evaded taxes. One should, however, be cautious in interpreting these findings as causal explanations of tax evasion, as they may constitute rationalizations on the respondents' part.

Comparing oneself with others may thus influence individual taxpaying behaviour. In this paper, social comparison theory (more specifically Rijsman's, 1974, 1983, elaboration of Festinger's, 1954, theory) was used to derive hypotheses about tax evasion behaviour. As will be made clear below, in the experiment subjects had to carry out a rather complex business management task. The rationale behind this was to investigate the question of whether people (taxpayers) refer to the position of others in order to obtain cues about how to behave in this particular situation. As almost everyone who took part had no personal experience of conducting a business, they would find it difficult to judge their performance during the business management task. A comparison standard is then needed as no objective information is present for the subjects (Festinger, 1954).

In the present experiment, participants had to manage a small shop and make decisions regarding advertising, information acquisition, pricing of products, and fiscal matters. Subjects were given information about their performance in relation to other individual (imaginary) participants. This information constituted the comparison standard which classified subjects' performance either as inferior, similar, or superior to the competitors' performance. This standard was presented quite saliently as it was expected that subjects would need to evaluate their business results in order to establish their dis/satisfaction with the "reward" for their performance (von Grumbkow & Wärneryd, 1986, p. 235). Presenting subjects with this information is believed to induce a motivation in them to change their behaviour in order to change their relative position. Changes are dependent on the relative position occupied by the comparison others and whether comparison takes place at an individual or group level. Given that people like to have as high an income as possible, one could consider obtaining income as an ability of a certain kind (in the present experiment certainly, but perhaps even more so in real life). In Festinger's (1954) terms, abilities and opinions form a basis on which people compare themselves with others in order to gain a positive image of themselves. The situation subjects were presented with may be characterised as a forced comparison of a competitive nature (Wheeler & Zuckerman, 1977).

Cross-national investigations may be undertaken to exploit natural differences in independent variables or to ascertain the extent to which theories and findings are general or confined to specific socio-cultural settings. The present study is of this second type. An important aim of this research was to describe the results of the present investigation in the light of previous research. This comparison should yield evidence on the cross-validation of the experimental technique.

Method

Subjects

A random sample from the local telephone directory was made of telephone numbers starting with a pre-selected code. Then a letter was sent inviting the recipient (or one of his family members over 21 with job experience) to participate in an economic behaviour research project involving microcomputers. A few days after this mailing the recipients were contacted by telephone and asked personally whether they were interested in taking part. Of 291 persons contacted, 22 women and 50 men agreed to participate, a response rate of just under 25%. The subjects were aged between 21 and 71, with an average of 40 years. All subjects were tested individually.

Design

Three between-groups factors were employed in the study, type of comparison (individual, categorical), nature of comparison (inferior, similar, superior), and period in which the tax return was audited. The first factor was manipulated by informing subjects that their business results were to be compared with those of another individual subject, or by telling subjects they were allocated to a cooperative of shop-keepers, whose results would be compared with those of another cooperative. Subjects were led to believe that the comparison thus was to be made on an individual performance level or a collective performance level.

By informing subjects that their performance was either inferior, similar, or superior to their competitors' performance, the second factor was operationalised. The performance of the subject in terms of net income was explicitly presented at the end of each period and at the end of each year. In the latter case, a statement about the subject's position relative to the comparison other/s was made. This information about relative performance was independent of subjects' actual performance and was stable across the years, i.e., subjects always received information pertaining to their initial relative position.

During the simulation, each subject was audited once; the audit occurred either in the first, fourth, seventh, or eleventh period.

The dependent measures were (a) the overall frequency of underdeclaring and the overall percentage of income declared, (b) the frequency of underdeclaring and the percentage of income declared in each of the three years of the simulation (there were four periods per year), and (c) the difference between the evasion measures for years 1 and 2, and for years 2 and 3.

Procedure

The study was divided into two parts, the first being the shop simulation and the second involving completing a questionnaire measuring sociodemographics, attitudes, norms, perceptions, personality attributes, and risk taking behaviour. Both parts took, on average, the same amount of time to complete for the subjects, 83 minutes in all.

To maximise comparability the shop simulation was the same as in Webley et al.'s (1988) second study with the text carefully translated into Dutch. After some information on how to operate the computer the subjects read, from the computer screen, instructions about the shop simulation. In brief, they were told to imagine that they had set themselves up as shopkeepers and would have to make a series of decisions (e.g., about the selling prices of their products) over a three year period. During the simulation they made pricing decisions on two product lines for each quarter of each year (twelve in all) and declared their income, also on a quarterly basis. In each quarter subjects were able to buy information (e.g., about seasonal variations in sales) and decide whether to advertise or not. At the end of each quarter the subjects were

126

informed whether they had been audited or not and their gross income, net income, and fines to date displayed. People were instructed to act as they themselves saw fit under the present circumstances, and to try to run their business as successfully as possible.

The questionnaire measured attitudes toward underreporting income and toward claiming unwarranted deductions (using semantic differentials, see Elffers et al., 1987), alienation (Zeller, Neal, & Groat, 1980), disinhibition (Hauber, Toornvliet, & Willemse, 1986, after Zuckerman, 1979), social support (a one item measure asking how people in the direct environment would react to the respondents' possible tax evasion behaviour: negative, indifferent, or positive), and social orientation (Liebrand, 1982).

Subjects received a bottle of red wine for their participation in the simulation study. For completing the questionnaire they were given a choice between a lottery-ticket with a chance of 1 in 100 of winning 100 guilders, a ticket with a chance of 1 in 25 of winning 25 guilders, and an unconditional reward of 2.50 guilders. This choice constituted a measure of behavioural risk-taking by the subjects. Prizes were paid immediately in cash or transferred by bank.

Hypotheses

Based on Rijsman's (1974, 1983) social competition theory two hypotheses were formulated about subjects' behaviour during the simulation. For subjects in the personal comparison condition, those in the inferior or equal performance conditions were expected to change their tax behaviour so as to obtain a higher income. Tax evasion would be more pronounced in these conditions than in the superior performance condition. The idea behind this is that people seek to distinguish themselves from others in a positive sense; they want to perform better. If people are already performing in a superior way, this drive necessarily will be less than when performing equally or in an inferior way.

For the subjects in the categorical comparison condition the reverse was expected; people in the superior condition would show a greater change in tax evasion behaviour than subjects in the inferior and equal performance conditions. Essential to this notion is the idea that "the only feasible way to build up... similarity with the status of the own category is to perform as the category does" (Rijsman, 1983, pp. 290-291). Conversely, for the inferior and equal conditions, this tendency to identify with the own category will be absent or very weak.

What was expected then, was interaction between type and nature of social comparison with regard to the changes in tax evasion behaviour elicited from year to year in the experiment.

Previous research showed a possibly larger deterrent effect when tax returns were audited earlier in taxpayers' careers. For instance, Webley et al. (1988) included the period in which a subject's return was audited as an exploratory variable. They found an indication that early audits were associated with less evasion, but not significantly so. The present study included an identical variable to explore this issue further.

Results

Simulation Data

First, the data obtained in the simulation were analysed using 2 x 3 x 4 analyses of variance with type of comparison (individual, categorical), nature of comparison (inferior, similar, superior) and period in which the audit occurred as between groups factors and the overall frequency of underdeclaring and overall percentage of income declared as dependent measures. The effect of nature of comparison nearly reached significance for the percentage of income declared ($F = 2.93$, $df = 2, 48$, $p < .063$) and a significant interaction was found between nature of comparison and the audit variable for frequency of underdeclaring ($F = 2.73$, $df = 6, 48$, $p < .05$) and for percentage of income declared ($F = 2.79$, $df = 6, 48$, $p < .05$). This interaction is somewhat complicated (see Table 1), but to simplify a little, those in the neutral and inferior conditions on average evaded more when audited in later periods (4th, 7th, or 11th) than when audited in the first, whereas for those in the superior condition this pattern was reversed. No other significant effects were found. With regard to the measures of change in tax evasion behaviour, no significant main or interaction effects were obtained.

Table 1: Frequency of Evading Taxes as a Function of Nature of Comparison and the Audit Variable

Nature of comparison	Period in which audit occurred[1]				
	1	4	7	11	
Inferior	4.8	4.3	7.3	4.4	**5.2**
Similar	2.3	4.3	4.9	4.7	**4.1**
Superior	6.8	3.4	6.0	3.3	**4.9**
	4.6	**4.0**	**6.1**	**4.1**	

[1] Selected quarters in a three year period.

Questionnaire Data

Table 2 shows the significant correlations between the various measures and tax evasion. Attitudes towards not reporting income and towards claiming unwarranted deductions, a strong sense of not

Table 2: Variables Significantly Related to Experimental Tax Evasion Behaviour

Variable	Correlation	Percentage not reported
Age[1]	−.21	
Employment status[2]	−.23	
Alienation[3]	.46	.23
Disinhibition[3]	.29	
Competitiveness[3]	.27	.29
Not reporting all income[3]	.37	
Unwarranted deductions[3]	.30	

[1] In years.
[2] 1 = Having a job, 2 = without a job.
[3] A high score indicates a stronger presence of that characteristic.

belonging to our society, a self-serving rather than other directed orientation (competitiveness), and a tendency to express oneself with socially proscribed behaviours (disinhibition) were all positively associated with frequency of underdeclaring. The percentage of income not declared was correlated with the alienation and the self-serving orientation measures. No relationships between the personality or attitude variables and the measures of change in tax evasion were found.

Cross-National Comparisons

The experimental results of this study can be compared to those of Webley et al. (1988), as the simulation is an exact replication. In both studies there were no significant effects of social comparison on any of the dependent measures. There is, however, a striking difference between

Table 3: Correlations Between Attitudes, Subjective Norms, Personality Attributes, and Tax Evasion Behaviour During the Simulation in Three Different Studies

Variables	Tax evasion behaviour		
	Robben et al.	Webley et al.	Hessing & Elffers
Attitudes			
Underreporting income	.37	n.s.	n.s.
False deductions	.30	n.s.	n.s.
Subjective norms			
Social support	n.s.	n.s.	n.s.
Personality attributes			
Alienation	.46	.28	.22
Competitiveness	.27	n.s.	.17
Disinhibition	.29		

the samples. In the Dutch sample far more evaders were present than in the British sample: 52 out of 72 evaded at least once compared to 30 out of 72 in the British sample ($x^2 = 12.5$, $df = 1$, $p < .001$).

The present data can also be compared with questionnaire data from Webley et al. and the findings of Elffers et al. (1987) (Table 3). Unlike the Elffers et al. and the Webley et al. studies, attitudes towards evading taxes by underreporting income and by overstating deductions correlated significantly with the number of periods in which tax was evaded. In the Webley et al. study competitiveness (self-serving orientation) was not positively related to tax evasion behaviour, whereas in this study it is, in accordance with the Hessing and Elffers (1985) model.

Discussion

As in previous experiments in which the effects of social comparison on tax evasion behaviour were investigated, no significant results were obtained (Webley, Morris, & Amstutz, 1985; Webley, Robben, & Morris, 1988) for any of the measures of tax evasion. One reason for this may be that the subjects clearly were not aware of the real (and hidden) meaning of the experiment. Research by Rijsman (1974, 1983) has shown that the predicted effects are obtained when the comparison dimension is made explicit to the subjects but, for obvious reasons, in this study tax evasion was not made salient to the subjects. However, nor on the dimension with respect to which they thought they were compared (final net income), were there any effects of social comparison although subjects were explicitly informed about their relative position. It thus appears that the social comparison variables did not motivate subjects to change their evasion behaviour.

From Table 2 we see that the decision to evade taxes (as represented by the frequency variable) and the magnitude of tax evasion are clearly distinct in that they are related to different demographic and personality variables. Only the alienation and self-serving orientation measures seem to form shared influencing parameters. The results suggest that people who are young, with a job, not society-oriented and with positive attitudes towards the behaviour are most likely to be associated with tax evasion behaviour. In contrast with other tax evasion experiments (Spicer & Becker, 1980; Spicer & Hero, 1985), no effect of sex was found on either the decision to evade taxes or the size of the misrepresentation of income.

By contrasting the present results with those obtained in research on documented tax evasion behaviour, one can get some idea of how well the experimental data match the pattern of variables that have been useful in explaining real behaviour. Webley et al. (1988) reported a similar comparison which generally supported the model delineated by Hessing and Elffers (1985). The Webley et al. and Hessing and Elffers studies indicated that personality variables represented the strongest correlates of tax evasion behaviour, with attitudinal variables being of little importance. In this study, on the other hand, attitudes toward evading tax correlated significantly with tax evasion behaviour. A possible explanation might be that in the present study, unlike the earlier ones, tax evasion behaviour and attitudes toward that behaviour were measured within a short time of each other. This may have made it more likely that subjects would provide answers to the attitude items that were congruent with their behaviour.

Conclusions

The results of the experiment showed that there were no effects of social comparison on tax evasion behaviour in either sample. This replicates the findings of Webley et al. (1988), and suggests that social comparison may have little influence on tax evasion behaviour. This is further accentuated by the absence of any association of the social support variable. Not only were subjects (in both samples) indifferent to the social comparison variables, but their perception of how others in their environment would react to their evading taxes was not related to tax evasion in the experiment.

The existence of significant behavioural differences between the national samples may stimulate (experimental) cross-national research on tax evasion. However, it seems that the different ratios of evaders and non-evaders may have an impact upon these differences, indicating that caution should be exercised in similar investigations.

References

Allingham, M.G., & Sandmo, A. (1972). Income tax evasion: A theoretical analysis. *Journal of Public Economics, 1*, 323-338.

Aronson, E., & Carlsmith, J.M. (1968). Experimentation in social psychology. In: G. Lindzey & E. Aronson (Eds.), *Handbook of social psychology, Volume 2*, 2nd ed., pp. 1-79. Reading, MA: Addison-Wesley.

Elffers, H., Weigel, R.H., & Hessing, D.J. (1987). The consequences of different strategies for measuring tax evasion behavior. *Journal of Economic Psychology, 8*, 311-337.

Festinger, L. (1954). Social comparison processes. *Human Relations, 7*, 117-140.

Friedland, N., Maital, S., & Rutenberg, A. (1978). A simulation study of income tax evasion. *Journal of Public Economics, 10*, 107-116.

Furnham, A., & Lewis, A. (1986). *The economic mind: The social psychology of economic behaviour.* Brighton: Wheatsheaf.

Grumbkow, J. von, & Wärneryd, K.-E. (1986). Does the tax system ruin the motivation to seek advancement? *Journal of Economic Psychology, 7*, 221-243.

Hauber, A.R., Toornvliet, L.G., & Willemse, H.M. (1986). Persoonlijkheid en criminaliteit. *Tijdschrift voor Criminologie, 2*, 92-106.

Hessing, D.J., & Elffers, H. (1985). Economic man or social man? A social orientation model for individual behavior in social dilemmas. In: H. Brandstätter & E. Kirchler (Eds.), *Economic psychology*, pp. 195-204. Linz: Trauner.

Hessing, D.J., Elffers, H., Weigel, R.H., & Kinsey, K.A. (1988). Tax evasion research: Measurement strategies and theoretical models. In: W.F. van Raaij, G.M. van Veldhoven, & K.-E. Wärneryd (Eds.), *Handbook of economic psychology*, Dordrecht: Kluwer.

Liebrand, W.B.G. (1982). *Interpersonal differences in social dilemmas; A game theoretical approach.* Groningen: State University of Groningen. Unpublished doctoral dissertation.

Rijsman, J.B. (1974). Factors in social comparison of performance influencing actual performance. *European Journal of Social Psychology, 4*, 279-311.

Rijsman, J. (1983). The dynamics of social competition in personal and social comparison situations. In: W. Doise & S. Moscovici (Eds.), *Current issues in European social psychology*, pp. 279-312. Cambridge: Cambridge University Press.

Spicer, M.W., & Becker, L.A. (1980). Fiscal inequity and tax evasion: An experimental approach. *National Tax Journal, 33*, 171-175.

Spicer, M.W., & Hero, R.E. (1985). Tax evasion and heuristics: A research note. *Journal of Public Economics, 26*, 263-267.

Spicer, M.W., & Lundstedt, S.B. (1976). Understanding tax evasion. *Public Finance, 31*, 295-305.

Wärneryd, K.-E., & Walerud, B. (1982). Taxes and economic behaviour: Some interview data on tax evasion in Sweden. *Journal of Economic Psychology, 2*, 187-211.

Webley, P., Morris, I., & Amstutz, F. (1985). Tax evasion during a small business simulation. In: H. Brandstätter and E. Kirchler (Eds.), *Economic psychology*, pp. 233-242. Linz: Trauner.

Webley, P., Robben, H., & Morris, I. (1988). Social comparison, attitudes and tax evasion in a shop simulation. *Social Behaviour, 3*, 219-288.

Wheeler, L., & Zuckerman, M. (1977). Commentary. In: J.M. Suls & R.L. Miller (Eds.), *Social comparison processes: Theoretical and empirical perspectives*, pp. 334-357. New York: Wiley.

Zeller, R.A., Neal, A.G., & Groat, H.T. (1980). On the reliability and stability of alienation measures: A longitudinal analysis. *Social Forces, 58*, 1195-1204.

Zuckerman, M. (1979). *Dimensions of sensation seeking: Beyond the optimal level of arousal*. Hillsdale, NJ: Erlbaum.

Richard Wahlund

Perception and Judgment of Marginal Tax Rates After a Tax Reduction

Abstract

Between 1983 and 1985, most marginal income tax rates were reduced in Sweden. Attitudes towards taxes had repeatedly been found to be very negative and marginal tax rates were assumed to be considered so unreasonably high by the general public that the national economy was ill-effected. The purpose of the tax reform was to reduce the unreasonableness of marginal tax rates in order to stimulate economic behaviour that would benefit the whole economy.

Through four successive surveys during the first phase of the tax reform, it was found that the cuts in marginal income tax rates were only partly perceived, not at once, and not at the same time by everybody. The time-lag was at least one year for any change to be perceived. At the same time, no reduction in the experienced unreasonableness of taxes could be observed, measured as the average difference between perceived marginal income tax rates and the corresponding marginal income tax rates considered reasonable at various income levels; nor were any changes found in the respondents' qualitative opinions about the Swedish income taxes.

By a system analysis technique – PLS (Partial Least Squares) – 38% of the variance in the theoretical construct "experienced un-reasonableness of marginal tax rates" was explained. The variables having the greatest direct **and** indirect impact upon the dependent variable were misperception of tax rates (the tendency to over- or underestimate tax rates in general), general attitudes towards taxes, political affiliation, the perceived height of one's own marginal tax rate, and attitudes towards tax evasion.

Author's address: Richard Wahlund, The Economic Research Institute at the Stockholm School of Economics, P.O. Box 6501, S-113 83 Stockholm, Sweden.

Background

Among politicians, business people, and other decision makers in society, as well as among economists and other social scientists, it is and has long been commonly believed that high marginal income taxes have a discouraging and impeding effect on various kinds of individual economic behaviour to the detriment of the whole economy. Sweden is far from an exception in accommodating this belief, although the country is well-known – or notorious – for its high taxes.

Between 1983 and 1985, an income tax reform was effected in Sweden, the purpose of which was to give taxation policy such a form that it "encourages work, productive efforts and saving and fights inflation, speculation, and tax frauds" (Reformerad inkomstbeskattning, 1982). As a result of the reform, marginal income tax rates were reduced within most income brackets, and deductions were made less favourable, especially for high income earners (henceforth, marginal income tax rates are referred to as "marginal tax rates"). The cuts in marginal tax rates were expected to result in changed behaviour, first and foremost by being experienced as a tax relief at the margin by most tax payers, and by changed – more positive – attitudes towards income taxes in general. As to the former, the marginal tax rates were expected to be seen as more reasonable or less unreasonably high than before the cut.

An intense discussion is currently going on in Sweden about a new tax reform to follow that of 1983-1985, the main purpose of which will be to reduce marginal taxes even more (Kommittédirektiv, 1987). So far, though, few have asked some of the most obvious questions that ought to be asked after the last tax reform: Did people perceive the reduction in marginal tax rates and did they experience the reduction as a tax relief or not? Did the cuts result in more positive attitudes towards income taxes in general? Finally, what explains the unreasonableness of marginal tax rates that people are assumed to experience?

The Purpose of the Paper

This paper analyzes whether or not the marginal tax rate cuts were perceived by Swedish tax payers during the first phase of the 1983-1985 tax reform; whether or not the changes in marginal tax rates made them be seen as less unreasonable than before and whether or not the changes in marginal tax rates resulted in changed attitudes towards income taxes; and finally, what explains the experienced unreasonableness of marginal tax rates? The paper will not look at the impact of tax attitudes on actual behaviour.

Method

The empirical data used for this paper derive from four surveys carried out within a research project that was begun in 1982 in order to follow up the tax reform by measuring household economic behaviour at four different points in time. The first survey was carried out in November/December 1982, just before the start of the tax reform. It was followed by a second in May/June 1983, a third in November/December 1983, and the fourth and last in May/June 1984.

A total number of 1752 (72.4%) men out of a total sample of 2421 Swedish male citizens, 20-65 years of age, were interviewed by telephone on the basis of a structured questionnaire. The interview time averaged 35 minutes. Tables which summarize the response and non-response rates for the different surveys can be found in Wahlund (1988b) and in Wahlund and Wärneryd (1988).

In order to collect some additional information, such as attitudes to Swedish taxes and to tax crime severity, perceived and expected rates of inflation, reasons for saving, and more exact figures for savings, interest received and paid, indebtedness, etc., an additional mail questionnaire was sent to all respondents. The latter was answered by 1427 (81.4%) out of the 1752 men interviewed.

In addition, information about age, civil status, family size, declared and taxed income in 1980 or 1981, etc., was ascertained for each respondent. This information made it possible to adjust for differing non-response in the various samples (see Wahlund, 1988b).

It is important to bear in mind that old-age pensioner households and households consisting of a single female or of only teenagers have been excluded from the surveys. Old-age pensioner households have shown different saving behaviour than other households (Lindqvist, 1981, 1983), and more than 20% of all households – about 17% of all individuals – were in this category (Statistics Sweden, 1985). The reason for not including old-age pensioners in the sample was that their differing economic behaviour would necessitate a larger sample. The main reason for excluding women was that it was very difficult to get the telephone numbers of female respondents due to the fact that men still dominate in the telephone directories.

The men sampled and interviewed were expected to speak not only for themselves, but also for their households.

In this paper, a weighted database has been used for all analyses. The data were weighted in order to make the distribution of age – within certain intervals – and civil status of the actual respondents identical with that of the total sample. The statistics for the total sample was the most representative statistics available for the studied population. The number of respondents in the weighted database is the same as in the unweighted database.

In addition, only the respondents who stated that they had a job and a monthly income of at least SEK 1000 (in real money value as of 1980) were included in the analyses. They amount to 1513 (86%) of all respondents in the weighted data-base (survey 1: 370; survey 2: 349; survey 3: 402, and survey 4: 392).

Apart from simple statistical tests of differences in means and variances between subgroups (t- and F-tests) a second generation multivariate analysis method called PLS (Partial Least Squares) was used to examine the direct **and** indirect impact and explanatory power of various variables òn the experienced unreasonableness of marginal tax rates and attitudes towards income taxes (World, 1975; Fornell, 1987). A Pearson product correlation matrix was used as input data.

Theoretical Aspects and Hypotheses

Perception of Marginal Tax Rates and of Changes Therein

In this study, the basis for finding out whether or not tax payers perceived a reduction in marginal tax rates during the income tax reform is group averages of perceived marginal tax rates at various points in time rather than individual perceptions or judgments of **changes**. Theories of perception can still be used as a source for hypotheses about the perception and categorization of changes. If tax payers perceive the reduction in marginal tax rates, it is assumed to result in a corresponding decrease in the averages of perceived marginal tax rates.

It is possible to use results from Weber's and his followers' studies of how large a change has to be in order to be noticed, from attention theory about what makes a person attend to stimuli, and from adaptation-level theory as to how changes are categorized and judged.

In perception theory, it is an established fact that changes have to be of a certain size to be perceived. Weber (1834) found that there is a "difference threshold," i.e., a difference between two stimuli must be of a certain magnitude before one can be distinguished from the other. This is often referred to as a "just noticeable difference." Weber proposed that the difference threshold tends to be a constant fraction of the stimulus magnitude. This implies that a change in a tax rate from, say, 40 to 30 percentage points is more likely to be noticed than a change from 80 to 70 percentage points, ceteris paribus. Fechner (1860) redefined what had become "Weber's law" by proposing that sensation increases as a logarithmic function of stimulus intensity. This redefinition of Weber's law has later been referred to as "Fechner's law" (Atkinson, Atkinson, & Hilgard, 1983).

Was the decrease in marginal tax rates in Sweden during the reform large enough to be noticed by the tax payers? The general hypothesis is that the greater the decrease in a marginal tax rate is in relation to its preceding level, the more likely it will be perceived, but if Weber's and Fechner's laws apply, the higher the marginal tax rate has previously been, the larger the change must be to have an effect.

It may be held that differences between amounts of money can always be discerned, irrespective of the size of the difference. Even so, perception of a change in tax rates may still be affected by factors such as exposure to the stimulus, the degree of attention and interest bestowed upon the stimulus, and the importance of the change to the individual.

Galanter (1962) proposed a number of factors that may influence attention. They can be separated into three groups: expectations, motives, and pay-off. If people expect a change in marginal tax rates, it is more likely to be perceived than without such expectations. Motives include attitudes, interests, needs, etc. The more pronounced the attitudes toward income taxes are (whether positive or negative), the greater the interest in taxes and the greater the need for a change (whether financially or ideologically based), the more likely a change in marginal tax rates is paid attention to.

The pay-off plays an important role in economics as a predictor of behaviour, and, according to Galanter, also of attention. It should be expected that the higher the (relative) pay-off of a change in marginal tax rates is to a tax payer, the more likely it is that he pays attention to the change.

In judging the importance of a change, the individual tends to use reference or anchoring points, the choice of which can influence the perception of, and the attention given to, the stimulus. Helson (1964) proposed an adaptation-level theory, according to which it is not only the focal stimuli that determine perception, but also the contextual (background) and residual (past experience) stimuli. The individual learns to associate a stimulus set with a reference point or adaptation level.

The perception of reduced marginal tax rates should hence be expected to be dependent not only upon the focal stimulus, i.e., the changes as such, but also upon context, background, and past experience, and upon attentional factors such as motives, expectations, and pay-off.

All qualitative information about the marginal taxes supplied by mass media and other sources could be classified as "background" stimuli or context. How well people perceive the current marginal tax rates may thus differ between points in time depending on how "hot" a topic tax rates are and what the message about the tax rates is, i.e., if they are described as still "extremely high" or as "rather acceptable" after having been reduced. The impact of background stimuli may, in turn, depend on the individual characteristics mentioned above (expectations, motives, and pay-offs).

As to the focal stimulus, it is rather difficult for many people to know what current marginal tax rates within different income brackets actually are, or will be. In the official information about the income taxes sent twice a year to all income earners, the total tax to be paid at different income levels is shown, i.e., the average or proportional rate of total tax. Marginal tax rates can be calculated, easily by some people and less easily by others, but some people may not discover that marginal tax rates can be calculated and still others may not be interested enough to go ahead and do it. Education level (past experience) and attentional factors such as interest in economic matters (motives and needs) may thus be important for how accurately marginal tax rates are perceived.

As to past experience, people running their own businesses and people actively managing their wealth, situations in which taking taxes into consideration is very important, should be more inclined than others to try to calculate the marginal taxes for the year to come and thus should perceive marginal tax rates more correctly.

However, since the self-employed also pay pay-roll taxes in addition to their income tax, they may systematically overestimate their income tax by including the pay-roll taxes in their calculation or perception of the income tax. This overestimation tendency may be reduced, though, due to the fact that the preliminary tax they calculate is the average tax rate, not the marginal tax rate, thus underestimating the latter. (Here it is assumed that the marginal tax rate is higher than the average total tax rate, but if pay-roll taxes are included in the latter but not in the former, then this may not be the case.) As a minimum, one would expect to find a smaller standard deviation in the perception of marginal tax rates among the self-employed than among employees. Since the self-employed are only a small fraction of the aggregate, their judgment will however influence the aggregate average rather little.

The wealth managers are usually found at higher income levels (Wahlund, 1988c; Wahlund & Wärneryd, 1988) and are thus accustomed to high marginal tax rates. People used to a high income and thus to high marginal tax rates would be expected to overestimate the marginal tax rate of a lower income while the opposite – underestimation of the marginal tax rate of a higher income – should be expected by those used to a lower income and to lower marginal tax rates. At the same time, people who make large deductions reducing the tax to be paid, may perceive marginal tax rates to be lower than people who do not reduce their tax through deductions. Wahlund (1983, 1988b) found a strong positive correlation between income and the size of deductions; the higher the deductions, the lesser an overestimation or greater an underestimation would be expected.

As to the perception of one's own marginal tax rate, one's past marginal tax rates may be more important than one's present ones, because past tax rates are much more assessable and certain than the one of the current year. The only time people will know for sure what their tax is, is when they have been taxed, i.e., in late autumn of the year following the income-earning year. This suggests that for many people a time-lag may exist in the perception of a change in marginal tax rates. This time-lag may very well be prolonged, the more prolonged the less often one's own tax is calculated.

To get to know what one's marginal tax rate was a year earlier, using the final information about the total tax (in monetary units) received in late autumn, people still have to make some calculations themselves, using the tax table received at the beginning of the year. Whether people do this or not will again depend on interest, motives, education level, size of taxable income, sex, age, etc.

People may also use the amount withdrawn from their monthly salary to get an idea about their tax rate. This tax rate, as well as the tax rate most easily calculated from the information received twice a year, is the **average** tax rate. At each income level this rate is lower than the actual marginal tax rate and does not change as much as marginal tax rates. This means that in general, underestimation of one's own marginal tax rate should be expected.

There are some studies showing that it is usual for people to underestimate the tax burden due to what Pommerehne and Schneider (1979) labelled a "fiscal illusion" or "tax illusion." Lewis (1978) found that people in a British town underestimated marginal tax rates at different income levels by 11% on the average. Wärneryd and Walerud (1981) also found an underestimation tendency, but not of the same magnitude as Lewis.

Finally, it should be pointed out that although marginal tax rates were cut at most income levels during the Swedish tax reform, they were not cut at all levels. In fact, at lower income levels they were slightly increased. Many people may also have moved to a higher income level during the course of the tax reform and may thus in fact have experienced no change or even an increase in their marginal tax rate. Even in these cases, the notion of a general tax reduction or tax relief will have been transmitted by the mass media or by other sources of information, causing marginal tax rates to be perceived as lower than before.

Judging the Reasonableness of Tax Rates

The reason for reducing marginal tax rates was that people were believed to consider the present rates as too high and thus to behave contrary to what is commonly considered to be "sound" economic behaviour and contrary to what is good for the national economy. In addition, a number of Swedish surveys had found strong negative attitudes toward the Swedish income taxes (e.g., Bylund, 1987; Hadenius, 1986; Laurin, 1986; Vogel, 1974; Wahlund, 1983, 1988a, b; Wärneryd & Walerud, 1981).

In order to be able to judge marginal tax rates as reasonable or unreasonable, people need a reference point. Wärneryd and Walerud (1981), as well as Lewis (1978), found such a reference point by asking the respondents to state what they thought was a reasonable tax on an income increment of SEK 1000 on top of various incomes.

Wärneryd and Walerud (1981) found that the difference between the reasonable marginal tax rate and the perceived marginal tax rate was – on the average – about 14 percentage points at the SEK 50,000 taxable income level and 21 percentage points at the SEK 150,000 level for the higher educated employees, and 18 percentage points at both income levels for the less educated employees (the marginal tax rate considered reasonable being lower than the perceived one). Using medians instead of averages resulted in still larger differences between reasonable and perceived tax rates. But what determines the reasonableness of marginal tax rates?

An assumption behind the tax reform must have been that the reference points up on which judgments of the reasonableness of a marginal tax rate is based, are rather stable over long periods of time. However, if Helson's adaptation-level theory, extended with the attentional factors suggested by Galanter (see above), also applies to these affective reference points, then the marginal tax rate considered reasonable at a certain income level and at a certain point in time should vary depending on the focal stimulus, differing background stimuli, differences in past experience among tax payers, and attentional factors such as motives and expectations.

In this case, the focal stimulus – the reasonable marginal tax rate – is in itself a function of the other types of factors and among these factors is the perceived marginal tax rate. Thus, when the perceived marginal tax rates go down, then the marginal tax rate regarded as **reasonable** should also decline. As to background stimuli and attentional factors, the same sources of variation and effects should be expected as in the judgment of marginal tax rates. Among other things, Wärneryd and Walerud (1981) found that political affiliation is an important predictor of the judged unreasonableness of marginal tax rates. As to past experience, the tax burden put on earlier incomes would be expected to influence the marginal tax rate considered reasonable today. That would also make earlier incomes and deductions to be of import. In other words, the higher the income tax and/or marginal tax rates one is used to, the higher the unreasonableness should be judged.

These findings suggest that the reference point for one's conception of what is a reasonable marginal tax rate may not be a static one. If marginal tax rates are reduced in general, one may accordingly adjust one's conception of what is a reasonable tax rate. So one starts to wonder: Does a reduction of the marginal tax rates at all result in the feeling of tax relief?

Hypotheses About Changes in Perception and Judgment of Marginal Tax Rates and in Attitudes Towards Taxes

The first three hypotheses concern aggregate averages and variability (as measured by the variances: $\hat{s}^2_{y_i}$) in perceived marginal tax rates. The next three hypotheses concern aggregate averages and variability in marginal tax rates considered reasonable and in the difference between the perceived marginal tax rates and the marginal tax rates considered reasonable. Hence, this difference is taken to define the "unreasonableness of marginal tax rates."

Hypothesis 1

The tax payers are – on the average – expected to underestimate marginal tax rates in 1982, i.e., in the year preceding the income tax reform.

There are two main reasons for this: (a) people in general are expected to be more familiar with average tax rates than marginal tax rates, the former being lower than the latter, and (b) the income tax rates had been increasing for a number of years at most income levels and it takes time before people adapt to new, higher tax rates.

Hypothesis 2

In general, a time-lag as to the perception of reduced marginal tax rates is expected. According to Weber-Fechner's law, the smaller the absolute and relative change in marginal tax rates, the less likely it is to be discovered by the average tax payer. How well a change is perceived depends also, according to attention theory and Helson's adaptation-level theory, on other factors related to the stimulus, and on factors related to the perceiver. These may vary over time and also have a delayed effect over time. Thus, the smaller the change (in combination with other factors influencing perception), the longer the time-lag, and the less of it will be perceived at a time – as measured by the average.

This means that the average incorrectness in perception of marginal tax rates is expected to be towards less underestimation – or greater overestimation – immediately following a reduction in marginal tax rates. Later on, as the change is slowly perceived, this incorrectness will move towards greater underestimation – or less overestimation – unless, as in this case, marginal tax rates are further reduced.

Hypothesis 3

An increase over time in the variances of perceived marginal tax rates as they are cut is expected due to differences in attention and in the learning process among tax payers. This also means that the variance of the incorrectness in perception will increase, at least at specified income levels where the marginal tax rate does not vary much. The latter is, of course, not the case when it comes to the respondents' own income. The respondents' own marginal tax rate will always have a high variance.

Hypothesis 4

As cuts in marginal tax rates are perceived, the marginal tax rate considered reasonable at differing income levels will be adjusted accordingly, i.e., no change is expected in the average difference between the perceived marginal tax rates and marginal tax rates considered reasonable.

The main reason for this is that the latter of the two variables is assumed to be a function of the former as well as of many of the variables that the perceived marginal tax rate in turn is a function of. It is also assumed that many of the factors influencing the perception of the reduction in marginal tax rates (e.g., mass media), influence the considered reasonableness of marginal tax rates in the same direction.

Hypothesis 5

The average difference between marginal tax rates as perceived and the corresponding marginal tax rates considered reasonable is expected to be greater at higher income levels than at lower income levels, as has been found in earlier studies.

Hypothesis 6

As marginal tax rates are reduced, an increase over time in the variance of the marginal tax rates considered reasonable is expected, due to differences in the adaptation process among the respondents.

Hypothesis 7

In accordance with Hypothesis 4, as marginal tax rates are reduced, no change is expected to be found over time in the opinions about or attitudes towards Swedish income taxes in general.

The Operational Definition of the Dependent Variables

The perceived marginal tax rates and the marginal tax rates considered reasonable by the respondents were related to three income levels: that of one's own income, that of an income of SEK 70,000, and that of an income of SEK 150,000. The questions asked in the surveys to measure the perception of marginal tax rates were:

"If you earned SEK 1000 above your ordinary income, how much of it would you have to pay in tax?" and "If a person has an annual income of SEK X, and happens to earn SEK 1000 extra, how much of the extra income do you think would go in tax?"; $X = \{70,000; 150,000\}$.

The question used to measure the marginal tax rate considered reasonable at each of the income levels followed immediately after the corresponding question about the respondent's perception of the marginal tax rate and it read: "How much of the SEK 1000 would you consider reasonable to pay in tax?" The reader should observe that it is the marginal tax in **monetary units** of an additional income at each income level that has been asked for, not the marginal tax in **per cent**. For simplicity, I will still talk about marginal tax **rates** instead of "marginal tax in monetary units" in the following.

To get the incorrectness in perceived marginal tax rates, the actual (true) marginal tax rate at each income level was calculated for each respondent. The true marginal tax rates of the three incomes in question were then simply subtracted from the corresponding perceived marginal tax rates. When calculating the marginal tax rate of the respondent's own income, twelve times the monthly income stated by the respondents was used, i.e., income from interest and capital gains as well as deductible costs were disregarded. Since local taxes differ (25%-34%) the actual marginal tax rate of the two specified incomes will also have a variance. Thus changes in local taxes have also been taken into account along with the changes in the state tax due to the income tax reform.

For all six questions, the respondents were given the option of answering "Don't know." Less than 10% of all respondents chose this option on any single question. How this proportion differed among the surveys and what characterized the "don't know"s will not be discussed in this paper.

A number of questions were used as indicators of people's attitudes towards Swedish income taxes in general. These are all spelled out in

Table 1 on p. 155-156. The first question – asking for people's general opinion about the income taxes – was measured using a seven-point scale where –3 meant "extremely negative," 0 meant "neutral," and 3 meant "extremely positive."

The next nine questions were measured by a four-point scale where –3 meant "disagree very much," –1 "disagree somewhat/rather," 1 "agree somewhat/rather," and 3 "agree very much." The last five were measured using a five-point scale where 0 meant that one considers the crime insignificant and 4 meant that one considers the crime very grave.

Results

Perception of Marginal Tax Rates

This discussion is based upon the results given in Table A:1 in the Appendix. The hypotheses will be discussed one by one in the order they were stated.

Hypothesis 1: Underestimation of Marginal Tax Rates in 1982

The respondents in the first survey in 1982 made more correct estimations of marginal tax rates, on the average, than did the respondents in Lewis (1978) and in Wärneryd and Walerud (1981). In 1982, the respondents' own marginal tax rate and that at the SEK 150,000 income level were, as hypothesized, underestimated by, on the average, 3.6 and 3.3 percentage points, respectively. At the SEK 70,000 income level it was slightly overestimated: by 1.7 percentage points.

One possible explanation of the latter finding is that higher income earners have a tendency to overestimate marginal tax rates of lower incomes, using their own marginal tax rate as a reference point, and that these overestimations have a greater impact on the aggregate average than other tax-payers' underestimation.

It is reasonable to assume that people have a more correct perception of the marginal tax rate of their own income than of that of other incomes. Still, in all four surveys the variation in the incorrectness in perception of one's own marginal tax rate is greater than the variation in

148

the incorrectness in perception of the marginal tax rate at the two specified income levels:

$$\hat{s}_{y_1}^2 > \hat{s}_{y_2}^2 \approx \hat{s}_{y_3}^2$$

where:

$\hat{s}^2$ = the variance (the standard deviations are shown in the Appendix),

y_1 = the incorrectness in perception of one's own marginal tax rate,

y_2 = the incorrectness in perception of the marginal tax rate at the SEK 150,000 income level,

y_3 = the incorrectness of perception of the marginal tax rate at the SEK 70,000 income level,

t = Autumn 1982, Spring 1983, Autumn 1983, Spring 1984.

One obvious explanation of this finding is that some people take their presumptive deductions and/or additional taxable incomes into consideration when estimating their own marginal tax rate, things that may affect the "true" marginal tax rate and make it different from the one I have calculated for the individual in question. Another explanation could be that the incomes of some people have changed very drastically and that they have not yet considered – or perceived – what this means for their marginal tax rate.

Hypothesis 2: Lagged Perception of Reduced Marginal Tax Rates

The hypothesized time-lag with respect to the perception of reduced marginal tax rates was found both for the two specified income levels and for the respondents' own income. As can be seen from Table A:1 (Appendix) and Figure 1 below, it took about one and a half years for any significant change in the means of perceived marginal tax rates to occur.

As a result, the perceived marginal tax rates became overestimated – at the SEK 70,000 income level more overestimated than earlier – immediately following the first reduction in marginal tax rates, as hypothesized. Between Spring 1983 (Survey 2) and Autumn 1983 (Survey 3), with constant marginal tax rates, the average incorrectness in perception moved in the hypothesized direction for all three incomes as the first reduction was slowly perceived.

149

At the SEK 150,000 income level, the average perceived marginal tax rate was about the same in all the first three surveys, despite the fact that the true marginal tax rate had been reduced by 4.7 percentage points. Then, in Spring 1984 (Survey 4), when the marginal tax rate had been cut by another 8.8 percentage points, the average perceived marginal tax rate dropped by four percentage points.

At the SEK 70,000 income level, where the actual decrease in the marginal tax rate between 1982 and 1983 was 6.7 percentage points, the average perceived marginal tax rate began to decrease at once (although not significantly). In 1984, when the marginal tax rate had been reduced by only another 1.8 percentage points, the average perceived marginal tax rate dropped by around three percentage points. These findings give support to the hypothesis that the greater the change, the shorter the time-lag.

Out of the total 8.5 percentage points that the marginal tax rate was cut by at the SEK 70000 income level, the respondents had perceived, on average, a reduction by 4.6 percentage points, i.e., about 50% of the reduction. At the SEK 150000 income level, the respondents had observed a reduction by 4.1 percentage points out of a total of 13.5 percentage points, i.e., about 30% of the total reduction. This gives support to the hypothesis that a reduction in an already high marginal tax rate is not as easily perceived as a reduction in a lower marginal tax rate, as Weber-Fechner's law suggests.

With regard to the effects that the cuts in marginal tax rates were expected to have on behaviour, the change in the perception of the marginal tax rate of one's own income is of greatest interest. The average actual (as calculated) marginal tax rate of one's own income decreased by about four percentage points in 1983, and then by another three percentage points in 1984. In 1983, hardly anything of the decrease was perceived – on average – and by Spring 1984, the average perceived marginal tax rate had dropped by only two percentage points, i.e., only about 30% of the total actual reduction in 1983 and in 1984. The latter corresponds to what was perceived of the reduction at the SEK 150,000 income level (also about 30%) but less to what was perceived of the reduction at the SEK 70,000 income level (54%). This may indicate that people in general considered themselves less positively affected by the income tax reform than other people. It could be the result of a preference drift not considered when the tax reform was designed. These

findings may also be influenced by some respondents taking into account
deductions and other taxable incomes not considered by the author when
calculating the "true" marginal tax rate of the respondents.

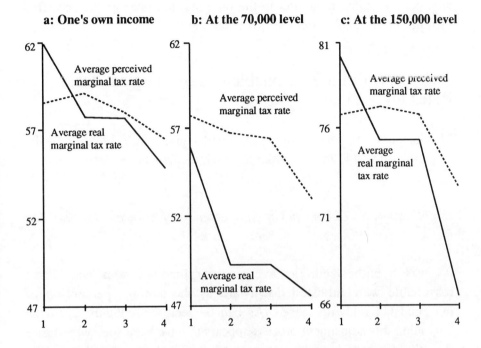

a: One's own income   **b: At the 70,000 level**   **c: At the 150,000 level**

**Figure 1: Average perceived and average real marginal tax rates for
three income levels at four points in time between 1982 and
1984.**

*Hypothesis 3: Increased Variance of Perceived Marginal Tax Rates Over
Time*

The hypothesized increase over time in the variances of the perceived
marginal tax rates and of the incorrectness in perception was found for
all income levels concerned, if only the first and the last surveys are
considered. (The significance levels for the respondents' own income and
at the SEK 70,000 income level were $p < 0.05$, and for the SEK 150,000
income level $p < 0.10$.) In 1983, the first year during which marginal tax
rates were reduced, the variance of perceived marginal tax rate increased
only for the respondents' own income, while it remained the same or
even dropped somewhat for the two specified income levels.

These findings suggest that the drop in one's own marginal tax rate, and later on also in the marginal tax rates of the specified incomes, was discovered faster by some people than by others, and that few people, if any, perceived the reduction in the marginal tax rates of the specified incomes immediately after the first reduction.

Judgments of the Reasonableness of Marginal Tax Rates Over Time

This discussion is based upon the results given in Table A:2 in the Appendix. It will follow the order in which the hypotheses were stated.

Hypothesis 4: No Change in Unreasonableness of Reduced Marginal Tax Rates

As was hypothesized, the average marginal tax rates considered reasonable were adjusted downward as the average perception of marginal tax rates decreased. As can be seen from Figure 2, in the beginning this adjustment process appears to have been somewhat faster than the decrease in average perceived marginal tax rates, but on the whole, these two adaptations kept abreast. This means that the average difference between perceived marginal tax rates and the marginal tax rates considered reasonable did not change as marginal tax rates were reduced. At no income level, nor between any two surveys (points in time), was a significant change found, although the variance of the difference increased significantly between 1982 and 1984 for one's own income and for the lower income level.

The former finding implies that the tax reform had not, on average and at least until the end of the first half of the reform, resulted in the expected feeling of a tax relief. The latter finding implies that some people did have the feeling of a tax relief, but that at the same time, others felt they were the victims of an increase in the tax burden which, in the aggregate, outweighed the tax relief perceived by the former.

As was suggested earlier on the basis of Weber's and Fechner's laws: Marginal tax rates may have to be cut by much more than they were during the tax reform, in order to be felt as a tax relief.

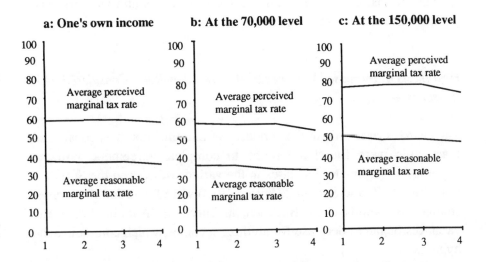

Figure 2: Average perceived marginal tax rates and average reasonable marginal tax rates for three income levels at four points in time between 1982 and 1984.

Hypothesis 5: A Positive Correlation Between Unreasonableness and Income

As was hypothesized, the average difference between marginal tax rates as perceived and the corresponding marginal tax rates considered as reasonable was higher at the higher income level than at the lower income level. The difference was about six percentage points: 28% on average at the SEK 150,000 income level as compared to 22% at the SEK 70,000 income level. Thus, although the unreasonableness of marginal tax rates was found not to change **over time** when tax rates were reduced, there is apparently a difference in unreasonableness between marginal tax rates of different heights at a certain **point of time**.

When comparing these findings with those of Wärneryd and Walerud (1981), it seems as if the experienced unreasonableness had increased during the first years of the 1980's, and much more than the marginal tax rates had increased. This is interesting, since the tax rates increased during this time. It may be explained, though, by the fact that the respondents in the Wärneryd-Walerud study were sampled from two special groups: employees with a university degree and workers. The populations are thus not comparable.

Hypothesis 6: Increased Variance of Marginal Tax Rates Considered Reasonable

The changes over time in the variances of marginal tax rates considered reasonable were found not to be in complete agreement with the hypothesis. Significant increases in the variances between the Survey 1 (Autumn 1982) and Survey 2 (Spring 1983) were found for all incomes studied, as hypothesized. But then, in Survey 3 (Autumn 1983), the variances began to decrease for all three incomes, which contradicts the hypothesis.

The first finding means that as marginal tax rates are reduced, some people are faster than others to make an immediate downward adjustment in "reasonable" marginal tax rates, and that probably some do it even faster than they perceive a reduction in the actual tax rates. Communicators, such as the mass media, thus seem to influence the **reasonableness** of marginal tax rates more than they influence the **perception** of marginal tax rates.

The second finding suggests that most people adjust their attitudes toward marginal tax rates more quickly than they perceive the actual changes. Again, background stimuli, mediating a notion of the importance of or need for lower taxes, may be more influential than the stimuli mediating the reduction in marginal tax rates. Mass media may play an important role.

Hypothesis 7: No Changes in Average Attitudes Towards Income Taxes Over Time

As hypothesized, F-tests showed no significant changes over time in the opinions about or attitudes towards the Swedish income taxes. Table 1 shows the mean, standard deviation, and number of respondents for each question in each survey (point in time).

154

Table 1: The Respondents' Attitudes Towards Income Taxes by Time/ Survey

		1982:1	1983:2	1983:3	1984:4	χ^2
Scales going from –3 to +3*						
What is your opinion about the income taxes in Sweden right now? Are you ...?	$\bar{x}$ s n	–1.10 (1.44) 370	–1.18 (1.42) 348	–1.20 (1.45) 400	–1.08 (1.42) 392	n.s.
The taxes take away money that is really mine	$\bar{x}$ s n	0.43 (1.82) 324	0.62 (1.77) 285	0.70 (1.77) 299	0.42 (1.85) 316	n.s.
The Swedish system of taxation is unjust	$\bar{x}$ s n	1.34 (1.54) 322	1.30 (1.60) 286	1.45 (1.50) 299	1.14 1.66) 314	n.s.
Considering the benefits that the state gives its citizens, the taxes are **not** too high	$\bar{x}$ s n	–0.06 (1.60) 324	–0.27 (1.64) 286	–0.18 (1.62) 300	0.00 (1.62) 315	n.s.
Because of the taxes it does not pay to work overtime or earn extra money	$\bar{x}$ s n	1.94 (1.56) 325	1.97 (1.48) 288	1.92 (1.56) 299	1.81 (1.53) 316	n.s.
There should be no tax on bank interest	$\bar{x}$ s n	0.64 (2.14) 324	0.78 (2.23) 286	0.56 (2.10) 299	0.65 (2.14) 316	n.s.
If you have a chance to reduce your taxes, you should take it, even if illegal	$\bar{x}$ s n	–1.40 (1.70) 324	–1.24 (1.80) 286	–1.35 (1.77) 299	–1.35 (1.77) 315	n.s.
People who do not declare extra income should be punished more severely than at present	$\bar{x}$ s n	1.35 (1.66) 323	1.37 (1.71) 286	1.25 (1.63) 298	1.16 (1.72) 316	n.s.
I would be prepared to pay an artisan "off the record" if I could get the job done cheaper that way	$\bar{x}$ s n	0.13 (2.12) 324	0.27 (2.04) 286	0.36 (2.03) 300	0.37 (2.17) 316	n.s.
It is highly inconsiderate to make too large deductions in your income tax return	$\bar{x}$ s n	0.69 (1.95) 318	0.88 (1.96) 284	0.54 (2.04) 298	0.62 (2.01) 312	n.s.

continued

155

Table 1, continued

		1982:1	1983:2	1983:3	1984:4	χ^2
Scales going from 0 to +4						
One doesn't declare extra income,	$\bar{x}$	1.70	1.69	1.58	1.55	n.s.
thereby making a gain of SEK	s	(1.25)	(1.10)	(1.21)	(1.22)	
1000	n	318	284	297	316	
One makes an "off the record"	$\bar{x}$	1.59	1.54	1.48	1.43	n.s.
payment to an artisan, thereby	s	(1.26)	(1.15)	(1.23)	(1.19)	
saving SEK 1000	n	320	285	298	313	
One makes deductions for	$\bar{x}$	2.63	2.62	2.60	2.53	n.s.
expenses that have not been	s	(1.18)	(1.17)	(1.21)	(1.14)	
incurred, thereby gaining	n	320	286	298	316	
SEK 1000						
One makes an agreement with	$\bar{x}$	2.26	2.34	2.23	2.32	n.s.
one's boss that part of one's income	s	(1.28)	(1.29)	(1.33)	(1.28)	
be paid "off the record", thereby	n	320	284	298	316	
gaining SEK 1000						

*For a description of the rating scales used, see p. 148.

Although no significant differences were found for mean values over time, an interesting tendency concerning questions on tax evasion should be pointed out. Out of eight variables measuring attitudes towards tax evasion, the means of six variables developed in a way which hints at relaxed morals. If this observation mirrors a true tendency, it would be in direct opposition to what was expected from the tax reform. The statistical test, however, does not reject the null hypothesis.

The Predictive/Causal Model of Unreasonableness of Marginal Tax Rates

So far, we have only been looking at what happened to perceptions and judgments of marginal tax rates and to attitudes towards taxes at the **aggregate** level, when marginal tax rates were lowered. We now turn to look at what explains differences between **individuals** in their assessment of the unreasonableness of marginal tax rates.

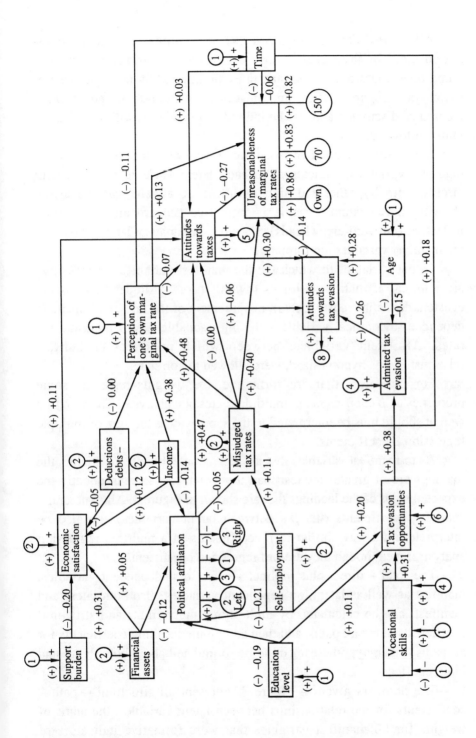

Figure 3: The predictive/causal model of unreasonableness of marginal tax rates.

All **hypotheses** about the direct and indirect effects of socio-economic, behavioural, and organismic variables on the unreasonableness of marginal tax rates are implied by the signs **within brackets** in Figure 3 below and most of them can be inferred from the theoretical discussion above. The individual hypotheses will be discussed in the following.

In Figure 3, all latent variables are drawn as squares. The number of manifest variables (indicators) to each latent variable are shown in circles, with hypothesized sign of influence attached to the arrow showing if the latent variable is formative (inward arrowheads) or reflective (outward arrowheads). To most explanatory latent variables, the manifest variables are formative.

Latent variables to which the the manifest variables are reflective are political affiliation, attitudes towards taxes, attitudes towards tax evasion, deductible costs (debts), misjudgment of tax rates, and the main dependent theoretical variable – the unreasonableness of marginal tax rates. All latent variables, between which no direct or indirect relationship was hypothesized, were allowed to correlate.

For indicators that are formative, the weights have the same properties as β coefficients in multiple regression analyses. The sign of a weight should thus be interpreted in the same way as the sign of multiple regression β coefficients.

As to manifest variables that are reflections of a latent variable, the loadings are of greater interest than the weights. It is consequently the expected signs of the loadings that are shown in Figure 3. All structural – "path" – coefficients (the β s between latent variables) can also be interpreted in a way similar to β coefficients in a multiple regression analysis, (even though they are **not** regression coefficients).

The total – direct plus indirect – effect of independent variables, manifest as well as latent, on dependent variables, also both latent and manifest, can be calculated by multiplying the weights and structural coefficients along all paths, and then adding the resulting coefficients for all paths. Thus, hypotheses need to be formulated about both direct and indirect effects.

The numbers given in Figure 3 represent all structural – path – coefficients for the relationships between latent variables, the signs of weights for all manifest variables that were formative indicators of explanatory latent variables, and the loadings of manifest variables that were reflections of latent variables, as estimated by a PLS analysis programme (Lohmöller, 1984). The weights, loadings, and communalities of all manifest variables are shown in Table A:3 in the Appendix.

As can be seen from a comparison of the signs within brackets and the actual, estimated coefficients, almost all hypotheses were supported (had the right sign), but some coefficients were insignificant, although they had the hypothesized sign, and others had a zero path coefficient. Table 2 shows the total effect coefficients (reduced path coefficients) for the relationships between all explanatory latent variables and every latent

Table 2: Total Effect (Reduced Path) Coefficients Between Latent Variables and Squared Multiple Correlation (Explained Variance) of Latent Variables

	1	2	3	4	5	6	7	8	9	10	11	12	13	14	15	16	17	18
10	0	-.05	.12	-.20	.31	0	0	0	0									
11	0	0	-.14	-.01	-.10	-.19	0	-.21	0	.05								
12	0	0	0	0	0	.11	.31	.20	0	0	0							
13	0	0	0	0	0	.04	.12	.07	-.15	0	0	.38						
14	.18	0	.01	0	.01	.01	0	.12	0	0	-.05	0	0					
15	-.02	0	.38	0	0	0	0	.06	0	0	-.02	0	0	.48				
16	.03	-.01	-.08	-.03	-.01	-.09	0	-.10	0	.14	.47	0	0	-.03	-.07			
17	.01	0	-.04	-.01	0	-.04	-.03	-.05	.32	.04	.14	-.10	-.26	-.04	-.08	.30		
18	0	0	.08	.01	.01	.03	0	.09	-.05	-.04	-.17	.01	.04	.48	.16	-.32	-.14	
R^2	0	0	0	0	0	0	0	0	0	18	16	14	19	5	38	24	31	38

The latent variables (theoretical constructs) are: 1) Time; 2) Deductions (debts); 3) Income; 4) Support burden; 5) Financial assets; 6) Educational level; 7) Vocational skills; 8) Self-employment; 9) Age; 10) Economic satisfaction; 11) Political affiliation; 12) Tax evasion opportunities; 13) Admitted tax evasion; 14) Misjudged tax rates; 15) Perception of one's own marginal tax rate; 16) Attitudes towards taxes; 17) Attitudes towards tax evasion; 18) Unreasonableness of marginal tax rates.

variable that they were hypothesized to influence. Table 2 also gives the squared multiple correlation (explained variance) for each dependent latent variable.

Only five variables were hypothesized to have a direct effect on the unreasonableness of marginal tax rates: time, the perceived height of one's own marginal tax rate, misjudgment of tax rates in general, attitudes towards taxes, and attitudes towards tax evasion. All other variables were expected to influence the unreasonableness of marginal tax rates only indirectly.

Hypothesis 8

Perception of one's own marginal tax rate was expected to have a high positive influence on the unreasonableness of marginal tax rates, both directly and indirectly, the latter by influencing attitudes towards taxes and towards tax evasion, which in turn were expected to influence the unreasonableness of marginal tax rates.

The reason for reducing the marginal tax rates was that they were assumed to be considered unreasonably high. This also means that the height of marginal tax rates was assumed to be the main explanation of its experienced unreasonableness, especially the height of one's own marginal tax rate. In order for this to be true, the marginal tax rates must be perceived correctly. It was therefore first and foremost hypothesized that the **perceived** height of one's own marginal tax rate would explain most of the unreasonableness in marginal tax rates. At the same time, other factors were also expected to influence the unreasonableness, making the impact of the perceived marginal tax rate of one's own somewhat uncertain.

The direct influence of the perception of one's own marginal tax rate was found to be lower than expected, the structural coefficient (hence called β) being only 0.13. The total path effect (β_3), including the influence via tax attitudes, was only somewhat higher: $\beta = 0.16$, i.e., the perceived height of one's own income explains only 2.6% of (the variation in) the experienced unreasonableness of marginal tax rates.

Hypothesis 9

A person's factual marginal tax rate, resulting from that person's income and deductions, was expected to be a major predictor of the perceived own marginal tax rate and indirectly to have a high positive effect on the unreasonableness of marginal tax rates.

Since one's real marginal tax rate is computed on the basis of one's income after deductions, income and deductible costs (measured by stated monthly income before tax and indicators of interest paid, respectively) should explain a great deal of the variation in the perceived own marginal tax rate. The indirect effects of income and deductions on the unreasonableness of marginal tax rates also give an indication of the impact of the height of one's real tax on the dependent variable.

The β between deductions and the perceived own marginal tax rate was found to be zero. This means that people, on average, do not at all take deductions into consideration when estimating their tax on an extra income. The β between income and perception of one's own marginal tax rate was 0.38. This means that a great deal of the variation in perceived own marginal tax rate is explained by something other than the real marginal tax rate. The β's would probably have been higher, though, if a curvilinear relation between income and deductions and perceived marginal tax rate had been estimated instead of a linear relation, as in this case.

Deductions and income were expected to indirectly influence the unreasonableness of marginal tax rates also through other constructs such as economic satisfaction and political variables. Here, I confine myself to pointing out that the total effect of one's income and deductions on the unreasonableness was rather low: $\beta_r = 0.08$ and $\beta_r = 0.00$, respectively. In other words, the height of one's own factual tax appears to give little explanation of how unreasonable one considers marginal tax rates to be.

Hypothesis 10

The under-/overestimating of tax rates in general, here measured as the misjudgment of the tax rates for SEK 70,000 and 150,000, respectively, was expected to have a direct influence on the perceived marginal tax rate of one's own.

The tendency to over- or underestimate marginal tax rates in general had a greater influence on the perception of one's own marginal tax rate than had income (a proxy for one's real marginal tax rate). The β was 0.48, which means that misjudgment in general of tax rates explains

23% of the variance in one's own perceived marginal tax rate. Many tax-payers appear ignorant of their own marginal tax rate.

Hypotheses 11 and 12

According to Hypothesis 11, the latent constructs "attitudes towards taxes" and "attitudes towards tax evasion" were both expected to have a direct negative effect on the experienced unreasonableness of marginal tax rates: the more positive or less negative the attitudes, the less unreasonable the marginal tax rates.

According to Hypothesis 12, the "attitudes towards taxes" construct was expected to have a direct effect on "attitudes towards tax evasion" and thus also an indirect negative effect on the experienced unreasonableness of marginal tax rates. The more negative towards taxes, the less seriously was a person expected to regard tax evasion.

Both attitudes towards taxes and towards tax evasion had the hypothesized negative effect on the unreasonableness variable: the βs were −0.27 and −0.14, respectively. Attitudes towards taxes also had the expected influence on attitudes towards tax evasion: $\beta = 0.30$. This means that the total effect of tax attitudes on marginal tax unreasonableness – the β_r – was −0.32, i.e., it explained more than 10% of the variation in the dependent variable.

Thus, if one is less negative about taxes than people usually are, one does not consider marginal tax rates to be as unreasonably high as others do. Also, if one has a more positive attitude towards taxes than others appear to have, one considers tax evasion to be a more serious crime.

Hypotheses 13 and 14

According to Hypothesis 13, the under-/overestimating of tax rates in general, here measured as the misjudgment of two different tax rates, was expected to have a direct influence on the unreasonableness of marginal tax rates.

According to Hypothesis 14, the under-/overestimating of tax rates in general was expected to indirectly influence the dependent variable by having an influence on the perception of one's own marginal tax rate –

the higher one perceived tax rates in general to be, the higher one would perceive one's own marginal tax rate – and by having an influence on attitudes towards taxes – the higher one perceived tax rates in general to be, the less positive or more negative towards taxes one would be expected to be.

The tendency to under- or overestimate – misjudge – tax rates in general was found to have the greatest direct and total impact on marginal tax unreasonableness: $\beta = 0.40$ and $\beta_r = 0.48$, i.e., it explains almost a fourth of the (variation in) marginal tax unreasonableness.

Misjudgment in general of tax rates was found to have no direct influence on attitudes towards taxes and only an insignificant indirect impact ($\beta_r = -0.03$) on this latent construct.

To sum up, unreasonableness seems, first and foremost, to be an **educational** problem. What explains misjudgment in general of tax rates should thus be of great interest. Unfortunately, only 5% of the variation in the misjudgment of tax rates is explained by the model.

Hypothesis 15

The lapse of time, during which tax rates were reduced, was expected to have a direct negative effect on the unreasonableness of marginal tax rates and on the perception of marginal tax rates, and a positive influence on attitudes towards taxes and on misjudged tax rates. The last influence is expected to lead to a positive indirect influence on the dependent variable, while all other indirect effects are expected to be negative, making marginal rates appear less unreasonable.

Time, as measured by the four surveys carried out at six-monthly intervals, consists of everything that happened in the Swedish society during the studied period: the changes in tax rates, everything that was written and said about taxes in general and the tax reform in particular, all opinions about taxes and the tax reform expressed by and discussed with collegues and friends, the development of the economic situation in the country as a whole, etc.

The directions (signs) of the influence of time on dependent variables were all found to be in accordance with the hypothesis, but the impact as such was much lower than expected (or at least than hoped for by politicians). The direct effect on the experienced unreasonableness was rather insignificant, $\beta = -0.06$, and the direct effect on attitudes was even lower, $\beta = 0.03$.

Time had some impact on the perception of one's own marginal tax rate, $\beta = -0.11$, which indirectly meant a negative effect on the unreasonableness, i.e., making marginal tax rates appear less unreasonable. Unfortunately, these "positive" effects on the unreasonableness were completely outweighed by the increase in misjudged tax rates during the time of the study: $\beta = 0.18$.

As was shown earlier in this paper, people had difficulties perceiving the cuts in the marginal tax rates. The total effect of time on the unreasonableness of marginal tax rates was found to be even less promising, $\beta_r = 0.00$. Still, this analysis provides further evidence that it is the general under-/overestimating tendency concerning tax rates that is the main problem.

Hypothesis 16

Political affiliation was measured by asking the respondents which political party they considered to be "the best" at present. A latent variable was constructed on which conservative and liberal affiliation loaded negatively and socialist and communist affiliation loaded positively. Political affiliation was expected to have an indirect negative effect on the experienced unreasonableness of marginal tax rates, first and foremost by having a strong positive influence on attitudes towards taxes, and secondly by having a negative influence on misjudged tax rates: the more conservative, the more negative towards taxes a person would be, and the greater the tendency would be to perceive tax rates higher than others do.

The party affiliation loading most negatively on the latent variable "political affiliation" was, as expected, the Conservative party (the "Moderates"). The loading was -0.85. The other two conservative-liberal parties, the liberal "People's Party" and the traditionally agrarian oriented "Center Party," loaded -0.08 and -0.09, respectively. The loading for the biggest party in Sweden, the Social Democratic Party, was the highest of those loading positively: 0.80. The Communist Party had a loading of 0.14. All other minor parties, as well as those answering "another party" and "don't know," had loadings between -0.04 and 0.05, i.e., very low loadings. This expected tax-related ideological construct is thus supported to a great extent.

As to the hypothesis, the expected directions of influence were supported by the analysis. Political affiliation had a strong positive effect on attitudes towards taxes: $\beta = 0.47$. Thus it is much less one's income tax as such or the perception of one's marginal tax rate that leads to negative attitudes towards taxes. Instead, political affiliation explains 22% of the variation in tax attitudes.

On the other hand, political affiliation had an insignificant influence on misjudged tax rates: $\beta = -0.05$. According to the sign of the coefficient, socialists would have a tendency to perceive tax rates slightly lower than would conservatives, just because of their political affiliation. The total effect of political affiliation on the unreasonableness of marginal tax rates was found to be the third highest: $\beta_r = 0.17$.

Hypothesis 17

Self-employment was expected to have an indirect positive effect on the unreasonableness of marginal tax rates: through a negative effect on political affiliation (self-employed being more conservative than others), through a positive effect on tax evasion opportunities and thereby indirectly on tax evasion, and through a positive effect on misjudged tax rates.

The positive effect of being self-employed on misjudgment of tax rates was expected to result from the fact that self-employed persons to some extent are assumed to include payroll taxes in their perception of income tax rates and to see more of the money they pay in taxes than others do. Such an effect was found: $\beta = 0.11$. Self-employed persons were also expected to support free-enterprise oriented (i.e., conservative) parties to a greater extent than others. This effect was also found: $\beta = -0.21$. Self-employed persons were furthermore expected to have greater opportunities to evade taxes, and this hypothesis was also supported: $\beta = 0.20$. The total effect of being self-employed on the experienced unreasonableness was still not among the highest: $\beta_r = 0.09$.

Hypothesis 18

Age was expected to have an indirect negative effect on the unreasonableness of marginal tax rates through a positive effect on attitudes towards tax evasion and through a negative effect on admitted tax evasion.

Older people were found to consider tax evasion to be a more serious crime than younger persons, $\beta = 0.28$, and they also admitted tax evasion to a lesser extent than younger interviewees: $\beta = -0.15$. The total effect of age on the unreasonableness of marginal tax rates was on the other hand low: $\beta_r = -0.05$.

Hypothesis 19

Admission of tax evasion was expected to cause less negative attitudes towards tax evasion and thus to have a positive influence on the unreasonableness of marginal tax rates.

A way to justify the evasion of taxes is to mentally reduce the seriousness of the crime. The more one has evaded taxes, the less serious would tax evasion be considered. Admitted tax evasion was found to have the hypothesized negative effect on attitudes towards tax evasion and thus also a positive effect on the unreasonableness of marginal tax rates: $\beta = -0.26$ and $\beta_r = 0.04$, respectively, i.e., the more one has evaded taxes, the more it would be justified to evade taxes by the unreasonable height of marginal tax rates. The effect on the unreasonableness was, on the other hand, insignificant.

Hypothesis 20

Tax evasion opportunities were thought to be one of many mediators of the effects of self-employment, educational level, and vocational skills on the unreasonableness of marginal tax rates by having a positive effect on admitted tax evasion.

It is a well-known fact from earlier research (see Wärneryd & Walerud, 1981, 1982) that "opportunity makes the thief." This hypothesis is again supported: $\beta = 0.38$. The total effect of tax evasion opportunities on unreasonableness of marginal tax rates is almost non-existent: $\beta_r = 0.01$.

Hypothesis 21 and 22

Vocational skills were expected to have a positive effect on marginal tax unreasonableness through tax evasion related variables.

The respondents were asked if they had any or more than one of six different types of vocational skills. Of these, skills in (a) bookkeeping, accounting, and other economic areas, (b) skills in transport, excavation, and the like, (c) skills in trades such as carpentry, electrical installation, plumbing, etc., (d) skills in technology and engineering, and (e) skills in law were expected to have a positive effect on tax evasion opportunities and thus positive weights. The only vocational skill expected to have a negative effect on tax evasion opportunities was (f) medicine: nursing, surgery, dentistry, etc.

The signs of all vocational skill variables were as expected except for the sign of skills in technology and engineering, which was also negative. Trademan skills had the highest positive weight, 0.96, and bookkeeping, etc., the next highest: 0.24. Although vocational skills had a high effect on tax evasion opportunities, $\beta = 0.31$, their indirect total effect on the unreasonableness of marginal tax rates through a number of variables related to tax evasion was zero.

Educational level was expected to have a positive effect on marginal tax unreasonableness through tax evasion related variables and through political affiliation.

The higher education people had, the more they were expected to affiliate with a conservative party. The hypothesis was supported: $\beta = -0.19$. The higher a person's education, the higher was the knowledge about possibilities to evade taxes and the more contacts making tax evasion possible were expected, resulting in a positive effect on tax evasion opportunities. The latter hypothesis was also supported: $\beta = 0.11$.

The total effect of educational level on the unreasonableness of marginal tax rates through political affiliation, attitudes towards taxes, tax rates perception constructs, and variables related to tax evasion was found to be insignificant: $\beta_r = 0.03$. Both educational level and vocational skills may still influence marginal tax unreasonableness in a non-hypothesized way, although they do not correlate at all with the dependent variable.

Hypothesis 23

Satisfaction with one's economic standard and monetary resources was expected to have an indirect negative influence on marginal tax unreasonableness by having a positive influence on attitudes towards taxes and on political affiliation.

Economic satisfaction was found to have a positive effect both on attitudes towards taxes and on political affiliation: the β's were 0.11 and 0.05, respectively. The latter was expected from the assumption that if one is satisfied with one's economic situation, then one is satisfied with the existing government, which at the time of the surveys was Social Democratic. Its impact on political affiliation was, on the other hand, insignificant. The impact of economic satisfaction on the unreasonableness of marginal tax rates had the hypothesized sign, but the impact was insignificant: $\beta_r = -0.04$.

Hypothesis 24

Support burden, i.e., the percent of the household members not contributing to household incomes, was expected to effect the unreasonableness of marginal tax rates positively by having a negative effect on economic satisfaction.

Support burden had the expected influence on one's perception of one's economic situation: $\beta = -0.21$. The total impact on the unreasonableness of marginal tax rates was, on the other hand, insignificant: $\beta = 0.01$.

Hypothesis 25, 26, and 27

According to Hypothesis 25, financial assets were expected to have a positive effect on the dependent variable by having a negative effect on political affiliation and, at the same time, to have a negative effect by influencing economic satisfaction positively.

According to Hypothesis 26, debts and deductible costs – interest paid – were expected to have a negative influence and income a positive influence on economic satisfaction.

According to Hypothesis 27, income was expected to influence political affiliation in such way that the higher the income, the more the conservative affiliation.

The latent variable "financial assets" consisted of two indicators measuring bank savings and other financial investments. The more assets and the higher income one has, the more one is satisfied with one's financial situation, and the more debts and interest one has to pay, the less one is satisfied with one's financial situation. All hypotheses were supported: $\beta = 0.31$, $\beta = 0.12$, and $\beta = -0.05$, respectively, although the last figure was insignificant.

This means, among other things, that the more satisfied one is with one's own financial situation, the less reason one has to complain about taxes and the less negative is one's attitude towards taxes. At the same time, the higher one's income, the more conservative the political affiliation: $\beta = -0.14$. This means that income, and the taxes one pays, simultaneously have a positive and a negative effect on the experienced unreasonableness of marginal tax rates.

The same opposing effects were found for financial assets. While this construct was found to have a negative effect on the unreasonableness through economic satisfaction, it was found also to have a positive effect by influencing political affiliation negatively: $\beta = -0.12$. Financial assets' total influence on the unreasonableness of marginal tax rates was found to be positive but insignificant: $\beta_r = 0.01$.

Summary and Discussion

As perception of marginal tax rates was measured here, the cuts in marginal tax rates during the 1983-1985 income tax reform were perceived, but only after some time, only partly, and not at the same time by everybody. Assuming that the reductions in marginal tax rates must be effectively perceived in order to influence behaviour, the expected changes in behaviour will consequently be less than proportional to the changes in marginal tax rates and to appear only after some time.

First of all, these findings seem to indicate that politicians need to be patient and possibly need to cut marginal tax rates more drastically in order to have the reductions perceived quickly and more broadly. As to the aim of enabling tax payers to experience a tax relief, it seems as if the tax reform has been rather unsuccessful, at least during its first phase. People seem quick to adjust the marginal tax rates they consider reasonable to their perception of reduced marginal tax rates.

The respondents considered their own marginal tax rate and the marginal tax rate of an income of SEK 70,000 to be, on the average, about 22 percentage points too high, and the marginal tax rate at the SEK 150,000 income level to be, on the average, about 27 percentage points too high, independent of the height of the marginal tax rates before and after they were cut. This indicates that the heights of marginal tax rates do matter, but only at a certain point in time, not over time as marginal tax rates are changed. In other words, an adaptation process appears to take place over time. It also means that the percentage of marginal tax that people considered they were paying in excess, on the average, increased as marginal tax rates were cut.

Will people consider even tax rates approaching zero too high? According to the findings at the aggregate level, at a certain point in time they would not, but if they were experiencing such a change over time, they would be more reluctant to accept it as an improvement. Still, theory suggests that this is true only when changes in tax rates are small. So the answer to the question: "Does reducing them really matter?" may be: "Probably, but only if they are changed drastically."

Of course, the way the dependent variables were measured in the study, may not render them true measures of perception and judgment of **reduced** marginal tax rates. People may have perceived the cuts in marginal tax rates to a greater extent than was found here, but may have had difficulties in translating the reduction into numerical terms in the requested fashion. Also, the changes found in the dependent variables may be at least partly due to perception of inflation rather than reduced marginal tax rates, at least for the two specified income levels, since the same levels were used in all four surveys.

At the same time, the way the dependent variables were measured in the four surveys resulted in meaningful data, i.e., the data could be subject to a meaningful analysis. At the aggregate level, people do seem to have a rather good numerical perception of marginal tax rates and to be able to assess them in numerical terms.

It has been suggested that people perceive a reduction of a high marginal tax rate less easily than a correspondingly large reduction of a lower marginal tax rate, in agreement with Weber-Fechner's law. This assumes that people look at the reduction in what they have to pay rather than at the increase in the money they receive. If a marginal tax rate is cut by 5 percentage points from 80% to 75%, this reduction is much less, in relative terms, than a corresponding monetary increase from 20% to 25%. The results do not refute the hypothesis that people take note of money earned, but the hypothesis that they take note of the tax they pay is more clearly supported by the results.

The analysis carried out in order to find explanations for the unreasonableness of marginal tax rates as experienced by the respondents, succeeded in explaining 38% of the variance of the dependent variable. The greatest impact on the unreasonableness of marginal tax rates had the general over- or underestimating tendency, i.e., the general misjudgment of tax rates. The total – direct plus indirect – effect (β_r) was 0.48. This suggests that first and foremost, the unreasonableness problem is an educational problem. Among other things, the findings show that people do not take their deductions into consideration when estimating their marginal tax on extra income.

As to the factual (marginal) tax rate one pays, here measured by the size of one's income and one's deductible interests, from which the taxes are calculated, its impact on the dependent variable was found to be very low: $\beta_r = 0.08$. The impact of one's own marginal tax rate as it was perceived was also unexpectedly low, $\beta_r = 0.16$, which makes it only the fourth most influential explanatory variable. This means that the height of one's own marginal tax rate, both the real one and the one perceived, is much less important than thought by many politicians and social scientists, in explaining how unreasonable people consider marginal tax rates to be.

The next most important explanation of the unreasonableness of marginal tax rates was the latent construct "attitudes in general towards taxes": $\beta_r = -0.32$. The hypothesized impact of misjudgment on attitudes towards taxes was found to be non-existing: $\beta_r = -0.03$. Thus, it appears as if two different types of mental dispositions together have the greatest impact on the unreasonableness of marginal tax rates: attitudes towards taxes and the general misjudgment of tax rates. The former was in turn found to be strongly influenced by one's political affiliation or belief, $\beta = 0.47$, making political affiliation the third most important explanation of the unreasonableness of marginal tax rates: $\beta_r = -0.17$.

The results show that people adjusted the perception of their own marginal tax rate downwards over time as tax rates were cut, and that this had a negative influence on the unreasonableness of marginal tax rates, i.e., made them less unreasonably high. It was also shown that people found the marginal tax rates successively less unreasonable over time: External influences during the period studied, viz., the tax reform as such and everything else that happened in society, had a direct, decreasing effect on judgments of unreasonableness. On the other hand and at the same time, the misjudgment in general increased over time as tax rates were reduced, i.e., there were difficulties in perceiving the reductions correctly. This means that time also had the effect of increasing the experienced unreasonableness of marginal tax rates, an effect which was found to completely offset the decreasing effects mentioned earlier.

Why different people generally under- or overestimate tax rates is thus an important question, which is not answered by this paper: political affiliation, self-employment, and time explained only 5% of the variation in this variable. It should be further investigated in future research, as should the impact of this and other of the examined variables on economic behaviour in general.

This paper has dealt with economic problems, using psychological theory and methodology, but the findings may also have contributed something to psychology. Firstly, at the aggregate level, they have given support to a micro-level hypothesis – Weber-Fechner's law. Hypotheses relating to aggregate level measures are common in economics, but too rare in psychology (cf. Katona, 1979). Secondly, if the unreasonableness of marginal tax rates can be considered an opinion, the results presented in this paper have given some hints as to how an opinion is formed: by ignorance, difficulties in perceiving (small) changes, attitudes to the subject matter, political-ideological values, and – but only to a very limited extent – the phenomenon itself, in this case, the height of marginal tax rates.

Appendix

Table A:1 Perceived Marginal Tax Rates at Three Income Levels and the Incorrectness of These Perceptions at Four Points in Time Between 1982 and 1984

a: One's own income

Year	Perception of the marginal tax rate				The approximate marginal tax rate				The incorrectness of perception			
	Mean	s	n	p	Mean	s	n	p	Mean	s	n	p
1982:1	58.6%	(16.4)	356		62.1%	(13.0)	362		−3.6	(15.9)	350	
				n.s.				<0.01				<0.01
1983:2	59.2%	(17.9)	300		57.9%	(12.4)	340		+0.8	(15.8)	294	
				n.s.				n.s.				n.s.
1983:3	58.0%	(17.7)	341		57.7%	(12.0)	388		−0.2	(16.0)	337	
				n.s.				<0.01				n.s.
1984:4	56.4%	(18.4)	355		54.8%	(10.6)	392		+1.3	(17.6)	349	

Significance levels

1982 <–> 1984: <0.05 <0.01 <0.01

b: At the SEK 70,000 level

Year	Perception of the marginal tax rate				The true marginal tax rate				The incorrectness of perception			
	Mean	s	n	p	Mean	s	n	p	Mean	s	n	p
1982:1	57.7%	(12.9)	356		56.0%	(1.3)	370		+1.7	(12.8)	356	
				n.s.				<0.01				<0.01
1983:2	56.7%	(12.8)	303		49.3%	(1.2)	349		+7.4	(12.7)	303	
				n.s.				n.s.				n.s.
1983:3	56.3%	(13.8)	360		49.3%	(1.2)	402		+6.9	(13.8)	360	
				<0.01				<0.01				n.s.
1984:4	53.1%	(14.2)	355		47.5%	(1.3)	392		+5.6	(14.1)	355	

Significance levels

1982 <–> 1984: <0.01 <0.01 <0.01

	Perception of the marginal tax rate				The true marginal tax rate				The incorrectness of perception			
c: At the SEK 150,000 level												
Year	Mean	s	n	p	Mean	s	n	p	Mean	s	n	p
1982:1	76.7%	(13.8)	355		80.0%	(0.1)	370		−3.3	(13.8)	355	
				n.s.				<0.01				<0.01
1983:2	77.2%	(12.4)	312		75.3%	(1.2)	349		+1.9	(12.4)	312	
				n.s.				n.s.				n.s.
1983:3	76.6%	(12.9)	355		75.3%	(1.2)	402		+1.3	(13.0)	355	
				<0.01				<0.01				<0.01
1984:4	72.6%	(14.8)	353		66.5%	(1.3)	392		+6.1	(14.8)	353	
Significance levels												
1982 <–> 1984		<0.01					<0.01				<0.01	

A one-tailed t test was always used. The pooled-variance t test was used when the two population variances were equal (when the F value was non-significant), and the separate-variance t test otherwise.

Table A:2 Perceived Marginal Tax Rate and the Marginal Tax Rate Considered Reasonable at Three Income Levels and the Difference Between These Two Rates at Four Points in Time Between 1982 and 1984

	Perception of the marginal tax rate				The marginal tax rate considered reasonable				Difference			
a: One's own income												
Year	Mean	s	n	p	Mean	s	n	p	Mean	s	n	p
1982:1	58.6%	(16.4)	356		37.2%	(14.9)	357		21.1%	(15.3)	349	
				n.s.				n.s.				n.s.
1983:2	59.2%	(17.9)	300		36.4%	(17.3)	320		22.6%	(18.1)	290	
				n.s.				n.s.				n.s.
1983:3	58.0%	(17.7)	341		35.8%	(15.6)	372		21.6%	(18.6)	336	
				n.s.				n.s.				n.s.
1984:4	56.4%	(18.4)	355		34.4%	(16.0)	364		21.6%	(18.0)	348	
Significance levels												
1982 <–> 1984:		<0.05					<0.01				n.s.	

b: At the SEK 70,000 level

Year	Perception of the marginal tax rate				The marginal tax rate considered reasonable				Difference			
	Mean	s	n	p	Mean	s	n	p	Mean	s	n	p
1982:1	57.7%	(12.9)	356		36.1%	(14.2)	354		21.5%	(15.0)	347	
				n.s.				<0.06				n.s.
1983:2	56.7%	(12.8)	303		34.3%	(15.7)	323		21.9%	(17.6)	296	
				n.s.				n.s.				n.s.
1983:3	56.3%	(13.8)	360		33.0%	(14.1)	366		23.1%	(17.5)	344	
				<0.01				n.s.				n.s.
1984:4	53.1%	(14.2)	355		31.8%	(14.6)	365		21.5%	(17.4)	340	

Significance levels

1982 <–> 1984:   <0.01   <0.01   n.s.

c: At the SEK 150,000 level

Year	Perception of the marginal tax rate				The marginal tax rate considered reasonable				Difference			
	Mean	s	n	p	Mean	s	n	p	Mean	s	n	p
1982:1	76.7%	(13.8)	355		50.0%	(18.4)	355		27.0%	(21.2)	347	
				n.s.				<0.08				n.s.
1983:2	77.2%	(12.4)	312		47.9%	(19.9)	315		28.8%	(21.9)	302	
				n.s.				n.s.				n.s.
1983:3	76.6%	(12.9)	355		48.1%	(19.4)	365		28.5%	(22.1)	345	
				<0.01				<0.08				n.s.
1984:4	72.6%	(14.8)	353		46.1%	(18.7)	362		26.5%	(21.3)	346	

Significance levels

1982 <–> 1984   <0.01   <0.01   n.s.

A one-tailed *t* test was always used. The pooled-variance *t* test was used when the two population variances were equal (when the *F* value was non-significant), and the separate-variance *t* test otherwise.

Table A:3 Weights, Factor Loadings, and Communalities of Manifest Variables

Variables	Weight	Load-ing	Commu-nality	Variables	Weight	Load-ing	Commu-nality
Time	100	100	100	**Tax evasion opportunities**			
				Says one has more opportunities	54	74	54
Deductions/debts				Believes that			
Interest paid	53	97	93	colleagues evade	28	57	33
Depts	50	96	93	Has helped somebody:			
				– repair a house	22	38	14
Income				– repair a car	21	33	11
Stated monthly income	89	94	89	– with vocational skill	38	67	45
Interest received	34	48	23	Has worked extra	15	22	5
Support burden	100	100	100	**Admitted tax evasion**			
				Paid black money	29	52	27
Financial assets				Received black money	69	88	77
Bank savings	68	89	79	Not declared income	27	45	20
Other investments	51	79	62	Too big deductions	21	58	34
Education level	100	100	100	**Misjudged tax rates**			
				Of SEK 70' income	55	88	77
Vocational skills				Of SEK 150' income	58	89	79
Economic	24	16	3				
Transport, etc.	16	33	11	**Perceived own rate**	100	100	100
Trades (carpentry, etc.)	96	92	85				
Medicine	–3	–5	0	**Attitudes towards taxes (cf. Table 1)**			
Engineering	–13	1	0	General opinion	43	76	57
Law	18	13	2	Consider benefits	36	72	52
				Extra work unprofitable	27	59	35
Self-employment				Tax system unjust	22	59	35
Self-employed	91	88	77	No tax on interest	26	51	26
Both self-employed and employed	48	43	18				
				Attitudes towards tax evasion (cf. Table 1)			
Age	100	100	100	More severe punishment	17	63	40
				Would pay off-the-record	21	71	51
Economic satisfaction				Too large deductions			
Economic standard	61	84	71	inconsiderate	15	49	24
Sufficient money	59	83	69	Would take chance	15	58	34
				Not to declare serious	19	78	60
Political affiliation				Pay off-the-record serious	20	84	70
The Moderates	–61	–85	72	False deduction serious	15	71	50
The People's Party	–6	–8	1	Off-the-record income			
The Center Party	–7	–9	1	serious	20	80	64
The Social Democrats	56	80	64				
The Communists	15	14	2	**Unreasonableness of marginal tax rates**			
The Greens	5	4	0	Of one's own	41	86	73
The Christian				Of SEK 70' income	38	83	70
Democrats	5	5	0	Of SEK 150' income	40	82	68
"Another party"	–2	–4	0				
"Don't know"	3	1	0				

References

Atkinson, R.L., Atkinson, R.C., & Hilgard, E.R. (1983). *Introduction to psychology.* 8th edition. New York: Harcourt Brace Jovanovich.

Bylund, E. (1987). *Tyck till om offentliga sektorn - Teknisk rapport* (Present your opinion about the public sector - Technical report). Stockholm: Statistics Sweden, I/Utredningsinstitutet.

Fechner, G.T. (1860). *Elements of psychophysics* (H.E. Adler, transl.). New York: Holt, Rinehart, & Winston. Reprint 1966.

Fornell, C. (1987). A second generation of multivariate analysis: Classification of methods and implications for marketing research. In: M. Houston (Ed.), *The Review of Marketing 1987*, pp. 407-450. Chicago: American Marketing Association.

Galanter, E. (1962). Contemporary psychophysics. In: R. Brown, E. Galanter, E.H. Hess, & G. Mandler (Eds.): *New directions in psychology, I*, pp. 87-156. New York: Holt, Rinehart, & Winston.

Hadenius, A. (1986). *A crisis of the welfare state? Opinions about taxes and public expenditure in Sweden.* Stockholm: Almqvist & Wiksell International.

Helson, H. (1964). *Adaptation-level theory.* New York: Harper & Row.

Katona, G. (1979). Toward a macropsychology. *American Psychologist, 34*, 118-126.

Kommittédirektiv (1987). *Utredning om reformerad inkomstbeskattning* (Official report on reformed income taxation). Dir. 1987:29. Stockholm: Ministry of Finance.

Laurin, U. (1986). *På heder och samvete. Skattefuskets orsaker och utbredning* (Upon my honour. The causes and extent of tax evasion). Stockholm: Norstedts.

Lewis, A. (1978). Perceptions of tax rates. *British Tax Review, 6*, 358-366.

Lindqvist, A. (1981). *Hushållens sparande – beteendevetenskapliga mätningar av hushållens sparande* (Household saving – behavioural measures of household saving). Stockholm: The Economic Research Institute at the Stockholm School of Economics.

Lindqvist, A. (1983). *Hushållens skuldsättning* (Household indebtedness). Stockholm: The Economic Research Institute at the Stockholm School of Economics. Studies in Economic Psychology:118.

Lohmöller, J.-B. (1984). *LVPLS 1.6 program manual.* Munich: Zentralarchiv, Hochschule der Bundeswehr.

Pommerehne, W.W., & Schneider, F. (1978). Fiscal illusion, political institutions, and local public spending. *Kyklos, 31*, 381-408.

Reformerad inkomstbeskattning (Reformed income taxation) (1982). Government Bill 1981/82:197.

Statistics Sweden (1985). Stockholm: Statistics Sweden.

Vogel, J. (1974). Taxation and public opinion in Sweden: An interpretation of recent survey data. *National Tax Journal, 27*, 499-513.

Wahlund, R. (1983). *The income tax system and working behaviour.* Paper presented at the 8th Colloquium of the International Association for Research in Economic Psychology (IAREP), Bologna, July 5-8.

Wahlund, R. (1988a). *People's perception and evaluation of reduced marginal income tax rates.* Stockholm: The Economic Research Institute at the Stockhom School of Economics. Research Paper 6339.

Wahlund, R. (1988b). *Skatteomläggningen 1983-1985, några konsekvenser* (The income tax reform 1983-1985, some consequences). Stockholm: The Economic Research Institute at the Stockhom School of Economics. Research Report 257.

Wahlund, R. (1988c). Varför och hur olika svenska hushåll sparar (Why and how different Swedish households save). In: K.-E. Wärneryd, S. Jundin, & R. Wahlund (Eds.), *Sparbeteenden och sparattityder,* pp. 115-186. Stockholm: Allmänna Förlaget.

Wahlund, R., & Wärneryd, K.-E. (1988). Aggregate saving and the saving behaviour of saver groups in Sweden accompanying a tax reform. In: S. Maital (Ed.), *Applied behavioural economics, Vol. I,* pp. 73-96. Brighton: Wheatsheaf.

Wärneryd, K.-E., & Walerud, B. (1981). *Skatter och ekonomiskt beteende 1* (Taxes and economic behaviour 1). Stockholm: The Economic Research Institute at the Stockholm School of Economics. Studies in Economic Psychology: 114.

Wärneryd, K.-E., & Walerud, B. (1982). Taxes and economic behaviour: Some interview data on tax evasion in Sweden. *Journal of Economic Psychology, 2*, 187-211.

Weber, E.H. (1834). *Concerning touch* (H.E. Ross, transl.). New York: Academic Press. Reprint 1978.

Wold, H. (1975). Path models with latent variables: The NIPALS approach. In: H.M. Blalock et al. (Eds.) *Quantitative sociology: International perspectives on mathematical and statistical model building*, pp. 307-357. New York: Academic Press.

Part III

Utility and Decision Theory

Erik Kloppenborg Madsen
Beyond the Expected Utility Proposition in Rational
Decision Making

Friedel Bolle
Levels of Aspiration, Promises, and the Possibility of
Revaluation

Klaus G. Grunert
Another Attitude Towards Multi-Attribute Attitude
Models

Joanna Sokołowska
Application of the Valence-Instrumentality-Expectancy
and Multiattribute Utility Models in the Prediction of
Worker Effort

Hector A. Munera
Prediction of Preference Reversals by the Linearized
Moments Model

Liisa Uusitalo
Economic Man or Social Man – Exploring Free Riding in
the Production of Collective Goods

Erik Kloppenborg Madsen

Beyond the Expected Utility Proposition in Rational Decision Making

Abstract

The normative aspects of the concept of rationality are explored. This exploration is based on a distinction between two aspects of the concept of rationality, the aspect of truth and the aspect of meaning. It is argued that basically rationality is a concept which refers to the practical ability of human beings to cope with complexity and uncertainty. Some ideas for moving beyond the expected utility proposition are suggested.

Author's address: Erik Kloppenborg Madsen, The Aarhus School of Business, Department of Marketing, Ryhavevej 8, DK-8210 Aarhus V, Denmark.

183

Rationality and Human Action

Broadly speaking, two opposite views may be identified as to the importance of the very idea of human rationality. At the one extreme there are those still maintaining the importance of the concept of rationality, but doing so in a manner which sees rationality as a very narrow and formal faculty of human beings. Mainstream microeconomics and decision theory are examples of this position. At the other extreme rationality is, roughly speaking, regarded as of no importance at all. In the general cultural debate "post-modernity" and "deconstructivism" are key words, and one can find instances of their influence in organizational theory and consumer behaviour. In short: Some people still believe in the possibility of planning and control based on foresight whereas others maintain the essential impossibility of all planning and control. There seems to exist a relationship between the two positions in that the validity of each claim is, at least partly, based on the supposed invalidity of the other.

In what follows, a strategy going beyond the two above-mentioned positions will be outlined. It is a strategy aimed at a broader understanding and interpretation of rationality, and it takes as its point of departure a perspective which might be termed "practical" or "moral" (those terms used synonymously). According to this perspective, rationality is a social and cultural phenomenon referring to a practical competence of human beings. Rationality, then, is regarded as being both a lot more and a lot less than the received theory of rational decision making proposes.

The expected utility proposition, stating that when given the choice between two or more risky alternatives, an agent – if rational – must always prefer the action or strategy with the highest expected utility, is criticizable on various grounds and for various reasons. This is due to the fact that the proposition can be interpreted in at least two different ways. According to one interpretation the proposition is taken as an empirical claim concerning human decision making. Hence, the right thing to do as a researcher is to test the claim against empirical realities. As many observers have maintained (see, e.g., Leinfellner, 1987), available evidence has actually falsified the proposition. It shows us that people do not follow or obey the axioms on which the expected utility proposition is resting. More about the consequences of unrealistic assumptions will be said later in this paper. According to the second interpretation, rationality is an evaluative and normative concept. That is, the concept is used for evaluating human action and as a standard for prescriptions.

I shall designate the two above-mentioned interpretations as the **aspect of truth** and the **aspect of meaning,** respectively. I shall furthermore argue for the importance of making this distinction when trying to understand what rationality is all about. It is for instance often assumed, I believe, that there is a certain association between the positive or descriptive dimension of the concept and the normative dimension. It is assumed that the empirically descriptive content of the proposition is a necessary and sufficient condition for its normative validity. From this follows that any falsification of the proposition as a hypothesis about the empirical world always and simultaneously must be regarded as a falsification of the proposition as an evaluation or prescription. But from the perspective taken in this paper, such a conclusion is wrong. If anything, the opposite is the case. Why make prescriptions for behaviour that is already rational? It is only to the extent that the proposition is falsified that the normative aspect of the proposition has any meaning. Meaning and truth, as those terms are used here, represent different ways of looking at the world, mutually exclusive but at the same time complementary.

In the following, special attention is given to the meaning aspect of rationality. This is, I think, justified by the fact that especially the aspect of meaning is poorly represented in most standard treatments of the concept of rationality. I shall supplement the above-mentioned distinction by further distinguishing between **information** and **communication** as two rather different but equally important aspects of rationality.

Although from a strictly theoretical point of view the above-mentioned aspects seem to be mutually exclusive, from a practical point of view this is not the case. There must be a link because theories affect the world. The pragmatic effect of the theory of rational decision making is the **rationalization** of the social world. Rationality and rationalization become linked to one another in a way corresponding to the relationship between what is traditionally referred to as theory and praxis, respectively. The terms theory and praxis signify different "ways of life" (see, e.g., Arendt, 1978) which correspond to the modern analytical distinction between positive and normative theories as well as the distinction between truth and meaning.

Thus, rationalization of the social world resembles our theoretical ideas about rationality. The concept of rationalization, which since Weber has been a key to the understanding and interpretation of modern Western culture, signifies demystification and scientification. This process of rationalization, it is argued, has taken place at the cost of other types and forms of rationality which were neither instrumental nor formal. "Purposive rationality" (Zweckrationalität), the specific result of this process, did not only eliminate other kinds of rationality, such as "value rationality," but became a value in itself. And rather paradoxically, purposive rationality has been established as a dominating value through the successful attack on the concept of value itself. The first step (Habermas, 1967) consisted in the elimination of values from science and rational decision making, declaring values to be irrational elements of those enterprises. The second step placed science and purposive rationality in the vacuum generated and thereby established instrumental – or calculative – rationality as the core of a new system of values.

This chain of events is well known and in one version or another is an important element of much critical debate about Western society and culture. The crisis of modern society – its apparent disability to solve or cope with its own problems – is according to this view closely connected with the process of rationalization and with the concept of rationality itself. The problem seems to be that not only is the concept of rationality, which is now dominating our institutions, unable to cope with the vital issues at stake, but also the very idea of instrumental rationality is itself constantly contributing to the misery. The dual character of rationality – as a theoretical concept and as a process of rationalization – is incomprehensible within the framework of the microeconomic theory of rational choice.

In order to cope with rationality in both its theoretical and practical aspects, one feels tempted to reintroduce the nearly forgotten idealistic distinction between "Verstand" and "Vernunft" or "intellect" and "reason" as Arendt (1978) has coined the pair. Apel (1984) makes a similar distinction between abstract analytical rationality and integrative rationality. Abstract analytical rationality is the hallmark of the fictitious decision maker within microeconomics, while the concept of integrative rationality seems to have no counterpart at all in economic theory. When scrutinizing theories of rational decision making and the normative content and orientation of those theories one is struck by the narrowness

186

and one-sidedness of the instrumental and formal concept of rationality. Rationality in the sense of rational choice may be only a minor part of reason and therefore only a minor component of the ability of human beings to cope with uncertainty and conflicts both in the outer environment and within themselves.

On the Implications of Unrealistic Assumptions in Models of Rational Choice

The realism of assumptions has been much debated in economics (see, e.g., Friedman, 1953; Machlup, 1978). At stake is a conflict between scientific realism and scientific instrumentalism. In short, realism holds that theories should truly describe the world and that basic assumptions should correspond to realities. Contrary to this, instrumentalism holds that theories are instruments for prediction. As a result theories can be neither true nor false. Now the kind of testing reported in the literature (see, e.g., the findings leading to the "Allais paradox," Leinfellner, 1987) is based on a realist point of view. That is, the sense of this procedure is dependent upon an assumption which states that the theory of rational choice is a theory about the factual or empirical world. The expected utility proposition is treated **as if** it were an empirical proposition or hypothesis. If no falsifying evidence exists the hypothesis may be regarded as true, at least temporarily. Therefore, to the student, be it of consumer or other behaviour, who cares about the degree of realism in theories and models, the expected utility proposition may be either true or false. However, as mentioned before, interpreted as an empirical hypothesis the proposition is already falsified, so one might legitimately ask why there is still research done which is based on this assumption. How can the hypothesis be justified in spite of its empirical falsehood?

A possible basis for its defence might be the concept of a "scientific research programme" (Lakatos, 1970). According to this view rationality as maximizing behaviour would be seen as the "hard core" for a research programme in microeconomics and decision theory (Latsis, 1976). The "hard core" signifies those parts of a research programme that for more or less conventional reasons are not put to any empirical test. Only the auxilliary hypothesis surrounding the hard core, the "protective belt," should – according to this view – be tested against empirical evidence. Questioning the concept of rationality itself simply means locating the debate **outside** the research programme which constitutes neoclassical microeconomics and the theory of individual decision making. The legitimacy of sustaining the neoclassical research programme is according to the Lakatosian point of view conditioned by its progressiveness. This means that if, based on the hard core mentioned but with some modification in the protective belt, one is able to predict new phenomena or "explain more" than before, then the preservation of the theory is justified.

The Lakatosian reconciliation of Popperian falsificationism and Kuhnian ideas about the development of science does, at least to some degree, make it plausible that any dynamic understanding of scientific fields has to accept not only concepts but also hypotheses which cannot themselves be empirically justified. Such conventionalist elements of theories are then justified with reference to success criteria connected with the research programme as a whole. So the fact that there is still a considerable belief, and a lot of work done, in the microeconomic programme in which individual rationality in the form of maximizing behaviour is an important assumption, seems to be well grounded.

Nevertheless, the question about assumptional realism is not irrelevant. This is seen most clearly in business economics and consumer behaviour. The very existence of marketing and consumer behaviour as academic fields is an indication thereof. Apparently, the theory of rational behaviour·cannot explain the behaviour of the **individual** firm or the **individual** consumer. Economic theory of the firm and of the consumer is intended to explain how markets function at the aggregate level but not really how individual actors in the economy are functioning and how they are made up. There is no firm in the theory of the firm as pointed out by Thorelli (1965, p. 249).

In order to make prediction possible at an aggregate level, economic theory sacrifices the realism of its assumptions. This in itself may or may not be problematic; the real cost is the loss of ability to explain or understand why it is possible to predict events. This, I think, is the reason why for instance Simon's (1967) behavioural theory of rationality has been so influential in business economics and why consumer behaviour has developed so rapidly as it has within the discipline of marketing.

But there is a further point to be made, a point connected with the above-mentioned "aspect of meaning." As far as unrealistic assumptions are allowed in theories and models, their only legitimation can be their potential value as instruments for prediction of behaviour. As instruments they can be neither true nor false, but only more or less instrumental. And exactly this constitutes the importance of another approach to the problem of rational decision making. As instruments, be it for prediction or advice, models are no longer accessible for empirical counterevidence. They can no longer be justified as approximations to the truth or as representations of the real world. They seem to be validated solely through their success as tools. But as soon as one looks upon theories of rational choice as instruments for prediction and advice the above-mentioned moral or practical point of view is implicitly introduced. This simply means that some further claims concerning the justifiability of models and theories are created. So, if one accepts the lack of empirical foundation of instrumental theories, but still demands some kind of justification, which is not simply the technological short-run efficiency of the model, then one has to look at the problem from another angle. When theories are no longer obliged to answer to claims of truth but only to claims of efficiency they are in danger of degenerating into instruments of specific interests and powers. The seemingly impossible task of finding any decontextualized and universal foundation of theories of decision making makes a strategy necessary which seeks to justify these theories, not with reference to any empirical foundation, but with reference to their acceptability by users of those instruments. And this is, I think, what makes the practical or moral point of view important.

So, contrary to the "scientific" point of view, one ought to reexamine the very meaning of the theory of rational choice. The difference between meaning and truth is, as mentioned before, that the meaning of a theory is not solely dependent on the empirical truth or falseness of theories. The question about truth is simply not asked by the interpreter investigating the theory. The question is rather: What does the theory accomplish and how does it perform? Those questions are rather pragmatical, but well grounded in the nature of the theory of rational choice itself.

There is a further aspect of the decision theory approach to be discussed, and that is its normativeness. The expected utility proposition is valid only for rational, not for irrational agents. This means that if the proposition is tested as an empirical hypothesis against actual behaviour and is falsified, the following conclusions may be drawn. Either the hypothesis is wrong or the agent is not rational. If it is concluded that the hypothesis is wrong, then something must by logical necessity be wrong with the axioms from which the theorem is derived. Several such shortcomings have been suggested (see, for example, Leinfellner, 1987). But if the second conclusion is drawn, which is not uncommon among economists, then we have the case of a Lakatosian research programme in which certain assumptions (the hard core) are regarded as irrefutable. The normativeness I am referring to here is not the trivial prescription of the expected utility proposition itself, which only tells us that if we are rational (in a certain narrow sense) then by necessity we shall obey certain axioms or rules. (If we do not, we are no longer acting rationally.) The interesting question is: What are the normative consequences of such a theory for the actors of the real world, i.e., all those actors who are not rational in the above sense? How are they affected by the norms and standards set by the theory of rational choice?

My point is the following. The theory of rational behaviour is normative in a double sense. Firstly it tells us how rational agents ought to behave. But this is a very trivial prescription because rational agents cannot behave otherwise. Therefore the real audience for theories of rational decision making must be the irrational actors. But the theory can on neither logical nor empirical grounds make any valid prescription for those actors, because they do not fulfil the condition of rationality. Nevertheless those actors are the only logical audience for the theory. Its normativeness therefore is closely connected with its potential pragmatic effects on these actors.

Contrary to the Lakatosian model, which professes to represent a realist point of view, theories of rational choice could also be regarded as part and parcel of the process of **rationalization.** In that case the meaning of models of rational choice must be understood as something different from their truth value. One should rather ask: Do the models contribute to the solving of vital conflicts in human affairs? Do they contribute in a way which develops the human ability to cope with risk and uncertainty connected with both the inner and the external environment of human agents? The answer to those questions presupposes some reflection with regard to the concept of rationality itself. The problem is no longer to test whether or not people are rational in the narrow sense mentioned, but rather to ask what rationality is and what it could be. Is human reason to be understood only in the narrow sense in which the decision theory approach treats it? Or is there possibly another approach through which rationality as an ability of human beings may be much more adequately developed in order to cope with conflicts and dangers in the world around them?

Beyond Empirical-Analytical Conceptions of Rationality – Rationality as Common Sense

To be rational in the sense of decision theory means that an agent should always prefer the choice with the highest expected utility. But the very possibility of having such preferences is conditioned by the agent's ability and will to act in correspondence with some rules or axioms which cannot themselves be grounded in any rational way. Thus, obedience to the axioms of the expected utility proposition cannot itself be justified as rational. Instead, the argument runs differently: If an agent wishes to act rationally, then he must by logical necessity follow certain rules. Because if he does not follow them he cannot possibly be maximizing and therefore cannot be rational. So it seems that rational behaviour is closely connected with not only the **ability** but also the **will** of human beings to stick to rules. Rational choice and logical inference therefore seem to be very much alike in the received view. In effect one can hardly see a difference.

Though the calculative faculty of logical inference and the capacity and willingness to act consistently are both part and parcel of the concept of rationality described above, they are quite different things. Rationality, therefore, has a complex meaning, mixing quite different capabilities of human actors. It consists of not only the **ability of logical reasoning or pure thinking** but also the **will to act in accordance with certain rules.** Rationality thereby constitutes a certain normativeness: the norm of obedience. The very idea that rationality is closely connected with behaviour which does not violate some given norms is of central importance. The nonviolation of say, the axiom of transitivity, represents in itself a preference or a norm which pure thinking cannot establish. And neither pure thinking nor the calculative faculty itself can justify the obedience of the actor. Obedience therefore must have its basis in either the will or some psychological or biological dimension beyond the reach of deliberate choice. So sticking to the rules is either a deliberate choice or the result of biological and/or psychological law-like forces acting through the agent.

If people are capable of following rules deliberately, then they must also be capable of breaking them. The point is that they seem to have a choice. But this choice in itself constitutes a problem for rationality and quite a paradoxical one at that because here we are talking about the process of breaking old rules and inventing new ones. People are not only rule-followers but also rule-makers. Actually, only computers are rational in the above-mentioned sense, because they do not and cannot break rules. One might argue that this is so because computers lack the abilities of emotion, common sense, and power of judgment and communication, and therefore are not capable of self-reflection and self-understanding. The hidden anthropology of the theory of rational decision making, so it seems, is based on a machine analogy.

Dreyfus (1987) has pointed to the very same problem when arguing that problem solving by rule-following behaviour is to a certain degree a kind of misrepresentation of human intelligence. In his five-stage model it is only the novice who is rational in the narrow manner outlined by the theory of rational decision making. The two first stages of the model, named "the novice" and "the advanced beginner," are characterized by actors who simply follow rules. The "competent performer" (Stage 3) adds conscious choices of plans and goals and reflects upon alternatives. The "proficient performer" (Stage 4) is strongly involved in his task and in organizing and understanding it on an intuitive basis. The "expert performer" (Stage 5) "neither solves problems nor makes decisions." He simply "does what works" (Dreyfus, 1987, p. 51). It is suggested by Dreyfus that one checks the model against one's own experience of driving a car. Although driving a car does not belong to the world's most complex tasks, the general ideas underlying Dreyfus' model point to some important aspects of the concept of rationality. Namely, that in as far as rationality has any connection with the ability of human beings to solve conflicts and cope with uncertainty in a complex environment, it is mainly due to the fact that the afore-mentioned strategy of rationalization has not fully succeeded. There is still some common sense, intuition, and practical sense left in the minds of people to make them capable of coping with a complex environment, this in spite of the abundant scientification and rationalization of practical affairs that are based on the narrow conception of rational decision making.

Constitutive vs. Regulative Rationality

Before going ahead with the task of defending a broader concept of rationality, a few words should be said about the distinction between regulative and constitutive ideas or rules. The importance of this distinction has been maintained by, among others, Searle (1969) in connection with the theory of speech acts, but it may be regarded as of central importance to the social sciences in general. The distinction may, I think, further clarify the concept of rationality. The question to be asked is the following: Is rationality in human behaviour to be considered as a regulative or a constitutive principle?

The immediate answer to this question is that the decision theory approach treats rationality as if it were a principle in the constitutive sense. Rules which are constitutive for a certain course of action are characterized by the fact that they define or even create the very possibility of a certain course of action. In the decision theory approach it is obedience to certain axioms which constitutes and thereby creates the subset of all possible actions which can be properly named rational actions. The falsifying evidence concerning obedience to the axioms of the expected utility proposition in a certain sense indicates that rules are not constitutive for human action in general. The theory of rational decision making tells us only that certain rules are constitutive for rational actors. But this simply means that the proposition is strictly analytical because the definition of rationality already contains the idea of rules as constitutive.

Contrary to the constitutive point of view, rationality may equally well be regarded as a regulative principle. Regulative rules do not define or create the conduct. They only regulate existing courses of action. According to this point of view, not only actions in general but also rational actions may exist without their obeying some preexisting constitutive rules. In order to illustrate the difference one could consider the difference between, say, having a dinner and playing a game of chess. I shall call the former activity an ill-defined game, and the latter a well-defined game. In the "ill-defined game" of eating, disobedience to table manners does not imply that one is not eating. In other words, table manners are not constitutive rules for eating, rather they have to be regarded as regulative rules. But in the "well-defined game" of chess, rules are constitutive for playing. Not following the rules of the game simply means that one is not playing chess.

The point is that in practical human affairs one cannot, neither principally nor in reality, make any a priori valid specification of the "rules of the game." This does not mean that rules do not exist, but rather that it is sometimes rational to break them and to invent new ones. Furthermore the validity of rules themselves has to be decided upon. This is, I think, where the concept of communication enters into the domain of rational decision making.

Information vs. Communication

Decision making as a rational activity has been closely related to the concept of **information.** It has been assumed that lack of wit is the only obstacle to rational conduct. (See, for instance, Simon, 1957, 1966.) So the gathering as well as the processing of information has been at the centre of theories of rational decision making. Given certain means and ends, models of decision making have been invented in order to give advice as to the behaviour of human agents, based on the idea that lack of knowledge about the situation in which the agents find themselves is the sole source of irrational conduct. Knowledge about facts and causal links between phenomena and logical reasoning is regarded as the sole source of rational problem solving.

Nevertheless, the limited success of the standard model with regard to both explanation and advice has created some scepticism and misbelief concerning the possibility of rational decision making. Simon's (1957) introduction of the concept of satisficing behaviour as an alternative to maximizing behaviour is an indicator of the defeat of the olympic theory of rationality. But the defeat, I submit, is only partly admitted in Simon's theory. It is still believed that knowledge about the situation in which the actor finds himself is the sole important source of rationality. Due to the complexity of the decision situation decision makers can have only incomplete knowledge. As a consequence decisions will of course also be incomplete. Nevertheless the received strategy has been the endeavour to improve decision making by means of information gathering and information processing.

If something is wrong with the concept of rationality, it is then also a problem for rationality itself. Instead of simply rejecting the importance of rationality, one should reconsider the nature and significance of the concept. Lack of wit is perhaps not the only bottleneck when it comes to improving decision making.

In my opinion, the scientification and rationalization of human practical affairs, the main task of decision theory, is biased in at least two respects. First and foremost the **communicative** aspects of decision making are nearly forgotten. As mentioned above, scepticism and disbelief concerning the possibility of rationality in decision making has essentially been rooted in the notion that people lack the wit necessary to act rationally. This is mainly so because rationality in the olympic sense is conditioned by objective knowledge about the environment in which the agent has to make his decision. The one-sided emphasis on objective knowledge and information leads to a rather paradoxical strategy. First a situation of nearly existential uncertainty is assumed, then by means of information gathering and information processing it is tried to transform this situation to one of certainty. The strategy is not only self-contradictory given the initial assumptions of genuine uncertainty but also impossible for yet another reason. Knowledge or information alone can never establish certainty in any subjectively relevant sense. Here, one must distinguish between the objective explanation and the subjective understanding of situations. Regarding the latter, communication has an important role to play. To communicate is not just to inform somebody about something, rather it is the process through which mutual understanding is created (Habermas, 1981). It is also the process through which involvement is created, making it possible to engage decision makers in non-empirical interpretations of importance for the decision at hand. This is precisely what the "aspect of meaning" of rationality is about.

From the point of view of rationality and rationalization, therefore, the improvement of decision making processes is complicated by not one but two bottlenecks: not only lack of wit but also dysfunctional communication. To consider rationality as a regulative idea and as a mainly practical ability of human beings is, I think, simultaneously to point to the integrative aspects of rationality of human conduct.

Communication is the means to integrate common sense and intuition in processes of decision making and thereby to broaden our concept of rationality. Communication is also the means whereby the gap between theory and praxis can be bridged because our communicative abilities are rooted in the social nature of human beings. As G.H. Mead (1984) once put it: "Man is a rational being because he is a social being." It is not the other way round. One may regard rationality in the sense of communicative competence as the outcome of a historical and social process of learning by which the powers of judgment and communicative ability have become transferred to individuals and social institutions alike. Rationality therefore is not – or not only – equal to analytical capacity, but rather to the ability to integrate knowledge and analysis in action and in social institutions.

References

Apel, K.-O. (1984). Das Problem einer philosophischen Theorie der Rationalitätstypen. In: H. Schnädelbach (Ed.), *Rationalität*, pp. 15-31. Frankfurt: Suhrkamp.

Arendt, H. (1978). *The life of the mind.* New York: Harcourt Brace Jovanovich.

Dreyfus, H.L. (1987). Misrepresenting human intelligence. In: R. Born (Ed.), *Artificial.intelligence – The case against*, pp. 41-54. London: Croom Helm.

Friedman, M. (1953). *Essays in positive economics.* Chicago: University of Chicago Press.

Habermas, H.J. (1971). Dogmatismus, Vernunft und Entscheidung – Zu Theorie und Praxis in der verwissenschaftlichten Zivilisation. In: H.J. Habermas, *Theorie und Praxis,* 4. Auflage, pp. 307-335. Frankfurt: Shurkamp.

Habermas, H.J. (1981). *Theorie des kommunikativen Handelns.* Frankfurt: Suhrkamp.

Lakatos, I. (1970). Falsification and the methodology of scientific research programmes. In: I. Lakatos & A. Musgrave (Eds.), *Criticism and the growth of knowledge*, pp. 91-195. London: Cambridge University Press.

Latsis, S. (1976). A research programme in economics. In: S. Latsis (Ed.), *Method and appraisal in economics*, pp. 1-41. Cambridge: Cambridge University Press.

Leinfellner, W. (1987). *The rise and fall of the expected utility hypothesis*. Paper presented at the 12th Annual Colloquium of the International Association for Research in Economic Psychology, Ebeltoft, Denmark, September 25-28.

Machlup, F. (1978). *Methodology of economics and other social sciences*. New York: Academic Press.

Mead, G.H. (1984). *Mind, self & society*. In: C.W. Morris (Ed.), *Works of G.H. Mead*, Vol. 1. Chicago: The University of Chicago Press.

Searle, J.R. (1969). *Speech acts*. Cambridge: Cambridge University Press.

Simon, H.A. (1967). *Models of man*. New York: Wiley.

Simon, H.A. (1966). *Administrative behaviour* (2nd ed.). New York: Free Press.

Thorelli, H.B. (1965). The political economy of the firm: Basis for a new theory of competition? *Revue Suisse d'Economie Politique et Statistique, 102*, 248-262.

Friedel Bolle

Levels of Aspiration, Promises, and the Possibility of Revaluation

Abstract

In decision theory we describe the choice of actions as made on the basis of a given body of values, usually a utility function (a profit function, a loss function). We often include the possibility that the utility function can change because of addiction, social interdependences, and other influences. In this paper, I am not so very interested in **these** revaluation processes, but wish to deal with revaluations which take place simply because the individual wants to change his or her own values. As far as I know, the question of whether, and to what extent, our values are at our own disposal has not aroused much attention among decision theorists. De gustibus non est disputandum!

A rough sketch of a way to introduce revaluations as alternatives in the set of feasible actions has been given in a former paper by the author (1983). While in that paper interest is focused on the nature of morals, here I want to discuss the revaluation process in more detail. In addition to making promises, the setting of levels of aspiration (LA setting) is shown to be another way of operating on one's own values. As revaluation options can be interpreted as the "freedom of will" and the limits of revaluation as limits of "will-power," the analysis provides an opportunity to discuss these otherwise rather vague concepts.

Author's address: Friedel Bolle, Department of Energy Economics, University of Cologne, Albertus-Magnus-Platz, D-5000 Cologne 41, West Germany, and Sozialökonomisches Seminar, University of Hamburg, von Melle Park 5, D-2000 Hamburg 13, West Germany.

As soon as he awoke, he made
up his mind to get up immediately,
to wash, to have his tea, to reflect
thoroughly. ... In spite of this
he stayed in bed for another half
an hour, suffering from this
intention of his.

Goncarov: Oblomov

Levels of Aspiration

We are used to hearing from sportsmen statements like "this year my goal is to win a medal in the Olympic Games" or "I will be content if I reach eight metres in this long jump." Also in everyday life we meet such a setting of goals, or Levels of Aspiration (LAs), e.g., to pass an examination with a certain grade, to find a job with a certain "satisfactory" salary, or simply to get up early enough to have an unhurried breakfast. The common observation in all these examples is that people establish criteria for their own performances, borderlines which separate success from failure.

Fritz Hoppe (1930) and Tamara Dembo (1931) were the first to analyze this kind of behaviour. Especially Hoppe's experiments and analysis guided investigations made in the following years. In their review article in 1944, Lewin, Dembo, Festinger, and Sears were already able to look back on a vast bulk of literature about the LA phenomenon. In this paper I want to concentrate on the question of how standard decision theory (utility theory) and LA theory are connected, stressing in particular the point that a revaluation takes place when an LA is set.

Since Simon (1955) called attention to LA setting behaviour in an outline of a theory of bounded rationality, this kind of behaviour is almost exclusively looked upon as a technique for simplifying the decision-making process (satisficing vs. optimizing). Unfortunately, only this aspect of LA setting has been absorbed in economics. The interests of the early investigators, however, seem to have focused on the process of dynamic valuation. People seek success and try to avoid failure, but success and failure are empty notions unless people also decide on what it takes to be successful, i.e., unless we decide on our LA.

Lewin et al. describe the choice of an LA as an optimization problem. (From the viewpoint of bounded rationality theories this is absurd. Instead of simplifying the decision-making process the introduction of an LA complicates it.) A "resultant weighted valence" is

(1)
$$
oV(A^h) = Va(Suc\ A^h)\ Prob(Suc\ A^h) \\
+ Va(Fail\ A^h)\ Prob(Fail\ A^h)
$$

defined where A^h is a possible LA, $Suc\ A^h$ is the event "A^h is reached," $Fail\ A^h$ is the event "A^h is not reached," $Va\ (.)$ describes the value (utility), and $Prob\ (.)$ the probability of an event. The A^h with maximal $oV(A^h)$ is chosen as the LA. This looks very much like ordinary maximizing of expected utility, but there is a crucial difference. In models for the maximization of expected utility the valuation is given and one looks for the best action, whereas here it is not a question of choosing an action but deciding on a valuation, viz., the condition of success.

Starbuck (1963) puts forward a model with the following simple structure:

(2)
$$
U^* = \begin{cases} U + S \text{ if the LA is reached} \\ U - F \text{ if the LA is not reached} \end{cases}
$$

with U = "normal" utility, S = value of success, F = negative value of failure. This simple model expresses very clearly the opinion of its author that the setting of an LA influences the utility function.

Let me emphasize once more that the revaluation aspect has been suppressed by many authors. For Siegel (1957), the LA is simply a point on the utility scale, and Simon (1955) is not far away from such a point of view either.[1]

Promises

The essence of LA setting behaviour can be described without invoking a social context – which does not mean that the experimenter, spectators, or group norms do not influence the LA. In social behaviour, above all in bargaining situations, we find other forms of revaluation. "I promise you, my dear child, that we will go swimming after you have finished your homework" or "I swear that I shall tell the truth" are examples in which future actions are revalued. The promised action gets a higher value and/or all other actions are devalued.

Let me try to formalize the effect of a promise. Before making a promise, my utility function is $u(s,a)$ where s is the state of the world (or sequence of states of the world) and a is an action (or a sequence of actions). After making the promise this utility function changes to

$$(3) \qquad u^* (s,a) = u(s,a) + m(s,a)$$

with $m(s,a) \geq 0$ if s is a state of the world in which the condition of my promise is fulfilled (my child finished his homework) and a includes the promised action (we go swimming), $m(s,a) < 0$ if I break my promise, and $m(s,a) = 0$ if the condition of the promise is not fulfilled. $m(s,a) > 0$ describes my good conscience because of keeping my promise, $m(s,a) < 0$ describes my bad conscience after breaking it. Apparently, this model does not force me to keep a promise. If I can win a larger utility u^* by breaking it, I will do so.

Only if other people think that my incentive to keep a promise is strong enough are they willing to rely on it, i.e., only under such a condition can I conclude contracts quickly and at low cost. One may object here that we do not need the incentive function $m(s,a)$ because the expected advantages from **future** contracts will make me keep my promise and remain trustworthy. Of course this is an important additional reason for keeping a promise, but this reason cannot explain why we feel committed to a promise made to a dying person or, more generally, to promises that have no means of being checked. Children are often required to make such promises as, for example, to cross the street only when the lights are green, or not to buy candy with the money they are given. Moreover, whether the truth is told after an oath has been taken cannot always be examined, at least not immediately.

A promise can be "energized" by more or less strong incentive functions, i.e., it seems to be possible to multiply m by factors within a certain range. It does not seem to be difficult to deviate from a course of action we have only **agreed upon**. On the other hand, there are people who risk their lives to carry out an action in order not to break a **solemn oath.**

We find this "social" type of revaluation also within individual decision-making. We observe that people make promises to themselves, for example, not to continue smoking. A more weakly energized form of such behaviour is to be **firmly determined** to do something. Ainslee (1975, p. 475) points out that even "in ordinary speech, one is said to **make** a decision, as if the choice has inertia." Many people feel a strong resistance to reconsidering a settled question.

What are the differences between setting an LA and making a promise to oneself? At present, I can merely conclude that promises are formulated for actions and LAs are formulated for states of the world, for "outcomes." Later, further differences will become obvious, but assuming that $m(s,a) = m(s)$ we can use Equation 3 to describe the setting of an LA, too.

When discussing promises I have pointed out that within a limited range, the individual can choose the "energy" of these promises, he can choose the strength of the bonds that confine him. However, as far as I know, it has never been discussed whether or not the amount of satisfaction involved in reaching one's LA (and the amount of disappointment when not reaching it) is at the disposal of the individual. Although Lewin et al., Starbuck, and other authors do not allow for such a choice, it seems quite reasonable to assume that the "energy" of LAs can also be swayed by the individual.

Will-Power, Counterpreferential Choice, and the Necessity to Construct a Dynamic Model

What we have learned so far is that we have the possibility of deliberately changing our subjective values. This is an exciting idea which has important consequences for decision theory, moral philosophy, and other fields. To prevent misunderstandings let me emphasize that these changes can be described reasonably well only in a dynamic context.

If we believe that it is at all possible to model human behaviour by means of utility theory (preference theory), then we must not oversimplify the preferences we use. We know that people have long-term preferences and we know that these preferences change in the course of time. A man with stable long-term preferences could – in a deterministic world – determine his future behaviour once and for all.

But we know that people often deviate from their planned course of action, even when not surprised by unforeseen events. Most alcoholics **plan** to stop drinking but they do not stop. Teachers often **plan** to be patient regardless of the behaviour of their pupils but they do not always succeed.

Dynamic utility theory assumes that an individual has a utility function

$$(4) \qquad u_i = u_i(...; s_{i-1}, a_{i-1}; s_i, a_i; s_{i+1}, a_{i+1}; ...)$$

with s_j = state of the world in period j, a_j = action in period j.

For $j > i$, s_j and a_j are expected states of the world and expected actions. In period i the individual can determine only a_i. But his utility is also influenced by states and actions of previous and later periods. Smoking, drinking, playing tennis, seeing movies, learning mathematics, as well as having made promises and set LAs in previous periods, influence today's preferences.

The statement that the preferences have changed from period i to period $i+1$ can be given precise meaning: In period $i+1$ all situations and actions up to s_i and a_i are determined and so we have to compare u_i and u_{i+1}, both as a function of $s_{i+1}, a_{i+1}; s_{i+2}, a_{i+2}; ..$. If u_i and u_{i+1}, regarded as functions of these arguments, are related by a monotonous transformation, 'their preferences have not changed from i to $i+1$; otherwise, they have. If preferences have changed, the optimal plan of period i – say, not to drink alcohol in period $i+1$ – might not be followed in period $i+1$.

From Equation 4 one can see that, as a by-product, every action of today can change tomorrow's preferences. In this paper our interest focuses on such actions, viz., the setting of LAs and the giving of promises, which change preferences purposefully and effectively, i.e., without "side effects." At time i my only goal is to maximize u_i and if it turns out that favourable future states and future actions (favourable from the viewpoint of u_i) can be expected after an LA is set, then such an LA will be set.

The notation of the rest of this paper is simplified by the suppressing of time indices. What is described in Equation 1, 2, 3, and all the following expressions are "tomorrow's preferences." The action a_i is the introduction of $m(s_{i+1}, a_{i+1})$ into tomorrow's preferences u_{i+1} $(...; s_i, a_i;$ $s_{i+1}, a_{i+1},...) = u(s_{i+1}, a_{i+1}) + m(s_{i+1}, a_{i+1}) = u(s,a) + m(s,a)$.

"Just what kind of freedom is the freedom of will?" asks Frankfurt (1971, p. 14). His answer is (p. 15): "Now freedom of action is (roughly, at least) the freedom to do what one wants to do. Analogously, then, the statement that a person enjoys freedom of the will means (also roughly) that he is free to want what he wants to want." On the one hand such an answer seems to be the only reasonable answer. One uses the terms "will-power" and "freedom of will" to describe certain situations and conflicts, and Frankfurt's definition seems to coincide with this usage. On the other hand, the definition is rather nebulous because a dynamic process is described by means of quasi-static expressions. Frankfurt is forced to introduce independent second-order values or preferences, i.e., preferences towards preferences, to get on track again.

In a dynamic context, Frankfurt's definition (which I do accept) has a far simpler meaning. Freedom of will means that today I can determine tomorrow's preferences; complete freedom of will means that this choice is not restricted (in reality it is, of course). The extent to which I can change tomorrow's preferences is called my will-power. If it is possible to complement the "natural" values of tomorrow $u(s,a)$, which imply my tomorrow's desire to smoke, by a sufficiently strong **incentive function** $m(s,a)$ so that $u(s,a) + m(s,a)$ imply my tomorrow's desire not to smoke, then I have **enough will-power** to give up smoking. If I do not have such a strong incentive function at my disposal, then I am **too weak**, then I do not have enough will-power for that purpose. Of course, the individual can also try to stop smoking by means of such external action as making bets with friends or going to a smokers' clinic. For a detailed discussion of such devices, see Schelling (1983).

The phenomenon of "counterpreferential choice" (Sen, 1977) has a clear meaning in such a dynamic model of choice. **Today** I would like to stop smoking from tomorrow on; **tomorrow** I prefer to smoke. The conflicting preferences are those of today and tomorrow. Today I always do what I prefer today (in the long-term perspective!) and tomorrow I do what I prefer tomorrow – but possibly I do not do tomorrow what I would like me to do from the viewpoint of today. "Will-power" means that I can (sometimes!) make myself act counter to the "original" preferences of tomorrow.

The attempt to explain conflicting preferences in a **static world** ends up in confusion. The statement that someone acts counter to his existing preferences is either a contradiction in itself or implies an unusual definition of "preferences." Second-order (and higher-order) preferences as introduced by Frankfurt, Sen, and others, have not been integrated into a model of decision-making by these authors: First-order and second-order preferences are neither connected with one another nor with actual decisions. In Bolle (1983) it is argued in more detail that we do not need independent second-order preferences for the explanation of the phenomena on which these authors base their arguments.

Today we do not know tomorrow's state of the world, we only have expectations about it. Tomorrow's natural preferences may be similarly uncertain. Under such circumstances we may underestimate the necessary will-power needed to give up smoking or – in Oblomov's case – to get out of bed. As a consequence we suffer from our fruitless attempt, we suffer from breaking the promise we made to ourselves. It is less frustrating simply to keep on smoking though "intrinsically we want to stop" (Bolle, 1981; Yaari, 1977) than to fight and be defeated.

When contemplating the introduction of revaluation options into a formal model of choice the most important question is: Which set of functions $m(s,a)$ are at the decision maker's disposal, and which restrictions on functions $m(s,a)$ have to be observed? Of course, the author is not able to give a complete answer, especially for the case when one leaves the simple "today-tomorrow" world and tries to analyze a world of many time periods. What I am able to do in the next section, is to try to isolate some rough restrictions which must be imposed on $m(s,a)$.

Restrictions on the Revaluation Options

If there are economies of scale, say in the building of a new barn, then it is more efficient when neighbours work together. The farmer whose barn is to be built last must rely on the promises of those whose barns are to be built first. Otherwise no cooperation would occur and labour would be wasted. Instead of expressing this efficiency-enlarging effect of promises in terms of an objective value like labour we can also express it in subjective values (utility) $u(s,a)$ from Equation 3. Without cooperation, everybody's utility would be smaller than that with cooperation.

The same type of problem can be found in the intertemporal decision-making of an individual (Ainslee, 1979; Elster, 1977; Strotz, 1956; Thaler & Shefrin, 1981; Yaari, 1977). Not to continue smoking can be an efficient course of action, i.e., it may give the individual larger utilities in all periods, but it may be impossible to follow such a course unless bound by a promise.

Operating on one's own values in this manner has the character of "repairing" them. Usually it is advantageous that tastes (for food, for locations, for companionship) are not completely rigid but develop as a response to pleasant and unpleasant experiences. Sometimes, however, this process leads to severe disadvantages, even to drug consumption or voluntary bondage. With the exception of extreme cases these degenerations can usually be removed by personal revaluation decisions.

Setting a level of aspiration can have the same efficiency-enlarging power as the making of a promise to oneself. A student, for example, who has difficulties in making himself learn something, may make a promise to himself to work eight hours a day, or he may set a level of aspiration to pass his final examination with a good grade.

Let me now give simple examples for incentive functions m, one belonging to an unconditional promise to oneself to stop smoking, α is the

$$(5) \qquad m(s,a) = \begin{cases} \alpha & \text{for } a = \text{not smoking} \\ -\beta & \text{for } a = \text{smoking} \end{cases}$$

with $\alpha, \beta > 0$,

and one belonging to a level of aspiration to pass an examination

$$(6) \qquad m(s,a) = \begin{cases} \alpha & \text{for } s = \text{passing the examination} \\ -\beta & \text{for } s = \text{not passing the examination} \end{cases}$$

again with $\alpha, \beta > 0$ (but usually not the same as in Equation 5).

good conscience when keeping one's promise or the value of success, respectively. $-\beta$ is the bad conscience after breaking the promise or the value of failure, respectively. Whether or not $m(s,a)$ is added to tomorrow's value is decided today where s and a are usually not definitely known. Let us further assume that today's utility depends roughly (among other influences) on tomorrow's expected utility $u(s,a) + m(s,a)$.

What restrictions should be imposed on $m(s,a)$ in a formal model?

Firstly, regarding our body of values as a body of information[2] about the best way to survive and reproduce we must suppose that there is a **maximum flow of value changes** just as there is a maximum flow of information into our long term memory (see Newell & Simon, 1972). Every revaluation decision has to be thought about so that the frequency of such decisions is necessarily restricted. Also the extent of revaluation in one decision, measured by $\alpha + \beta$, should usually not be too large because "mistakes" could otherwise have catastrophic consequences. In reality, there are some exceptions with large $\alpha + \beta$. We have already mentioned that for some people, the power of a solemn oath is so strong that they would prefer to die rather than break it.

Secondly, value changes for the sake of enlarging efficiency should not have an expected value of their own, i.e., **the expected value of $m(s,a)$ should be near 0 for promises.** If it were smaller than 0, efficiency-enlarging promises would not be given in many cases. If it were larger than 0, promises would be given which are efficiency-decreasing, in order to win the positive value of $m(s,a)$. As promises usually can be kept and are kept, we must expect the α / β ratio to be small, i.e., that the otherwise bad conscience is the essential motivation to keep a promise. The small α / β proportion includes an interesting implication: A promise cannot be removed by another promise. If I make the promise not to smoke and try to remove it by the promise to smoke, then, provided both incentive functions have the form of Equation 4, the aggregate value is $\alpha - \beta < 0$ for smoking as well as for not smoking. If α / β were larger than 1 it would be advantageous to promise to carry out an arbitrary action and to promise not to do so at the same time.

Thirdly, **in LA setting behaviour the expected value of $m(s,a)$ is larger than 0.** In the best known examples of LA setting, individuals do not set goals with an intrinsic value of their own, i.e., in $u(s,a) + m(s,a)$, $m(s,a)$ depends only on whether the goal is reached or not. LA setting behaviour was "discovered" when subjects who were involved in another experiment began to "play" with the material of this experiment (Hoppe, 1930). They set **themselves** tasks in order "to kill time" and their satisfaction depended on their performance with these tasks. The setting of a task corresponds to the introduction of an incentive function m and it is clear that in such cases it would be irrational to add an incentive function to future utilities if the expected value were negative. Additionally, the probability that a goal is reached is usually smaller than the probability that a promise will be kept. Both reasons imply that the α / β ratio is larger for LAs than for promises. From experiments we know that – for similar tasks – α, β, and the subjective probability of reaching a goal are connected. α is negatively correlated with this probability, and β is positively correlated (see Lewin et al., 1944). So the ratio α / β decreases with the increasing probability of reaching the goal. When there is a choice between setting an LA or making a promise to oneself, the former is always chosen. If its power is not strong enough, promises will be made as well or an attempt made to precommit one's "later self" (see Parfit, 1973) by external means.

Conclusion

In general, the possibility of operating on one's own values seems to complicate the decision-making process considerably. But that is not a necessary consequence. One of the great difficulties of dynamic decision making is the necessity to reconsider in every time period the planned course of action (except for a special class of intertemporal utility function, see Strotz, 1956). In a model where we choose a course of action in the first period and give it enough inertia by **making up our minds** to follow this course, decision-making is far easier. Thus it is not certain that models in which also valuations can be swayed will be more complicated than those without this possibility.

If we can affect our values we are also – at least partly – responsible for them. (Whatever the moral meaning of responsibility is.) We are not only responsible for what we are **doing** – for drinking alcohol, eating candy, talking with friends, reading poems – but also for **liking** activities so much that we carry them out, viz., for the motives behind our behaviour. The arbitrariness that lies in such development of values raises the inescapable question about the long-term implication of freedom of will, namely whether "one can, at last, do everything" (Elster, 1977, p. 481, interpreting Descartes). Personally, I do not believe in such a possibility: The restrictions on the deliberate revaluation process are severe and the "energy" of this process certainly does not have a magnitude above that of other influences such as addictive processes, social interdependences of values, and the mere effect of ageing.

Notes

1. See the example of LA setting behaviour in the appendix of Simon's 1955 article. Curiously, however, this example is not at all in the spirit of the main body of the article.

2. Changes of utility caused by additional information are hypothesized and described by Cyert and de Groot (1980).

References

Ainslee, G. (1979). Specious reward: A behavior theory of impulsiveness and impulse control. *Psychological Bulletin, 82*, 463-496.

Bolle, F. (1981). Comments on dynamic decision-making: Is there a conflict between rationality and efficiency? *Erkenntnis, 16*, 131-136.

Bolle, F. (1983). On Sen's second-order preferences, morals, and decision theory. *Erkenntnis, 20*, 193-205.

Cyert, R.M., & de Groot, M.H. (1980). Learning applied to utility functions. In: A. Zellner (Ed.), *Bayesian analysis in econometrics and statistics*, pp. 199-268. Amsterdam: North-Holland.

Dembo, T. (1931). Der Ärger als dynamisches Problem (Untersuchungen zur Handlungs- und Affektpsychologie X. Hrsg. K. Lewin). *Psychologische Forschung, 15*, 1-144.

Elster, J. (1977). Ulysses and the sirens: A theory of imperfect rationality. *Social Science Information, 16*, 469-526.

Frankfurt, H.G. (1971). Freedom of will and the concept of a person. *Journal of Philosophy, 68*, 5-20.

Hoppe, F. (1931). Erfolg und Misserfolg (Untersuchungen zur Handlungs- und Affektpsychologie IX. Hrsg. K. Lewin). *Psychologische Forschung, 14*, 1-62.

Lewin, K., Dembo, T., Festinger, L., & Sears, P.S. (1944). Level of aspiration. In: J.M. Hunt (Ed.), *Personality and behavior disorders*, pp. 333-378. New York: Ronald Press.

Newell, A., & Simon, H.A. (1972). *Human problem solving*. Englewood Cliffs, NJ: Prentice-Hall.

Parfit, D. (1973). Later selves and moral principles. In: A. Montefiore (Ed.), *Philosophy and personal relations*, pp. 137-169. London: Routledge & Kegan Paul.

Schelling, T.C. (1983). Ethics, law, and the exercise of self-command. In: S.M. McMurrin (Ed.), *The Tanner lectures on human values*, pp. 43-80. Salt Lake City, UT: University of Utah Press.

Sen, A. (1977). Rational fools: A critique of the behavioral foundations of economic theory. *Philosophy and Public Affairs, 6*, 317-344.

Siegel, S.A. (1957). Level of aspiration and decision making. *Psychological Review, 64*, 253-262.

Simon, H.A. (1955). A behavioural model of rational choice. *Quarterly Journal of Economics, 69*, 99-118.

Starbuck, W.H. (1963). Level of aspiration. *Psychological Review, 70*, 51-60.

Strotz, R. (1956). Myopia and inconsistency in dynamic utility maximization. *Review of Economic Studies, 23*, 165-180.

Thaler, R.H., & Shefrin, H.M. (1981). An economic theory of self-control. *Journal of Political Economy, 89*, 392-406.

Yaari, M.E. (1977). Endogeneous changes in tastes: A philosophical discussion. *Erkenntnis, 11*, 157-196.

Klaus G. Grunert

Another Attitude Towards Multi-Attribute Attitude Theories

Abstract

The paper argues that multi-attribute attitude theories, in spite of their widespread use, are not very successful in predicting behaviour, have flaws in their theoretical foundations, and are usually combined with measurement procedures of questionable validity. A meta-analysis of some 20 studies trying to predict consumer choice is used to support the first criticism. Cognitive psychology, especially insights about knowledge representation systems, is used to delineate theoretical flaws. The criticism of the measurement procedure is based on arguments from the qualitative/quantitative controversy. The paper closes with suggestions for alternative theoretical models and measurement procedures.

Author's address: Klaus G. Grunert, The Aarhus School of Business, Ryhavevej 8, DK-8210 Aarhus V, Denmark.

213

The "Law of Multi-Attribute Market Reaction"

In the sciences, the term "law" is normally used to designate a theory which is widely accepted and seems to be true without qualifications as regards timespan or geographical area. "Natural law" is, at least in everyday language, a much more widely used term than social law or economic law, mirroring the much greater progress that has been made in the natural sciences compared to the social sciences.

In a 1981 paper, Lutz formulated the *law of multi-attribute market reaction:*

A consumer's attitudinal and behavioral responses to any market offering are a function of the salient perceived consequences to the consumer of purchasing that offering and the desirability of those consequences to the consumer (Lutz, 1981, p. 13).

What made Lutz think that this is a law?

Lutz's assertion is based on the widespread use of a certain class of theories to explain economic behaviour and especially consumer behaviour. This class of theories has become known as multi-attribute attitude theories (MAAT). The most well-known member of this class of theories is the attitude theory of Fishbein and Ajzen (e.g., 1975). Other versions that have been used are the attitude theories of Rosenberg (1956), Anderson (1971), and several simplifications or complications of these theories that were developed in marketing to better adapt these theories for the purpose of explaining consumer behaviour (see Silberer, 1981, or Wilkie & Pessemier, 1973, for overviews).

Three assumptions form the core of this group of theories:

1. Behaviour towards an object is determined by the attitude towards that object or by the attitude towards that behaviour.

2 . Attitude in turn is determined by the cognitive structure with regard to the attitude object.

3. Cognitive structure with regard to the attitude object is conceptualized as the linking of a small number of attributes to the attitude object. Hence, the term multi-attribute attitude theories.

The Predictive Power of Multi-Attribute Attitude Theories

As already noted, these theories have been widely used in attempts to explain consumer behaviour. A closer look reveals, however, that there have been hardly any summary treatments of the predictive ability of these theories in consumer research (see Geise, 1984, for an exception). In social psychology, on the other hand, there have appeared quite a number of reviews of the predictive abilities of attitude theories (e.g., Benninghaus, 1976; Meinefeld, 1977; Wicker, 1969), most of them with rather devastating results. If Lutz still believes that there is a law of multi-attribute market reaction in consumer research, then either the theories must be more successful here than in other areas, or the widespread use of these theories is taken as a surrogate indicator for their predictive power.

Exhibit 1 (see Appendix) contains summary information on 18 publications comprising 26 studies having the following characteristics:

– the relationship between attitude and behaviour or behavioural intention is investigated

– the attitude object is a consumer good or the purchase of a consumer good

– the attitude is computed as a sum score of belief strengths and evaluations, i.e., a MAAT framework is used.

If several model variants were investigated in one study (e.g., with and without a normative component), only the more successful variant is included in Exhibit 1.

Of course, the list is not comprehensive (e.g., unpublished studies have not been included). Still, it is probably representative for the research that has been conducted. Information on additional, mostly unpublished studies can be found in tables by Geise (1984), and Wilkie and Pessemier (1973).

In most cases, simple or multiple correlation coefficients have been used to assess predictive ability. Hence, this indicator is used in Exhibit 1 as well, even though it has been shown that the computation of product-moment correlations with values that were obtained by multiplying two components is warranted only if these components were measured on a ratio scale (Bagozzi, 1984; Orth, 1985). A few studies used a

215

dichotomous measure as the dependent variable, in which case predictive success is given as a percentage of cases which were correctly predicted.

Looking at the last column of Exhibit 1, one can see that the multiple correlation coefficients range all the way from .18 to .69. However, the studies differ widely in the way the dependent variable was measured, and also in the version of MAAT that was used to predict the dependent variable. The most important differences are the following.

1. In order to predict buying behaviour with regard to a consumer product, some studies use the attitude towards that product, while others use the attitude towards the act of buying that product.

2. Some studies use an additional independent variable termed the normative component. This extension, which is supposed to measure social pressures towards performing or not performing a certain act and the motivation to comply with these pressures, was proposed by Fishbein and obviously goes beyond the law of multi-attribute market reaction.

3. In some studies, the dependent variable is not behaviour, but a construct called behavioural intention, which is supposed to be close to behaviour.

4. If behaviour itself is measured, an important distinction is whether it is measured concurrently with attitudes and in some cases behavioural intentions, or whether there is a separate measurement.

The latter point is especially important, because concurrent measurement of behaviour usually means asking respondents either to retrospectively report previous behaviour, or to perform some behaviour in a laboratory setting. In both cases the validity of behaviour measurement can be questioned, because the data collection situation is beset with strong demand effects, with a bias towards consistent answering.

In order to get a clearer view of how these various factors affect predictive success, a meta-analysis was performed, the results of which are presented in Tables 1 and 2. Correlation coefficients were transformed to Fisher z-scores and used as the dependent variable in a regression analysis using the various descriptors of study design just mentioned as independent dummy variables. If predictive success was given in percentages of correct predictions, these were made comparable to correlation coefficients by taking square roots. Since, however, a dichotomous dependent variable is most probably more reliable than a continuous one, the distinction between dichotomous and continuous dependent variables was also included in the analysis. Finally, one study was based on aggregate instead of individual data, which also increases reliability, thus complicating the comparison of correlation coefficients. Hence this, too, was taken into account.

Table 1 gives results first for the full model, and Table 2 for a reduced model that was estimated using only those descriptors that proved to have a significant influence. The results can be interpreted as follows.

Table 1: Meta-Analysis of MAAT Studies: Results for Full Model

	Estimated z-score	Standard error of estimate	p
Basic model			
Independent variable: attitude towards the object			
Dependent variable: behavioural intention			
Measurement of dependent variable: continuous, individual data	1.164	.117	.000
Effects of deviations from basic model			
Independent variable:			
attitude towards the act	−.459	.200	.034
normative component	+.603	.189	.005
Dependent variable:			
behaviour, concurrent measurement	−.360	.355	.325
behaviour, separate measurement	−.745	.343	.044
behaviour, c.m., when intention was also measured	−.087	.199	.665
behaviour, s.m., when intention was previously measured	−.872	.363	.028
behaviour, aggregate data	−.105	.342	.763
Measurement of dependent variable: dichotomous	+1.136	.422	.015

$R^2 = .67$, $F = 4.41$, $p < .005$, $n = 26$

As for the explanatory variables, attitude towards the product leads to more correct predictions than attitudes towards the act of buying the product. This is somewhat astonishing, because it is contrary to the assumptions made in most writings in this area (see, e.g., Ajzen & Fishbein, 1977). Inclusion of a normative component variable in addition to the attitude variable increases predictive success.

Table 2: Meta-Analysis of MAAT Studies: Results for Reduced Model

	Estimated z-score	Standard error of estimate	p
Basic model			
Independent variable: attitude towards the object			
Dependent variable: behavioural intention and/or behaviour, concurrent measurement or behaviour, separate measurement with aggregate data			
Measurement of dependent variable: continuous	1.135	.083	.000
Effects of deviations from basic model			
Independent variable:			
attitude towards the act	−.483	.175	.012
normative component	+.594	.156	.001
Dependent variable:			
behaviour, separate measurement with individual data	−.776	.231	.003
Measurement of dependent variable: dichotomous	.805	.193	.004

$R^2 = .65$, $F = 9.67$, $p<.001$, $n = 26$

Concerning the dependent variable, it comes as no surprise that predictive success is highest when not behaviour itself, but only behavioural intention is to be explained. When behaviour itself is measured, the use of aggregate data leads to amounts of explained variance that are about the same as when predicting behavioural intentions only. Also, when behaviour is measured concurrently with attitude, the correlations are not significantly lower than when measuring behavioural intention only. Only when behaviour is measured separately from attitude, do correlations drop significantly, unless a dichotomous measure of behaviour is used.

Separately measured behaviour is the crucial test for the theory, because it is the only research design not beset with demand effects leading to a bias towards consistent responses. Using individual data, a continuous measure of behaviour, and attitude towards the object as the only explanatory variable, the model estimates a correlation between attitude and behaviour of .17, i.e., about 3% of explained variance. On this basis, it hardly seems justified to talk about a law of multi-attribute market reaction.

Given the small number of studies included in the analysis, leading to a large number of empty cells in the design matrix of the meta-analysis, the results must be interpreted with caution. A cursory glance at Exhibit 1 reveals that out of three studies using separate measures of behaviour, one resulted in a correlation of only .18, one was based on aggregate data, and one included the normative component as an additional explanatory variable.

A possible conclusion from this analysis would be that the causal chain cognitive structure –> attitude –> behaviour is much too simple, and that constructs such as normative components and possibly others are necessary to supplement it. However, it might also be worthwhile to check whether the way cognitive structure is conceptualized in MAAT could be a reason for the low predictive ability.

The Concept of Cognitive Structure

As already noted, cognitive structure, or at least the part of it that is supposed to determine attitude, is conceived in MAAT as the linkage of a small number of attributes, usually 5-10, to the attitude object. If the attitude object is a behaviour rather than a material object, then these attributes are usually regarded as consequences of performing the behaviour. A link between the attitude object and an attribute is called a belief. Beliefs are usually characterized by two criteria. Their strength, mirroring the subjective probability of the existence of a relationship between attitude object and attribute, and their evaluation, meaning the extent to which the attribute is viewed as desirable or undesirable.

This model of cognitive structure can be presented graphically as in Figure 1a. It is a very simple associative structure, and hence can be viewed as a special type of a more general class of models of cognitive structure that have become known as associative networks. This class of models, which is widely used in cognitive psychology (see Chang, 1986, for an overview), can be drawn upon to point out a number of limitations of the concept of cognitive structure used in MAAT.

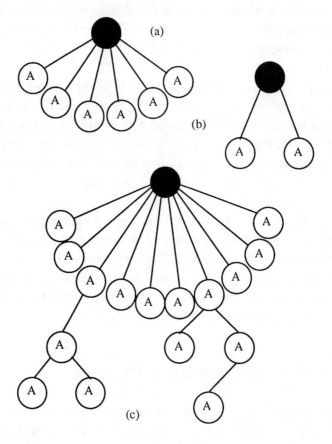

Figure 1: Different types of cognitive structure.

A first limitation is the assumption that all cognitive structures have the same format, that of Figure 1a, no matter whose cognitive structure it is and no matter which attitude object is involved. Cognitive structures are learned, and as knowledge about a certain object increases over time, cognitive structure will mirror these increases. One might argue that while cognitive structure changes, the part of it affecting attitude will always remain the same and appear as in Figure 1a, but this seems very unlikely.

At this point, one should perhaps recall what an attitude was originally considered to be. While definitions of attitude abound, a consensual definition may be that an attitude is a learned disposition to behave consistently in a negative or positive way towards an attitude object (Fishbein & Ajzen, 1975, p. 6). This presupposes a minimum level of familiarity with the attitude object. Below this level, there may still be a rudimentary cognitive structure with regard to that object, but it will not lead to consistent behaviour. In this case, it is doubtful if one should talk about attitudes. This rudimentary structure could look like the one depicted in Figure 1b, i. e., different from the one assumed in MAAT in that there is only a very small number of attributes linked to the object. On the other hand, as knowledge increases, it seems likely that cognitive structures develop into more complicated configurations than the one in Figure 1a. A possible, more complicated structure is depicted in Figure 1c. It differs from the basic model in Figure 1a in two ways: Firstly, the number of cognitions linked to the attitude object is larger than 10, and secondly, associations are formed not only by direct, but also by indirect links: to use a term from graph theory, associations can consist of paths of different length.

Figures 1a-c show that cognitive structures can be assumed to vary in two dimensions: horizontal and vertical complexity. MAAT assume these dimensions to be constant over all persons and all attitude objects, which seems highly unlikely. This may be one possible reason for the low predictive power of these theories.

A second limitation is that MAAT make assertions about cognitive structure, but not about cognitive processes. Any observable human behaviour that is governed by cognitive factors is, however, a joint result of both structure and process. By simply observing behaviour, no matter whether "real" behaviour or giving answers in a data collection situation, we cannot conclude whether information used or uttered was simply retrieved from cognitive structure, or was inferred on the basis of more general knowledge at the time of use. The distinction is important, because information actually stored in cognitive structure that becomes behaviourally relevant today will in all likelihood also be relevant tomorrow, while information inference is highly situation-specific, and the way information is inferred in a data collection situation may be quite different from the way this is done in everyday behaviour.

In the early versions of MAAT it was rather clear that the intention was to predict behaviour from stored information: The cognitive processes involved were implicitly assumed to be simple retrieval operations. But in later versions, this assumption becomes more doubtful. If we talk about attitude not towards an object, but towards a behaviour, which may be highly specific like the attitude towards buying a piece of cake for tea this afternoon, it becomes much less plausible that consequences of this specific behaviour are stored in a person's cognitive structure. It appears much more likely that these consequences are inferred at the time of use from more basic knowledge, e.g., about the general consequences of eating cake. This may explain why, at least when the aim was to predict consumer purchases, attitude towards the product was more successful than attitude to the behaviour itself, as demonstrated in Tables 1 and 2.

Thus, it is possible that if the simple concept of cognitive structure used in MAAT and the way it is linked to behaviour were replaced by a more complete cognitive model, the predictive abilities of such a model would exceed those now observed.

This section was concerned only with possible flaws in the theory. Naturally, there may also be flaws in the way cognitive structure is usually measured. This is the topic of the next section.

Measurement of Cognitive Structure

Cognitive structure within the context of MAAT is usually measured in a two-step process. First, a small qualitative study is undertaken to find possible beliefs or attributes that could form part of a cognitive structure with regard to the attitude object. Those mentioned most frequently are then used in a larger standardized survey, where these beliefs are presented to respondents in order to be rated according to strength and evaluation (see Ajzen & Fishbein, 1980).

Thus, strictly speaking, only the small qualitative pre-study is an attempt to measure cognitive structure, because only then do respondents have the opportunity to voice the information they have actually stored in their memory. In the main study, respondents no longer have this chance. Rather, they are presented with other people's beliefs, and have to rate these with regard to strength and evaluation, no matter whether they actually form part of their own cognitive structure or not. The assumption seems to be that this approximates respondents' cognitive structure as it would have manifested itself in a more open measurement procedure.

This assumption is difficult to justify for at least two reasons. Firstly, it would presuppose that the qualitative study of beliefs was executed with great care. The fact that there is hardly ever any published information or methodological discussion on how the qualitative study was carried out, documents that this is not the case. In fact, in many cases it is omitted altogether; the researcher himself sits down and thinks up some possible beliefs. We know hardly anything about the reliability and validity of this qualitative step. Even if it is carried out in a reasonable way, it is usually based on a convenience sample, and it seems very doubtful that the beliefs these people have in their cognitive structure can be readily generalized to other populations.

The second reason is that the standardized survey not only limits responses to those beliefs that were uttered by other people, but its administration actually changes the cognitive structure of the respondents. Using an extreme case for illustration, it is possible that respondents did not even know beforehand about the existence of a certain attitude object, but that, during the interview, they build up a cognitive structure with regard to this object, because relevant beliefs are so readily supplied to them. The cognitive structure to be ascertained is thus changed by the measurement itself. It seems difficult to expect valid measures from such a type of procedure.

Towards Alternatives in Theory and Measurement

Within the scope of the present paper, it is not possible to specify in any detail alternative theories and measurement procedures. One can, however, list a number of prerequisites that an alternative approach should meet.

On the theoretical side, it should be more flexible with regard to the type of cognitive structure entailed, i.e., it should allow for differences in horizontal and vertical complexity. It should also spell out by which kind of processes cognitive structure is transformed to behaviour, both in real life and in a data collection situation. As for theories about cognitive structure, semantic networks, which have found modest application in consumer research (e.g., Grunert, 1982, 1986), may be a feasible approach. The results of research on information retrieval and judgment processes could be fruitfully applied to the question of how stored information is used.

As for measurement, it should allow respondents to air their own beliefs, and hence should be an open procedure. Reservations with regard to the use of open procedures have usually been related to their cumbersomeness and to the difficulties of turning them into quantitative estimates. Recent advances in computer-assisted content analysis and in the analysis of free recall data may point out ways in which these problems can be circumvented (Grunert, 1988; Grunert & Bader, 1986).

Appendix

Exhibit 1: Summary Information on 26 MAAT Studies

Study	Independent variable	Dependent variable	Attitude model	Item selection	Attitude objects	Subjects	N	Results*
Assael & Day (1969)	attitude (object)	behaviour (market shares, s.m.)	Thurstone	?	pain reliever, deodorant, coffee	national random sample	?	ø r = .43**
Bass, Pessemier, & Lehman (1972)	attitude (object)	behaviour (observed, lab setting, c.m.)	adequacy-importance	?	soft drinks	students, secretaries	264	37% correct predictions
Brislin & Olmstead (1973)	attitude (behaviour), normative component	behaviour (observed, lab setting, c.m.)	semantic differential	?	detergents	housewives	132	r = .39
Cowling (1973)	attitude (behaviour), normative component	behavioural intention	Fishbein	?	soft drinks, diet foods, luxury good	?	?	ø r = .30
Kraft, Granbois, & Summers (1973)	attitude (object)	behaviour (reported, c.m.)	adequacy-importance	focus group	paper tissue, fruit juice, coffee	housewives	173	66% correct predictions***
Sheth (1973)	attitude (object)	behavioural intention	adequacy-importance	?	foods	housewives	954	ø r = .49
Bonfield (1974)	attitude (object), normative component	a) behavioural intention b) behaviour (diary, s.m.)	semantic differential	focus group, depth interviews	fruit juice	consumer panel	261	a) ø r = .69 b) ø r = .37
Ginter (1974)	attitude (object)	behaviour (observed, lab setting, c.m.)	adequacy-importance	focus group	household cleaner, desinfection spray	housewives	453	36% correct predictions
Sheth (1974)	attitude (object)	behaviour (diary, s.m.)	adequacy	depth interview	foods	housewives	954	ø r = .18

Study	Independent variable	Dependent variable	Attitude model	Item selection	Attitude objects	Subjects	N	Results*
Mazis, Ahtola, & Klippel (1975)	attitude (object)	a) behavioural intention b) behaviour (reported, c.m.)	i) adequacy-importance ii) Fishbein iii) Rosenberg	free association list selection	deodorant, shampoo, restaurant	students	26-44	a) i) r = .53 a) ii) r = .44 a) iii) r = .48 b) i) r = .49 b) ii) r = .43 b) iii) r = .46
Raju, Bhagat, & Sheth (1975)	i) attitude (object) ii) attitude (behaviour)	behavioural intention	i) Rosenberg ii) Fishbein	?	car	students, housewives	243	i) r = .39 ii) r = .47
Wilson, Mathews, & Harvey (1975)	attitude (object), normative component	behavioural intention	semantic differential	?	toothpaste	housewives	162	ø r = .67
Bearden & Woodside (1977)	attitude (behaviour), normative component	behavioural intention	semantic differential	focus group, depth interviews	soft drinks	consumer panel	172, 184	ø r = .48
Ryan (1978)	attitude (behaviour), normative component	behavioural intention	Fishbein	free association	toothpaste	students	97	ø r = .47
Möller (1979)	attitude (object), normative component	behavioural intention	vector model	free association	toothpaste, tv set	?	411	ø r = .69
Smith & Swinyard (1983)	attitude (object)	a) behavioural intention b) behaviour (observed, lab setting, c.m.)	Fishbein + "confidence"	?	snack	students	79	a) ø r = .42 b) ø r = .36
Gresham, Bush, & Davis (1984)	attitude (object)	behavioural intention	Fishbein	free association	cereal, soap, detergents, soft drinks	students	48	ø r = .34

226

Study	Independent variable	Depentent variable	Attitude model	Item selection	Attitude objects	Subjects	N	Results*
Schnedlitz (1985)	attitude (behaviour), normative component	behavioural intention	Fishbein	depth interview	lemonade, skirts	students	120	$\varnothing$ r = .62

* average multiple correlation coefficient, unless otherwise noted
** aggregate data
*** "multiple act measure"
s.m. = separate measurement of behaviour
c.m. = concurrent measurement of behaviour

References

Ajzen, I., & Fishbein, M. (1977). Attitude-behavior relations: A theoretical analysis of empirical research. *Psychological Bulletin, 84*, 888-918.

Ajzen, I., & Fishbein, M. (1980). *Understanding attitudes and predicting social behavior*. Englewood Cliffs, NJ: Prentice-Hall.

Anderson, N.H. (1971). Integration theory and attitude change. *Psychological Review, 78*, 171-204.

Assael, H., & Day, G. S. (1969). Attitudes and awareness as predictors of market share. *Journal of Advertising Research, 8*(4), 3-10.

Bagozzi, R.P. (1984). Expectancy-value attitude models: An analysis of critical measurement issues. *International Journal of Research in Marketing, 1*, 295-310.

Bass, F.M., Pessemier, E.A., & Lehman, D.R. (1972). An experimental study of relationships between attitudes, brand preferences, and choice. *Behavioral Science, 17*, 532-541.

Bearden, W.O., & Woodside, A.G. (1977). Testing variations of Fishbein's behavioral intention model within a consumer behavior context. *Journal of Applied Psychology, 62*, 352-357.

Benninghaus, H. (1976). *Ergebnisse und Perspektiven der Einstellung-Verhaltens-Forschung*. Meisenheim: Hain.

Bonfield, E.H. (1974). Attitude, social influence, personal means, and intention interactions as related to brand purchase behavior. *Journal of Marketing Research, 11*, 379-389.

Brislin, R.W., & Olmstead, K.H. (1973). Examination of two models designed to predict behavior from attitude and other verbal measures. In: *Proceedings, 81st Annual Convention, American Psychological Association*, pp. 259-260. Washington, DC: American Psychological Association.

Chang, T.M. (1986). Semantic memories: Facts and models. *Psychological Bulletin, 99*, 199-220.

Cowling, A.B. (1973). Determining and influencing consumer purchase decisions. *European Research, 1*, 26-31.

Fishbein, M., & Ajzen, I. (1975). *Belief, attitude, intention and behavior*. Reading, MA: Addison-Wesley.

Geise, W. (1984). *Einstellung und Marktverhalten*. Frankfurt: Deutsch.

Ginter, J.L. (1974). An experimental investigation of attitude change and choice of a new brand. *Journal of Marketing Research, 11*, 30-40.

Gresham, L.G., Bush, A.J., & Davis, R.A. (1984). Measures of brand attitude: Are cognitive structure approaches really needed? *Journal of Business Research, 12*, 353-361.

Grunert, K.G. (1982). *Informationsverarbeitungsprozesse bei der Kaufentscheidung: Ein gedächtnispsychologischer Ansatz.* Frankfurt: Lang.

Grunert, K.G. (1986). Cognitive determinants of attribute information usage. *Journal of Economic Psychology, 7*, 95-124.

Grunert, K.G. (1988). *A method to estimate cognitive structure from qualitative data in market research.* Aarhus: The Aarhus School of Business, Department of Marketing. Working Paper No. 12.

Grunert, K.G., & Bader, M. (1986). Die Weiterverarbeitung qualitativer Daten durch computerunterstützte Inhaltsanalyse. *Marketing - ZFP, 4*, 238-247.

Kraft, F.B., Granbois, D.H., & Summers, J.O. (1973). Brand evaluation and brand choice: A longitudinal study. *Journal of Marketing Research, 10*, 235-241.

Lutz, R.J. (1981). *Lessons learned from a decade of multi-attribute attitude research in marketing.* Los Angeles: University of California, Center for Marketing Studies. Working paper.

Mazis, M.B., Ahtola, O.T., & Klippel, R.E. (1975). A comparison of four multi-attribute models in the prediction of consumer attitudes. *Journal of Consumer Research, 2*, 38-52.

Meinefeld, W. (1977). *Einstellung und soziales Handeln.* Reinbek: Rowohlt.

Möller, K. (1979). Attitudinal and social influences on color television and toothpaste buying intentions. In: *Proceedings of the 8th Annual Meeting of the European Academy of Advanced Research in Marketing*, pp. B69-B93. Groningen: EAARM.

Orth, B. (1985). Bedeutsamkeitsanalysen bilinearer Einstellungsmodelle. *Zeitschrift für Sozialpsychologie, 16*, 101-115.

Raju, P.S., Bhagat, R.S., & Sheth, J.N. (1975). Predictive validation and cross-validation of the Fishbein, Rosenberg, and Sheth models of attitudes. In: M.J. Schlinger (Ed.), *Advances in consumer research*, Vol. 2, pp. 405-415. Chicago: Association for Consumer Research.

Rosenberg, M.J. (1956). Cognitive structure and attitudinal affect. *Journal of Abnormal and Social Psychology, 53*, 367-372.

Ryan, M.J. (1978). An examination of an alternative form of the behavioral intention model's normative component. In: H.K. Hunt (Ed.), *Advances in consumer research*, Vol. 5, pp. 283-289. Chicago: Association for Consumer Research.

Schnedlitz, P. (1985). *Einstellungen und soziale Beeinflussung als Bedingungen von Kaufabsichten*. Frankfurt: Peter Lang.

Sheth, J.N. (1973). Brand profiles from beliefs and importances. *Journal of Advertising Research, 13*(1), 37-42.

Sheth, J.N. (1974). An investigation of relationships among evaluative beliefs, affect, behavioral intention, and behavior. In: J.H. Farley (Ed.), *Consumer behavior: Theory and application*, pp. 89-114. Boston: Houghton-Mifflin.

Silberer, G. (1981). Einstellungen und Werthaltungen. In: M. Irle (Ed.), *Marktpsychologie als Sozialwissenschaft*, pp. 533-625. Göttingen: Hogrefe.

Smith, R.E., & Swinyard, W.R. (1983). Attitude-behavior consistency: The impact of product trial versus advertising. *Journal of Marketing Research, 20*, 257-267.

Wicker, A.W. (1969). Attitudes versus actions: The relationship of verbal and overt responses to attitude objects. *Journal of Social Issues, 25*(4), 41-78.

Wilkie, W.L., & Pessemier, E.A. (1973). Issues in marketing's use of multi-attribute attitude models. *Journal of Marketing Research, 10*, 428-441.

Wilson, D.T., Mathews, H.L., & Harvey, J.W. (1975). An empirical test of the Fishbein behavioral intention model. *Journal of Consumer Research, 1*, 39-48.

Joanna Sokołowska

Application of the Valence–Instrumentality–Expectancy and Multiattribute Utility Models in the Prediction of Worker Effort

Abstract

According to the cognitive approach to motivation and decision, the choice among alternative actions is in fact the choice among outcomes that differ in their value and their probability. These outcomes can either be goals in themselves or the means of achieving goals (i.e., instrumental values). Clear examples of choices associated with the first type of outcome are moral decisions, while examples of choices connected with the second type of outcome are economic decisions.

The first study reported in the present paper was designed in order to compare two models for predicting choices among alternative efforts in a work setting. The second study was designed in order to investigate possible reasons for the lack of predictive success of this whole class of models. This study too was carried out in an industrial setting.

Author's address: Joanna Sokołowska, Department of Psychology, Polish Academy of Sciences, Pl. Malachowskiego 1, 00-063 Warsaw, Poland.

Evaluation of Multiattribute Outcomes of Work

One of the central issues of work organization is how to obtain and maintain a high level of performance from the personnel. One of the most important factors determining performance is motivation. A number of approaches to work motivation have been used. Expectancy theory is the most widely accepted approach and the one that has the greatest empirical support (Mitchell, 1979) .

Vroom (1964) hypothesized that the choice of a given action (connected with a certain amount of effort) is determined by the multiple combination of the valence of first-level outcomes, the instrumentality of these outcomes for the attainment of second-level outcomes, and the individual expectancy (belief concerning the probability) that the action will be followed by the outcome of interest. Thus:

$$(1.1) \qquad V_j \quad = \sum_{k=1}^{n} (V_k \times I_{jk})$$

$$(1.2) \qquad F(A_i) \quad = \sum_{j=1}^{n} (E_{ij} \times V_j)$$

where:

V_j = the valence of the first level outcome j,
V_k = the valence of the second level outcome k, i.e., the valence of consequence k of outcome j,
I_{jk} = the perceived instrumentality of outcome j for consequence k,
E_{ij} = the expectancy that a given action i will lead to outcome j,
$F(A_i)$ = the force of motivation for a given action i.

According to Vroom's model, the valence (utility) of first level outcomes varies proportionally with its instrumentality in relation to second level outcomes (e.g., rewards, punishments, and other consequences possibly connected with the first-level outcome) which are regarded as valuable or painful. Two kinds of expectancies are included in the above model – the expectancy that a given action will lead to a given outcome (i.e., the subjective probability that a given effort will lead to a given first-level outcome), and the expectancy that the contingency between a first-level outcome and its consequences exists. Vroom (1964) described the former as the degree to which a person believes that a great effort on his/her part will lead to high performance. This type of expectancy has been treated as a subjective probability. The term instrumentality has been applied to the link between a first-level outcome and its possible consequences. The link is in fact a network of connections in which a number of consequences are associated with any given outcome; it, too, is subjectively perceived. Vroom described instrumentality as the perceived correlation between first-level outcomes and their possible consequences.

In line with the above considerations, it can be noted that the VIE model is based on the following assumptions:

1. an individual chooses among independent alternatives,
   (a) the holistic valence (utility) of each outcome is evaluated separately and independently,
   (b) the holistic judgments about the utility of the alternatives are compared,

2. no interactions exist between different outcome dimensions (attributes), i.e., consequences of an outcome,

3. an outcome valence (utility) is computed in a compensatory way, i.e., trade-offs between different outcome attributes are made,

4. the choice among alternatives is done on the basis of a comparison of all given alternatives (internal criterion),

5. the choice among alternatives is based on the Subjective Expected Utility (SEU) decision rule.

These general assumptions suggest conceptual similarities between the VIE model and the MAU model used in psychological decision theory. The latter can be written as follows, if using the Valence-Instrumentality-Expectancy theory terms:

$$(2.1) \qquad V_j \qquad = \sum_{k=1}^{n} (V_k \times W_k)$$

$$(2.2) \qquad F(A_i) \quad = \sum_{j=1}^{n} (E_{ij} \times V_j)$$

where:

V_j = the utility of a given outcome j,
V_k = the utility of an outcome j on an attribute k,
W_k = the weight assigned to the attribute k,
E_{ij} = the subjective probability that an outcome j will occur if
            alternative i is selected,
$F(A_i)$ = the force of the tendency to choose alternative i.

According to this model, the utility (valence) of a given outcome j is a function of the sums of the interactions of the utilities of all its attributes and the perceived weights assigned to these attributes. The choice is a product of a given outcome utility and the subjective probability of its occurrence.

These two models include the same concept (valence or utility and expectancy or subjective probability) and the same cognitive rules for gathering information. The only difference is in the meaning of the concept "utility of a given outcome." In the MAU model, the utility of a given outcome is regarded as a sum of products of utility of attributes and their weights. In the VIE model, the utility of a given outcome is a sum of products of utility of attributes and instrumentality of the outcome of interest for the attainment of these attributes. The difference is not only technical in character, it originates from different theoretical frameworks. The weights used in the MAU model are nothing but more precise information about the utility of outcome attributes. These weights are the reflection of an individual's hierarchy of values. On the other hand, Vroom's instrumentality concept is the reflection of an individual's belief concerning the frequency of the simultaneous occurrence of certain values. This suggests that the instrumentality concept is nearer to the probability concept than to the utility one. Some researchers have treated it that way (Dachler & Mobley, 1973; Lawler & Porter, 1967; Nebeker & Mitchell, 1974). Nevertheless, there are at least two reasons to be sceptical about conceiving instrumentality as probability.

234

1. The instrumentality concept originates from social learning theory (Rotter, 1954), and was created in order to describe the generalization of individual and social experiences with regard to cause-effect relations. The probability concept is not useful in such a situation. Its provides us with information about frequency of events, not about causal relations.

2. If we were to interpret instrumentality as probability then it would mean that a conditional probability concept would be included in the VIE model. Research in behavioural decision theory has shown that people do in fact not behave in accordance with the laws of conditional probability.

According to the above models, the utility of a multiattribute outcome is a function of the following factors:

1.   the utility of an outcome's attributes,
2.   the weights assigned to these attributes,
3.   the instrumentality of a given outcome for attainment of these attributes.

It seems that outcomes of interest can be divided into two classes. An outcome can be either the goal in itself or the means whereby such a goal is achieved. Clear examples of the first type of outcome are moral decisions, while examples of the second type of outcome are economic decisions.

Here, it is proposed that the VIE model is more appropriate for describing economic decisions than the MAU model. This was investigated in the context of employees' decisions about work effort.

Study 1: A Comparison of the Predictability of the VIE and MAU Models With Regard to Employee Productivity

Subjects

Two hundred employees of the Warsaw Auto Factory were included in the study – 50 engineers working at the factory's research unit (designers and technologists), and 150 blue-collar workers.

Research Techniques

Measure of Work Motivation

This variable was measured with three batteries of items within one questionnaire. Battery 1 measured two types of expectancies (in line with the Vroom model – see Equations 1.1 and 1.2):

E = the expectancy that one's own effort (here: "a great work effort") will lead to a given outcome (here: a high performance level), i.e., the subjective probability of achieving this performance level.

I = the expectancy that a high performance level will lead to given consequences (material and non-material ones, internal and external ones), i.e., the perceived instrumentality of a high performance level for 16 selected positive and negative work consequences.

Battery 1 consisted of 17 items concerning the above relations. The subjects were asked to rate on a five-point Likert-type scale (always, often, sometimes, seldom, never) the frequency of situations described. The following examples show two:

For the measure of E:

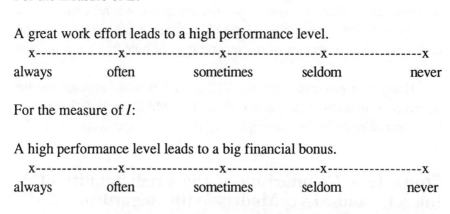

A great work effort leads to a high performance level.

```
x----------------x------------------x------------------x-----------------x
always         often            sometimes           seldom            never
```

For the measure of I:

A high performance level leads to a big financial bonus.

```
x----------------x------------------x------------------x-----------------x
always         often            sometimes           seldom            never
```

Battery 2 measured the utility of 16 selected consequences (e.g., high salary, big financial bonus, promotion, a certificate of appreciation) on a five-point Likert-type scale (from "I would like this very much" to "I wouldn't like this at all"). These 16 consequences (dimensions) of the level of performance could be classified into the four following categories: money, promotion, professional prestige, satisfaction from work.

These four categories were included as items in Battery 3. Subjects were asked to order these value categories from the most important to the least important.

The force of motivation to exert a "great work effort" was computed on the basis of Batteries 1 and 2 jointly, in line with the VIE model (see Equation 1.2), and forms **Indicator 1.**

The tendency to choose a "great work effort" was computed on the basis of answers to the subjective probability items from Battery 1, to the questions about utility dimensions from Battery 2, and information about the dimensions' weights from Battery 3 (see Equation 2.2), thereby forming **Indicator 2.**

Additionally, a joint index, including both the instrumentality concept and the weight, was computed: **Indicator 3**, in line with Equations 3.1 and 3.2:

$$(3.1) \qquad V_j = \sum_{k=1}^{n} (V_k \times W_k \times I_{jk})$$

$$(3.2) \qquad F(A_{ij}) = \sum_{j=1}^{n} (E_{ij} \times V_j)$$

Measure of Actual Performance Level

Data on work performance were collected for all subjects. For the 150 blue-collar workers the **index of achievement level (LP)** was the ratio of the performance to the norm achieved in the given department. Performance level was measured over the three months preceding the investigation.

It was much more difficult to assess the performance level for the 50 designers and technologists since no objective criteria exist to evaluate their effectiveness. Thus in this case evaluations by superiors had to suffice. The superiors rated their subordinates on a four-grade scale (poor, sufficient, good, very good) according to the following aspects: how well assignments were carried out, quality of submitted designs, what correction was needed in designs (none at all, minor details, normal corrections, major changes), and independence in work. Superiors were also asked to rate the different teams and laboratories on the fulfilment of assignments and the quality of results. The mean rating for all aspects was the objective index of performance level for engineers. A comparison of individual and group evaluations was also carried out.

Results

The distributions of the three indicators of the motivation to exert a "great work effort" are given in Figure 1.

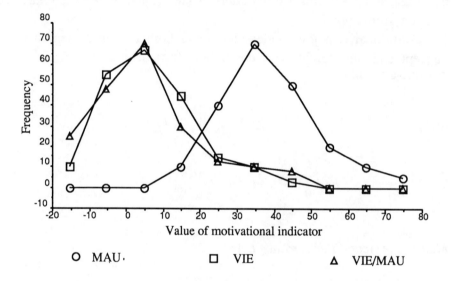

Figure 1: **Distribution of motivational indicators.**

It appears that all three distributions are similar in shape, and that the shape is close to that of the Gauss' curve. Significant correlations (Pearson's r) were found among the three indicators (Indicators 1 and 2: $r = .59$, $t =12.96$, $p < .001$; Indicators 1 and 3: $r = .53$, $t =10.88$, $p< .001$; Indicators 2 and 3: $r = .58$, $t =12.59$, $p< .001$).

The correlation between each of the three above indicators of the motivation to exert a "great work effort" and actual performance level was then checked. No correlation was found.

On the basis of the above data no difference in predictability was found for the three indicators, based on the MAU model and the VIE model, respectively.

238

Discussion

The lack of predictive success of all investigated indicators for actual performance level may have resulted from the following factors:
– false theoretical assumptions in both the MAU and the VIE models,
– inadequate design of the empirical research,
– specific conditions of the investigated environment which negate the models' generality.

As far as the first two factors are concerned, many studies have been done in order to test the predictability of the VIE model. Although this model is widely accepted as a good tool for predicting individual motivation, the empirically obtained correlations between measures of motivation based on the VIE model and other measures of effort are in fact rather low. They have not even exceeded 0.25 (e.g., 0.23 in Mitchell & Nebeker, 1973; 0.18 in the study by Lawler & Porter, 1967; 0.18 in Pritchard & Sanders, 1973). The relationship between the motivation computed by means of the VIE model and the actual performance level of workers has also been studied. Results are ambiguous. Zedeck (1977) found ten studies of this relationship – three of these indicated that the VIE model has a predictive value, the others showed no correlation.

Many authors have suggested that methodological deficiencies are the main reason for such findings. Firstly, cause-effect relations have been investigated in surveys rather than in experiments. Secondly, the measures used have not been precise enough.

The first problem results from the fact that it is hard to carry out a quasi-laboratory experiment in an industrial setting. Lawler and Suttle (1973), while rejecting the traditional questionnaire survey, have suggested a new schema of two-step questionnaire research, which allows inferences about causal relations with the use of a double correlation method. However, the results of some research in which questionnaires and experimental methods were used simultaneously did not differ significantly (e.g., Arvey, 1977; Broedling, 1975; Jorgenson & Dunnette, 1973).

As to the second problem, identified by Pritchard and De Leo (1973), it is clear that the scales used have usually been ordinal or Likert-type. Schmidt (1973) discussed some reasons why Likert-type rating scales, when multiplied together, may produce inconsistent tests of the VIE theory. Mitchell (1974) noticed that the complexity of the theory may have exceeded the measurement methods employed to test the theory. Mitchell and Beach (1979) and Zedeck (1977) have also suggested that many of the measurement difficulties encountered in prior expectancy studies could have been avoided by the use of behavioural decision theory to test the VIE theory.

Many studies of behavioural decision theory have dealt with how individuals process information about multiple attributes in order to arrive at a job choice decision. Most decision theory research on job preferences has assumed compensatory relationships through the use of additive linear mathematical models to represent combination processes (e.g., Feldman & Arnold, 1978; Zedeck, 1977). These studies have generally achieved high predictive value using additive linear models (e.g., Goldberg, 1968; Stahl & Harrel, 1981, 1983). Fischer (1976), however, who was interested in both the predictive capacity of the MAU model and its accuracy in depicting the way decisions actually are made, found that the simple linear models may produce good statistical predictions of preferences for multiattribute outcomes but that these models cannot represent the judgment processes of all individuals.

Because no difference was found in the predictive capacity of the two models in this study, it seems that besides methodological considerations set out above, some situational factors might have affected the general relationship posited by the VIE model. Two such factors, specific to the current Polish situation could be the following:

– shortages of goods on the official market and extremely high prices for the same goods on the free or black market result in low perceived utility of money, especially in comparison with other material benefits,

– specific criteria of promotion result in low perceived instrumentality of actual performance level for reinforcements.

The second factor was partly supported in this study. Empirical results showed clearly that most of the subjects did not perceive any relationship between performance level and reinforcements. The data are found in Table 1.

In line with Graen (1969) it can be stated that for the VIE model to be of predictive value, a reciprocating climate is required. On the basis of Table 1, one must conclude that this condition was not fulfilled.

Table 1: The Percentage of Subjects Who Believed That an Increase in Performance Level Led to:

Type of rewards	Increase in rewards %	No change %	Decrease in rewards %
Financial rewards	11. 5	83. 5	5. 0
Promotion	14. 5	78. 0	7. 5
Professional prestige	14. 5	77. 5	8. 0
Work satisfaction	36. 0	59. 0	5. 0

The first factor which could weaken the predictive value of the VIE model was investigated in the second study carried out in an industrial setting. Study 2 was designed in order to get information about the perceived utility of money and other reinforcements among blue-collar workers and low and medium level managers.

Study 2: Perceived Utility of Rewards and Punishments Used in Polish Industry

Subjects

Interviews were made with 352 blue-collar workers and low and medium level managers working at two factories in Warsaw (Kasprzak Radio Plant and Ursus Mechanical Plant).

Research Techniques

The first step was to construct a list of reinforcements used in Polish industry. The list was constructed on the basis of a pilot study and amended with items available in the literature. The result was a list of 131 items consisting of reinforcements which can be classified as follows:
- task characteristics
- physical working conditions
- human relations
- professional prestige
- promotion

– material reinforcement (monetary rewards and punishments, salaries, and other goods, e.g., a flat provided by the employer, a coupon to purchase a car, or some other attractive article, being awarded a holiday paid for by the employer, etc.)

– compliments and reprimands.

The subjects were asked to rate the attractiveness of these reinforcements on a nine-point Likert-type scale (from "I would like this very much" to "I wouldn't like this at all").

Each survey delving into values and social relations should include a check of the social desirability of its questions. Thus all items were investigated from this point of view by means of Edwards' Social Desirability Scale (Edwards, 1957 a, b).

Results

Ten items out of 131 having high social desirability loadings were excluded from further analysis.

The rewards allotted the highest positive utility are presented in Table 2 and the punishments allotted the highest negative utility in Table 3.

Table 2: Rewards With the Highest Ranks of Positive Utility

Types of rewards	Median		Mean	
	value	rank	value	rank
Getting a flat from the employer	8.53	1		
Help in getting a cooperative flat	8.42	2		
Good organization of production	8.40	3	8.25	1
Being liked by workers	8.39	4	8.10	3
Work with popular superiors	8.31	5.5	8.20	2
Attractive holidays	8.31	5.5		
Good physical condition of work	8.25	7	7.95	8.5
Doing a so-called good job	8.20	8	8.02	6
Freedom in the way of doing job	8.18	10	8.09	4
Annual financial rewards	8.19	9	8.04	5
Higher bonus			7.97	7
Team-work with an expert boss			7.95	8.5
Independence in completing difficult task			7.94	10

From Table 2 it can be seen that the assistance of the employer in getting access to a flat at the official price or to live in a company-owned flat were perceived as the most attractive rewards by at least half of the subjects. Other highly estimated rewards were well organized production in the enterprise and good human relations. As was expected, lower ranks were assigned to monetary rewards. Disciplinary dismissal from work, a reprimand recorded in the personal file, and other dismissal from work had the highest ranks among punishments (Table 3). Monetary punishments, similarly to monetary rewards, ranked lower.

Table 3: Punishments With the Highest Ranks of Negative Utility

Types of punishments	Median		Mean	
	value	rank	value	rank
Disciplinary dismissal from work	1.14	1	1.45	1
Reprimand recorded in the personal file	1.26	2	1.74	2
Other dismissal from work	1.30	3	1.83	3
Reprimand by the boss in the presence of the management of the plant	1.49	4	2.13	7
Poor physical condition of work	1.53	5	1.93	4
Loss of bonus	1.62	6	2.01	6
Plant produces junk	1.66	7	2.00	5
Boss neglects the workers' opinion	1.77	8	2.33	11
Reprimand in the presence of subordinates	1.81	9	2.25	8
Slighted by fellow workers	1.83	10	2.26	9
Passed over for a raise	1.85	11	2.29	10
Poor organization of work	1.98	12	2.36	12
Reprimand in the presence of fellow workers	1.88	13	2.41	13
Demotion	2.03	14	2.41	14
Reduction of bonus	2.08	15	2.49	16
Not liked by the boss	2.09	16	2.47	15

The results support the hypothesis that relatively low utility is assigned to monetary rewards under the condition of market good shortages.

References

Arvey, R.D. (1972). Task performance as a function of perceived effort-performance and performance-reward contingencies. *Organizational Behavior and Human Performance, 8,* 423-433.

Broedling, L.A. (1975). Relationship of internal-external control to work motivation and performance in an expectancy model. *Journal of Applied Psychology, 60*, 65-70.

Dachler, H.P., & Mobley, W.H. (1973). Construct validation of an instrumentality-expectancy-task-goal model of work motivation: Some theoretical boundary conditions. *Journal of Applied Psychology Monograph, 58*, 397-418.

Edwards, A.L. (1957a). Social desirability and probability of endorsement of items in the interpersonal check list. *Journal of Abnormal Psychology, 55*, 394-396.

Edwards, A.L. (1957b). *The social desirability variable in personality assessment and research.* New York: Dryden Press.

Feldman, D.C., & Arnold, W.J. (1978). Position choice: Comparing the importance of organizational and job factors. *Journal of Applied Psychology, 63*, 706-710.

Fischer, E.W. (1976). Multidimensional utility models for risky and riskless choice. *Organizational Behavior and Human Performance, 17*, 127-146.

Goldberg, L.B. (1968). Simple models or simple processes? *American Psychologist, 23*, 483-496.

Graen, G. (1969). Instrumentality theory of work motivation: Some experimental results and suggested modifications. *Journal of Applied Psychology Monograph, 53*, 2, Part 2.

Jorgenson, D.O., & Dunnette, M.D. (1973). Effects of the manipulation of a performance-reward contingency on behavior in a simulated work setting. *Journal of Applied Psychology, 57*, 271-280.

Lawler, E.E., & Porter, L.W. (1967). Antecedent attitudes of effective managerial performance. *Organizational Behavior and Human Performance, 2*, 122-142.

Lawler, E.E., & Suttle, J.L. (1973). Expectancy theory and job behavior. *Organizational Behavior and Human Performance, 19*, 482-503.

Mitchell, T.R. (1974). Expectancy models of job satisfaction, occupational preference, and effort: A theoretical, methodological, and empirical appraisal. *Psychological Bulletin, 81*, 1053-1077.

Mitchell, T.R. (1979). Organizational behavior. *Annual Review of Psychology, 30*, 243-282.

Mitchell, T.R., & Beach, L.R. (1979). A review of occupational preferences and choice research using expectancy theory and decision theory. *Journal of Occupational Psychology, 49*, 231-248.

Mitchell, T.R., & Nebeker, D.M. (1973). Expectancy theory predictions of academic effort and performance. *Journal of Applied Psychology, 57*, 61-67.

Nebeker, D.M., & Mitchell, T.R. (1974). Leader behavior: An expectancy theory approach. *Organizational Behavior and Human Performance, 11*, 355-367.

Pritchard, R.D., & De Leo, P.J. (1973). Experimental test of the valence-instrumentality relationship in job performance. *Journal of Applied Psychology, 57*, 264-270.

Pritchard, R.D., & Sanders, M.B. (1973). The influence of valence, instrumentality, and expectancy on effort and performance. *Journal of Applied Psychology, 57*, 55-60.

Rotter, J. B. (1954). *Social learning and clinical psychology*. New York: Prentice-Hall.

Schmidt, F.L. (1973). Implications of measurement problems for expectancy theory research. *Organizational Behavior and Human Performance, 10*, 243-251.

Stahl, M.J., & Harrel, A.J. (1981). Modeling effort decision with behavioral decision theory: Toward an individual differences model of expectancy theory. *Organizational Behavior and Human Performance, 27*, 303-325.

Stahl, M.J., & Harrel, A.M. (1983). Using decisions modeling to measure second level valences in expectancy theory. *Organizational Behavior and Human Performance, 32*, 23-34.

Vroom, V.H. (1964). *Work and motivation*. New York: Wiley.

Zedeck, S. (1977). An information processing model and approach to the study of motivation. *Organizational Behavior and Human Performance, 18*, 47-77.

245

Hector A. Munera

Prediction of Preference Reversals by the Linearized Moments Model

Abstract

Both in experimental and in theoretical contexts, it is often the case that two or more decision problems are at first sight equivalent to the decision analyst. It is noted that in the case of "preference reversals" the choice problems may not be equivalent. A careful description of the problem in terms of decision trees is suggested.

The empirical observations in preference reversal experiments may be predicted by the linearized moments model (LMM). The LMM contains transitive preferences, but not the substitution principle of expected utility theory. This places the LMM and the EURDP model (expected utility with rank dependent probability) in the same class. Some advantages of the LMM are noted.

Author's address: Hector A. Munera, Quantum Mechanical Institute, A.A. 52976, Bogota D.E., Colombia (South America).

247

Introduction

It is a well known fact from experimental psychology that many decision-makers (DMs) confronting a choice between lotteries *A* and *B*, may prefer *A* to *B* in a direct choice, but may ask more for *B* than for *A* in a selling situation (S-bids) or may pay more for *B* than for *A* in a buying situation (B-bids). See, for instance, Lichtenstein and Slovic (1971), Lindman (1971), and Slovic and Lichtenstein (1983).

If we accept the premise that DMs try to be self-consistent we have to conclude that – excepting experimental mistakes – there is no such thing as a "preference reversal." There are at least two simple explanations for the apparent inconsistency in the experimentally observed choices:

1. The choice situations are not exactly alike. In some ways this is the approach of regret theory (e.g., Loomes & Sugden, 1983) where an ulterior feeling of regret or joy is entered to explain the difference between the (assumed by the decision analyst) similar choice situations. More recently, in an interesting paper, Karni and Safra (1987) (K-S henceforth) show that in the typical experimental set-up to test preference reversals the choice situations are not the same, and, moreover, that the expected utility model cannot be consistent with observation.

2. The expected utility model (EUM) – whose predictions are contradicted by the observed choices – is not applicable. In a weak form, this is the approach of some followers of the orthodoxy that have proposed ad-hoc variations to the basic EUM; examples are Fishburn's (1985) intransitive preferences and K-S's "rank dependent probabilities."

It is the long-standing view of this author (Munera, 1978) that many choice situations deemed to be equivalent are not. Indeed, by simply drawing the decision trees the difference may be obvious. This assertion is substantiated in the next section for the four choice problems described by Lichtenstein and Slovic (1971), namely: (a) direct choice, (b) S-bids, (c) B-bids, (d) compound lotteries. After that, the so-called preference reversal phenomenon is defined.

In the third section, a summary description is given of the linearized moments model LMM (see, for instance, Munera, 1988). In the fourth section predictions of the LMM are obtained for the three experiments of Lichtenstein and Slovic (1971) (L-S henceforth). It is found that all behavioural patterns actually observed are predicted, including "unpredicted preference reversals" that according to L-S are "hard to rationalize under any theory of decision making" (p. 48). A closing section summarizes the main results and points out differences and similarities with the model of expected utility with rank dependent probabilities (EURDP).

Definition of the Problem

The Four "Equivalent" Choice Situations

In their early paper L-S described four choice situations that – in the context of the EUM – were assumed to be behaviourally equivalent (see Note 1). They were: (a) a direct choice between two lotteries; (b) selling the right to enter a lottery (S-bid); (c) buying the right to enter a lottery (B-bid); (d) giving the certainty equivalent for a (rather complex) compound lottery.

In the following, each of these four cases is analyzed. It should be noted that the initial individual state of wealth is emphasized, a factor that has been unjustly neglected in many analyses. Such a factor may be at the root of some problems, such as the "framing effect" (Slovic & Lichtenstein, 1983; Tversky & Kahneman, 1981).

Direct Choice

An individual decision maker (DM) with initial state of wealth c is offered the possibility of entering either one of two **free** lotteries $A = (w,x; p,1-p)$ or $B = (y,z; q,1-q)$ where w,y are gains and x,z are losses or neutral outcomes; typically, $p > q$ and $y > w$. In the L-S paper, prospect A is the "p-lottery" and prospect B is the "$-lottery." The decision tree representing this problem has three branches as shown in Figure 1.

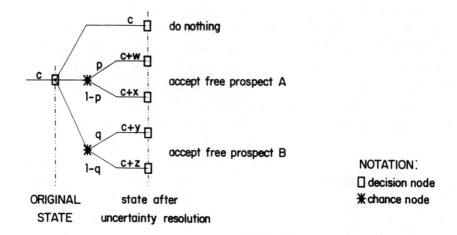

Figure 1: Direct choice between prospects A and B.

S-Bids

The initial state of wealth of the DM is an amount c **plus** the right to enter a lottery A. If the selling price s for A is $s = a$, then the initial state is behaviourally equivalent to $c + a$. The decision tree for this problem has two branches only. As shown in Figure 2a the leaves of the tree are the initial state $(c + a)$ in one branch, and $(c + w)$ and $(c + x)$ in the other one; the latter can algebraically be rewritten as $[(c + a) + (w - a)]$ and $[(c + a) + (x - a)]$. This means that – relative to the initial state $(c + a)$ – the outcomes of the lottery are $w - a$ and $x - a$ which are smaller than w and x as intended by the designer of the experiment. The decision tree for prospect B is similar.

Clearly, a set of additional assumptions is required to claim that two separate trees (one for A, another for B) with different initial wealths $[(c + a)$ and $(c + b)]$ are equivalent to the direct choice of Figure 1.

B-Bids

The initial state of wealth is c; let the price for a ticket t to play prospect A be $t = a$. The corresponding decision tree has two branches as shown in

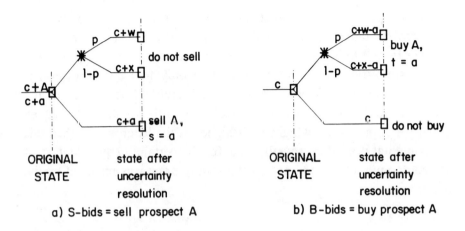

a) S-bids = sell prospect A

b) B-bids = buy prospect A

Figure 2a + b: Selling and buying prospects.

Figure 2b. Note that the leaves of the tree are the initial state c and the **net** outcomes relative to the initial state c: $c + (w - a)$ and $c + (x - a)$. Comparing parts (a) and (b) of Figure 2 it appears that both trees have the same structure: same net outcomes $w - a$ and $x - a$ relative to different initial states $c + a$ and c (also, it is quite possible that the numerical values of a for s and t may be different). The decision tree for prospect B is similar.

Compound Lottery

More often than not, the previous three decision problems are posed in an imaginary context. To avoid criticisms towards such experimental setup, L-S and other psychologists (see references in L-S and K-S) have devised a procedure whereby some of the choices are actually played for money (see Experiment III in L-S and the K-S paper for details). Briefly, the experiment runs as follows.

The initial state of wealth of the DM is c **plus** the right to enter a lottery A. The DM is asked by the decision analyst for what amount $s = a$ the DM would trade the right to play the lottery. Up to now the experiment is a simple S-bid. However, at this point the experimenter announces that he will not pay a but rather will either pay a **random** counteroffer $d > a$ or will force the DM to play the lottery if $d < a$, the decision depending upon a and the outcome of a roulette (for every bid a counteroffer table was prepared assigning different values d to each number from 1 to 36).

A simplified decision tree (including only four counteroffers) is shown in Figure 3. Depending upon the individual perception of the (unknown to the DM) counteroffers table, the initial wealth state may be either $c + A$ or $c + A^*$, whichever is higher. If the latter is true, then this experimental procedure actually asks for the certainty equivalent s^* of the compound lottery and not for the selling price s as intended by the decision analyst.

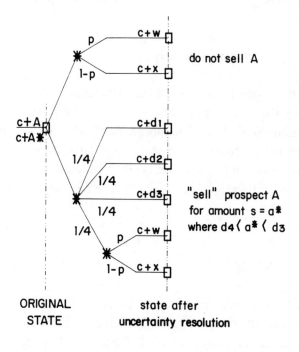

Figure 3: Compound S-bids = "sell" prospect A.

The Preference Reversal Phenomenon

Three experiments were designed and carried out by L-S in order to test the existence and persistency of preference reversals.

Experiment I: Direct Choice vs. S-Bids

Six pairs of lotteries A and B were used as summarized in Table 1. The first part of the experiment asked whether A was preferred to B, or conversely (this is the choice problem in Figure 1). The second part obtained certainty equivalents a and b for lotteries A and B in S-bid situations; each case is an application of Figure 2a.

It is this author's contention that these three decision problems are different because the corresponding trees differ. Hence, all four choice patterns shown in Table 2 are potentially observable in a given experiment, as indeed reported by L-S. However, according to the EUM the only allowed patterns are those showing no reversals (I and IV).

Table 1: Prospects Used in the Three Experiments of L-S Study (1971)

Exp.	Pair	Prospect A				Prospect B			
		w	x	p	E(A)	y	z	q	E(B)
I	1	4.00	−1.00	0.99	3.95	16.00	−2.00	0.33	3.94
	2	2.50	−0.75	0.95	2.34	8.50	−1.50	0.40	2.50
	3	3.00	−2.00	0.95	2.75	6.50	−1.00	0.50	2.75
	4	2.00	−2.00	0.90	1.60	5.25	−1.50	0.50	1.88
	5	2.00	−1.00	0.80	1.40	9.00	−0.50	0.20	1.40
	6	4.00	−0.50	0.80	3.10	40.00	−1.00	0.10	3.10
II	1	1.00	−0.20	10/12	0.80	9.00	−2.00	3/12	0.75
	2	1.10	−0.10	9/12	0.80	9.20	−2.00	3/12	0.80
III	1	4.00	−1.00	35/36	3.86	16.00	−1.50	11/36	3.85
	2	2.50	−0.50	34/36	2.33	8.50	−1.50	14/36	2.39
	3	3.00	−2.00	34/36	2.72	6.50	−1.00	18/36	2.75
	4	2.00	−2.00	33/36	1.67	5.00	−1.50	18/36	1.75
	5	2.00	−1.00	29/36	1.42	9.00	−0.50	7/36	1.35
	6	4.00	−0.50	32/36	3.50	40.00	−1.00	4/36	3.56

The thrust of the L-S experiment was to show that there existed choices depicting preference reversals, thus opposing the EUM. Their experiment was designed to observe pattern II; therefore, they were somewhat surprised when pattern III was observed as well.

Table 2: Patterns of Choice in L-S Experiments

Pattern	Direct choice	S-bid	Remarks
I	*A* preferred to *B*	*a > b*	No preference reversal
II	*A* preferred to *B*	*b > a*	"Conditional predicted reversal"
III	*B* preferred to *A*	*a > b*	"Conditional unpredicted reversal"
IV	*B* preferred to *A*	*b > a*	No preference reversal

Although the differing decision trees imply that all four patterns are possible, they do not provide a guide as to whether there exists a theory predicting such patterns, or as to how a given individual would choose in a given situation. Later in this paper it is shown that the linearized moments model (LMM) predicts the existence of consistent individuals depicting the four behavioural patterns of Table 2, and allows prediction of how a given individual would choose in every case. Hence, experimental observations like those of L-S may be interpreted as a test of the choice theory rather than a test of the individual subject. Therefore, in Popper's (1959) sense, the L-S results falsify the EUM, but corroborate the LMM.

Experiment II: Direct Choice vs. B-Bids

This experiment is entirely similar to the previous case, substituting B-bids for the S-bids. L-S used 49 lottery pairs, but in their paper there are only two numerical examples, included in Table 1. Since the decision trees of Figures 1 and 2b are different, the same four patterns of choice summarized in Table 2 are potentially observable, as confirmed by the experiment. L-S report that the proportion of unpredicted reversals was higher than in Experiment I.

Experiment III: Direct Choice vs. Compound Lottery

The first part of the experiment was a direct choice between *A* and *B* as in Figure 1. The second part comprised two separate applications of Figure 3: one for *A*, another for *B*. Again, the four patterns of choice of Table 2 are possible and were observed in the six lottery pairs used by L-S (see Table 1).

The compound lottery is a complex problem, whose potential outcomes depend upon the bid a^* or b^*; moreover, their variation is not smooth but presents 36 discontinuities (one at each counteroffer). This assertion may be more easily grasped by considering the related (but different) problem illustrated in Figure 4: the direct choice between *A* and A^*.

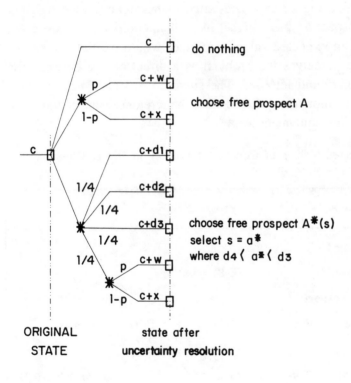

Figure 4: Direct choice between prosepects A and A*(s).

For the sake of the illustration we give a **simplified** numerical example assuming that there were only four counteroffers (each with probability 0.25) located at

$$(1) \qquad d_1 = w - (w - x)/8$$

$$d_2 = w - 3(w - x)/8$$

$$d_3 = w - 5(w - x)/8$$

$$d_4 = w - 7(w - x)/8$$

and similarly for lottery B^*. For the lottery pair III-1 in Table 1, the expected values of A^* and B^* as function of the bid are shown in Table 3. For the particular counteroffers of Equation 1, it is seen that simple prospect A has a higher expected value than simple prospect B, but compound prospect B^* has a higher mean than compound prospect A^*. That is, even an expected-value-maximizer would exhibit preference reversals if he perceives the problem as a direct choice between the simple and compound lotteries. The situation in Experiment III (see Figure 3) is even more complicated since the reference state contains the unknown certainty equivalent for A^*.

Table 3: **Expected Values of Compound Lottery in Direct Choice. Example III-1 in L-S (1971)**

Prospect A		Prospect B		
Simple prospect				
E(A) = 3.8611		E(B) = 3.8472		
Compound prospect				
Bid range	E(A)	Bid range	E(B)	Remarks
−1.00 to −0.375	1.50	−1.50 to 0.6875	7.25	
−0.375 to 0.875	2.56	0.6875 to 5.0625	8.04	Optimum bid for B
0.875 to 2.125	3.31	5.0625 to 9.4375	7.74	
2.125 to 3.375	3.74	9.4375 to 13.8125	6.34	
3.375 to 4.00	3.86	13.8125 to 16.00	3.85	Optimum bid for A

As a conclusion, given that in a direct comparison A and A^* are different, it is hard to argue that Experiments I and III may be equivalent. This view was also recently expressed by Karni and Safra (1987).

Moreover, the design of Experiment III may easily lead to a game theoretical condition. Since the counteroffer table is unknown to the DM, his decision would depend on his particular guess as to the values contained in the table. The DM might select strategic responses s^{**}, trying to outguess the experimenter in order to optimize his revenue from the compound lottery.

The Linearized Moments Model (LMM)

As an alternative to the EUM, the present author has proposed (Munera, 1978, 1985a, 1986) a linearized moments model (LMM) that contains both the EUM and Kahneman and Tversky's (1979) prospect theory as particular cases, that solves the paradoxes addressed to the EUM, and that does not contain the controversial axiom of substitutibility fundamental to EUM. Moreover, the LMM may be expressed in terms of axioms (Munera, 1985b) and is completely compatible with the experimental evidence, in particular with observations violating EUM (Munera, 1988), including preference reversals (this study).

The LMM assumes the existence of an **index of preference** $h(z)$ mapping **sure states** $z \ \varepsilon\{Z\}$ onto the real line such that if state a is preferred to state b, then $h(a) > h(b)$, and conversely. Index $h(.)$ is a **deterministic** or "riskless" construct similar to value functions (see Keeney & Raiffa, 1976, Chapter 3); $h(.)$ encodes the strength of preference and does not have any risk content whatsoever. Hence, in general, $h(.)$ is not equivalent to the utility function $u(.)$ of the EUM (e.g., v. Neumann & Morgenstern, 1944).

Consider now a probability distribution P over outcomes X, where "probability" is understood in a **physical** sense (see Note 2): (a) frequentist, if applicable; (b) linked to physical and/or frequentist realities plus "expert judgement" (which must not reflect the assessor's attitudes towards risk/randomness/uncertainty). Assuming that individual decision makers (DMs) are capable of assigning certainty equivalents e $\varepsilon\{Z\}$ behaviourally equivalent to the non-deterministic alternatives $A(X,P)$, we can effectively map the space (X,P) onto the real line; in symbols: $h(e) = H(A)$, where $H(.)$ is a functional. We focus here on discrete alternatives

$$A = (x_1, x_2, \dots, x_n; p_1, p_2, \dots, p_n), \text{ with } p_1 + p_2 + \dots + p_n = 1$$

For monetary gain prospects most DMs may be represented by a simple LMM, namely the "pessimistic" three-moments model (TMM) (Munera, 1988):

$$(2) \qquad H(A) - h(c) = r_1 M_1 - r_2 M_2 + r_3 M_3$$

where the linearized moment of order k is $M_k = [m_k]^{1/k}$ and

$$(3) \qquad m_k = \sum_i p_i [h(x_i+c) - h(c)]^k \text{ for } k = 1, 2, 3$$

is a kth-moment of the preference indices, relative to some reference state c.

The coefficients r_k are the attitude-towards-randomness parameters (ATR-parameters) obtained by fitting Equation 2 to observation (for details see Munera, 1978, 1985a, 1988). All individuals consistent with three logically appealing prescriptive conditions (see Note 3) must have

$$(4) \qquad r_1 + r_2 + r_3 = 1$$

and a pair r_2, r_3 falling in the hatched region of Figures 5 and 6 (Munera, 1978; 1985a; 1988).

The objective input to Equation 2 is formed by the probability density functions (PDFs), or probability mass functions in the case of discrete distributions. The subjective input to Equation 2 is contained in two components:

– The shape of the preference index for monetary gains/losses, $h(z)$. A Taylor series expansion around a reference state c gives:

$$(5) \qquad h(z) = h(c) + (z - c)h'(c) + \dots$$

In the numerical illustrations in this paper we will keep only two terms in Equation 5, which is consistent with the empirical observation that $h(.)$

often is linear (Munera, 1978, 1988), especially for small monetary sums.

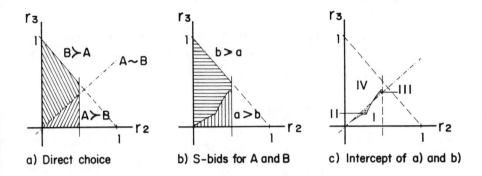

a) Direct choice   b) S-bids for A and B   c) Intercept of a) and b)

Figure 5: Regions of ATR space in experiment I-3 (L-S, 1971. Individuals in II and III exhibit "preference reversals" (see Table 2).

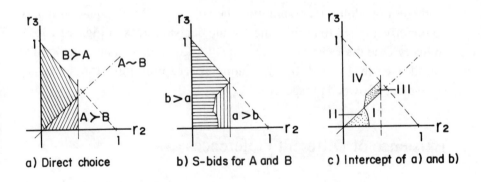

a) Direct choice   b) S-bids for A and B   c) Intercept of a) and b)

Figure 6: Regions of ATR space in experiment III-3 (L-S, 1971). Individuals in II and III exhibit "preference reversals" (see Table 2).

– The values of the ATR-parameters, which reflect the relative importance of different parts of the PDF. A given individual is thus a point in the plane r_2 - r_3. If the point is inside the hatched area of Figure 5a the DM is fully consistent with the three prescriptive conditions of the LMM (Note 3).

Substituting Equation 5 into Equation 2 we find that the left hand side reduces to $H(A) - h(c) = h(c + a) - h(c) = ah'(c)$. Thus the certainty equivalent a for prospect A is

$$(6) \qquad a = r_1 M_1 - r_2 M_2 + r_3 M_3$$

with

$$(7) \qquad m_k = \sum_i p_i [x_i]^k$$

It is remarkable that our final expression Equation 6 is independent of both the local slope $h'(c)$ and the reference state c.

Predictions of the LMM

Without any additional assumption the simple LMM of Equation 6 may be directly applied to each branch of the decision trees in Figures 1 to 3. In every case the reference state c to enter Equations 2 and 3 is the total initial wealth formed by the monetary capital plus the certainty equivalent of owned prospects.

Existence of Different Preferences

We only have to find whether there exist regions inside the shaded area of Figures 5 and 6 depicting different preferences towards the prospects studied by L-S (see Table 1).

Direct Choice

Prospect *A* is equivalent to *B* if *H(A)* = *H(B)*. Substituting Equations 6 and 4 in this equality one gets the linear expression

(8)
$$r_3 = \alpha + \beta r_2$$

which partitions the r_2 - r_3 plane into two regions: *A* preferred to *B* (below) and *B* preferred to *A* (above) as illustrated in Figure 5a. Clearly, there exist individuals depicting either preference. All numerical examples in Table 1 are similar, the position of the line "A equivalent to B" depending upon the moments of prospects *A* and *B*.

S-Bids and B-Bids

The left hand side of Equation 6 for prospect *A* in Figure 2 is $h(c + a)$ - $h(c + a)=0$ (and similarly for prospect *B*). This means that the problem reduces to accepting a "free" prospect *A*, starting from state $c + a$ (or, respectively, $c + b$). From Equation 7 the moments are

(9)
$$m_k = p(w - a)^k + (1 - p)(x - a)^k$$

Equation 6 thus implies that for every value of *a* there exist points (i.e., DMs) located along a straight line, similar to Equation (8), consistent with that particular selling value. The same is true for prospect *B*. Moreover, the point where the line $s=a$ for prospect *A* crosses the line $s=b$ for prospect *B* represents the individual asking *a* for *A* **and** *b* for *B*. By following this procedure it is easy to (numerically) find loci in the r_2 - r_3 plane corresponding to different selling combinations $(s=a, s=b=a+\Delta)$. In particular, the locus $s=a=b$ partitions the space into two regions: individuals asking more for *B* than for *A* (above) and individuals asking more for *A* than for *B* (below), as illustrated in Figure 5b.

It is clear that the regions in parts (a) and (b) of Figure 5 are not the same. However, as seen in part (c) of the same figure the two regions intercept, which implies that the four behavioural patterns of Table 2 are possible in this numerical example. Similar results were obtained for the other five examples corresponding to Experiment I in Table 1.

The treatment for B-bids is exactly alike. The results for the two numerical examples of Table 1 are similar.

Compound Lotteries

Again, the problem is to find the certainty equivalent a^* for the compound prospect A^*, such that $h(c + a^*)=H(A^*)$, with a reference state $(c + a^*)$. As in the previous paragraph, this leads to a left-hand-side equal to 0 in Equation 6. An analysis similar to that of the previous section allows construction of the locus $a^*= b^*$ to represent those individuals asking the same amount for the compound prospects A^* and B^*. The only particularity is that this locus is not continuous due to the discontinuities in the compound lotteries. To the left and above lies the region of $b^* > a^*$, which in all six examples of Table 3 intercepts a large section of the region "A preferred to B," as seen in the example of Figure 6. Thus, as empirically observed by L-S, it is predicted that more individuals will depict preference reversals in Experiment III than in Experiment I.

Predictions for Particular Individuals

For a given individual – defined by the pair $r_2 - r_3$ – it is a simple matter to check in what region of Figures 5 or 6 his point lies for each of the L-S experiments. We carried out the exercise for six typical individuals as follows: A = (0,0); B = (0.05,0.05); C = (0.10,0.05); D = (0.15,0.09); E = (0.30,0.18); F = (0.40,0.32). Their choice patterns for lotteries of Experiments I and III (see Table 1) are summarized in Table 4.

In Figure 1 of their paper, L-S show histograms for the four items of Table 4. Our theoretical results qualitatively reproduce the empirical observations of L-S in the following senses:

(a) Regarding the number of times that prospect A was chosen:

– Depending upon the individual, prospect A may be selected any number of times from 0 to 6, in both Experiments I and III.

– Since the majority of individuals in Experiment I (about 73%) preferred A three or four times, it is suggested that the majority of respondents may be similar to our examples C and D.

Table 4: Individual Patterns of Choice in L-S Experiments[1]

Experiment	Individual						Reversals	
	A	B	C	D	E	F	P	U
I-1	I	IV	I	I	I	III	0	1
1-2	IV	IV	III	III	I	III	0	3
I-3	V	IV	I	I	II	III	1	1
I-4	IV	IV	IV	IV	II	IV	1	0
I-5	V	IV	II	II	II	IV	3	0
I-6	V	IV	I	IV	I	IV	0	0
Number of occurrences of:								
A preferred to B	1	0	4	3	6	0		
$a > b$	1	0	4	3	3	3		
Predicted reversals[2]	0-0	0	1-25	1-33	3-50	0	5	
Unpredicted reversals[3]	0-0	0-0	1-50	1-33	0	3-50		5
Experiment								
III-1	II	IV	II	II	II	IV	4	0
III-2	IV	IV	II	II	II	IV	3	0
III-3	IV	IV	II	II	I	III	2	1
III-4	IV	IV	IV	II	II	III	2	1
III-5	II	II	II	II	II	IV	5	0
III-6	IV	IV	II	II	II	IV	3	0
Number of occurrences of:								
A preferred to B	2	1	5	6	6	0		
$a > b$	0	0	0	0	1	2		
Predicted reversals[2]	2-100	1-100	5-100	6-100	5-83	0	19	
Unpredicted reversals[3]	0-0	0-0	0-0	0	0	2-33		2

[1] See Table 2. Pattern V: *A* indifferent to *B* and $a = b$.
[2] The number after the "-" is the proportion (%) of reversals relative to the number of times that *A* was preferred.
[3] The number after the "-" is the proportion (%) of reversals relative to the number of times that *B* was preferred.

– In Experiment III the proportion in the tails (5/6 and 1/2) increases relative to Experiment I. In our example, for individual A the lower tail increases, but the higher one increases for individuals C/D.
(b) Regarding preference reversals:

– Our results are consistent with L-S findings in Experiment III: Most subjects made predicted reversals and unconditional reversals were rare (L-S, p. 52).

Concluding Remarks

A careful description of several seemingly equivalent decision problems may bring out significant differences. It is suggested that decision trees may be used for such purposes. Indeed, we found that the direct choices, the S-bids, the B-bids, and the compound lotteries used to study preference reversals are different objects. An important component – typically left out – is the initial individual state of wealth.

The use of indices of preference based on the linearized moments model (LMM) allows a meaningful comparison of all branches of the decision trees. The LMM requires the explicit introduction of subjective value-judgements represented by two parameters encoding individual attitudes-towards-randomness (ATR). We simulated the process of choice for several individuals (i.e., different ATRs). Our model explains the existence of both **predicted** and **unpredicted** preference reversals, as empirically observed by several psychologists, for instance Lichtenstein and Slovic.

An alternative model also capable of explaining preference reversals is expected utility with rank dependent probability (EURDP) proposed by Karni and Safra (1987). This theory uses a utility over "sure outcomes" similar to our deterministic index of preference $h(.)$. In the numerical examples here a general approach for $h(.)$ was used: the first linear term of a Taylor expansion. Contrariwise, K-S use an ad-hoc function for $u(.)$ with three linear sections in a very short monetary interval. Regarding probability, the LMM handles prospects as exogenous given data (for instance, probabilities associated with random devices are taken at face value). On the contrary, EURDP introduces an ad-hoc "probability transformation function" with four sections for the same short utility interval. In summary, the paucity of empirical parameters (only two in our model) is a significant point in favour of the LMM.

Finally, as also noted by Karni and Safra, in order to explain preference reversals there is no need to give up transitivity of preferences, just the substitution principle.

Notes

1. At a theoretical level, a difference between S- and B-bids (the cost to enter the lottery) is acknowledged in the EUM. At the experimental level, however, the two situations are deemed to be comparable. As it happens, the interpretation of this paper coincides with the experimental view.

2. In the only other working and general moments model, that of Hagen (1972), probability is very similar: a rational estimate of objective probability (where "rational" means that "the estimate is the same whether the event is desirable or not").

3. The three prescriptive conditions imposed on the pessimistic TMM are:
   (a) First-degree-stochastic dominance (FDSD) over unfavourable prospects which leads to all $r's$ positive.
   (b) Pessimism = consistency with certainty for losses, which leads to Equation 4.
   (c) Randomness-abhorrence = a DM would pay for not entering a free homogeneous favourable prospect. Exclusion of such extreme behaviour leads to $r_2 < 0.5$.

References

Fishburn, P.C. (1985). Nontransitive preference theory and the preference reversal phenomenon. *Rivista Internazionale di Scienze Economiche e Commerciali, 32,* 39-50.

Hagen, O. (1972). A new axiomatization of utility under risk. *Teorie a Metoda, 4* (2), 55-80.

Kahneman, D., & Tversky, A. (1979). Prospect theory: An analysis of decision under risk. *Econometrica, 47,* 263-291.

Karni, E., & Safra, Z. (1987). "Preference reversal" and the observability of preferences by experimental methods. *Econometrica, 55,* 675-685.

Keeney, R.L., & Raiffa, H. (1976). *Decisions with multiple objectives: Preferences and value tradeoffs.* New York: Wiley.

Lichtenstein, S., & Slovic, P. (1971). Reversals of preferences between bids and choices in gambling decisions. *Journal of Experimental Psychology, 89,* 46-55.

Lindman, H.R. (1971). Inconsistent preferences among gambles. *Journal of Experimental Psychology, 89,* 390-397.

Loomes, G., & Sugden, R. (1983). A rationale for preference reversal. *American Economic Review, 73,* 428-432.

Munera, H.A. (1978). *Modeling of individual risk attitudes in decision making under uncertainty: An application to nuclear power.* Berkeley, CA: University of California. Doctoral dissertation.

Munera, H.A. (1985a). The generalized means model (GMM) for non-deterministic decision making: Its normative and descriptive power, including sketch of the representation theorem. *Theory and Decision, 18,* 173-202.

Munera, H.A. (1985b). A theory for technological risk comparisons. In: G. Yadigaroglu & S. Chakraborty (Eds.), *Risk analysis as a decision tool*, pp. 14-58. Cologne: Verlag TÜV Rheinland.

Munera, H.A. (1986). The generalized means model (GMM) for non-deterministic decision making: A unified treatment for the two contending theories. In: L. Daboni, A. Montesano, & M. Lines (Eds.), *Recent developments in the foundations of utility and risk theory*, pp. 161-184. Dordrecht: Reidel.

Munera, H.A. (1988). A large scale empirical test for the linearized moments model (LMM): Compatibility between theory and observation. In: B.R. Munier (Ed.), *Risk, decision, and rationality*, pp. 291-311. Dordrecht: Reidel.

Popper, K.R. (1959). *The logic of scientific discovery.* London: Hutchinson.

Slovic, P., & Lichtenstein, S. (1983). Preference reversals: A broader perspective. *American Economic Review, 73,* 596-605.

Tversky, A., & Kahneman, D. (1981). The framing of decisions and the psychology of choice. *Science, 211,* 453-458.

v. Neumann, J., & Morgenstern, O. (1944). *Theory of games and economic behavior.* Princeton, NJ: Princeton University Press.

Liisa Uusitalo

Economic Man or Social Man – Exploring Free Riding in the Production of Collective Goods

Abstract

The paper takes up the conflict between expressed preferences for collective goods, such as environmental quality, and actual behaviour in society. In discussing possible reasons for this attitude-behaviour inconsistency found in empirical studies, a distinction is made between preferences and choices.

The inconsistency of preference orderings and possible biases in preference revelation are first analyzed. The major part of the paper deals with the strategic behaviour of individuals when they choose whether to cooperate or act as free riders. Various actor types and appropriate incentives for creating cooperative behaviour are discussed in detail. Finally, societies are categorized according to their principal ways of attempting to secure the provision of collective goods.

Author's address: Liisa Uusitalo, Helsinki School of Economics, Runeberginkatu 14-16, SF-00100 Helsinki, Finland.

Introduction

The individual-collective paradox is present more than ever in to-day's modern societies. The satisfaction of a number of welfare needs depends to a greater extent than before on the availability of public or collective goods which require cooperation from everyone. At the same time, however, individualism and individual utility are very much emphasized both ideologically and methodologically in present-day economic and social thinking.

A good empirical instance of this paradox is the conflict between the expressed demand for environmental quality on the one hand, and behaviour that maximizes individual utility on the other hand. Attitudes towards environmental protection are very positive, and there seems to be a genuine desire among the public to improve environmental quality. However, corresponding changes in politics and legislation as well as in the behaviour of individual citizens have been very slow. Results from a large survey show that environmental attitudes and behaviour have a positive but very weak correlation (Uusitalo, 1986b). Consequently, environmentally positive attitudes do not always lead to environmentally sound choices in the respondents' own life or in society.

When we are studying the conditions of rational behaviour, this inconsistency between preferences and behaviour becomes theoretically very interesting. The minimal requirements for rational behaviour usually assume that people act consistently according to their beliefs, and that their actions are based on consistent and transitive preference orderings. The reasons for the failure of this formal rationality are presented before going into the broader definitions of rationality which this paper seeks to outline.

The importance of studying preferences and choices independently is to be emphasized. The need for this distinction becomes particularly evident in the case of public or collective goods with which we are dealing. The demand for public or collective goods which have previously been free or underpriced cannot be revealed by market behaviour. Moreover, collective goods involve several possibilities for individual free riding. Free riding, that is, efforts to enjoy collective goods without contributing oneself, can occur both at the stage of preference revelation (in voting or other forms of preference expression), and at the stage where individuals choose between cooperation and defection when they are required to contribute to the production of the collective good.

The research, so far, has tried to reveal existing preferences in favour of collective goods (and the willingness to pay for them). However, it is equally or even more important to reveal mechanisms that either prevent or further the cooperation among citizens which is needed for the production of the goods. It is true that some environmental goods can be provided by representative organs such as the government (e.g., founding of national parks). However, very many collective goods require collective action in a broader sense; cooperation is required of all or at least an overwhelming majority of actors having common intentions (for example, less polluting behaviour of almost all consumers or firms is required in order to reach lower noise and pollution levels).

Within economic theory the real conflict between "economic" and "moral" man has so far often been neglected. The prisoners' dilemma situation that very clearly exemplifies the discrepancy between preferences and action has not been fully understood: It is a description of the necessity to introduce cooperative behaviour as the best means of securing individual interests as well. In those cases where need satisfaction is dependent on how other people behave, individual utility maximizing does not lead to an optimal result even for the individual himself.

The Goals of the Analysis

This paper aims first at discussing possible reasons for failures of preference-behaviour consistency. Strategic choice behaviour, where actors try simultaneously to get their share of the accepted collective goal and to maximize their individual utility, is a major problem that will be discussed.

Then the different combinations of individual utility seeking and collective welfare seeking behaviour will be summarized, and I will discuss some suitable means of encouraging different "types" of actors to contribute to the collective good. Gradually the analysis moves towards a type of behaviour that assumes a broader definition of rationality than the formal rationality of economic models. Finally some parallels will be drawn between the different actor types and corresponding types of societies.

Inconsistent and Conflicting Preferences

We cannot as a matter of course impute to people complete, consistent preference orderings. People may act randomly if their action is based on indifference or inconsistent preferences concerning the different collective goals. People may wish to engage in several states of affairs simultaneously, and the choice situation, the given set of alternatives, and the perceived risks involved in them can influence the order of preference (Elster, 1983; Kahneman & Tversky, 1979, 1984; Tversky, 1969). It is quite possible that due to time preferences, for instance, the fact that people tend to give more weight to immediate need satisfaction, environmental protection may be underemphasized in attitude surveys (Elster, 1983, pp. 7-8). Environmental protection often deals with securing life quality in the distant future and for future generations and, therefore, may be underemphasized in the present need hierarchy. On the other hand, it can in some cases also be overemphasized, for example, if the immediate risks involved in environmental pollution are perceived as very high (catastrophic situations).

Biases can also occur depending on whether survey questions are presented to respondents in a way that encourages or discourages free riding in preference revelation. However, in contrast to voting or choice situations, in a survey there are no (or extremely weak) incentives for "strategic" answers. Consequently, distorted preference revelation, a possible reason behind the found inconsistency between stated preferences and behaviour, does not get support from empirical findings. Respondents' free riding when they are expressing their preferences, or exerting "lip service" to what are perceived to be generally accepted goals in society, is not a major reason for the attitude-behaviour inconsistency. The majority is honestly of the opinion that environmental protection should be improved and is willing to accept collective measures in favour of that goal. It is also difficult to prove a hypothesis of incomplete preference orderings for different social goals; people are not indeterminate or acting randomly when giving their preferences (Uusitalo, 1988).

Thus, a strong free riding hypothesis is not supported when we deal only with preferences for environmental protection. The picture changes totally if we examine free riding involved in the choice of one's own action. The incompleteness or inconsistency of preferences for different social goals (among others, environmental protection) seems not to be the most central problem. In fact, the many conflicting social goals per se cause the actor much less trouble than does the conflict between his/her preference for these social goals on the one hand, and his/her striving for individual utility on the other.

Each actor's inner conflict, which basically is the conflict of the whole society, has led many writers to suggest that preferences should actually be divided into two separate classes. Attempts to distinguish conceptually between individual utility seeking preferences and social welfare preferences have been made, for example, by Arrow (taste vs. values), Buchanan (individual vs. citizen preferences), Harsanyi (personal vs. social welfare or ethical preferences), and Margolis (private S-preferences vs. group G-preferences). (For summary of these, see Margolis, 1982.)

Some writers have simply assumed that the actor's personality determines whether individual or social welfare preferences dominate in his utility function (e.g., Harsanyi, 1977). Margolis, in turn, assumes two utility functions for each individual. He claims that both previous unselfishly vested resources and expected future benefits from group altruism are important determinants when the individual is choosing an equilibrium between selfish and unselfish behaviour. This "fair share argument" is, of course, consistent with utility theory. Actually it is in Margolis's model only a choice between individual selfishness and group selfishness; real social commitment cannot be included in the model. By social commitment we mean behaviour which is based on adopted moral norms and ideals and in which utility considerations do not play any role. This type of socially committed behaviour is of course far less common than behaviour in favour of collective goals the attainment of which also provides a share of private gains.

In addition to any "fair share" or "private side bet" argument (implied already by Hobbes in Leviathan, see Hobbes, 1968, and later taken up by Elster, 1979; Margolis, 1982; Olson, 1965; Stroebe & Frey, 1982, among others), I would like to add that the type of information available to the actor is decisive for the choice between individual utility seeking and commitment to social goals. In the atomistic, competitive "consumer society" where individual utility and individual success are much more emphasized than collective goals, there is a kind of "information bias" which makes it hard to create socially committed preferences and behaviour without private side bets.

In addition, there can also exist an information or consciousness gap in society with respect to the quality of public goods and to the factors affecting it. For example, members of the public may be generally aware of environmental problems but have no idea of how serious they are or how their own actions contribute to them.

My hypothesis is that the two types of information available – social welfare information and individual utility information – both have an influence on behaviour. It is possible that at present, expressed attitudes already reflect **new metapreferences** in favour of environmental quality, and that these are based on social welfare information, i.e., on the knowledge or experience of environmental damages. On the other hand, **behavioural preferences** as regards individual consumption and ways of life can still be determined by individual utility information based on material welfare ideals. This two-type information hypothesis would give one plausible explanation of the weakness of correlation between environmental attitudes and behaviour which was found in empirical research.

It is doubtful, however, whether the conflict between two kinds of preferences – that is, the individual utility vs. collective welfare dilemma – can ever be totally solved, because it seems to be a structural property of most societies to utilize both as motivational bases. Still there can exist large differences between various societies and in different time periods as to which one is emphasized more. Hirschman (1982), for example, assumes a cyclical development where too far-reaching individual utility seeking will after a while automatically turn into a growing interest in collective ideals and action, and vice versa. (In his model, the turning point from private to public affairs is caused by psychological frustration with the private goods as well as by deprived needs for the public ones.)

Whether or not one believes in the self-adaptation of society and the emergence of collective preferences when they are needed, and even if approximate unanimity of metapreferences in favour of environmental quality or other collective goods could be gradually reached, the integration of preferences and actual behaviour remains to be achieved. It implies solving the problem of free rider behaviour and overcoming the difficulty of changing the rules of the game from non-cooperative to cooperative ones.

Preferences and Action in Conflict – The Problem of Free Rider Behaviour

The strategic situation where the individual actor has to choose between contributing his/her own effort to the production of a collective good and defecting, taking only the self-interest into account, is usually described as a prisoners' dilemma (PD), a non-cooperative, non-zero sum game. Free riding is often taken as a general, many-party case of the prisoners' dilemma: a case where the universal defection is Pareto-inferior to universal cooperation while, at the same time, defection is the dominant strategy for each individual (which means that the lonely cooperator will not produce such an amount of the collective good that his/her cost or efforts would be rewarded; see, e.g., Hardin, 1982; McMillan, 1979; Pettit, 1986; Taylor, 1988).

In the PD conceptualization, a central assumption is that the actor is not aware of the actions of the other players. This means that each party uses only individual utility information as the basis of his/her decision. Moreover, the collective good produced by the cooperators will be nonexcludable and available to the lonely defector anyway. If the number of actors is very large, the probability that one actor could have an influence on the quality of the public good becomes even smaller, which again decreases cooperation and increases the tendency to free riding.

Under these conditions, for each party who desires the public good but has only individual utility information available, defecting – while all others cooperate – becomes the most preferred alternative (e.g., Axelrod, 1984; Pettit, 1986; Sen, 1973, 1982; see also Uusitalo, 1985). However, if every party takes the individually rational decision to free ride, the collective good will not be produced at all, which would be against the actors' own preference order (in which universal cooperation is preferred to universal defection). The requirements of formal rationality are fulfilled, but the choice is not collectively "reasonable" (e.g., von Wright, 1985, pp. 169-188).

It is clear, however, that in a many-party case it will often be enough if a certain majority acts as cooperators and secures the production of the collective good. A minor number of defectors usually cannot endanger it, and in practice it is even less probable that lone defectors can make the cooperators worse off than under universal defection. (For this type of "foul dealer" problem, see Pettit, 1986.)

It is more or less an empirical question how large a majority is needed for different types of collective goods to be produced, and how to encourage cooperators to continue cooperating instead of following the example of the lonely free riders. A serious problem is that when a large majority of a very big group (e.g., the whole population) would need to cooperate, the incentives to free riding also tend to be at their greatest. Free riding is easier to combat in small groups because of the quick learning process and because each actor can more easily see the connections between his/her action and the collective outcome.

In the present context we are considering such collective or public goods that can be produced only by collective cooperation among the majority of actors. Consequently, the problem can be perceived as similar to a PD. In contrast, free riding is not a major problem in cases where some legitimate representatives of the collective can bring about the desired public good without the help of actors themselves. In such cases of "collective action" the problem is reduced to revealing the collective preferences (existing we-intentions) and to legitimizing the action, i.e., establishing the right of the representative actor or governing body to carry out the collective intentions.

Free riding can take place under rules of pure economic rationality, in a situation where some people do not really care about the public good and others – maybe the majority – are interested in producing the public good but where there are no integrative procedures to guide people's behaviour. What, then, can be done to change the atomistic, non-cooperative game into a co-operative one?

Appealing to the Economic Man

In the case of deliberate free riders who do not care about the collective good, the most fruitful method is probably to try to create forms of incentive-compatible cooperative behaviour, and appeal directly to the pure self-interest which in this case is the very reason for non-cooperative behaviour. Setting a price on the non-cooperative behaviour – or introducing social sanctions – means that private side bets are given to those who cooperate and a language is used which the economic man understands.

Many economists have proposed this decentralized solution for the production of collective goods. It is hoped to reach an optimal common solution by way of self-interested behaviour. However, it has also been shown theoretically how difficult it is to solve the free rider problem in this fashion. It is impossible to reach a dominant equilibrium (a dominant incentive-compatible strategy for the actor) and Pareto-efficiency at the same time (see, e.g., McMillan, 1979; Smith, 1980).

Many practical problems are also associated with finding the right level of incentive, that is, an efficient "price" for non-market collective goods. Likewise it has been difficult to define property rights for collective goods that have previously been free (Uusitalo, 1986a). The traditional situation in which collective goods (such as air and water) have been used freely without any restrictions has made many economic agents (business firms, farmers, and consumers) behave "as if" they had property rights to the collective good in question although they have none. When property rights are established and given to society, which is typical for such collective goods as the ones mentioned, protests arise against paying or against making other sacrifices in order to obtain those goods. The interested parties still tend to see themselves as property owners, and consequently want to be treated as sellers – not buyers – of those goods. Hence, in opposition to "the polluter-pays-principle," they ask for compensation from society if they are to cooperate in the production of the good.

The different types of actors in the category Economic Man are described in Figure 1. Despite all the difficulties involved, incentives and the fair share-argument can contribute towards encouraging a Rational Egoist to act as an Incentive-Compatible Cooperator if he may expect to have private side bets, that is, if beside the collective good he gains additional individual utility from acting cooperatively. The same goes for Foul Dealers, although the incentives or sanctions must probably be higher in this case.

Secondly, there can exist Rational Fools who actually have a preference for the collective good but who – due to the information gap

		Action directed towards		
		Individual utility maximization		Collective utility including one's own private interest
Preferences directed towards	Individual utility	**Rational Egoist** and/or **Foul Dealer**	(Incentives) (Fair share argument) ------------>	**Incentive- Compatible Cooperator**
	Collective utility including one's own private interests	**Rational Fool**	(Social welfare information) ------------>	**Informed Consequentialist**

Figure 1: Types of economic man.

or biased information – do not realize that their rational individual utility seeking behaviour actually goes against their own very interest (the PD paradox). The proper kind of information can turn them into Informed Consequentialists, whereupon they will act in a cooperative way which better secures their own interests too.

All the aforementioned types (Rational Egoist, Rational Fool, Incentive-Compatible Cooperator, and Informed Consequentialist) have turned up in economic welfare literature, and they are variations of Economic Man, a man whose preferences and actions are directed at maximizing individual utility. Economic Man selects collectively rational behaviour if he can be made to believe that it is the best way to secure his private interests. In the case of Economic Man, increased information, incentives, and the manipulation of the feasible set of choices (e.g., by legislation) are feasible means of decreasing free riding. For economic agents such as business firms they seem to be the only conceivable means. But there are also actors who behave as Moral Men or who fall in between the pure types of Economic Man and Moral Man as shown in Figure 2.

		Action	
		Individual utility maximization	Socially committed behaviour
	Individual utility	1. **Economic Man**	3. **"As-If" Moral Man**
Preferences			
	Commitment to social goals	2. **Free Rider**	4. **Moral Man**

Figure 2: Types of social commitment.

Appealing to Social Commitment

Some people can have socially committed preferences but they can still act as typical **free riders** for several reasons: because of the weakness of will, because the behavioural norms are too weak, or because of the veil of insignificance which makes their effort look insignificant from the point of view of the final outcome. These people represent Type 2 in Figure 2.

There are several ways of preventing this common type of free riding. With the help of information we can fight against the "weakness of will" of the actors, and help them develop their character by strengthening their will-power. Different measures of securing "second best rationality" (the person knows that he acts inconsistently and takes precautions against it) can be taken (Elster, 1979). Usually this means the "Ulysses' strategy": Previously made agreements or accepted social norms are employed to govern action in certain roles or situations. (On the cooperative function of norms, see, e.g., Ullman-Margalit, 1977.) Important in the justification of these agreements is the equal treatment of the participants. People are willing to move from a PD game to a cooperative game (or a game with an equilibrium point that contains cooperative strategies) provided that others do so, too. One example is the "assurance game." In contrast to the PD, in this game – when assured that others cooperate too – an actor prefers cooperation to lonely defection (see, e.g., Sen, 1973, pp. 96-99).

It has been proposed that moral sentiments do not bring a solution to the collective goods problem because of the so-called volunteer's dilemma (VoD), a situation where volunteers are needed for the production of the collective good, but where it cannot be produced if **all** volunteer. This means that we have a game with several asymmetrical points of equilibrium (e.g., Diekmann, 1985; Holler, 1986).

VoD is perhaps not a very relevant problem when we deal with environmental quality as the collective good we want to produce. Usually, the more volunteers there are to produce the collective good (e.g., those who obey speed limits), the better is the outcome. However, VoD problems are conceivable. For example, environmental quality would improve if people volunteered for a simple, non-consumeristic alternative way of life with a high amount of non-market activity and self-sufficient home production. Yet, the society may collapse if all were to adopt this way of life.

The veil of insignificance refers to the – often justified – feeling that one person's choice has an insignificant impact upon the final outcome. This is a very influential reason for free riding (e.g., Kliemt, 1986). The veil of insignificance becomes stronger as groups grow larger. In small experimental groups it has been more difficult to find free riding, because there the effect of everybody's contribution can be perceived more easily.

Not only the absolute size of the actor group is significant, however. In a dynamic context, the relative number of cooperating actors is also important. If a person perceives that the majority is free riding, this increases the probability that he/she too will act in this way in the next sequence. If, on the contrary, the feedback tells that the majority is cooperating, this enforces one's own cooperative behaviour.

In attempting to reduce this motive for free riding, information could be used to remind people of agreements and accepted social norms, to increase collective consciousness, and to reduce the feelings of insignificance among the public. Instead of "advertising" the model of free riding, the attention of the public could be drawn to the fact that, in most cases, the majority is not free riders and is acting in a cooperative way. A rapid information feedback about successful cooperation can further increase the number of cooperators in the next time sequence.

Another group of people falling in between pure Economic Man and Moral Man comprises those who basically are not committed to the common goals and have not internalized the social ideas but who nevertheless are willing to behave in a cooperative way in favour of collectively rational behaviour. They behave as if they were Moral Men (Type 3 in Figure 2).

The As-If Moral Man can feel sympathy for other members in society, or the cooperative activity itself may be necessary for him to feel as an accepted member of society. The As-If Moral Man is not much different from the Incentive-Compatible and Informed Consequentialist types of Economic Man; he only expects slightly different kinds of information and incentives.

Moral Man, finally, refers to the ideal case of an actor whose preferences and actions are both largely socially committed. If he has adopted social ideals, he acts consistently according to them without paying attention to his own private interest. Moreover, Moral Man exerts self-reflexivity in that he continuously evaluates his metapreferences and does not stiffly stick to those once adopted. A Moral Man is aware of the need of a constant metaranking of rankings, and of the necessity to sometimes take precautions against the weakness of will.

Moral Men and truly altruistic behaviour do exist, but can hardly be more than unattainable ideals for most people. A vast majority of the population tends to be located in categories falling between the pure egoist, Economic Man, and Moral Man, depending on the collective issue in question. For most people the inner conflict between individual self-interest and collective welfare remains a permanent conflict whether they are conscious of it or not.

Societies and the Individual vs. Collective Dilemma

Referring to the different motivational bases of **actors**, we can also draw a parallel with the corresponding types of **societies**. The characterization of societies displayed in Figure 3 is, of course, a very rough one. However, it may still help in analyzing various kinds of societies and in pin-pointing each type's major problems in the production of collective goods.

		Action primarily	
		Self-interested	Socially committed
Preferences primarily	Self-interested	**Atomistic, Economically Efficient Society**	**Coercive Imposed-Law Society**
	Socially committed	**Alienated Society**	**Cooperative Self-Reflexive Society**

Figure 3: Societies corresponding to different degrees of social commitment.

The first type of society, Atomistic, Economically Efficient Society, relies on the market mechanism for producing collective goods. There are only few commonly accepted cooperative norms or sentiments of solidarity, and cooperative behaviour is assumed to take place only under circumstances where the public interests can be combined with the private ones. Social welfare information and socially committed behaviour are not utilized as means to produce collective goods or to strive for collective pursuits. The coherence of the society rests on its economic – not social – goals. Society acts as a rational business firm rather than as a community of shared values and ways of life.

In the second type of society, Alienated Society, there are cooperative goals and shared values concerning the collective goods but not sufficient mechanisms for ensuring that behaviour conforms to these goals. Action is alienated from goals. Public preferences and the true demand for collective goods often remain unrevealed to the decision makers. Information on social consequences is lacking or is distorted towards emphasizing individual utility. Social norms are too weak to encourage cooperative behaviour. The situation is perceived as a PD-type non-cooperative game where everybody tries to secure his/her own interest although everybody would prefer universal cooperation.

In the third type, Coercive Imposed-Law Society, attempts are made to utilize cooperative games and secure the production of collective goods with the help of mutually binding agreements. It is hoped that preferences will change accordingly in favour of the cooperative solutions, or at least that incentives and imposed sanctions are effective enough to secure the amount of cooperative behaviour needed for the production of collective goods.

In Alienated Society legal norms and economic incentives are too weakly developed when compared with people's collective goals, whereas in Coercive Imposed-Law Society usually much social information is needed to make the reasons for the collective agreements clear for those who are not aware of them. In Alienated Society efforts must be concentrated on the development of mechanisms for integrating goals and behaviour; in Coercive Imposed-Law Society actions must be taken to legitimate norms and increase collective consciousness.

The fourth type, Cooperative Self-Reflexive Society, represents the ideal communicative and cooperative society (in the sense of Habermas) in which individual preferences and actions are consistent with collective welfare goals and where some kind of harmony exists between individual interests and collective goals.

Metaranking of preferences takes place continuously, and legitimation takes place through self-reflexive "rational" discussion and argumentation. Rationality is now understood in a broader sense than that of formal requirements only. Rationality can be evaluated at various levels and by using different validity criteria for different discourses as Habermas (1981) has proposed. The rationality of factual statements is based on their truthfulness, and this is established in scientific discourse. The validity of norms and normative statement is based on arguments of universality, of their "rightness" or "justness" for everybody. Even the rationality of preferences can be discussed on the basis of investigations of their autonomy vs. manipulability.

In a communicative society the conflict between individual utility and collective welfare may not be solved but at least it is consciously taken into consideration in the process of self-reflection and metaranking.

References

Axelrod, R. (1984). *The evolution of cooperation*. New York: Basic Books.

Diekmann, A. (1985). Volunteer's dilemma. *Journal of Conflict Resolution, 29*, 605-610.

Elster, J. (1979). *Ulysses and the sirens – Studies in rationality and irrationality*. Cambridge: Cambridge University Press.

Elster, J. (1983). *Sour grapes – Studies in the subversion of rationality*. Cambridge: Cambridge University Press.

Habermas, J. (1981). *Theorie des kommunikativen Handelns*. Band 1 und 2. Frankfurt: Suhrkamp.

Hardin, R. (1982). *Collective action*. Baltimore: Johns Hopkins.

Harsanyi, J. (1977). *Bargaining equilibrium in games and social situations*. Cambridge: Cambridge University Press.

Hirschman, A. (1982). *Shifting involvements – Private interest and public action*. Princeton, NJ: Princeton University Press.

Hobbes, T. (1968). *Leviathan*. (Orig. 1651.) Harmondsworth: Penguin.

Holler, M. (1986). Moral sentiments and self-interest reconsidered. In: A. Diekmann & P. Mitter (Eds.), *Paradoxical effects of social behaviour*, pp. 223-233. Vienna: Physica-Verlag.

Kahneman, D., & Tversky, A. (1979). Prospect theory: An analysis of decision under risk. *Econometrica, 47*, 263-291.

Kahneman, D., & Tversky, A. (1984). Choices, values, and frames. *American Psychologist, 39*, 1-10.

Kliemt, H. (1986). The veil of insignificance. *European Journal of Political Economy, 2*, 333-344.

Margolis, H. (1982). *Selfishness, altruism, and rationality*. Cambridge: Cambridge University Press.

McMillan, J. (1979). The free rider problem: A survey. *Economic Record, 55*, 95-107.

Olson, M. (1965). *The logic of collective action*. Cambridge, MA: Harvard University Press.

Pettit, P. (1986). Free riding and foul dealing. *Journal of Philosophy, 83*, 361-379.

Sen, A. (1973). *On economic inequality*. Oxford: Clarendon Press.

Sen, A. (1982). *Choice, welfare, and measurement*. Oxford: Basil Blackwell.

Smith, V. (1980). Experiments with a decentralized mechanism for public good decisions. *American Economic Review, 70*, 584-599.

Stroebe, W., & Frey, B. (1982). Self-interest and collective action: The economics and psychology of public goods. *British Journal of Social Psychology, 21*, 121-137.

Taylor, C. (1988). *Possibility of cooperation.* Cambridge: Cambridge University Press.

Tversky, A. (1969). Intransitivity of preferences. *Psychological Review, 76*, 31-48.

Ullman-Margalit, E. (1977). *The emergence of norms.* Oxford: Clarendon Press.

Uusitalo, L. (1985). *Rational consumers – Irrational citizens?* Berlin: International Institute for Environment and Society of the Science Center Berlin. Discussion Paper 85-20.

Uusitalo, L. (1986a). *Environmental impacts of consumption patterns.* Aldershot: Gower.

Uusitalo, L. (1986b). *Suomalaiset ja ympäristö – tutkimus taloudellisen käyttäytymisen rationaalisuudesta* (Finns and the environment – A study in the rationality of economic behaviour). Helsinki: Helsinki School of Economics. Publication A:49.

Uusitalo, L. (1988). *Environment and other social goals – Exploring inconsistency and differentiation of social goal preferences.* Helsinki: Helsinki School of Economics. Discussion Paper F-192.

von Wright, G.H. (1985). *Filosofisia tutkielmia* (Philosophical essays). Helsinki: Kirjayhtymä.

Part IV

Consumer Behaviour

Solveig R. Wikström et al.
From the Consumption of Necessities to Experience-
Seeking Consumption

Susanne C. Grunert
Personality Traits as Elements in a Model of Eating
Behaviour

Lorenz Lassnigg
The "New Values" and Consumer Behaviour – Some
Empirical Findings From Austria

Dominique Lassarre and Christine Roland-Lévy
Understanding Children's Economic Socialization

Marek Wosinski
A Model of Consumer Behaviour in the Situation of
Shortages

Solveig R. Wikström, Ulf Elg, and Ulf Johansson

From the Consumption of Necessities to Experience-Seeking Consumption

Abstract

The focus of this article is the proposition on an evolving new consumption pattern, increasingly fragmented and experience-oriented and controlled by psychological rather than material needs.

The starting point is different theories of human needs and the possibilities for consumption to play new roles. The changing consumption pattern and the inherent logic of the emerging trends are described by means of a conceptual model. The pervasiveness of the phenomenon is illustrated by a set of examples.

This project has been financed by the Swedish Council for Management and Work Life Issues whose support we gratefully acknowledge.

Authors' addresses: Solveig R. Wikström, The Swedish Council for Management and Work Life Issues, P.O. Box 5042, S-102 41 Stockholm, Sweden; Ulf Elg and Ulf Johansson, Department of Business Administration, University of Lund, P.O. Box 7080, S-220 07 Lund, Sweden.

Introduction

The consumption patterns of the 1980s are full of contradictions. With disposable incomes no longer growing as they have been doing over recent decades, it seems logical to find a growing demand for simple products and a new awareness of prices; it does not seem equally logical that the consumption of luxury goods and sophisticated products and services is also growing. Another paradox is that people with low incomes are devoting themselves to exclusive consumption, while the wealthy can often be seen in low-price stores or choosing simple product varieties. Yet another inexplicable phenomenon is the growth of the "second-hand" market, at a time when mass production and distribution of new products have never been more efficient. People appear to be saving with one hand and squandering with the other. What they save on, and what they indulge in, form a pattern that has not been seen before.

This complex and puzzling picture of consumption causes problems for companies responsible for supply. They wonder – with justification – just what it is that consumers really want: Are they looking for cheap, good, serviceable varieties, or sophisticated quality products? And, they may well wonder as well, what role does price play in all this?

The confusion is also a headache to policymakers. It is obviously difficult to support the interests of the consumers on the market, if nobody quite knows what they want or what they consider important. It was easier when the idea of the rational decision process and the hegemony of material values was paramount. Policy goals were clear: to promote the development of good serviceable products at reasonable prices, and to help consumers in their buying decisions by providing accurate price information, buying advice, and appropriate product descriptions. How adequate is such a policy to the consumers of the 1980s?

In the following we analyse the new pattern of consumption, attempting to identify and explain its structure. We look first at some theories of basic human needs, and analyse consumption in terms of its ability to satisfy these needs. Secondly we discuss the various forces that have engendered the changes in consumption. We describe and explain the new consumption pattern in a model, and demonstrate its inherent logic.

288

Human Needs and the Functions of Consumption

The question of why people consume has long engaged the attention of the various social sciences. All the foremost names of consumption research from Veblen (1899/1953) and Riesman (1950) to Hirsch (1976), Scitovsky (1977), Leiss (1978), and Fromm (1978) have addressed the issue. There is general agreement that consumption has two basic functions which can be discerned in all human action: to satisfy material needs and to fulfil immaterial psychological needs.

In the various hierarchic motivation theories which explain human behaviour, physiological and material needs occupy the lowest rungs.[1] Only when these are adequately met does our interest turn towards the higher needs: the need for self-respect and winning the approval of other people – the building blocks of personal identity; the need for community and closeness; and, finally, the striving for personal development and growth.

With regard to consumption it is the first of these functions, to satisfy material needs, which has long been regarded as the most important. So long as living standards are low and people are living in straitened economic circumstances, the material consumption that is necessary to survival obviously comes first, and anything not contingent on the vital material needs must take second place. Thus, even in this context, human needs are conceived as forming a specified hierarchy. Only when the survival needs have been satisfied is there room for the higher immaterial and psychological needs.

But the categories are not fixed once and for all. The boundaries to what are considered vital material needs have been extended in the course of evolution. Thus in **The Joyless Economy** (1976) Scitovsky assigns two roles to consumption, namely comfort and pleasure, and he lets comfort represent the fundamental pain-reducing consumption needs. Thus he claims that all the goods and services required by the good life are geared to the satisfaction of material needs. Consequently, cars, washing machines, and instant foods are all fulfilling fundamental material needs in the developed society, although this does not mean that the same products cannot also fulfil psychological needs. The second major function, the psychological function, has quite another purpose. We consume not only to counteract unpleasantness, but also to experience pleasure, to find stimulation and enjoyment. In **Man for Himself**

(1978) Fromm introduces a classic dichotomy similar to Scitovsky's. He speaks of scarcity behaviour and affluence behaviour. The former is aimed at reducing want, the latter towards the experience of happiness and pleasure. Several other researchers (see, e.g., Maddox, 1981; Swan & Combs, 1976) have put forward similar ideas, i.e., that there is an essential difference between the two categories of needs, which can in no way substitute for one another. The fulfillment of the material needs provides a comfortable life, but no permanent enjoyment or pleasure. Only the psychological needs can provide for this form of satisfaction.

It is easy to understand the important role which the consumption of goods and services plays in the satisfaction of material needs. The role of consumption in the satisfaction of psychological needs, on the other hand, is not so obvious. But it is there, in various guises.

Above all consumption can give prestige and the approval of other people. It helps to place people in the social hierarchy. In Veblen's world as described in **The Theory of the Leisure Class** (1899), prestige plays an important part in consumption, as it does in Riesman's **The Lonely Crowd** (1950), where the individual, controlled by extraneous forces, is seen as the central figure in the mass consumption society. The consumer choices of such individuals are steered by what other people think and what other people regard as suitable.

As well as commanding prestige, consumption can establish and confirm personal identity. In relationships with others, in interactions between individuals, self-awareness develops. We become someone in our own eyes. In our choice of products and life style, the picture of our own identity evolves, both in ourselves and in relation to others. In this context Veblen has shown how consumption can provide self-respect. In the life style postulated by Fromm, consumption is crucial in just this sense. It prevents anxiety and confirms identity.

In the hierarchy of needs postulated in motivation research, there are two further needs: for community and for self-realization. But these needs are barely mentioned in consumption research. Could this be because they are not regarded as particularly important in themselves, or is it felt that consumption cannot fulfil them? In personality research the driving forces of human behaviour are graded according to a different scheme. Two fundamental human needs are distinguished: autonomy, which is somewhat similar to what the motivation researchers call self-realization, and homonomy, a parallel to "relatedness," i.e., community and closeness (Angyal, 1941). We have concluded from this comparison that the need for self-realization and closeness is fundamental, and thus extremely strong. If these needs find inadequate outlets in human lives in other ways, it is reasonable to suppose that people will seek to satisfy them by way of consumption.

Looking first at the need for community or belonging, it seems to us that consumption offers abundant opportunities here: in eating, in sport and other leisure activities, in the consumption of culture, and so on. Community can also be experienced without direct physical closeness. By being part of a well-defined value community or an ideology, people can fulfil their need for belonging.

The interactions between people belonging to various groups in which values are shared, experiences exchanged, and identities developed in the course of consuming goods and services, obviously fulfil the need for human warmth and closeness.

When individuals involve themselves in problems and activities which demand the full exploitation and even the development of their capacity, when they have to learn new things and build on their skills and confidence, then we can talk of self-realization. The personal identity expands. Specialized and exclusive consumption, which presupposes continual learning and competence development, thus offers rich opportunities for satisfying just this need. It seems to us that committed consumption provides opportunities for people to grow and expand their own existential scope.

Change and the Limits of Consumption

Whereas human nature and human needs are given, consumption changes as time passes. There are other factors besides human needs which determine what is ultimately consumed.

The amount that is consumed is determined by economic conditions, by incomes and prices. While material conditions set the limits to consumption, other forces determine what is consumed, and how, within the given boundaries. Every period has its own consumption pattern. The values and norm systems obtaining at any given point represent important determining factors. Naturally the supply situation also affects the issue.

In the pre-industrial society consumption resources were small, and consumption subject to tradition. The content of existing consumption was determined by the norms prevailing in the class to which the consumer belonged. Consumption was extrinsically determined, to use Riesman's concept. The flow of new products on to the market was slight during this period.

In the subsequently evolving industrial society, the economic resources increased. Consumption expanded. New products appeared on the market. Social mobility increased and class boundaries became increasingly blurred. New categories of people now affect consumer choices. Friends and acquaintances, work colleagues, and, indirectly, the mass media take on the normative role. They indicate in various ways what it is acceptable to like, to think, to consume. Class behaviour is replaced by group fashion. Individuals who are controlled from without have no need to adopt the norms and customs of their class; rather, they can turn their attention to particular groups and then try to imitate and adapt to them. In this way the groups become increasingly standardized both in taste and behaviour. Mass consumption now dominates the picture of society.

The next phase, which has not yet been definitively named but which is often called the neo-industrial or service society – and which, to be both concrete and simple, we regard as having started at the threshold of the 1980s – looks rather different. Economic growth has slackened and private consumption stagnated. Fewer and fewer genuinely new products and services are appearing on the market. Norms are breaking down. Lyttkens (1988) speaks of "collective individualism." Each individual seeks to assert his or her specific character, even vis-à-vis the group to which he or she belongs. In terms of consumption, this means that group control is being replaced by individual control. There is more scope for expressing individual preferences and needs.

For obvious reasons the literature can provide little guidance when it comes to describing and explaining this period. But scattered observations and reflections have been made. For instance the idea is sometimes heard that there are limits to consumption, that the standard products of the industrial society lead to satiety (see, for example, Asplund, 1967; Scitovsky, 1976; Uusitalo, 1986). There are different views about the implications. Asplund believes that other more particularized areas of consumption will become more attractive.

Scitovsky, on the other hand, holds the opposite view: The dreariness and monotony of consuming standardized mass-produced goods and services creates a constant need for new varieties and demand is thus insatiable.

Scitovsky goes further and asks himself what will ultimately happen, human nature being what it is. Because of their standardization, mass-produced goods provide little stimulation, and any novelty value which they may possess never lasts long. In the long run pleasure will nonetheless win the day, at the cost of comfort. Static comfort, in his view, will not be enough to satisfy us. Our curiosity will lead us to seek experiences involving an element of enjoyment. Enjoyment, with its superior qualities, is certain to surpass comfort as a source of stimulation.

Uusitalo develops a similar line of argument, suggesting that a shift is occurring away from "convenience consumption" which aims at saving time and effort, towards the kind of consumption which brings us pleasure, enjoyment, and stimulation as a result of our own efforts. She also points out that production in the home, which used to be motivated on economic grounds, has now acquired an expressive function as a means of self-realization. Once economic and technological development has reached a certain level, she claims, the non-economic post-industrial values can more readily find expression. Consumption, both of products or services, becomes more specialized, more refined, and more varied. (See also De Geer et al., 1986; Elg, Johansson, Tollin, & Wikström, 1987.)

Starting from these theories and ideas, we have analysed the changes in consumption in Sweden, and have identified certain discernible patterns. But the developments outlined below are by no means specific to Sweden. On the contrary, we believe that similar developments are taking place in all mature industrial societies.

A Descriptive Model

Although it has long been recognized that consumption has both material and psychological causes, it has proved difficult to explain consumption unequivocally by reference to these two factors. It has often been claimed that certain types of consumption are best understood in terms of material needs, while other types should be explained in terms of psychological needs. It seems to us, however, that the various consumption patterns can

293

best be understood by considering the material and the underlying psychological motives simultaneously, and by evaluating all consumption in light of them both.

In the model described below we define consumption along two dimensions, "degree of necessity" and "degree of stimulation." What we call the degree of necessity indicates the more material needs which consumption has to satisfy. However, we do not limit "necessity" to that which is necessary to mere physical survival – food and shelter for instance. It also includes what is regarded as indispensable to the functioning of everyday life in modern society – for example, refrigerators, TV, telephone, cheap ready-made clothing, and instant foods. Up to a point this dimension is objective, i.e., everyone must make roughly the same assessment; so, for example, norms exist for what is standard equipment in all homes. At the same time, however, these norms change as society develops. Furthermore, to some extent personal values decide what is necessary to a good and comfortable life. These norms and values can of course vary with age, family structure, occupation, etc. The degree of necessity is thus neither static nor unequivocal.

At one end of the necessity scale we find the kind of consumption that is regarded as indispensable to a good life, measured in present-day terms. At the other end is the kind of consumption without which life could still go on without visible disturbances. We turn to it once the necessities of life have been fulfilled. Consumption at a low level of necessity is interchangeable and thus in many cases transient. It is quick and easy to transfer from one area to another which seems more attractive.

This leads us directly to the other more markedly psychological dimension, the degree of stimulation. We use the concept of the degree of stimulation as an overall designation for consumption providing for psychological values. It may be a question of prestige, self-respect, belonging, or self-realization, i.e., needs associated with the ego and relationships with the world around us.

Stimulative consumption can be attained in different ways. In terms of products, the very fact that these are new and unfamiliar can provide some stimulation. The greater the novelty, the greater the stimulation. There are also products especially destined to provide stimulation, and we should not forget what human ingenuity can do to generate excitement from simple raw materials. At the other end of this scale are the products which are only slightly stimulative; "slightly" because the products are so familiar and ordinary that they are no longer capable of arousing much interest, or because the type of goods as such is perceived as uninteresting.

Although consumer behaviour research has long addressed the importance of psychological dimensions, among other things in the study of purchasing motives at the product and brand level, most of this interest has its roots in the material and the rational. The main focus of the research is: How do consumers collect information, and with the help of this information how do they decide which product is best suited to solving a particular problem? This approach has been called the "information processing view" (see, e.g., Bettman, 1979). But in fact interest has been largely directed towards the evaluation of products according to what we have called the degree of necessity. This type of research assumes that consumption can be explained in terms of the material needs which it is intended to satisfy; the problem that then interests the researcher is why a consumer chooses to satisfy his material needs in a particular way.

This approach has been criticized in some quarters, and it has been pointed out that certain kinds of consumption cannot be explained in this way. According to Holbrook and Hirschman (1982), for example, the information processing view cannot be applied to any consumption connected with leisure-time activities or to what they call hedonic consumption. A different approach is needed, they say, if we are to understand this type of consumption; they call it the "experiential" approach whereby consumption is explained in terms of the subjective symbolical meaning, the aesthetic value, and the enjoyment and pleasure involved. This largely coincides with the determinants of our degree of stimulation.

Unger and Kernan (1983) also discuss components which we regard as crucial to the degree of stimulation. Unger and Kernan are explicitly addressing the concept of "leisure" and what determines an activity's classification as a leisure pursuit. They introduce six determinants, which seem also to us to coincide with the components in our overall concept of stimulating consumption, namely: (a) intrinsic satisfaction, (b) perceived freedom, (c) involvement, (d) arousal, (e) mastery, and (f) spontaneity.

Thus, Unger and Kernan restrict themselves to leisure activities, while Holbrook and Hirschman quote entertainment, art, and leisure pursuits as being suitable subjects for their experiential approach. When it comes to other types of consumption, the utility-oriented view is apparently still regarded as more appropriate.

We suggest, however, that all consumption should be seen in relation to the degree of necessity it contains and the degree of stimulation it provides. By combining these two scales we get four cells, illustrating different types of consumption; see Figure 1.

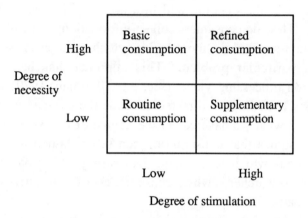

Figure 1: Four different types of consumption.

Basic consumption is the type of consumption which is regarded as indispensable, but which provides little personal stimulation. It is almost the same as compulsory consumption. It is necessary to the smooth and convenient functioning of our lives. Examples could be television sets, telephones, ordinary food, refrigerators, raincoats, and bedroom curtains. This type of consumption brings little joy, but any malfunction causes extreme irritation.

Refined consumption represents that part of our necessary consumption to which we devote particular interest and which thus provides us with stimulation – with the gilding on the necessary gingerbread. It may be a specially cooked meal, with gourmet dishes or more homely fare, or a dream kitchen in which even the refrigerator can add to the pleasure, an exclusive bathroom, or a prestigious car.

We might expect the **routine consumption** box to be empty: Who, after all, wants to consume things which are not necessary and which do not provide any stimulation either? But the box is not entirely without content. Certain activities, certain types of consumption, operate mainly as a way of regaining strength; or they are simply part of our "being in a rut." Examples: passive TV viewing, or the routine purchase of an evening paper.

Supplementary consumption provides life's silver lining. This is the consumption which we allow ourselves because, although not necessary, it provides stimulation and palpable personal satisfaction. This is where our personal interests can develop; supplementary consumption embraces, for example, most leisure pursuits and hobbies. Here (in so far as resources allow) there is scope for trying out new and exciting products which might provide us with fresh experience. What Holbrook and Hirschman mean by the experiential side of life is largely catered for in this cell.

Dynamics

Figure 2 serves to illustrate consumption trends over the last few decades.

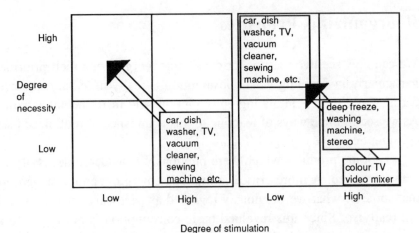

Figure 2: The movement of products towards high degree of necessity and low degree of stimulation.

Ever since the end of the war a growing number of new and technologically advanced products have been appearing on the market.

They first arrived as relatively luxurious products, which at the same time were unfamiliar and exciting. As prosperity spread, more households had the resources to buy these products, and as people became accustomed to them their functions were perceived increasingly as

297

essential to the good life. But as these products became an accepted element in practically every home, they also became less interesting and therefore provided less stimulation. Their consumption was becoming part of what we have called basic or compulsory consumption. For a long time it was possible to obtain fresh stimulation by adding new items to the established ranges; but these too were soon regarded as necessities. It is just this type of consumption that Scitovsky describes in The Joyless Economy.

Gradually, however, problems arose. As disposable incomes ceased to rise it became impossible to go on consuming new products while also retaining the entire range of earlier consumption. Perhaps, too, some kind of saturation point (in Asplund's sense) had been reached. People's lives had become so loaded with basic consumption that there was no time or scope or energy left for continually consuming more and yet more goods. At this point we are approaching Scitovsky's vision of the future – and our own present.

Reorganizing Priorities

We can now see two reasons for consumers reorganizing their priorities, particularly in deciding what consumption is really necessary: the need for new and more stimulating consumption, and instrumental satiation. As we see it, three ways of reacting to this abundance of routinized basic consumption have emerged (Figure 3).

1. Some products which were previously considered necessary are being revalued. A more critical attitude is emerging, and a recognition that some of what we previously regarded as necessary consumption is not really so. Since this revalued basic consumption is not regarded as stimulating either, it is reduced or terminated. Examples: Some households decide they do not need a car, others that they do not want a television, yet others do without a dishwasher or a washing machine of their own, or they sell their holiday cottage.

2. Other products cannot be avoided, even though it seems impossible to make their consumption stimulating. So some effort is made to devote the least possible resources to this kind of consumption. Examples: to be satisfied with good but standard foods, to buy a cheap second-hand car, or to use the simplest type of refrigerator or freezer.

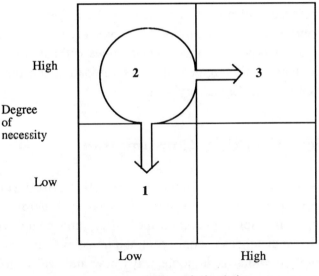

Degree of stimulation

Figure 3: Possible reactions to an increase in routinized basic consumption.

3. The consumption of certain basics can be made more stimulating by choosing to specialize in exclusivity; they then enter the ranks of refined consumption. The necessary resources can be released by reducing other basic consumption according to alternatives (1) and (2). Examples: Food consumption can be made more exciting by concentrating on gourmet cooking or health food; we can take a special interest in the interior decoration of our homes (cf. the dream kitchen), or we can buy that new exciting and longed-for car.

We see the decline that has hit many traditional basic markets, and the shifts that have occurred between different areas of consumption, as evidence of such a reorganization of priorities. Further evidence is the ongoing fragmentation of consumption, since it is obvious that the whole population does not follow the same pattern in changing its priorities; the reorganization is based on individual needs and values. This helps to explain why there is scope for sophisticated and luxurious products with their related service activities (for those who find that particular area stimulating), as well as for simple products stripped of all but the essentials (for those who want to minimize consumption in a particular field).

The resources released by a reduction in basic consumption can also be redirected into the consumption of completely new and stimulating products. Here too personal interest and values will naturally determine choice. In other words fragmented or discriminating consumption does not occur only in the compulsory area.

Experience-Seeking Consumption

In light of this argument an interesting question arises: For what do people use their released resources? What is regarded today as stimulating consumption? Despite the variety and complexity of the picture, we can distinguish certain common traits, as well as an approach to consumption which is in some ways new and which affects both sophisticated basic consumption and the new ego-intensive consumption.

There are signs that stimulation is achieved today by a more active type of consumption than before. It is no longer enough to be a passive mass consumer; people take steps to seek stimulation rather than waiting to be stimulated. We suggest that consumption has become increasingly associated with self-realization, in the guise of what we call "experience-seeking consumption." This is not a particularly surprising development. As living standards increase, we reach ever higher levels in the hierarchy of needs. Personal growth is high among the psychological needs – above social prestige, for example. Experience-seeking consumption means that we are not consuming products as ends in themselves; rather products are chosen because they suit the individual consumer's field of interest. Thus experience-seeking consumption stems from a variety of particularized interests. In order to find an outlet for these, the individual consumer combines items drawn from different sources but which fit into the totality which he desires and which constitutes the experience.

Experience-seeking consumption has something in common with what Hirschman and Holbrook (1982) call hedonic consumption. By this the authors mean consumption devoted to the satisfaction of emotional human needs. The products which they regard as important in this context are art, concerts, films, etc. They point out that the consumption of these products calls for considerably more consumer commitment than the consumption of the more materially oriented products.

However, experience-seeking consumption is not synonymous with the products consumed. Rather, the decisive factor is the context, and the way in which the consumption occurs. Nor does it consist only of products specially geared to the satisfaction of emotional needs without making any contribution to the more material needs, i.e., it is not simply a question of supplementary products. Even products representing a high degree of necessity can be included because they fit a particular sphere of interest or a totality. Thus the totalities will embrace the refined consumption of necessities as well as the often ego-intensive supplementary type of consumption. Experience-seeking consumption has several characteristic features which can be identified with the help of the following buzz-words (see Figure 4).

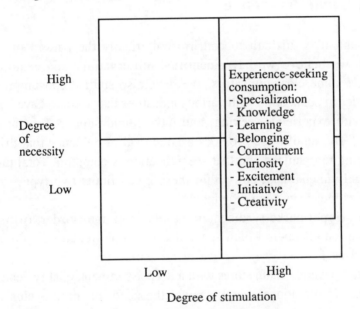

Figure 4: **Features of experience-seeking consumption.**

In order to specialize in a particular field of interest, knowledge is required. The possibility of learning more and increasing our knowledge is an important ingredient in experience-seeking consumption. Unless there is an opportunity for developing and expanding our special interest, we will simply be engaged in purely routine consumption – exactly the opposite of what we wanted. Another important element in experience-seeking consumption is the sense of belonging to a group, of being able to develop and enhance an interest together with other like-minded people.

Curiosity and the joy of discovery also characterize this type of consumption. People take the initiative, they consume products and activities in a personally creative way, they are actively involved. At the same time they expose themselves to risk. This is an inevitable condition of the chance to expand their own existential scope.

Since this type of consumption involves the combination of various goods and services into a totality which constitutes the actual experience, it also means that production and consumption become intertwined. The consumer's "production role" is even more obvious in experience-seeking consumption than it is in other types of consumption.

Empirical Evidence

Although it is difficult to confirm empirically the pattern of change which we believe we have identified, observations and examples do provide some clear indicators. We have also studied consumption and activities in connection with various industries that seem to have a natural link with experience-seeking, and have found support for our theses there.[2] The retail trade provides a good deal of evidence that priorities are being reorganized and that specialization is common. Total turnover is largely unchanged, but within these given limits two types of retail organizations have been growing:

1. Hypermarkets, discount stores, and mail-order firms, i.e., distribution channels which specialize in simple functional products at low prices.

2. Specialist chain stores with a deep assortment, quality department stores, and boutiques, which answer the need for more exclusive and sophisticated products and ranges.

A similar dichotomy can be seen in the Electrolux Group.[3] During the 1960s sales of capital goods to households had the form of a normal distribution in the specialist dimension, i.e., products with an average degree of sophistication accounted for the highest sales. During the 1980s sales have been mainly in two categories: products which offer basic functions only without supplementary qualities, and highly specified variants such as stoves with built-in gas grills, warming cupboards, and hot plates, refrigerators for wine storage, and so on. In our terminology it is thus a question of sales for basic consumption and refined consumption, respectively.

Our analysis of book publishing – a sector which can be expected to reflect the kind of shift in interests that we have pinpointed – shows that between 1970 and 1985 there has been a clear concentration on the experience-seeking area. While total numbers published have risen by 20%, the number of book titles dealing with art, food and health, fishing and other practitioner sports, keep-fit and body-building have multiplied many times over. Books on music and the theatre have also increased substantially.

An examination of the Swedish journal and magazine market also shows fragmentation and a new orientation towards the experience-seeking field. While total sales fell by 25% between 1978 and 1985, the actual number of different journals has almost doubled. The new entrants cater for the same type of special areas that we noted in book publishing. The expansion has occurred mainly at the expense of the large general-interest family magazines.

The shift in interest is revealed not only in changing reading habits but also in other respects: artistic, theatrical, and musical events are becoming increasingly common and the supply more diversified and sophisticated.

But people are not simply content to enjoy other people's creativity. They are increasingly active themselves. We need only consider the enormous growth in interest in participative sports and various kinds of exercise. Although we are unable to provide any statistics, there are indications that the increase has been substantial. The abundance of books and journals alone would suggest this, and there are many other pointers. What has happened is that the great popular sports have broken up into a huge variety of different specialities. At the same time sports are being practised in a more sophisticated way – or so the demand for equipment seems to suggest. Take the example of sports-shoe sales. Whereas people used to wear the same shoes for all sporting and leisure activities, there are now – and particularly since the beginning of the 1980s – special shoes for different activities. For jogging, for example, there are shoes allowing for the jogger's weight, his jogging style, and jogging intensity.

In the sporting field new movements have emerged aiming at the physical development of the body. The "Keep Fit" movement is an example. "Jump and Sweat," a Swedish association to promote exercise under qualified leadership, had 1,500 members in 1978 and about 50,000 in 1985. Only a shortage of leaders and premises prevents the movement growing even more quickly. The programme is based on jogging and canoeing, skiing holidays, wind surfing, and various ball games. Body building is another growing health movement. According to the magazine Body Building 200,000-250,000 people in Sweden regularly train together, and many more do so at home in private.

Similar developments are to be found in singing and music. According to a recent investigation, in 1987 half a million Swedes belonged to choirs, of which there were between 12,000 and 17,000 in the country. Choral singing has thus developed into a popular movement.

On a somewhat smaller scale the number of people playing in orchestras of various kinds – chamber music, jazz, and pop – is also growing.

Fragmentation and specialization have also affected travel. The volume of package travel has remained more or less constant, but the focus has changed. Mass tourism is giving way to guided tours under knowledgeable leaders. The programmes can range from exotic foreign travel, art and music tours, nature tours, to excitement and adventure in the shape of shooting the rapids, log rafting, igloo tours in Greenland, dog-team driving in the north of Sweden, mountain climbing, etc.

Specialization has also left its mark on the world of the theatre and film. Small theatres are proliferating; Stockholm alone boasts 53 theatres, which makes it the most theatre-intensive city in the world relative to its population, and the productions on offer are widely varied. The same thing is happening in the cinema. Big cinemas are being split into several small ones, allowing for greater variety and the satisfaction of many interests.

Why Just Now?

One can ask why consumption patterns, activities, and ways of behaving have started to change so noticeably during the 1980s, as our examples show that they have done. A change of such magnitude stems not from a single cause but from several in combination.

The dissolution of established norms is probably the most important explanatory factor. Previously much consumption was predetermined, controlled extraneously by prevailing ideas about how people in particular categories – age, occupation, family type – were expected to behave and consume. The new priorities and specializations spring from the greater freedom people have acquired to follow their own inner needs and desires.

But several forces are probably working in the same direction. When individualism replaces collectivism, prestige attaches not to the imitation of group behaviour but to unique individual behaviours and forms of consumption. The value systems of today also contain elements of élitism. It is more prestigious to excel in one field than to be equally good in many. Thus external norms are still at work, but now combined with more opportunity for following personal and individual needs.

Specialization, giving priority to some particular area or areas, has positive side-effects. To know one field well, to be an expert, engenders self-confidence and self-respect. The continuous learning that accompanies refined consumption, increases the payoff; the enjoyment is all the greater. This type of consumption also encourages initiative. It utilizes the whole of a person's capacity, thus satisfying the need for self-realization and personal development. Consumption is being moved higher and higher up the hierarchy of needs.

Another related aspect is the growing interest in immaterial things and activities, which manifests itself in two rather different ways.

One is in concern for individual physical and mental well-being. Sports and keep-fit activities, preventive health care, and the emphasis on active leisure are expressions of this interest. Once again it is a question of a shift in values from the group to the individual.

The second is the growing interest in spiritual values, aesthetics, culture, and ethics. This can be seen as an expression of material satiation, a reaction against the excessively rational, and the dearth that has accumulated over the years of objects and activities to answer the needs of the soul.

Originally consumption was supposed to meet our material needs. But as consumption has risen, the importance and power of the psychological values have grown. What the consumption patterns of the 1980s signify is that people are seeking to express needs that could previously be satisfied in other roles – in working life, in the family, and in the community at large.

Even in the new consumption pattern mass-produced goods and services still play an important part. They represent the conditions for a comfortable life. But their availability and their high quality are taken for granted today, and growth is now found largely in the kind of consumption that addresses a variety of perceived gaps. Industrial society has concentrated on productivity and efficiency, and has done so with great success. But the price has been the physical and mental well-being of the individual. In his introductory address to the World Future Society's Professional Members Forum in Salzburg, 27-30 June 1988, the peace and futures researcher Robert Jungk talked about the missing link in futures studies: aesthetics and art – neither of which are of any material use. Art and beauty appeal to the emotions and to people's undernourished souls. The present art and beauty boom, Jungk continued, is a compensation for a society with rationality in plenty; but man longs for something else besides – science and art, comfort and pleasure. Thus it is products and services promoting health and physical vitality or satisfying spiritual values – aesthetics, ethics, and culture in various forms – which offer the greatest potential for the future. Consumption that contributes to a long active and rich inner life is the kind that is growing.

Thus the contradictions in the consumption of the 1980s which we touched upon in our introduction are not a disconnected or incomprehensible phenomenon. The pattern in these contradictions can be seen as a logical consequence of the forces of change which have reshaped industrial society and released the human need for self-development, identity, and context. That the pattern of consumption has simultaneously become more individualized, more creative, more experiential – but also more confusing and paradoxical – is of course no coincidence. In the society of gilded necessity the consumer is also a producer with a chance to consume his way into a life of creativity, individualized to his own special conditions. Individual creating and learning is consumption's new function. It is a function that will not make life easier for the producers of goods and services, nor for consumption researchers and makers of consumer policy.

Notes

1. Cf. Maslow's typology of needs, which includes five categories: physiological needs, safety, love, esteem, and self-actualization (Maslow, 1954), and Barnes's modification of Maslow: physiological needs at the bottom and a higher level made up of self-esteem, esteem for others, and belongingness (Barnes, 1960). Harrison (1966) suggests a similar scheme with the physiological-economic needs at the bottom. Upon satisfaction of these needs, a higher level of social ego needs is then sought. Alderfer (1969), combining the elements of Maslow's need hierarchy, assumes that a human being has three core needs: material existence needs, relatedness needs (including all the needs which involve relationships with significant others), and growth needs (including all the needs which involve the individual in producing creative or productive effects on himself and his environment).

2. This work represents part of an ongoing study of the renewal of consumer goods companies, which is being carried out by the authors of the present article.

3. This information comes from an interview included in an ongoing study. See Note 2.

References

Alderfer, C.P. (1969). An empirical test of a new theory of human needs. *Organizational Behavior and Human Performance, 4*, 142-175.

Angyal, A. (1941). *Foundations for a science of personality.* New York: The Common Wealth Fund.

Asplund, J. (1967). *Om mättnadsprocesser* (On satiation processes). Uppsala: Argus.

Barnes, L. (1960). *Organizational systems and engineering groups.* Boston: Harvard Graduate School of Business.

Bettman, J.R. (1979). *An information processing theory of consumer choice.* Reading, MA: Addison-Wesley.

de Geer, H., Ekstedt, E., Elvander, N., Henning, R., Lyttkens, L., Norgren, L., Sjölund, M., & Wikström, S. (1987). In the wale of the future. Swedish Perspectives on the Problems of Structural change. Aldershot: Gower.

Elg, U., Johansson, U., Tollin, K., & Wikström, S. (1987). *Matens metamorfos* (The food metamorphosis). Stockholm: LT:s förlag.

Fromm, E. (1978). *To have or to be*. London: Cape.

Harrison, R. (1966). *A conceptual framework for laboratory training*. Mimeo.

Hirsch, F. (1976). *Social limits to growth*. Gambridge, MA: Harvard University Press.

Hirschman, E., & Holbrook, M. (1982). Hedonic consumption: Emerging concepts, methods, and propositions. *Journal of Marketing, 46* (2), 92-101.

Holbrook, M., & Hirschman, E. (1986). The experiential aspects of consumption: Consumer fantasies, feelings, and fun. *Journal of Consumer Research, 9*, 132-140.

Leiss, W. (1978). *The limits to satisfaction*. London: Marion Boyars.

Lyttkens, L. (1988). *Politikens klicheér och människans ansikte* (The clichés of politics and the face of man). Stockholm: Akademeja.

Maddox, R.N. (1981). Two-factor theory and consumer satisfaction: Replication and extension. *Journal of Consumer Research, 8*, 97-102.

Maslow, A.H. (1954). *Motivation and personality*. New York: Harper.

Riesman, D. (1950). *The lonely crowd*. New Haven, CT: Yale University Press.

Scitovsky, T. (1978). *The joyless economy*. Oxford: Oxford University Press.

Swan, J.E., & Combs, L.J. (1976). Product performance and consumer satisfaction: A new concept. *Journal of Marketing, 40*(2), 25-33.

Unger, L.S., & Kernan, J.B. (1983). On the meaning of leisure: An investigation of some determinants of the subjective experience. *Journal of Consumer Research, 9*, 381-392.

Uusitalo, L. (1986). *Environmental impacts of consumption patterns*. Aldershot: Gower.

Veblen, T. (1953). *The theory of the leisure class*. New York: Mentor Books. (First edition 1899.)

Susanne C. Grunert

Personality Traits as Elements in a Model of Eating Behaviour

Abstract

Many more factors than physiological needs determine eating behaviour, and several disciplines have offered different explanations to enlighten the manifold aspects of eating behaviour and food habits. A review of these is given, which reveals that an integrated model, supported by empirical findings, is still missing. The importance of an individual's personality traits has been given little attention so far. In this paper, the attempt is made to move towards such an integrated model by considering those personality traits that may be particularly relevant in shaping the cognitive, emotional, and conative components of an individual's eating behaviour. The traits considered here are self-consciousness, body consciousness, and locus of control.

Author's address: Susanne C. Grunert, University of Hohenheim, Institute for Consumer and Home Economics (530), P.O. Box 70 05 62, D-7000 Stuttgart 70, West Germany.

Investigating Eating Behaviour – Basic Ideas

According to the Advanced Learner's Dictionary of Current English, nutrition means "the process of supplying and receiving nourishment" as well as "the science of food values." These definitions are at the same time simple and revealing as both imply an important fact – that physiological needs are of decisive importance in shaping eating behaviour: To maintain the body functions, the organism needs a well-regulated intake of food and fluid. For an efficient regulation, meeting these requirements, the organism must be able to recognize the signals of nutrient needs, to initiate eating behaviour, and to control it in such a way that food intake will be terminated when the supply of nutrients is sufficient. Sensations of hunger and thirst are such necessary signals, leading to a motivational state in which a general and/or specific physiological shortage of the organism interacts with the totality of genetic, structural, and dynamic dispositions of an individual, giving rise, together with environmental factors, to a certain eating behaviour.

The term "nutrition" deals primarily with the physiological needs of the body in terms of specific nutrients and the means of supplying these nutrients through adequate diets, whereas "eating behaviour" is defined as all planned or spontaneous activities directed towards the procurement, preparation, and consumption of food, also including the social, symbolic, and ritual uses of food (Diehl & Leitzmann, 1985). With the term "food habits" one describes recurrent performances of food-related behavioural sequences by which an individual or social group selects, prepares, or consumes food, directly or indirectly, as a part of cultural, social, and religious practices.

In addition to the natural sciences which have contributed much to our knowledge of the physiological aspects of nutrition, the following four fields of social science have tried to assess the factors which influence eating behaviour and food habits: Economics, both at the macro and micro levels, sociology, anthropology, and psychology. Looking at the major outcomes of these research efforts, it seems that one important concept – with regard to so-called normal eating behaviour – has been neglected so far: the individual's personality traits. It is argued here that personality traits play a strong role in the psychological control of food intake, thus shaping the cognitive, emotional, and conative components of an individual's eating behaviour. Personality traits are interpreted in this context as latent variables underlying the manifest food habits. Those deemed especially relevant can be described by the following key-words: Self-consciousness, body consciousness, and locus of control. Together with other explanatory factors they should be of help in the development of an integrated model of eating behaviour which might then be subjected to empirical testing.

Social Science Contributions to the Understanding of Eating Behaviour

Economics

Out of the manifold aspects of the phenomenon of eating behaviour or food habits, economic analysis has concentrated on a very limited subset, viz., the way in which quantities and types of food bought by consumers reflect changes in prices and consumer incomes. The roots of this analysis are found in the 19th century, and are associated with well-known names – Gossen, Engel, and Giffen.

Gossen put forward the law of diminishing marginal utility: A need looses its intensity while being satisfied. When satiety sets in, continued consumption results in reluctance. Engel demonstrated that with increasing income, the expenditure on food increases in absolute terms, but decreases as a relative proportion of income as the income elasticity of demand for food is less than one. A special case of an anomalous demand curve was exemplified by Giffen who showed that an increase in the price of an inferior good, e.g., bread, can lead to increased demand for this good when household income is low and, therefore, the negative real income effect more than compensates for the substitution effect.

It is interesting that these three "classic" economic laws were first formulated in the context of consumers' food expenditures, and were only afterwards applied to other areas of consumption. This might be due to the fact that nutrition is the basic prerequisite for human survival. It is evident, however, that sufficient food supply for everybody was more critical in the last century than it is now, also in those countries which today are characterized by abundance. The question can be raised whether the old laws remain valid in affluent societies.

Summarizing the main findings of economic analysis on the relationships between consumption, income, and prices, one has to conclude that in general anything can happen. Expenditure on food can either decrease or increase when prices rise. Since the Giffen case is a rare exception, though still relevant for some developing countries, it can usually be assumed that the demand reacts inversely, but not at the same rate as price rises (Tangermann, 1986). However, price and income elasticities of food demand have upper as well as lower limits, because food is at the same time a necessity and a saturation good. Looking at the long-term development of food consumption, it becomes evident that food as such – the physical raw material contained in food products – is subject to natural saturation, whereas the processed part of food is consumed in increasing amounts. Hence, the income elasticity of the demand for processing is greater than that for the raw product content of food (Buse, 1986; Strecker, Reichert, & Pottebaum, 1976).

A closer look should thus be taken at factors like "consumption habits," "preferences," or "tastes" which usually are not in the focus of economic analysis. According to Hirschman (1982), the disinterest in food consumption analysis shown by most economists relates to the fact that the income elasticity of demand is lower for perishable goods than for durable goods and services. He criticizes this low esteem and labels food as "truly nondurable goods" which provide pleasures that are simple, familiar, yet intense and indefinitely renewable because these pleasures are based on the body's recurring physiological need for energy food supplies: Foodstuffs disappear precisely when conveying their energy to the organism, and their disappearance is essential to the pleasure felt in the act of consumption. Hirschman's view is empirically supported by Silberberg (1985), who demonstrated that the law of diminishing marginal utility, applied to food nutrients, should be interpreted as follows: With increasing income, consumers shift toward the pleasurable aspects of food consumption and attach less importance to the production of nourishment.

That these aspects have so far not been investigated in more detail, seems to be related to the fact that the progress made by economic theory in analysing consumers' food consumption lies mainly in explaining market demand for a general product class (Meulenberg, 1985), rather than in explanations of choices of specific product variants.

Sociology

A sociological perspective on human eating behaviour can hardly be found. Although sociology deals with every aspect of the life of human beings in groups and, in particular, studies the influence of group life on individual behaviour and identity, very few sociologists have devoted their research efforts to food consumption patterns.

One of the few is Elias (1969) who illustrates his interesting analysis of the civilizing process with, inter alia, the historical development of table manners towards a more and more regulated and comprehensive control of individual behaviour. Analogous to this approach of so-called figurational sociology, Mennell (1986) describes the "civilizing of appetite" as strongly related to the increasing security, regularity, reliability, and variety of food supply. Furthermore, he claims that the possibility of consuming large quantities of food as an expression of social superiority has reached its limits, whereas the qualitative possibilities are inexhaustible. Evident signals for this development are the proliferating refinements of cooking recipes, the growing publication of cookbooks and magazines, and the many ways of demonstrating a gourmet's knowledge.

Using a similar socio-historical approach, Bourdieu (1984) concentrates on a sociology of tastes. He regards tastes, and the distinctions which they substantialize, as a cultural system which determines the relationships among the social classes, and at the same time expresses the standards which membership of these classes involves. Therefore, tastes in food can be related, as tastes in art and popular culture, to the body images which the classes hold, and are also a symbol of the relationship between the sexes. Tastes are socially transmitted and are, thus, carriers of the order of things in general, and of the order of society in particular. This view can be illustrated by considering two basic cultural attributes of food: strength and health. All foods can provide strength, though meat is seen as the best source as it is associated with masculinity, courage, and virility. Health is connected with vegetarianism which is associated with femininity, purity, and naturalness (Twigg, 1984).

Recently, a "sociology of nutrition" has been called for in the proposal of a framework to investigate food consumers' motivations and behaviour (Kutsch, 1985). This framework stretches from a macro perspective to the individual level by identifying and structuring the social conditions of eating behaviour in four contexts:

– a cultural context, including historical perspectives and intercultural aspects;

– a socio-structural context, considering consumption norms as well as role and class specific behaviour;

– a group context, concerned with family and peer group influences;

– a personal context, limited to the three constructs interpersonal influence, opinion leadership, and reactance to advertising.

Although this framework is a first systematization of sociological perspectives on eating behaviour, a theory regarding the sociological aspects of food consumption patterns is still missing.

Anthropology

Studying a group's way of life as it is passed on from generation to generation, anthropology, unlike sociology, has developed its own methodology of investigating food habits. The integration of dietary-nutritional themes with anthropological issues has a long tradition. It can be traced back to descriptions provided by ancient societies in China, Egypt, or Italy (see Grivetti, 1981), was stimulated by colonialism which facilitated the observation of dietary patterns of natives (e.g., Adlung, 1912) and led to a search for the complex relationships among natural environment, human physiology, and culture (e.g., de Garine, 1979).

Although clear differences cannot be defined, four main lines of research may be distinguished. One deals with a wide range of aspects that relate food consumption patterns to ethnic identity, culinary tradition, social structure, social status, and cultural change. For example, Richards (1932) demonstrated that food production and distribution patterns were core elements of social structure. Fischler (1981) described recent changes in culinary traditions as a crisis of gastronomy where, on the one hand, the power of the "empire of snacks" increases, while on the other hand a state of "gastro-anomy" is attained, where food faddists, diet freaks, and gourmets all search for new dietary goals and norms.

A second line of research stresses the individual cognitive aspects of food, analysing its non-physiological meanings as, e.g., expressions of prestige and status, fear reducing and rewarding functions, and pleasure aspects (Pumpian-Mindlin, 1954; Woods, 1960).

A third group concentrates on "cultural nutrition," defining nutritional anthropology as a subfield. There are different methodological approaches:

– Environmentalism: Food intake is seen as regulated primarily by environmental conditions and climatic factors;

– Cultural determinism: Culture is viewed as the main determinant of diet because humans are regarded as having the capacity to mould their environment at will;

– Functionalism: Food habits are explained on a non-nutritional basis, i.e., they are not regarded as founded on physiological needs but as markers to identify the age, gender, class, and social status of the consumer.

The common basic idea, however, is that humans seek food, not nutrients, and that dietary patterns are best understood through examination of cultural, economic, environmental, and historical determinants (Grivetti, 1981).

The fourth approach calls for a comprehensive biocultural perspective, explaining eating behaviour as the result of both biological and cultural forces which are inseparably intertwined. It also uses a concept of human ecology which interprets food as the means of transferring energy among ecosystem components and nutritional requirements as conditioned by a multiplicity of ecological factors. Hence, the nutritional system is defined "as a series of biocultural transitions, mediated by human decisions at every stage from food production, through dietary intake, to nutritional status and its health, and behavioural consequences" (Kandel, Jerome, & Pelto, 1980).

In conclusion, nutritional anthropology is concerned with a wide range of factors influencing eating behaviour and presents an extensive research agenda under the heading "you are what you eat" (Murcott, 1986).

Psychology

Concentrating the research efforts on the level of individual behaviour, psychology seems to have an ambiguous attitude towards eating behaviour. A multitude of studies have emerged in the last decades, but they concentrate almost exclusively on aberrant food patterns and neglect the normal range of eating behaviour.

A general model of individual behaviour (Sherif & Sherif, 1969) can serve as a basic conceptual framework for nutrition psychology. It uses as the frame of reference the totality of interrelated external and internal factors that are operative at a given moment in time. In the context of nutrition, the eating behaviour of an individual is then the result of central structuring and processing of external and internal determinants, none of which have a single, direct, and independent influence. Examples of external factors are availability of food, relationships with family members and other reference persons, messages in the mass media, and the time, place, and occasion for eating. Physiological needs, nutritional knowledge, attitudes, self-concept, emotions, and personality traits belong to the internal determinants. Factors that influence eating behaviour both internally and externally are, e.g., education, culture, religion, and status (Diehl, 1980).

Given this basic scheme, empirical psychologically oriented studies deal with different aspects of eating behaviour by assessing the determinants of:
- abnormal eating habits leading to obesity, anorexia, or bulimia;
- the development of eating behaviour;
- individual food aversions;
- food faddisms.

There are two basic limitations in the psychological research published to date. First, the emphasis on deviating eating behaviour is striking and well documented by the large number of studies conducted in this area. This is perhaps because deviant eating behaviour can be operationalized in a simpler fashion, and because a comparison of extreme groups results in a higher probability that hypotheses get confirmed (see Wilson, 1979, for an annotated bibliography; Diehl, 1980, for a comprehensive literature review and analysis). Second, there is a striking lack of investigations of personality traits as determinants of eating behaviour – except for a psychoanalytic approach to the "oral character" and, again, studies of eating disorders like obesity, anorexia, and bulimia. It is difficult to believe that personality traits should not be relevant in shaping also normal eating behaviour.

Evaluating the Contributions

The main objectives of this admittedly rather summary review have been, first, to demonstrate that eating behaviour has indeed been of interest in several different research traditions; second, to illustrate that despite all the interesting and important findings an integrated model or conceptual framework is still missing.

In the remainder of this paper, an attempt to fill this gap will be made by putting the emphasis on personality traits of individuals. They are regarded as the variables that determine to what extent economic, socio-cultural, and anthropological factors are allowed to manifest their influence on human eating behaviour.

A Model for the Regulation of Eating

Beside economic, sociological, anthropological, and psychological factors, physiological needs play an important role in shaping eating behaviour. As has been stated above, the organism must be able to recognize signals of nutrient needs, to initiate eating behaviour, and to control it in such a way that the food intake will be terminated when the supply of nutrients is sufficient. Given the manifold determinants of food consumption patterns, it is obviously necessary to find a common framework for classification. The "boundary model for the regulation of eating" in Figure 1 is such an attempt to integrate as well as to distinguish between physiological and psychological determinants (Herman & Polivy, 1984).

The basic assumption is that food intake is regulated by two boundaries. These boundaries designate the state of hunger on the one side, of satiety on the other. The area in between is called the range of biological indifference. Thus, hunger and satiety are regarded as two separate processes which influence food intake of the organism only outside the range of biological indifference. Within this range, psychological factors determine the eating behaviour of an individual. These factors, however, can also have limited spill-over effects in the physiological zones of hunger and satiety, and, more importantly, individuals can differ in the width of their range of biological indifference.

317

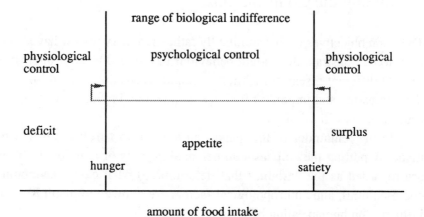

Figure 1: The boundary model for the regulation of eating (Herman & Polivy, 1984).

Eating Behaviour and Personality Traits

Three eating-related concepts are helpful in finding out which personality traits might be relevant for explaining eating behaviour. Although emerged from studies of eating disorders, they can, at a first stage, help also to explain important aspects of normal food habits (Ruderman, 1986):

— the first concept, **emotionally induced eating**, designates food intake caused by emotions like anger, uncertainty, or loneliness (e.g., Menzies, 1970);

— the second concept, **externally stimulated eating**, based on Schachter and Singer's cognitive-physiological theory of emotions (1962), assumes that the eating behaviour of individuals can be relatively independent of internal body signals and thus is largely controlled by external food cues;

— the third concept, **restrained eating**, describes persons who keep their body weight problems within limits by permanent light dieting (e.g., Herman & Mack, 1975).

These three concepts all deal with the behavioural intention or actual behaviour of individuals under stress conditions, i.e., individuals who try to compensate unpleasant feelings or emotional disturbances through

318

food intake. It is rather the wish to eat as such that counts, than the kind or quantity of food consumed (although this latter aspect should be subject to further research). While the first two concepts, emotionally induced and externally stimulated eating behaviour, describe strategies to cope with frustrations, the third concept of restrained eating is more concerned with the possible outcome of these strategies: After consuming larger food quantities due to emotions or external stimuli, individuals counterregulate by restricting their food intake during a certain period until they regain their usual body weight. The major common aspect of these behavioural intentions and actual behaviour is that they all disregard physiological signals of hunger and satiety and manifest their influence within the range of biological indifference. Thus, emotional states, external stimuli, and restriction should be part of the psychological control of food intake (Grunert, 1988).

Other psychological determinants will complement and/or interfere with these three factors. It is natural to conceive personality traits as intervening variables which determine the extent of influence an individual "allows" emotional or external factors to exert. With regard to nutritional reactions to external and internal stimuli, there are especially three personality trait concepts which may be relevant: Self-consciousness, body consciousness, and locus of control. They have been explicitly chosen because they are known to distinguish between those individuals who are highly aware of their self and body, their needs and capacities, and those individuals who are to a much greater extent subject to external, cultural, emotional, and social influences.

Recently, Buss and Finn (1987) proposed a classification of personality traits which distinguishes among instrumental, affective, and cognitive traits, all three groups being divided into self-related and other-related aspects as well as socially relevant and non-socially relevant aspects (see Figure 2).

When compared with Figure 2, the model launched in this paper includes only self-related cognitive traits of a social or non-social nature. The main reason for this is that normal eating behaviour implies an ability to be cognitively aware of bodily states. Nevertheless, future research has to look into possible relationships between eating behaviour and personality traits like anger, fear, well-being, excitement seeking, or impulsivity as they may also, to a considerable extent, influence the control of food intake.

	Instrumental traits		Affective traits		Cognitive traits	
	Power	Prosocial	Self	Nonself	Self	Nonself
Social	Dominance (M) Rebelliousness (M) Aggressiveness (M) Macchiavellianism Impression management	Sociability Altruism (F) Nurturance (F) Succourance (F)	Shyness Shame	Empathy (F) Resentment	Public self-consciousness Locus of control Morality	Perspective of others Interpersonal trust Sensitivity to expressive behaviour in others
Non-social	Activity (M) Excitement seeking (M) Impulsivity Achievement		Guilt (F) Well-being	Anger (M) Fear (F)	Private self-consciousness Self-esteem Gender identity	Absorption Blunter-monitor

(M) indicates that men score higher on the trait; (F) indicates that women score higher on the trait.

Figure 2: A classification of personality traits (Buss & Finn, 1987).

Self-Consciousness

The process of a person focussing attention on his/her own self as an object has been described by the theory of objective self-awareness (Duval & Wicklund, 1972). According to Fenigstein, Scheier, and Buss (1975), however, self-awareness refers only to a transitory state because the existence of self-directed attention is the result of situational variables. In contrast to this, they introduce the term self-consciousness, defined as a constant and consistent tendency of a person to direct his/her attention more inwardly or more outwardly. In this sense, self-consciousness is a permanent behavioural disposition.

Fenigstein et al. (1975) distinguished two separate aspects of self-consciousness. One dimension consists of a cognitive, private reflecting on the self, the other describes a concern with the self as a social stimulus in the sense of being subject to public attention. A third dimension of their scales assesses social anxiety, which refers to a reaction to the aforementioned processes of self-focused attention. This trait is relevant in the context of emotionally induced and externally stimulated eating as a strategy for coping with the unpleasant feeling of uncertainty. With regard to restrained eating and social anxiety, it is conceivable that an individual may control food intake by permanently dieting in order to avoid social sanctions due to overweight. The private aspect of self-consciousness accounts for the tendency to attend to one's inner thoughts and feelings. This inward attention should comprise an attentive monitoring of internal bodily signals, which results in an appropriate regulation of eating – this monitoring process is the basis for eating within a normal range of food intake (Cappon, 1973). Contrary to this, public self-consciousness should be more related to the concern over one's body appearance and could thus lead to a quantitative control of food intake, similar to the effect of social anxiety.

Another aspect of private self-consciousness is interesting in the context of eating. Mullen and Suls (1982) conducted a study to examine the ameliorative effect of private self-consciousness on stressful life events in relation to physical health. Their results suggest that individuals scoring high on this trait are more likely to notice their psychological and somatic reactions to stressful situations and take instrumental actions which ameliorate their reactions to stressors. Hence, these persons are, for example, supposed not to mix up internal hunger feelings with emotional distress.

Body Consciousness

Does the private-public distinction as regards self-consciousness also apply to the awareness of one's own body? Analogous to the above-mentioned self-consciousness inventory, a body consciousness questionnaire has been developed (Miller, Murphy, & Buss, 1981). Using this questionnaire, these authors have demonstrated that there are three separate personality dispositions concerning body consciousness.

One is called body competence, an evaluative factor concerning strength and grace of the body. The corresponding items endorse effective body functioning. Thus, this factor should be negatively related to the three aspects of eating behaviour in focus here since they imply an ineffective control of food intake in the sense of disregard of physiological bodily signals. The public dimension of body consciousness consists of a chronic tendency to be concerned with and focus on the external appearance of the body, that is the observable aspects of one's body. The difference from public self-consciousness lies in a more distinct formulation of the corresponding items, which, in the Self-Consciousness Scales, are only indirectly addressing body image aspects. The private dimension of body consciousness describes a disposition to concentrate on internal bodily sensations.

Correlation analysis of the two inventories revealed that an interest in the psychological aspects of one's self, i.e., self-consciousness, is significantly associated with an interest in the bodily aspects of oneself, regardless of whether the focus is private or public. The two public dimensions appear to be essentially the same, whereas the two private aspects, although related, seem to be distinct personality traits. Experiments have shown that private body consciousness is the pre-eminent determinant of awareness of bodily sensations, whereas private self-consciousness only adds to the awareness for those who already score high on private body consciousness (Miller et al., 1981).

As Cappon (1973) emphasizes, normal eating behaviour presupposes an ability to be cognitively aware of hunger and satiety signals, independent of external stimuli. Therefore, it appears reasonable to suggest that those individuals high in private body consciousness should regulate their food intake according to internal bodily states to a higher degree than those who are low in private body consciousness and, thus, more susceptible to external cues.

Locus of Control

The perception of which control instances decide one's personal success or failure, is a variable considerably influencing consumption and life styles (e.g., Arbuthnot, 1977). The construct of "locus of control of reinforcement" has been introduced by Rotter (1966) and comprises generalized expectancies of individuals about the possibilities to influence their own fortunes. Internal control refers to individuals who ascribe success or failure to their own behaviour, capacities, or attributes. External control refers to individuals who are convinced that powerful others, luck, or coincidences are mainly responsible for their fate. Empirical studies indicate a strong relationship between internal-external control and other personality traits. Internals are more tolerant, sociable, intellectual, and achieving, whereas externals are more anxious, frustrated, aggressive, and dogmatic (Joe, 1971). With specific relation to health issues, research shows that, faced with health problems, internals are more likely to make adaptive responses than are externals (Kristiansen, 1987; Strickland, 1978).

With regard to eating behaviour, the construct of internal external control should be helpful in revealing where individuals perceive the responsibility for their food intake to lie, how resistant they are to external influences, and to what extent they conform to socially established nutritional norms. Internals are supposed to know better why, what, and when to eat and, thus, to be more likely to mould their environment according to their needs – for example by keeping a healthy and well-balanced diet or by being concerned with ecological problems related to food. By contrast, it is suggested that externals are more susceptible to situational influences and more conforming to fashion trends like, e.g., fast-food eating styles.

Hypotheses

Summarizing these theoretical notions, two sets of hypotheses can be formulated:

Hypotheses A: Negative relationships exist between emotionally induced, externally stimulated, and restrained eating behaviour and (1) private self-consciousness, (2) private body consciousness, (3) body competence, (4) internal locus of control.

This set of hypotheses is based on the assumption that those individuals who score high on the traits mentioned under (1) to (4) regulate their food intake predominantly in response to internal physiological signals of hunger and satiety. Their range of biological indifference is correspondingly small.

Hypotheses B: Positive relationships exist between emotionally stimulated, externally induced, and restrained eating behaviour and (1) public self-consciousness, (2) public body consciousness, (3) social anxiety, (4) external locus of control.

323

Individuals who score high on these traits are supposed to disregard internal signals of hunger and satiety and to rely mainly on non-physiological cues when "regulating" their food intake. Thus, their range of biological indifference is wide.

Empirical Findings

These sets of hypotheses were tested in a study carried out in 1987 using the above described variables as the independent ones, i.e., as those factors which influence the regulation of food intake within the range of biological indifference, and as dependent variables emotionally induced, externally stimulated, and restrained eating behaviour. The concept of locus of control was not included. This concept has to be assessed with specific scales (Joe, 1971) and no such inventory for measuring eating-related locus of control orientations has been developed so far – a gap to be filled in the near future. Emotionally induced, externally stimulated, and restrained eating behaviour was measured on the basis of self-report statements contained in the Dutch Eating Behaviour Questionnaire (Van Strien et al., 1986).

All scales were translated into German by the author. The Self-Consciousness Scales consist of 23 items, of which ten ascertain private self-consciousness, seven public self-consciousness, and six social anxiety. The Body Consciousness Scales contain 15 items, five for the assessment of private body consciousness, six for public body consciousness, and four for body competence. The German version of the Eating Behaviour Inventory is composed of ten items for each of the three behavioural dispositions (Grunert, forthcoming). The sequence of items within each inventory followed those of the original scales. Answering to the statements was by five-point scales with the adverbial modificators never, seldom, sometimes, often, and very often. Questions assessing the demographic data gender, age, weight, and height preceded the inventories. The questionnaire was self-administered by the respondents who were undergraduate students at the University of Hohenheim. 119 questionnaires were included in the data analysis. Results of scale and item analyses are reported elsewhere (Grunert, 1987).

Correlation coeficients (Pearson's r) were computed between the sum scores of the subscales of the respective inventories for testing all the hypotheses except A(4) and B(4). As Table 1 reveals, none but Hypothesis A(3) was completely confirmed. Hypotheses B(1), B(2), and B(3) were partially confirmed; B(1) and B(2) with regard to restrained eating behaviour, B(3) with regard to emotionally induced and externally stimulated eating behaviour. Hypotheses A(1) and A(2) were rejected in the sense that instead of the predicted negative correlations a lack of significant relationships was observed indicating that private self-consciousness and private body consciousness have little to do with any of the three aspects of eating behaviour.

Table 1: Correlations Between Different Aspects of Eating Behaviour and Personality Traits

	Private self consciousness	Public self consciousness	Social anxiety	Private body consciousness	Public body consciousness	Body competence
Emotionally induced eating	.10	−.07	.32***	−.02	.00	−.26**
Externally stimulated eating	−.06	−.07	.30***	.30	−.10	−.33***
Restrained eating	.13	.22**	.05	−.08	.39***	−.21*

Note: * $p<0.05$, ** $p<0.01$, *** $p<0.001$.

With regard to Hypotheses B(1) to B(3), the expected relationships between public self-consciousness and public body consciousness on the one side and emotionally induced as well as externally stimulated eating behaviour on the other, and between social anxiety and restrained eating behaviour, respectively, did not emerge. The positive correlation between social anxiety and emotionally induced and externally stimulated eating behaviour may be explained by the fact that individuals marked by a high degree of social anxiety possess a heightened reactivity to emotional cues and external stimuli; a similar pattern has been demonstrated with feelings of fear (Schachter, Goldman, & Gordon,

1968; Slochower, 1983). There is a link between public self-consciousness, public body consciousness, and social anxiety in the sense that individuals scoring high on these traits are concerned with their public appearance and with the impression they arouse in other people. As the data revealed, these concerns lead to different reactions with regard to eating behaviour. Whereas the public aspects of self-consciousness and body consciousness relate to a restrained food intake involving a cognitive appraisal of one's body contours, social anxiety is associated more with a coping strategy, i.e., with compensating one's unpleasant feelings of insecurity through eating. The finding that social anxiety is not linked to restrained eating behaviour seems to illustrate that dieting calls for a strong will and continuous effort which is somewhat incompatible with social anxiety, a trait which includes feelings of helplessness and incompetence.

The confirmation of Hypothesis A(3), i.e., finding negative relationships between body competence and all aspects of eating behaviour, is in accordance with one of the results reported by Miller et al. (1981). Using the Emotionality Scale of the EASI (Emotionality, Activity, Sociability, Impulsivity) Temperament Survey (Buss & Plomin, 1975), they found negative correlations between body competence and the negative end of emotionality, e.g., tendencies to become frightened, upset, or angry.

Because only some of the personality traits investigated were related to eating behaviour in the predicted way, it is of course appropriate to ask whether personality traits do indeed influence the psychological control of food intake. In this exploratory phase, a definite rejection cannot be made however. Firstly, other personality traits might also be relevant in this context and considered in future research. Secondly, there is a methodological caveat. The internal consistency (Cronbach's alpha) of the scales employed proved to be sufficient, but highly satisfactory only for the eating behaviour inventory (Grunert, 1987). It is thus conceivable that the hypothesized relationships would emerge through the use of improved versions of the Self-Consciousness and Body Consciousness Scales. Moreover, it would certainly be desirable to administer the scales to non-student respondents and a larger sample.

A regression analysis with the three aspects of eating behaviour as dependent variables and the personality variables as the independent ones, by and large confirmed the correlation results and indicated that the variables investigated here account for up to 28% of the variance in self-reported eating behaviour (Table 2).

Table 2: Results of the Regression Analysis

Dependent variables	Constant	Regression coefficients (standard error)						r^2
		Independent variables						
		Private self-conscious-ness	Public self-conscious-ness	Social anxiety	Private body con-scious-ness	Public body con-scious-ness	Body Compe-tence	
Emotionally induced eating	21.32 (6.95)	.30 (.17)	–.46 (.27)	.47** (.16)	–.22 (.26)	.22 (.23)	–.55* (.25)	.17
Externally stimulated eating	37.38 (5.37)	–.08 (.14)	–.03 (.21)	.29* (.13)	.26 (.20)	–.13 (.18)	–.66*** (.19)	.19
Restrained eating	19.06 (7.36)	.14 (.19)	–.08 (.28)	.01 (.17)	–.68* (.28)	1.18*** (.24)	–.73** (.26)	.28

Note: * t <0.05, ** t <0.01, *** t <0.001.

Conclusion: Proposing an Integrated Model of Eating Behaviour

The three personality traits of self-consciousness, body consciousness, and locus of control are hypothesized to be important variables influencing normal eating behaviour within the range of biological indifference. Empirical findings indicate that – with the exception of locus of control which could not be assessed – these traits do account for some part of the regulation of food intake.

Figure 3 is an attempt to integrate the determinants of consumers' eating behaviour that have been discussed in this paper. The model is intended to serve as a basis for developing a research design that can be subjected to more detailed empirical testing, e.g., by causal analysis

(Bagozzi, 1980; Bentler, 1980), in order to assess the extent to which each of the factors determine eating behaviour.

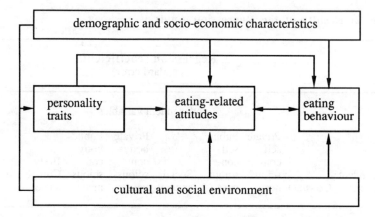

Figure 3: A model of eating behaviour including personality traits.

The concept of eating-related attitudes is introduced here as a mediator between personality traits, demographic and socio-economic characteristics, and environmental factors, on the one hand, and eating behaviour on the other hand. The relationship between attitudes and behaviour is a highly controversial topic (Benninghaus, 1976; Wicker, 1969). The low predictive power of attitudes may, however, be due to the fact that attitudes have been regarded as determined wholly by the cognitive structure with respect to the attitude object (Fishbein & Ajzen, 1975), disregarding personality traits altogether. As a mediator between general dispositions and specific behaviour, attitudes on food consumption may turn out to be useful; the mediator function representing the generative mechanism through which a focal independent variable is able to influence the dependent variable of interest (Baron & Kenny, 1986). In effect, it would be surprising if aspects such as health-related attitudes, expression of social contacts, and aesthetical, ethical, and religious beliefs (van Raaij, 1984) would not play a role in the determination of eating behaviour.

References

Adlung (1912). Die wichtigsten vegetabilischen Nahrungsmittel der in den deutschen Schutzgebieten lebenden Eingeborenen. *Der Tropenpflanzer, 10*, 547-551.

Arbuthnot, J. (1977). The roles of attitudinal and personality variables in the prediction of environmental behavior and knowledge. *Environment and Behavior, 9*, 217-232.

Bagozzi, R.P. (1980). *Causal models in marketing*. New York: Wiley.

Baron, R.M., & Kenny, D.A. (1986). The moderator-mediator variable distinction in social psychological research: Conceptual, strategic, and statistical considerations. *Journal of Personality and Social Psychology, 51*, 1173-1182.

Benninghaus, H. (1976). *Ergebnisse und Perspektiven der Einstellungs-Verhaltens-Forschung*. Meisenheim: Hain.

Bentler, P.M. (1980). Multivariate analysis with latent variables: Causal modeling. *Annual Review of Psychology, 31*, 419-456.

Bourdieu, P. (1984). *Distinction: A critique of the judgement of tastes*. London: Routledge & Kegan.

Buse, R.C. (1986). Is the structure of the demand for food changing? Implications for projections. In: O. Capps Jr. & B. Senauer (Eds.), *Food demand analysis. Implications for future consumption*, pp. 105-130. Blacksburg, VI: Virginia Polytechnic Institute and State University.

Buss, A.H., & Finn, S.E. (1987). Classification of personality traits. *Journal of Personality and Social Psychology, 52*, 432-444.

Buss, A.H., & Plomin, R. (1975). *A temperament theory of personality development*. New York: Wiley.

Cappon, D. (1973). *Eating, loving, and dying. A psychology of appetites*. Toronto: University of Toronto Press.

de Garine, I. (1979). Culture et nutrition. *Communications, 31*, 70-92.

Diehl, J.M. (1980). *Ernährungspsychologie*, 2. Aufl. Frankfurt/M.: Fachbuchhandlung.

Diehl, J.M., & Leitzmann, C. (1985) (Eds.). *Measurement and determinants of food habits and food preferences*. Wageningen: Stichting Nederlands Instituut voor de Voeding.

Duval, S., & Wicklund, R.A. (1972). *A theory of objective self-awareness*. New York: Academic Press.

Elias, N. (1969). *Über den Prozess der Zivilisation. Soziogenetische und psychologische Untersuchungen*, 1. Band, 2. Aufl. Bern: Francke.

Fenigstein, A., Scheier, R.F., & Buss, A.H. (1975). Private and public self-consciousness: Assessment and theory. *Journal of Consulting and Clinical Psychology, 43*, 522-527.

Fischler, C. (1981). Food preferences, nutritional wisdom, and socio-cultural evolution. In: D.N. Walcher & N. Kretchmer (Eds.), *Food, nutrition and evolution*, pp. 59-67. New York: Masson.

Fishbein, M., & Ajzen, I. (1975). *Beliefs, attitude, intention, and behavior*. Reading, MA: Addison-Wesley.

Grivetti, L.-E. (1981). Cultural nutrition: Anthropological and geographical themes. *Annual Review of Nutrition, 1*, 47-68.

Grunert, S.C. (1987). *Ergebnisse einer testkritischen Überprüfung von vier individualdiagnostischen Indikatoren.* Stuttgart: Universität Hohenheim, Institut 530, Lehrstuhl für Konsumtheorie und Verbraucherpolitik.

Grunert, S.C. (1988). Consumers' nutrition behaviour: An approach involving the concept of autonomy. *Journal of Consumer Studies and Home Economics, 12*, 213-224.

Grunert, S.C. (forthcoming). Ein Inventar zur Erfassung von Selbstaussagen zum Ernährungsverhalten. *Diagnostica*.

Herman, C.P., & Mack, D. (1975). Restrained and unrestrained eating. *Journal of Personality, 43*, 647-660.

Herman, C.P., & Polivy, J. (1984). A boundary model for the regulation of eating. In: A.J. Stunkard & E. Stellar (Eds.), *Eating and its disorders*, pp. 141-156. New York: Raven Press.

Hirschman, A.O. (1982). *Shifting involvements. Private interest and public action*. Princeton, NJ: Princeton University Press.

Joe, V.C. (1971). Review of the internal-external control construct as a personality variable. *Psychological Reports, 28*, 619-640.

Kandel, R.F., Jerome, N.W., & Pelto, G.H. (1980). Introduction. In: N.W. Jerome, R.F. Kandel, & G.H. Pelto (Eds.), *Nutritional anthropology. Contemporary approaches to diet and culture*, pp. 1-11. New York: Redgrave.

Kristiansen, C.M. (1987). Social learning theory and preventive health behavior: Some neglected variables. *Social Behavior, 2*, 73-86.

Kutsch, T. (1985). Zur Programmatik der Ernährungssoziologie. *Hauswirtschaft und Wissenschaft, 33*, 51-56.

Mennell, S. (1986). Über die Zivilisierung der Eßlust. *Zeitschrift für Soziologie, 15*, 406-421.

Menzies, I. (1970). Psychosocial aspects of eating. *Journal of Psychosomatic Research, 14*, 223-227.

Meulenberg, M.T.G. (1985). Towards a multidisciplinary analysis of food consumption. In: J.E.R. Frijters (Ed.), *Consumer behaviour research and marketing of agricultural products*, pp. 1-25. The Hague: Nationale Raad voor Landbouwkundig Onderzoek.

Miller, J.C., Murphy, R., & Buss, A.H. (1981). Consciousness of body: Private and public. *Journal of Personality and Social Psychology, 41*, 397-406.

Mullen, B., & Suls, J. (1982). "Know thyself": Stressful life changes and the ameliorative effect of private self-consciousness. *Journal of Experimental Social Psychology, 18*, 43-55.

Murcott, A. (1986). You are what you eat - Anthropological factors influencing food choice. In: C.Ritson, L. Gofton, & J. McKenzie (Eds.), *The food consumer*, pp. 107-126. Chichester: Wiley.

Pumpian-Mindlin, E. (1954). The meanings of food. *Journal of the American Dietetic Association, 30*, 576-580.

Richards, A.J. (1932). *Hunger and work in a savage tribe*. London: Routledge.

Rotter, J.B. (1966). Generalized expectancies for internal versus external control of reinforcement. *Psychological Monographs, 80* (1), 1-28.

Ruderman, A.J. (1986). Dietary restraint: A theoretical and empirical review. *Psychological Bulletin, 99*, 247-262.

Schachter, S., & Singer, J.E. (1962). Gognitive, social, and physiological determinants of emotional state. *Psychological Review, 69*, 379-399.

Schachter, S., Goldman, R., & Gordon, A. (1968). Effects of fear, food deprivation, and obesity on eating. *Journal of Personality and Social Psychology, 10*, 98-106.

Sherif, M., & Sherif, C.W. (1969). *Social psychology*. New York: Harper & Row.

Silberberg, E. (1985). Nutrition and the demand for tastes. *Journal of Political Economy, 93*, 881-900.

Strecker, O., Reichert, J., & Pottebaum, P. (1976). *Marketing für Lebensmittel*. Frankfurt: Umschau-Verlag.

Strickland, B.R. (1978). Internal-external expectancies and health-related behaviors. *Journal of Clinical and Consulting Psychology, 46,* 1192-1211.

Tangermann, S. (1986). Economic factors influencing food choice. In: C. Ritson, L. Gofton, & J. McKenzie (Eds.), *The food consumer,* pp. 61-83. Chichester: Wiley.

Twigg, J. (1984). Vegetarianism and the meaning of meat. In: A. Murcott (Ed.), *The sociology of food and eating. Essays on the sociological significance of food,* pp. 18-30. Aldershot: Gower.

van Raaij, W.F. (1984). Een model van het voedingsgedraag. *Voeding, 45,* 376-382.

Van Strien, T., Frijters, J.E.R., Bergers, G.P.A., & Defares, P.B. (1986). The Dutch Eating Behavior Questionnaire for the assessment of restrained, emotional and external eating behavior. *International Journal of Eating Disorders, 5,* 295-315.

Wicker, A.W. (1969). Attitudes versus actions: The relationship of verbal and overt behavioral responses to attitude objects. *Journal of Social Issues, 25*(4), 41-78.

Wilson, C. (1979). Food custom and nurture. An annotated bibliography on sociocultural and biocultural aspects of nutrition. *Journal of Nutrition Education, 11,* 211-261.

Woods, A.E. (1960). Psychological dimensions of consumer decision. *Journal of Marketing, 24*(1), 15-19.

Lorenz Lassnigg

The "New Values" and Consumer Behaviour – Some Empirical Findings From Austria

Abstract

The study examines the relationship between individual attitudes on a "materialism – postmaterialism" scale and the consumption level of the household in which the interviewed individuals live. The study was based on oral interviews of a representative sample of Austrians. It provides cross-sectional data, and hence can indicate differences in values, but not really value changes.

The results achieved at the total aggregate level were very plausible: The "postmaterialists" have a higher standard of living than the "materialists," although their attitudes tend to have the effect of lowering the level of consumption.

When dividing the total sample into subgroups it appears, however, that the results are not very clear-cut: The interrelationship between attitudes and consumer behaviour is far more complex than the model assumptions could account for.

For critique and discussion, the author is indebted to his friends and colleagues Georg Fischer, Karl Müller, and Karl Pichelmann, and to an unknown referee.

Author's address: Lorenz Lassnigg, Department of Sociology, Institute for Advanced Studies, Stumpergasse 56, A-1060 Wien, Austria.

Introduction

This paper deals with the question as to whether relationships can be established between value orientations and the consumption standard of households in Austria. It is based on a cross-sectional empirical study. Hence, it can give insights about differences in consumer behaviour and how these are linked to different values, but not really about value changes.

Although such relationships are rarely discussed explicitly, discussions of "changing values" are still rooted in implicit assumptions and expectations about the links between values and the "working society," "achieving society," or "consumer society." On closer scrutiny, however, these assumptions and expectations prove to be contradictory and ambivalent.

On the one hand, it is assumed that the new values tend to be appreciated by those segments of the population who have satisfied their principal material needs, who enjoy a relatively high income and, consequently, a high level of consumption. On this basis, these people will turn towards "postmaterialistic" needs. In Austria, this view is mainly taken by those political forces of the social democratic and trade union movements who are strongly oriented towards industrial growth and raising the standard of living in the traditional sense: The new values as represented by the attitude of the privileged middle classes, of those "who can afford it."

On the other hand, the new values are being related to the new social movements, on the assumption that these attitudes tend to coincide with decreasing consumer needs or at least with attitudes critical of consumption. For instance, one study comparing the new social movements internationally states "a distinct relationship, frequently confirmed empirically, between the spreading of 'postmaterialistic' value patterns and a greater sensitivity for issues raised by the new social movements" (Brand, 1985, p. 329).

In discussions about changes in the value orientation in Western societies, however, reference is seldom made to empirical investigations of the actual behaviour of people. It sometimes appears as if value changes serve as a type of "deus ex machina" explanation of facts that cannot be explained otherwise, or as a kind of substitute for explanations one does not want to accept. This may be illustrated by the attempts to consider changing value orientations as the cause of inflation (cf., e.g., Steinmann, Büscher, & Pfister, 1984).

Recently, it has become popular to stress that attitudes of individual consumers have a considerable influence on their behaviour – not least because of the poorness of predictions based on aggregate consumption functions. In the conclusion to his well-known comparative study of the USA and the Federal Republic of Germany, Burkhard Strümpel states that "attitudes, expectations, and motifs" are "not only arabesques of economic dynamics" and that "changes of mood in the consumers have resulted in decreasing demand, particularly with respect to housing, cars, mobile and other durable consumer goods, thus aggravating an economic crisis" (Strümpel, 1977, p. 86; cf., also Katona, Strümpel, & Zahn, 1971).

An extensive investigation of the structure of consumption in Austria yielded findings which to a surprising extent deviate from similar studies in other countries. They can be explained neither by differences in the level of development (measured by the per capita national product) nor by differences in affluence. Hence the authors of the study suggested that more detailed analyses of the "relationship between consumers' moods and the spending behaviour of Austrians" was necessary (Wüger, 1985, p. 717). On the one hand, differences were found in saving behaviour. When, in recent times, the rates of saving increased and the rate of consumption decreased in other countries, the rate of saving decreased in Austria, while the rate of consumption increased. On the other hand, considerable differences were found in the structure of consumption compared to the FRG, the USA, and Belgium: "The fact that in an international comparison Austrians spend relatively much on food and luxuries, clothes, and shoes, and on transportation and communication, but less on education, entertainment, and recreation, does not depend so much on the income situation as on preferences, the prevailing relative price levels, etc." (Wüger, 1985, p. 715).

The Investigation

The analysis to be presented here is based on a random sample (N = 1478) of oral standardized interviews carried out by an opinion polling institute in the summer of 1985 (Balog, Cyba, & Lassnigg, 1985, 1988). The "new

335

values" are represented by the variable "Materialism – Postmaterialism" according to the well-known formulation of Inglehart (1977, pp. 27-53, 1979).

The MAT-POST-variable was constructed as follows. From a list of eight items the respondents had to choose those three items that they favoured as the most desirable and place them in order of preference. Four items were defined as indicators of materialism:

– Maintaining a high rate of economic growth
– Making sure that the country has strong defense forces
– Maintaining order in the nation
– Fighting rising prices.

The other four items indicated "postmaterialistic" values:

– Seeing to it that the people have more of a say in how things get decided at work and in their local communities
– Trying to make the country's cities and countryside more beautiful
– Giving the people more of a say in important government decisions
– Protecting the freedom of speech.

The respondents were classified as "materialists" if they placed MAT-items in the first three places and as "postmaterialists" if there were POST-items in the first three places. The remaining respondents formed a mixed "middle group" without a pronounced orientation on the MAT-POST-variable.

Although the materialism – postmaterialism dimension has been criticized in many ways, and is indeed to be viewed critically, it was chosen because of its clear, widely known definition, and because it is sufficiently suitable for preparing items for the purpose at hand (regarding criticisms, see Herz, 1987).

An "inventory concept" was the starting point for the operationalization of consumption, i.e., a count was made of durable consumer goods possessed and the frequency of the consumption of goods or services was noted. A monetary assessment of the value of goods, as performed by Schmölders and Biervert (1972), was not made: It would have been be very difficult to carry out for services and non-durables. The elements of the consumption indices are presented in Table 1. As a result of several conversions, three metric variables were defined in order to measure the different aspects of consumption.

Table 1: Elements of Consumption

A: Consumer durables[1]		% available in:			
		Total sample	MAT	0	POST
"Standard goods":	telephone	84.5	81.5	84.9	86.7
	vacuum cleaner	91.7	91.7	91.7	90.7
	washing machine	92.5	94.0	92.3	92.0
	refrigerator	96.9	95.8	96.6	98.7
	gas or electric cooker	94.4	92.3	94.5	98.7
"Luxury goods":	stereo	38.7	26.2	39.4	57.3
	dishwasher	22.6	16.7	23.5	24.0
	video recorder	10.0	7.1	11.1	2.7
	personal computer	3.8	1.2	4.2	4.0
	microwave cooker	2.6	1.8	2.6	4.0

B: Consumer goods and services[2]	% regular consumption				% no consumption			
	Total sample	MAT	0	POST	Total sample	MAT	0	POST
sweets	10.0	9.2	10.3	8.0	15.9	21.5	15.2	12.0
alcohol	15.3	9.8	16.2	16.0	12.8	17.7	12.1	10.7
hairdresser	23.1	23.0	23.4	20.0	9.2	13.0	7.7	20.0
restaurants	7.2	3.7	7.8	8.0	27.1	29.2	27.7	14.7
laundry	7.9	5.0	8.3	9.3	34.8	37.5	33.8	41.3
holidays/travel	12.4	9.3	12.2	21.3	35.3	47.8	34.7	16.0
tobacco	24.3	17.7	25.1	29.3	*	*	*	*
shoes	7.1	4.3	7.0	14.7	*	*	*	*
fruit/vegetables	*	*	*	*	1.0	1.2	1.1	0.0

C: Indicators	Mean	Std. Dev.	Min	Max
1. Total index (Possession and Expenditure)[3]	0.61	3.68	−11.00	+11.00
2. Possession of consumer durables	0.77	2.01	−5.00	+5.00
3. Expenditure on consumer goods and services	−0.18	2.44	−8.00	+9.00

1. Possession: Sum of "standard goods" + the squared sum of "luxury goods" (limited to a maximum of 3). The distribution was then curtailed (the maximum value was set to 10), and the mean adjusted to zero.
2. Expenditure: "regular consumption" = +1, "never consumed" = −1, * = not evaluated; index = sum of these values.
3. Total consumption = sum of Possession + Expenditure.

1. Possession of consumer durables ("Possession"). According to the extent to which the goods were available in the population, a list of durables was divided into two sections: one referring to "standard goods" (telephone, vacuum cleaner, washing machine, refrigerator, gas or electric cooker) and one referring to "luxury goods" (stereo equipment, dishwasher, video recorder, personal computer, microwave cooker). All standard goods were given a value of 1 and summed; luxury goods were summed in the same way (although limited to a maximum of 3) and the sum squared. "Possession" is the sum of these two measures (after curtailment and mean adjustment, cf. Note to Table 1).

2. Expenditure on consumption goods and services ("Expenditure"). From a list of non-durable consumer goods and services an index was constructed according to the regularity of consumption in the households. "Regular" consumption was given the value +1, "never" consumed −1, and the index is the sum of these values. (The list encompassed sweets, alcohol, hairdresser, restaurants, laundry, holidays/travels, tobacco, shoes, fruit/vegetables).

3. Total index ("Possession" and "Expenditure"). The partial indices for the possession of consumer durables and for expenditures on non-durable goods and services were added to form the total index of household consumption.

In order to investigate the stability of the results, not only the total sample but also three groups were analyzed:

– Housewives
– Heads of households
– Paid employees living in their own households.

The rationale behind this grouping was the assumption that the groups would differ with respect to the process of generating as well as that of spending the household income. If similar results were to be obtained for all three subgroups, this would constitute a strong confirmation of the importance of the MAT-POST-variable.

Tables 2-4 contain information about the random sample and the subsamples. The entire sample displayed characteristic differences with respect to age, which do not appear within the subgroups.

**Table 2: Distribution of Sample With Respect to the Materialism –
Postmaterialism Scale**

	MAT	0	POST	N (=100%)		
Total	14.2	79.5	6.3	1187		
Adolescents (pupils, students)	11.9	74.3	13.8	109		
Housewives	16.2	77.8	6.0	167	χ^2	= 24.38
Total number of employees	12.1	80.8	7.1	603	df	= 6;
Retired persons	17.9	79.9	2.3	308	p	= .0004
Head of household	14.6	80.5	4.9	575	χ^2	= 4.01
Other household members	13.7	78.6	7.7	612	df	= 2;
					p	= .1349
15-19 years	9.2	79.8	11.0	109		
20-29 years	5.6	81.7	12.7	197		
30-39 years	9.2	81.0	9.8	184	χ^2	= 61.18
40-49 years	16.9	77.9	5.2	172	df	= 10;
50-59 years	19.4	78.2	2.4	211	p	= .0000
60 years and older	19.1	79.0	1.9	314		
Total number of paid employees[1]	10.1	82.2	7.7	454		
Unskilled manual employees	11.5	80.5	8.0	87	χ^2	= 6.48
Skilled manual employees	12.5	84.1	3.4	88	df	= 6;
Non-manual employees (low level)	12.0	79.7	8.3	133	p	= .3715
Non-manual employees (medium and high level)	6.2	84.2	9.6	146		

1) All paid employees, including those not living in a household of their own (e.g., in the parents' household). "Paid employees" are the total number of employees minus the self-employed.

Table 3: Materialism – Postmaterialism According to Age Groups and Subsamples

Age group	Total	House- wives	Heads of households	Wage earners, living in their own households
		% Materialists		
15-19	9.2	-	-	12.9
20-29	5.6	0.0	2.2	5.0
30-39	9.2	5.6	9.9	6.7
40-49	16.9	24.2	14.4	14.3
50-59	19.4	20.9	16.7	17.1
60 and older	19.1	22.2	17.8	12.5
Total	14.2	16.2	14.6	10.3
		% Postmaterialists		
15-19	11.0	-	-	6.5
20-29	12.7	21.1	13.0	9.2
30-39	9.8	11.1	11.1	11.5
40-49	5.2	3.0	5.2	5.1
50-59	2.4	0.0	2.5	3.9
60 and older	1.9	2.8	2.2	0.0
Total	6.3	6.0	4.9	7.6

Table 4: Household Income per Capita (in Austrian Schillings)

MAT	6,177	5,074	6,457	6,954
0	6,625	5,594	6,915	7,423
POST	7,383	4,200	8,926	8,212
Total	6,611	5,424	6,946	7,435
One-way analysis of variance				
F	4.3294	2.1806	6.5196	1.6899
p	.0134	.1163	.0016	.1858
Bartlett-Box homogeneity of variances				
F	2.006	3.439	2.995	1.068
p	.135	.032	.050	.344

Results for the Total Population

Table 5 relates differences in consumption levels in the total sample to attitudes as measured by the materialism – postmaterialism variable. The differences between the groups with different attitudes are statistically significant, and it can be seen that with respect to all three dimensions of consumption, the "materialists" consume least and the "postmaterialists" most. Table 4, however, makes it clear that in all subsamples except housewives, the "materialists" have the lowest current (weighted) household income per capita, and "postmaterialists" the highest. Therefore it appears to be necessary to control for the influence of income.

Table 5: Mean Consumption Values for the Materialism – Postmaterialism Categories

	Total consumption		Possession		Expenditure	
	Mean	(N)	Mean	(N)	Mean	(N)
MAT	−.65	(158)	.27	(168)	−.93	(158)
0	.76	(904)	.84	(944)	−.10	(904)
POST	1.41	(75)	.96	(75)	.45	(75)
Total	.61	(1137)	.77	(1187)	−.18	(1137)
Analysis of variance						
F	12.0589		6.2160		10.6007	
p	.0000		.0021		.0000	
Bartlett-Box homogeneity of variances						
F	1.327		6.489		.933	
p	.266		.002		.394	

To this end, an analysis of covariance was carried out based on the assumption that the attitude variable exerts its influence – if at all – as an intervening variable. Therefore a model was set up which made it possible to estimate the amount of consumption for any given level of income. Income, age, and family status were used as covariates. Family

341

Table 6: **Analysis of Covariance: Controlling the Effects of Age, Income, and Family Status on Consumption**

Variable	Total consumption		Possession		Expenditure	
	F	*p*	*F*	*p*	*F*	*p*
Age	129.4	.000	100.5	.000	68.9	.000
Income	194.5	.000	135.4	.000	117.6	.000
Family status	9.7	.000	8.7	.000	6.2	.000
MAT-POST	5.3	.005	3.0	.048	4.9	.008
R^2	.245		.188		.161	
MCA	Deviation	Eta	Deviation	Eta	Deviation	Eta
Unadjusted		.15		.10		.14
MAT	−1.32		−.51		−.81	
0	.15		.07		.08	
POST	.91		.24		.68	
Adjusted		.09		.07		.09
MAT	−.80		−.26		−.54	
0	.14		.07		.08	
POST	−.08		−.28		.21	

status included: single persons without children, couples without children, single persons or couples with children.

The model assumptions, however, were only partly fulfilled: The homogeneity of variances is obviously violated with regard to age, and the homogeneity of regressions seems not to be given. As shown in Table 6, the model explains approximately 20% of the variance and results in significant, though weak effects for the MAT-POST-variable.

When one considers the total consumption level, the results indicate that the standard of living of the "postmaterialists" would be substantially higher if they had a different attitude: The adjusted value for the consumption level is still higher than that of the materialists, but slightly below the middle group level.

The two consumption components behave differently: As a consequence of controlling the covariates, the possession of durable consumer goods is reduced for the "postmaterialists," but not the consumption of non-durables and services.

According to this outcome, both views presented in the introduction seem to be correct: In absolute terms, the postmaterialists enjoy a higher material standard of living than the other two groups, but in relation to their consuming power, on average they spend less than would be expected. In the main, they refrain from purchasing goods produced by the industrial system that is under criticism from the new social movements.

Results for the Subpopulations and General Discussion

When the data are examined with respect to the various subsamples (Table 7), it becomes evident that for the paid employees there exists no statistically significant relationship at all between the materialism – postmaterialism variable and level of consumption. In fact, the effects become insignificant for **all** subgroups as soon as the background variables are controlled for (Table 8).

Table 7: Results for the Subsamples: Analysis of Variance for the MAT-POST Categories

Subpopulations	Total consumption		Possession		Expenditure	
	F	p	F	p	F	p
Housewives	4.2371	.0161	3.4598	.0338	2.8091	.0633
Heads of households	3.9131	.0205	1.5626	.2105	5.5871	.0040
Paid employees with their own households	.9536	.3851	.5943	.5524	1.9737	.1402

One possible explanation of this result is of a statistical nature. It could be that the effects investigated are typically small, and would be evident only in larger samples. But there are arguments that suggest a substantial interpretation.

Firstly, the results can be taken to indicate that the influence of attitude variables on economic matters is of little importance.

Secondly, our results can be used by those who doubt the validity of the materialism – postmaterialism variable.

Table 8: **Analysis of Covariance: Significance of MAT-POST in the Subsamples (Controlled for Background Variables)**

Subpopulations	Total consumption		Possession		Expenditure	
	F	p	F	p	F	p
Housewives[1]	2.303	.103	2.348	.099	1.415	.246
Heads of households[2]	1.069	.344	1.565	.210	1.678	.188
Paid employees with their own households[3]	.210	.811	.278	.757	.171	.843

1) Controlled for age and income.
2) Controlled for age, income, and family status.
3) Controlled for age, income, professional position, and number of paid employees in the household.

Thirdly, I would like to point out the problem implicitly contained in most evaluations of the influence of individual attitudes on consumers' behaviour in general. Consumption was registered at the level of households, which may well be a reasonable method; however, normative attitudes concern individuals. Therefore there are actually two aggregation problems which distort the relationship between individual attitudes and household consumption: (a) In what way do individual members of a household influence decisions about the level of consumption? (b) To what extent are households homogeneous with respect to their normative attitudes?

On the basis of these considerations, the differing results could also originate from the phenomenon of "truncation of variance" in the subgroups, which was brought forward in connection with estimations of subgroup wage functions, based on human capital theory (cf. Cain, 1976, p. 1246). In this case, lack of homogeneity of variances would be given a substantive interpretation and the actual interaction of household members would have to be examined. Such considerations suggest that the extent of the influence of value orientations on the consumption behaviour of households will depend on the actual homogeneity of households. Another investigation could start from this point.

References

Balog, A., Cyba, E., & Lassnigg, L. (1985). *Arbeitsbezogene Werthaltungen und Ansprüche an die Arbeit.* Vienna: Institute for Advanced Studies. Research Report.

Balog, A., Cyba, E., & Lassnigg, L. (1988). Ansprüche an die Arbeit und arbeitsbezogene Werthaltungen. *SWS-Rundschau, 28,* 56 65.

Brand, K.-W. (1985). *Neue soziale Bewegungen in Westeuropa und in den USA.* Frankfurt: Campus.

Cain, G.C. (1976). The challenge of segmented labor market theories to orthodox theory: A survey. *Journal of Economic Literature, 14,* 1215-1257.

Herz, T.A. (1987). Werte, sozialpolitische Konflikte und Generationen – Eine Überprüfung der Theorie des Postmaterialismus. *Zeitschrift für Soziologie, 16,* 56-69.

Inglehart, R. (1977). *The silent revolution. Changing values and political styles among western publics.* Princeton, NJ: Princeton University Press.

Inglehart, R. (1979). Wertwandel und politisches Verhalten. In: J. Matthes (Ed.), *Sozialer Wandel in Westeuropa*, pp. 505-533. Frankfurt: Campus.

Katona, G., Strümpel, B., & Zahn, E. (1971). *Aspirations and affluence.* New York: McGraw-Hill.

Schmölders, G., & Biervert, B. (1972). Level of aspiration and consumption standard: Some general findings. In: B. Strümpel, J.N. Morgan, & E. Zahn (Eds.), *Human behaviour in economic affairs. Essays in honor of George Katona*, pp. 213-227. Amsterdam: Elsevier.

Steinmann, G., Büscher, R., & Pfister, J. (1984). Gesellschaftlicher Wertwandel und makroökonomisches Zielsystem. In: H.J. Klages & P. Kmieciak (Eds.), *Wertwandel und gesellschaftlicher Wandel*, pp. 97-121. Frankfurt: Campus.

Strümpel, B. (1977). *Die Krise des Wohlstands.* Stuttgart: Kohlhammer.

Wüger, M. (1985). Der private Konsum im Strukturwandel. *Monatsberichte des Österreichischen Instituts für Wirtschaftsforschung (WIFO), 58,* 708-717.

Dominique Lassarre and Christine Roland-Lévy

Understanding Children's Economic Socialization

Abstract

Different methods were employed to investigate children's sources of economic information. Children, aged 11 to 12 years and in the first year of secondary school, were observed in supermarkets, interviewed, and asked to play the role of advertisers or economic message transmitters. Three types of information sources were identified: active, entertaining, and social information sources. It was shown that shopping is an important and new source of information at this stage in life. As regards entertaining information, attitudes of boys and girls towards TV commercials differed: While boys consider advertising as a source of information, girls look at it as entertainment. The location of social information sources moved from the family to larger settings: entering high school gives autonomy to children, they can go shopping on their own, they are accepted as partners in adults' conversations. All these conditions make this period of life amenable to economic education.

Authors' address: Laboratoire de Psychologie Sociale, Université René Descartes, 28 Rue Serpente, F-75006 Paris, France.

Purpose of the Study

The general topic of the present study is children's knowledge, understanding, and behaviour in the economic world. It is a part of what is generally called "naive economics," the economics of non-specialists (Albou, 1984). In the French educational system, economics is not a school subject. Nevertheless, even young children have some familiarity with the economic world: They are consumers in their own right, they buy or request products for their own use, such as toys or candy, they choose or propose goods for the whole family such as food or household equipment and most of them have savings or even a bank account. Children become involved also in macroeconomic issues: With their families, they share major socio-economic problems, such as poverty, unemployment, and inflation, and they know they will soon have to choose a job or, at least, a school orientation. Economic information takes on many different forms. As consumers, children are often the target of television advertising, but they are also more or less voluntary receivers of information not intended for them, such as TV news. Along with the mass media, there is a flow of informal communication within the family and within the peer group.

This paper is focused on the sources of economic information used by children of 11 and 12 years: From where stems their economic knowledge? Do information sources have different impacts depending on the topic? Can these sources be used as a basis for introducing economic education in secondary schools?

Theories of Economic Socialization

Socialization can be defined (Ziegler & Child, 1969) as "a broad term for the whole process by which an individual develops through transaction with other people, his specific pattern of socially relevant behaviour and experience." It is related to the general problem of education in all societies.

The Two Main Theoretical Approaches

Two main theories dominate the field: the Piagetian developmental-cognitive approach and the environmentalistic learning theory.

As the notion of purely endogenous maturation has never been supported by empirical evidence, Piaget proposed a transactional process, viz., "equilibration," which links children's cognitive stages to their experience of the world. This model emphasizes the primacy of children's actions in their development. Learning theory (behaviourism), on the contrary, stresses the effects of the environment on children's behaviour. A functional behaviour is reinforced or imitated because "it works," it is rewarded.

As Youniss (1978) indicates, there is nothing really incompatible between these two models:

(a) the cognitive model is applied to the development of thinking processes while learning theory explains behaviour. Piaget provides the framework and the behaviourists the content of socialization;

(b) the first model stresses intraindividual differences as the child grows up while the second describes interindividual variations at the same age more accurately;

(c) both theories assume that contacts with social reality are necessary for the build up of a predictable pattern of behaviour.

Applications to Economic Socialization

Although its relevance for the study of economic socialization can be questioned, the Piagetian model is at the moment the favourite one among researchers in the field.

Except in his early work on "The Moral Judgment of the Child," Piaget essentially studied children's understanding of the physical world, a reality where the child can carry out its own experiments through direct interaction with the environment. Applying the model to the social world, Furth (1978) sees interpersonal situations as direct experiences. He studied (1980) the understanding of social and economic phenomena in which children are involved, such as shopping, traveling by bus, or going to school. He assumes that social knowledge grows as the field of the child's interactions gets wider. But economics is more than interpersonal interaction; it is a system which implies many phenomena such as banking, inflation, international exchange, etc., all related to one another by an abstract structure. Interpersonal relationships portray only a part of the economic roles. For instance, by shopping the child learns the selling role of the shopkeepers but nothing about their employer or accountant roles. Economics has two levels of meaning (Granger, 1967): (a) the actual consequences (living standards, salaries) of individual behaviour (consumption, work) and collective behaviour (taxes, strikes), and (b) the satisfaction of ideals (e.g., as regards social and economic justice) through human organization (regulation). The first aspect is behavioural and the second purely cognitive.

Some authors (Jahoda, 1979; Leiser, 1983) assume that the construction of complex systems is achieved by the integration of different subsystems: The understanding of banking results from the successful combination of knowledge about profit and about employment.

As a result of these complexities, most studies, although referring to a Piagetian framework, do not use a Piagetian methodology. They use interviewing centred on knowledge, understanding, and even behaviour (Ward, Wartella, & Wackman, 1977), but it is rare to see **active** methods such as role-playing or problem-solving (Jahoda, 1979) in use as well as analyses of the impact of a study's methodology on children's cognitive processes (Jahoda, 1981).

The Role of Sources of Information in Economic Socialization

Information is the basis of many forms of economic socialization. Piaget assumes that information has an impact on the logical structure of the mind: Economic **thinking** (understanding the economic world) needs information to develop. By organizing this information, the child will develop economic **knowledge:** Economic thinking is the basis of economic knowledge. Both thinking and knowledge are related to the abstract, logical conception of the economy, the child's idea of how it works.

Analyzing the content of children's misperceptions, Strauss (1952) noticed that errors are not only **similar** in their cognitive structure but also have an identical content (knowledge): for instance, for most young children, money comes from God or gold mines. This content derives from different sources of information, viz., religious education and fictional stories, transmitted by parents and cultural and mass media (novels, television programmes).

By observing adult behaviour conveyed by different sources of information, children also build up their own **representation** of economic phenomena which includes a pattern of affective and cognitive responses, **opinions.** "Children have to acquire relevant information from their social environment in order to be able to construct a correct representation of economic systems" (Jahoda, 1981, p. 56).

A study of how children deal with economic information should be the first step on our way to understanding the different factors that determine children's economic outlook. The reception of messages, combined with the awareness of being a target who can be influenced, and the rational use of the various sources of information are necessary conditions for becoming a mature consumer and a responsible citizen in a society facing economic crisis.

Merging Different Perspectives on Children's Sources of Economic Information

As an introduction to our own studies, a review is given of the main results obtained in previous research in this extremely wide field. Previous research can be classified into two main categories: studies of economic socialization and of information processing.

Economic Socialization

Since children are not all the same, much research deals with differentiating factors. Economic socialization is a process which goes through stages as the child grows up; this implies differences according to age. It occurs in specific educational environments; this implies differences according to gender and social class.

Developmental Studies

Many studies have compared children's awareness about economics at different ages, usually from 6 years of age to 14. Other studies have focused on the age at which children perceive and memorize advertising messages; here, studies start at 3 years. Although founded in Piaget's theory, these studies remain more descriptive than structuralist. Sometimes authors have selected children of 6, 9, and 12 years, in order to comply with the definite Piagetian stages (Burris, 1983; Siegal, 1981), and there is no doubt that they have found different reactions at each age. Other researchers interviewed children of all ages and found a general development of thinking but with so many differences of content that it is difficult to arrive at a precise structure of children's economic reality (Danziger, 1958; Furth, 1980). There has also been no agreement about the age at which it is meaningful to evaluate children's economic knowledge, or what this knowledge is to be compared with. Could a control group of young adults be used for comparison purposes, or is there something like an ideal consumer who can be used as a yardstick?

Although children's opinion about the economy and their representations of economic phenomena have been very little studied (Cummings & Taebel, 1978; DeFleur & DeFleur, 1967), it is noticeable that conformity and consistency increase as children get older.

Cross-Sectional Studies

Such research has essentially dealt with three factors: gender, the cultural environment, and the family's socio-economic level. In studies of economic thinking, research did not show any difference between boys and girls. Such differences appear very clearly, however, in numerous studies of economic knowledge, especially about advertising (Cullingford, 1984; Lassarre, 1985) but also about more general topics such as occupations (DeFleur & DeFleur, 1967).

Girls generally take a larger part in activities related to consumption (shopping, cleaning, meal preparation). They are given less pocket money than boys of the same age. They appear more interested in advertising but less gullible. Does this indicate a greater maturity for girls? It is clear that educational habits are not the same for boys and girls.

Perhaps these differences are smaller in higher social classes. Social class is the most frequently investigated factor in studies of economic knowledge (Berti, Bombi, & Lis, 1982; Jahoda, 1981). Upper class children soon become familiar with banking vocabulary and the prestige of occupations while children whose fathers work in large factories acquire good knowledge and understanding of industrial relations. In this case, the observed differences may not only be related to social class but also to the occupation or educational level of the parents, especially that of the mother (Kapferer, 1985). Lautrey (1980) showed that parents' cognitive structures and educational styles directly influence the quantity, type, and diversity of information that is "admitted" into the family, determines informal socialization through conversation, and leads to differences in the family's consumption habits.

Reviewing the literature on the topic, Lea, Tarpy, and Webley (1987) quote a large number of cross-cultural studies. It appears that children from different countries have more or less the same knowledge and understanding of economic phenomena at approximately the same age. For example, Burris's (1983) results obtained with American children are very similar to those found among Egyptian children and by Danziger (1958) with Australian children. Jahoda and Woerdenbagch (1982) showed that the development of ideas about the banking system is the same among Scottish and Dutch children. Hong Kwang and Stacey (1981) found that the development of economic concepts among Malaysian Chinese children was very similar to that reported for Western children. On the other hand Harris and Heelas (1979) have pointed out that "in cultures in which the money is 'primitive,' children will not move through the stages as Western children do, not because they are incapable of formal thinking, but because the collective representation in that domain is unsophisticated" (Lea et al., 1987, p. 377). As Webley (1983) explains, authors who have shown that children from different cultures reach the same level of economic knowledge at the same age have used similar research strategies and asked similar questions. Thus the consistency found could be explained mainly by the similarity of the methods used.

Information Processing: How Children React to Different Sources of Information

The second category of studies is related to the fact that the different sources of economic information have to be treated separately. In particular, how do children use different sources of information? It also concerns the functional analysis of economic communication, the analysis of the interaction between emotional reactions, behaviour and cognitive processes: in other words, the "subjectively" oriented analysis of the effects of economic communication.

Different studies (see Beaudichon, 1982) have shown that in order to explain their purchases children refer to four main sources of economic information: parents and family habits, peers, advertising especially on television, and products themselves (brand, packaging, price). More general economic information comes from other sources: different news media, adults' informal conversations, and school subjects such as history or geography. There is a link between the source of the message and the type of communication that is established: for example, whether the communication becomes unidirectional or interactive, referential or persuasive, whether the child is the target of the message or just an occasional receiver. Likewise, communication will be didactic between the teacher and the child, functional with the parents, entertaining when it comes from media, phatic with peers, and so on.

By means of content analysis, economic messages can be analyzed with respect to their accuracy and their logic (Durandin, 1982) as well as with respect to the rhetoric and setting used. This has been done for TV commercials (Durandin et al., 1981) and series (DeFleur, 1964), but rarely for news or parents' messages to children.

Most analyses of the use of information as well as of the contents of messages are "objective," external to the person; but it is also necessary to study the experiences of the children themselves: the analysis then becomes "subjective." A subjective analysis entails studying children's cognitive and emotional reactions towards the sources of the communication as well as towards the message itself. In the case of commercial messages, children under the age of 13 seem to have great difficulties in distinguishing between the information included in the message and its spectacular aspects (Durandin et al., 1981; Lassarre, 1985). The evaluation of the content of the message is contaminated by the evaluation of its form: Both the source of the message and the message itself are often rejected at the same time! By rejecting persuasion, the child may erroneously be perceived to react rationally and critically even if the behaviour may be due to a bad mastership of persuasive messages.

Purchase is often quoted by children as the only way of verifying the truth of advertising. One wonders why other ways of verifying the truth of messages are not used such as, for example, the comparison of different sources (typically used, say, with respect to sexual matters).

Five Pilot Studies of Children's Different Sources of Economic Information

The specific questions our research was intended to answer were the following:

− From where stems the economic knowledge of 11 and 12 year old children? What are the impacts of different sources of information? How do children trust these different sources? What are their opinions about general economic phenomena?

− To what extent do children trust and use information from media? Are there differences between televised and written information, between information from advertisers and consumer organizations? Are peers an important source of information?

− What do children know about television advertising? Do they perceive it as a source of information?

− Is purchasing a source of information? Are boys and girls similarly motivated to go shopping? Do they behave the same way in supermarkets?

− Has early family education any impact upon children's representation of economic life?

Method

The investigations focused on the use of sources rather than on content or quality of the information received. The approach was not developmental: In all the studies, the subjects were boys and girls aged 11 and 12. In most cases, they were in their first year of secondary school

(French "colleges") in Paris and its suburbs. The social status of their parents is representative of the population of this area. Differences between boys and girls were at the centre of our attention.

Study One: Semi-Structured Interviews

In semi-structured interviews sources of information about three economic matters were ascertained: a consumer product (soft drinks), a service (insurance), and a social problem (the employment of young people). Different economic opinions were also subject to inquiry. Half of the 46 interviews were made at school and the other half at the interviewer's home. Children at the end of the last level of primary school were compared with children at the beginning of the first year of secondary school (Roland-Levy, 1987). The results of this study were used as a background for the later studies.

Study Two: Laboratory Study With Experimental Task

Here, the use of written and televised information and advertising about the same three matters (soft drinks, insurance, and employment) was investigated. The study was carried out at school with 72 children either individually or in couples of the same gender. Different topics were addressed in different groups. The instructions were:

Suppose you have just created a new soft drink for young people/started a new insurance company/suppose you are a Minister and you have found a way to give jobs to young unemployed people. How will you let this be known? How will you be able to convince others that your soft drink/insurance/employment plan is the best one? To help you, written and televised information is available. You can look at it as you like.

When ready to answer, the child was given a sheet of paper on which to write down its propositions. Results are based on the observation of the number and category of documents the child investigated. The different documents were: (a) articles extracted from consumer information magazines, (b) ads from magazines, and (c) TV commercials. A very simple content analysis of the child's propositions was also carried out.

Study Three: Interviews and Experimental Tasks

This study consisted of interviews about the way TV commercials are made, with open end questions followed by two experimental tasks, analysis of a TV spot, and production of advertising messages. In all, 96 children were interviewed either individually or in groups of three (boys or girls) at school (first year of secondary school). The session started by asking the children to explain the role of TV advertising and the way a TV commercial is designed and produced. They were then asked to describe in words their own design for a TV spot for cheese. Finally, they had to analyse a spot for cheese.

Study Four: Observations in Supermarkets Followed by Questionnaires

Forty-nine children were observed during all their activities when visiting small supermarkets. Special attention was given to their information-seeking behaviour as purchasing is often quoted as the only way to learn about products. The method of observation was based on Barker's ecological psychology with its focus on behaviour episode units (Barker, 1968, 1978).

A supermarket is a behaviour setting. Barker (1963) regards "behaviour episodes" as a combination of acts and/or speech of an inhabitant of the setting which constitutes a "fundamental molar unit of the behaviour stream." It is impossible to decompose it into smaller units. When series of behaviour episodes are observed, it is noticeable that there is no total correspondence between stimuli (neither environmental nor social) and behavioural responses: Some stimuli do not elicit any response and numerous behaviour episodes are not caused by stimulation estimating from the setting, but rather have their causes in motives inherent to the person.

Each of the 646 observation units included one place in the setting (which generally means a product category) and/or one behaviour (walking, appentency, purchasing, giving up, seeking information, making a request, responding) and/or a stimulus. Each child was alone, with another child, or with an adult. At the end of their shopping they were interviewed separately about "the different things that they found interesting in the supermarket." The interviewer tried to find motives for the observed behaviour.

Study Five: Projective Tests

Four hundred children 11 and 12 years old were asked to draw up a short story on the basis of pictures of two purchasing situations (a woman looking at a shop window and a view of an open air market) and two hierarchical work situations (one male and one female).

These tests were made at home with children from different cultural communities (French, Portuguese, Algerian, Moroccan, and Antillean). The children were all born and educated in France, but – apart from the French group – their parents were foreigners. Observing family habits is the primary source of information about the economic world, but the effect of this source can only be illuminated by interviewing children from very different groups which enables one to separate the effects of

Methods	Topics	Psychological processes	Main independent variables
1. Semi-structured interviews	. soft drinks . insurance . employment	. information-seeking habits . knowledge and its sources . credibility of the different sources . opinions	. gender . school level
2. Laboratory study with experimental task	. soft drinks . insurance . employment	. information-giving behaviour . credibility of different sources	. gender . information sources . situation (alone/ with peers)
3. Interviews and experimental tasks	. TV commercials	. knowledge about television advertising . trust in efficiency of attractive/ informative aspects of advertising	. gender . situation
4. Observations in supermarkets followed by questionnaires	. consumption products	. purchasing behaviour . information-seeking behaviour . motivation	. gender . situation (alone/with a peer or an adult)
5. Projective tests	. consumption . employment	. representation of two economic situations (purchasing/hierarchical relationships at work)	. gender . cultural community (early family education)

Figure 1: Methods, topics, psychological processes, and main independent variables explored within the different studies.

early family education from the wider environmental socialization. Data were collected in the suburbs of Tours. The stories were subjected to both a clinical-psychological analysis, and a content analysis focusing on motives and economic roles.

The variables investigated with the aid of the different methods are summarized in Figure 1.

As the studies will not be reported in detail, we have chosen to present only those results which show differences between variables which are significant at $p<.05$. x^2-tests were used for non-parametric data and Student t or analysis of variance for parametric data.

Results

The findings can be used to develop faster and more accurate methods of investigating the topics addressed as well as children's economic socialization in general. The purpose of this particular paper, however, is first and foremost to arrive at a synthesis of results about the use of information sources. We categorized the sources into three types:

1. **Active information**. It is acquired in a natural situation characterized by involvement (purchasing or choosing a school orientation) or an artificial pedagogical situation, similar to experimentation. The informative process is conscious and voluntary.

2. **Entertaining information**. It is acquired through the mass media. It can have the form of purposive messages (advertising or news) or of marginal information included in fiction (novels, films, TV series). The child can use this information consciously or not; this is what DeFleur and DeFleur (1967) called incidental education.

3. **Social information**. It stems from the family or conversations with friends of equal or higher age.

Active Information

We studied the acquisition of active information by observation in supermarkets, experimental tasks in school, and projective tests.

This type of information is very salient during children's shopping. It represents 30% of their activities in the supermarket. It includes

- reading labels
- looking for a particular product on a shelf
- trying out products
- looking at prices, adding up expenses, and counting money
- seeking the advice of the accompanying person, child or adult
- putting a question to the shop assistant.

This behaviour was frequent in food departments which had shop assistants (meat, delicatessen, seafood, fruit, vegetables), in cereal and other breakfast product departments, and on the way from one department to another. There was no particular difference between boys and girls.

The child spent a longer time searching for information when alone (40% of behaviour units) than when accompanied by an adult (25%).

There are few links with other behaviour in the supermarket: 63% of the purchases were made without previously seeking any information in the setting; only 22.5% of appentency behaviour was followed by information-seeking activity. But what we call appentency (touching products, smiling, talking about the product), can be considered as a pre-information-seeking behaviour as at this age information is still strongly affective. Appentency was the most important behaviour; it represented 43% of activities in the supermarket and was not connected with purchase. Thus we can assert that information-seeking is a very important and independent activity in supermarkets. "To look for information" was mentioned as a motive to go to the supermarket only in 5.5% of the interviews and children became aware of its importance only when they were interrogated about their sources of information **in the very setting**. Then, 53% said that their source of information about products was shops and supermarkets (while in Study One, when interviewed at home or at school, only 12% of the children referred to this source of information). In the purchase setting, they invoked this source of information for sweets, do-it-yourself products, clothes, and books.

In the projective tests, information through shopping appeared in 29% of the stories about "the marketplace" and in 49% of the stories about the "shop window." Looking at the price and asking the shop assistant were the most important information-seeking activities. Information-seeking was equally common as a behaviour for both boys and girls, but it appeared as a motive less often for the girls (11%) than for the boys (29%): "she's looking at the window because she wants to know the prices in different shops before choosing a new dress; she's invited to a wedding" or "she is just window shopping."

Entertaining Information

In the interviews, 43 children (out of 46) mentioned TV commercials as a source of information about products and economic matters, but in the supermarkets, advertising was quoted as a source of information by only 3 children out of 49 and only for household products such as washing powders or electric batteries.

Interviews centred on TV commercials were made at school with the intention of discovering more about the knowledge of children: How is a TV commercial made? Who does it and why? (Study Three.) Here, the main finding is the difference between boys and girls. We already knew that girls of this age spend a longer time watching television (Welcomme & Willerval, 1986). But our study shows that they are primarily watching it as an entertainment while boys expect to get information from commercial television.

At 12 years of age, all children know the commercial purpose of TV spots (Kapferer, 1985), but boys also mention other financial aspects such as advertisements subsidizing TV programmes. Boys think that advertisements on television are useful because they are informative, while girls appreciate the aesthetical means used to enhance the value of the product.

The knowledge about the way TV commercials are made depends on these differences in perspective. All boys quoted the roles of both advertisers and advertising agencies. Only two thirds of the girls did so, whereas they emphasized the roles played by movie production, studios, actors, and directors. One might be led to conclude that girls are romantic while boys are realistic; the second part of Study Three (the experimental task) shows that the matter is more complex than that.

When children were asked to recall a TV spot about cheese which they had just seen, they cited an equal number of attractive and informative details, but one third of the details they cited were really not contained in the TV spot they had been shown. The invented details were informative and mainly given by boys; thus it appears that boys "supply"

TV spots with the information they are looking for. Their analysis is factual, for instance they reject special effects, and to make it more factual they add informative details. "They said that cheese is good for health because there are some proteins and vitamins in it," alas, there is no mention of proteins or vitamins in the spot. Girls do not expect information. They focus on the attractive aspects of the show and appreciate special effects: "to show that eating cheese is like drinking milk, they show the amount of milk getting less as the nice little boy is eating cheese"; "the boy was well dressed and good-looking." Interested by the formal aspects of the advertisement, girls consider it as fiction whose information content is not to be taken seriously.

Table 1: Conditions and Results of Study Two

	Soft drinks	Insurance	Employment
Available information			
Number of articles	8	15	9
Number of ads (magazines)	8	14	9
Number of TV commercials	16	5	5
Results			
Articles consulted (mean)	4.4	5.9	3.3
Advertisements consulted (mean)	3.3	–	3.4
Articles + ads (weighted means)	0.41	0.37	0.31
TV spots consulted (mean)	8.7	4.7	4.5
TV spots (weighted means)	0.54	0.94	0.9

How children use information from advertising and non-advertising media depends essentially on the topic (see Table 1). For soft drinks, children were more attentive to neutral consumer information than to advertising but the material they themselves produced (always advertisements) was more attractive than informative. In Study Three, both boys and girls included a great number of attractive details (66%) in spots they invented for cheese. It seems that in spite of their attention to consumer information, the attractive aspect dominates their image of food advertising. For insurance and employment, whether the written information came from advertisements or not did not matter, but we can see from the weighted means in Table 1 (number of consulted articles, ads, or spots divided by the number of available articles, ads, or spots) that television advertising is relatively more important. For insurance, productions were half advertising, half non-advertising. This material was informative (especially for boys), because, as the interviews divulged, children did not know which information to give. They felt insecure with this topic, so they asked for verification of information: "One shouldn't tell stupid things; the government should control it." For the issue of youth employment, the produced material never took the form of advertising. The children proposed personal media, and their messages were informative: "the Minister should appear on the TV news and explain everything," "I would send information by mail to all young unemployed people." In the interviews, children said that they knew about employment through TV news and people they knew. It is noticeable that in the production task, they duplicate their own sources of information.

The interviews showed that other TV programmes, such as series, are a source of information for children. As we did not include them explicitly in our research, we cannot exactly know their impact. Most series come from the U.S., and it would certainly be interesting to know how American consumption and economic patterns are transposed by children to the French society.

Social Information

Studies of younger children (Durandin et al., 1981) have pointed to two sources of social information, family and friends, and we can add another source that children aged 11-12 years often refer to as "other people." By this is meant conversations among adults that are overheard or conversations they have with adults outside the family. Table 2 shows that these relationships are important for checking the veracity of information.

Entering high school means a great change in the respective importance of parents and friends in their informative roles. At the end of primary school, parents and TV commercials are the main sources of information. Three months later, in secondary school, friends and purchase settings have a stronger informative power. Social life has replaced the family context. In the interviews, parents' friends and friends' parents appeared as another adult reference for insurance and employment.

Table 2: **Social Sources of Information Quoted Spontaneously in the 46 Interviews (Study One)**

	Friends	Parents	Other people	No social source quoted
General information	19	11	3	13
Checking veracity	8	7	11	20
Soft drinks	5	17	8	16
Insurance	0	14	13	19
Employment	0	11	7	28

In supermarkets, family was invoked as a source of information for sweets and beauty products. The presence of an adult in the setting is not necessarily positive. There was more social stimulation when the child was with a friend than with its mother. There was less information-seeking behaviour with parents (25%) than with friends (34%).

We assume that representation of economic situations in the projective test was influenced by information acquired in the family. It is noteworthy that in this test, information-seeking behaviour, especially looking at prices, was very important for Algerian and Portuguese children, 65% and 62% respectively, and very low for French children, 17%, from the same economic stratum.

Only 28% of the children saw a job situation in the picture of two women. The majority of the French children perceived the women to have complementary roles, whereas children from foreign communities perceived the relationship to be a hierarchical one. But in both groups, the story appeared to be non-conflictive, and sometimes there was even a happy ending: "she had been looking for a job and the lady behind the desk tells her that she has just got one for her." Only 22% of the children saw a job situation in the picture of two men, and the majority were migrant children. Only the Portuguese children were quite prone to imagine a conflict: "he didn't wash the stairs; his boss tells him he must find another job." It is rather obvious that the family context makes the children more or less sensitive to employment problems.

Friends were reported as a source of information for sweets, toys and games, and books. During the experimental tasks, children who were alone were more attentive to all kinds of information than when they were in groups. Their production, oral in Study Three, written in Study Two, was more stereotyped when in a group situation. In supermarkets, girls more frequently than boys were observed together with a friend of the same age. Their behaviour was very social: They chattered while queuing for vegetables or other food products. They explored beauty and school equipment departments with a lot of appentency and information-seeking behaviour.

Conclusion

The multiple approach to the study of children's sources of economic information at this particular turning point, the beginning of high school, appears quite fruitful. It makes it possible to explain the findings of one study by those of another one; for instance, our interviews provided explanations of the differences among topics noticed in the message production task.

Some contradictions appear. For instance, the relative importance attributed to TV advertising is much lower in the supermarket setting than at home or at school. These differences between short and long term information processes ought to be explored in more depth.

Among the main results of these studies are the following:

– children from secondary schools use a wider array of information sources than those from primary schools, and they seem to choose their sources according to the topic;

– there are differences between girls and boys in their attitudes towards commercial television as well as differences in their behaviour in supermarkets;

– these gender differences seem to be overruled by differences in subcultures, a finding which underlines the strong effects of family education.

There are also some educational consequences to be drawn. If used in schools, a structural approach can certainly make children more conscious of the existence and functions of what we have called entertaining information. It is possible to use tasks of active information search to develop a sense for other sources of information and for the need to compare source reliability with respect to different topics.

References

Albou, P. (1984). *La psychologie économique*. Paris: PUF.

Barker, R.G. (1963). On the nature of environment. *Journal of Social Issues, 19*, 17-38.

Barker, R.G. (1968). *Ecological psychology: Concepts and methods for studying the environment of human behaviour*. Stanford, CA: Stanford University Press.

Barker, R.G. (1978). *Habitats, environments, and human behaviour*. San Francisco: Jossey Bass.

Beaudichon, J. (1982). *La communication sociale chez l'enfant*. Paris: PUF.

Berti, A.E., Bombi, A.S., & Lis, A. (1982). The child's conceptions about means of production and their owners. *European Journal of Social Psychology, 12*, 221-240.

Burris, V. (1983). Stages in the development of economic concepts. *Human Relations, 9*, 791-812.

Cullingford, C. (1984). *Children and television*. London: Gower.

Cummings, S., & Taebel, D. (1978). The economic socialization of children: A neo-marxist analysis. *Social Problems, 26*, 198-210.

Danziger, K. (1958). Children's earliest conception of economic relationships. *Journal of Social Psychology, 47*, 231-240.

DeFleur, M.L. (1964). Occupational roles as portrayed on television. *Public Opinion Quarterly, 28*, 57-74.

DeFleur, M.L., & DeFleur, L.B. (1967). The relative contribution of television as a learning source for children's occupational knowledge. *American Sociological Review, 32*, 777-789.

Durandin, G. (1982). *Les mensonges en propagande et en publicité*. Paris: PUF.

Durandin, G., Cave, F., Feertchak, H., Joyeux, B., Lassarre D., Ludwig, D., & Perez-Bourguet, A. (1981). *L'enfant et la publicité télévisée*. Paris: Université René Descartes, Laboratoire de Psychologie Sociale. ATP du CNRS 3376.

Furth, H.G. (1978). Young children's understanding of society. In: H. McGurk (Ed.), *Issues in childhood social development*, pp. 228-256. London: Methuen.

Furth, H.G. (1980). *The world of grown-ups*. New York: Elsevier.

Granger, G.G. (1967). Epistémologie économique. In: J. Piaget (Ed.), *Logique et connaissance scientifique*, pp. 1019-1055. Paris: Gallimard NRF.

Harris, P., & Heelas, P. (1979). Cognitive processes and collective representations. *Archives Européennes de Sociologie, 20*, 211-241.

Hong Kwang, R.T., & Stacey, B.G. (1981). The understanding of socio-economic concepts in Malaysian Chinese school children. *Child Study Journal, 11*, 33-49.

Jahoda, G. (1979). The construction of economic reality by some Glaswegian children. *European Journal of Social Psychology, 9*, 115-127.

Jahoda, G. (1981). The development of thinking about economic institutions: The bank. *Cahiers de Psychologie Cognitive, 1*, 55-73.

Jahoda, G., & Woerdenbagch, A. (1982). The development of ideas about an economic institution: A cross-national replication. *British Journal of Social Psychology, 21*, 337-338.

Kapferer, J.N. (1985). *L'enfant et la publicité*. Paris: Dunod.

Lassarre, D. (1985). De l'attitude envers le spot au comportement de prescription: Quelques effets de la publicité télévisée sur les enfants de 9 à 10 ans. *Proceedings of the XIIème Séminaire International de Recherche en Marketing*, pp. 109-136. Aix en Provence: IAE Aix Marseille.

Lautrey, J. (1980). *Classe sociale, milieu familial, et intelligence*. Paris: PUF.

Lea, S.E.G., Tarpy, R.M., & Webley, P. (1987). *The individual in the economy*. Cambridge: Cambridge University Press.

Leiser, D. (1983). Children's conceptions of economics. *Journal of Economic Psychology, 4*, 297-317.

Roland-Lévy, C. (1987). *Understanding the economic behaviour of children*. Paper presented at the XIIth Colloquium of the International Association for Research in Economic Psychology, Ebeltoft, Denmark, September 25-28.

Siegal, M. (1981). Children's perceptions of adult economic needs. *Child Development, 52*, 379-382.

Strauss, A. (1952). The development and transformation of monetary meanings in the child. *American Sociological Review, 17*, 275-286.

Ward, S., Wackman, D.B., & Wartella, E. (1977). *How children learn to buy*. London: Sage.

Webley, P. (1983). Economic socialization in the pre-adult years: A comment on Stacey. *British Journal of Social Psychology, 22,* 264-265.

Welcomme, G., & Willerval, G. (1986). *Juniorscopie.* Paris: Larousse, Bayard Press.

Youniss, J. (1978). The nature of social development: A conceptual discussion of cognition. In: H. McGurk (Ed.), *Issues in childhood social development,* pp. 203-227. London: Methuen.

Ziegler, B., & Child, I. (1969). Socialization. In: G. Lindzey & E. Aronson (Eds.), *Handbook of social psychology,* Vol. 3, pp. 450-555. Reading, MA: Addison-Wesley.

Marek Wosinski

A Model of Consumer Behaviour in the Situation of Shortages

Abstract

This paper introduces a model of consumer behaviour in the situation where consumers need a particular product which is not available on the market. In such a situation a consumer may use alternative strategies to the strategy used in a normal market situation. One, namely the use of an intermediary, seems to have important consequences for consumers, for social relationships, and also for the economy in general. A description of this strategy and its consequences constitutes the main part of the model considered.

The model has been developed on the basis of data specific to Polish conditions, but can be applied generally to situations of economic shortage.

The author wishes to thank The Swedish Institute for financial support and Karl-Erik Wärneryd for organizing facilities for this study. The author also owes a special debt of gratitude to Barbara Czarniawska-Joerges for her comments and to Tony Newbold for corrections to the manuscript.

The first version of this paper was presented as Research Paper No. 6326 of The Economic Research Institute, Stockholm School of Economics, June 1987.

Author's address: Marek Wosinski, Department of Social Psychology of Education, University of Silesia, ul. Tyszki 53, 40-126 Katowice, Poland.

Shortages

The aim of this paper is to introduce a model of consumer behaviour in the shortage economy and to discuss the most important consequences of this behaviour for society and the economy in general, as well as for consumers themselves.

According to Nove (1983), shortage means that buyers with a legitimate claim on resources cannot obtain what they want or need, even though they have money. Though it concerns both consumers and managers, in this paper I will focus only on the effects shortages have on individual consumers. It is not my intention to discuss the causes of shortages, as these are treated elsewhere (e.g., Bauer, 1978; Kornai, 1980; Krasinski, Piasny, & Szulce, 1984; Nove, 1983). The most detailed analysis of the economics of shortage can be found in Kornai's book (1980). He refers mainly to the Hungarian experience, one of the East European countries where shortages occur. It should be noted, however, that shortages may occur more or less temporarily in any country, at least for a given type of product.

Kornai describes consumer behaviour in the situation of shortages in terms of a two-level dilemma. Firstly, a consumer has to decide whether to apply to the administration for access to the centrally or locally distributed goods, instead of searching for this product on the market. Secondly, when present in the shop and on seeing the product, a consumer has to make a take-it-or-leave-it decision. It concerns all situations where there is no differentiation among types, quality, or sizes of a particular product (see also Krasinski et al., 1984) which means that in reality it is a producer who decides what is bought. Shortages create "shopping under pressure," a situation in which consumers buy everything that is available just because they anticipate future shortage or increased prices.

The analysis of the relationships between the Polish level of production, the supply on the market, and the standard of living in particular households shows that the mechanisms for distributing consumer goods must be much more complicated than what is implied by contracts between sellers and buyers. It is characteristic that people complain about shortages of both basic and luxury goods, yet in their homes they have most of those goods which are supposedly in short supply. Thus one must be able to obtain those goods by means other than normal shopping procedure. In this case, models of consumer behaviour need to take into consideration more factors than those included in traditional psychological models.

Traditional Models of Consumer Behaviour

Several models of consumer behaviour have been constructed since psychology entered the field of economics. Some of the most commonly quoted in textbooks on consumer behaviour and marketing are: Engel, Kollat, and Blackwell's Model of Buyer Behavior (1978), the Dyadic Model of Consumer Behavior (Bonoma, Bagozzi, & Zaltman, 1975), Kerby's Model of Consumer Behavior (1975), and Nicosia's Model of Consumer Behavior (Nicosia, 1967). These models were constructed with the intention of expounding the factors which influence consumer behaviour as well as describing the psychological mechanisms involved in the behaviour itself. Two features are characteristic for all these models.

Firstly, they are purely cognitive and describe consumer behaviour mainly in terms of information processing and decision making. In this view, a consumer is a person with a problem to solve: how to satisfy a particular need by choosing the right kind of products. Problem solving and decision making processes are based both on individual experience and on information about the utility of particular products, their availability, etc.

Secondly, they describe consumer behaviour in markets, where the consumer's main task is to choose among different available products (or rather a subset hereof, as the consumer is usually familiar with only a few of them).

These two features reveal that the models mentioned above have limited relevance with regard to consumer behaviour in the so-called shortage economy. For consumers, shortages create a situation where buying becomes more of a social than an individual behaviour (see also Verhallen, 1984). It means that in order to acquire a particular product a common (cooperative) activity is needed, involving more parties than merely buyer and seller. Using the terms of Tomaszewski (1983), we may consider shopping as a "collective action" instead of an "individual action."

All models of consumer behaviour are constructed at a very high level of generalization. Nevertheless, their explanatory and predictive value seems to be limited in situations where consumer behaviour becomes an element of complex social interaction. Obviously, cognitive processes are also involved in such situations, but when a further party intervenes between a buyer and a seller, new variables must be taken into consideration in order to understand both the consumer behaviour and its social and economic consequences.

A large number of factors have been described as influencing consumer behaviour in a normal market situation. Psychologists strongly emphasize the importance of social influences, as consumers always act in a particular socio-economic context (Wärneryd, 1987). Beside individual factors such as personality, motives, perception, and experience, all those factors which influence "life-style," viz., a particular culture, a system of values, demographic factors, social status, reference groups, the type of household, have an important impact on consumer behaviour in a particular situation of choice. The traditional models, however, do not take into account the specific network of personal contacts and the activity which is necessary (or at least helpful) if one is to obtain products that are unavailable in the shops.

Relatively little has been written, too, about the consequences of consumers' behaviour for social relationships and the social environment as a whole (for an exception, see Uusitalo, 1983, although in her book, little is said about the individual consumer). In a shortage situation, the behaviour of consumers can have manifold consequences for the socio-economic situation in which they are placed. These consequences probably become more apparent with increasing disparity between consumer needs and what is being offered by the market.

Empirical Studies

To gather some preliminary information about how people behave in the situation of shortages we carried out an anonymous survey of 200 randomly selected persons (50% women, 50% men) aged 25-45. The participants were required to answer the following question: "How do you act if you need a particular product which is not available on the market? Please describe what you do in the greatest possible detail." After the answer to this question had been given, we asked the following: "If you seek the help of any intermediary, please describe all your thoughts, feelings, and behaviour related to this interaction." Data about the income of each person in the family, and about the respondent's education and profession were also collected. Data from this pilot study as well as from everyday observations were used as a basis for constructing the model described below.

We have made two further studies analysing particular aspects of consumer behaviour when faced with shortages. The first of these (Pietras & Wosinski, 1988) describes consumers' experience of injustice connected with shortages. The second (Wosinski, 1988) compares the behaviour of consumers belonging to five different professional groups: workers, clerks, medical doctors, teachers, and owners of small businesses ("private sector").

Some examples from these studies will be used as illustrations in the following.

Consumer Behaviour When Faced With Shortage: Resignation

Usually the need for a particular product causes a person to search for it on the market. Visits to several stores and information acquired from other people result in an estimate of the probability of finding the product on the market. Such an estimate may be strongly influenced by previous experiences, leading to an a priori assumption that the product is unavailable. Any further search would be mainly to confirm this assumption, so that little effort is expended before one decides to abstain from further search and from the consideration of other possibilities (see Figure 1).

Resignation seems to assume one of two forms. Some people tend to reassess the previously desired good and apply various kinds of rationalization to justify why they do not need it. Sometimes they find a substitute, sometimes they ignore its objective usefulness. Over a longer time this type of resignation may lead to some changes in the consumer's system of values (cf. Sévon, 1988); it certainly means changed consumption patterns. It should be mentioned that people reporting this type of resignation, 22% of interviewed persons, usually do not connect negative emotions with the situation. This type of resignation might be designated as "accepted passivity."

373

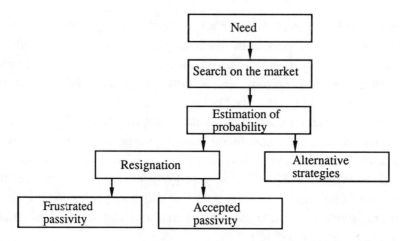

Figure 1: A general model of consumer behaviour in the situation of shortages.

Almost the same percentage of respondents (18%) spoke about resignation of a quite different type. The value of the desired product is still perceived as high, and when the probability of obtaining it is estimated to be low, people feel uncomfortable and usually complain strongly about the situation. This type of resignation may be called "frustrated passivity" and may have all the symptoms usually observed as reactions to stress. (Similar types of passivity were seen in our studies on the experiences of injustice connected with economic events, Wosinski, 1988; Wosinski & Wosinska, 1985.)

In the more detailed inquiry made in the study of a group of 133 consumers representing five professional groups, we found that only 25% became fully resigned, whereas after a few days (weeks, months), 49% began searching again in the shops.

Several differences were observed between the various professional groups in this respect (see Table 1).

It turned out that clerks constitute the group which resigns most frequently (43%) and which rather seldom returns to searching after a few days (14%). Workers also often abandon further search (34%), but 50% of them make another inquiry after some time. In comparison with other groups, workers infrequently apply alternative strategies (only 26%).

Table 1: General Reaction to Shortages (in Percentages)

Type of reaction	Workers	Medical doctors	Clerks	Teachers	Private sector	Average
	n = 30	n = 29	n = 28	n = 24	n = 22	n = 133
Resignation	33.6	10.3	42.8	16.6	13.4	23.4
Searching again after a few days	33.3	34.5	0	41.6	40.8	30.0
Searching again after a few weeks	13.3	7.2	10.7	25.0	18.6	16.9
Searching again after a few months	3.3	0	3.6	4.1	4.5	3.1
Alternative strategies	26.4	41.4	35.7	41.6	45.0	38.0

Asked about the reasons for resignation, different groups reported different types of arguments (see Table 2). Objective difficulties were

Table 2: Subjective Rationalization of Resignation (in Percentages)

Type of reason	Workers	Medical doctors	Clerks	Teachers	Private sector	Average
	n = 30	n = 29	n = 28	n = 24	n = 22	n = 133
Objective difficulties	9.9	27.6	10.7	33.2	31.8	22.6
Helplessness	36.6	13.8	0	25.0	13.6	18.0
Unavailability of alternative strategies	19.9	20.7	32.1	29.1	9.1	22.2
Effort larger than possible payoff	6.6	27.6	32.1	25.0	25.0	20.1
Ability to adapt	19.9	20.7	14.3	4.1	27.4	17.3

Table 3: Evaluation of Particular Situations as Social Injustice

Type of situation	Passive (%) $n = 35$	Active (%) $n = 15$	z
Shortage			
- in general	71.4	26.7	2.94*
- of home equipment	68.6	33.3	2.31*
- books	48.6	26.7	1.44
- food	60.0	26.7	2.16*
- flats	74.3	26.7	3.15*
- medicines	74.3	26.7	3.15*
Waiting			
- inefficient waiting	60.0	26.7	2.16*
- "lists" of waiting people	57.1	26.7	1.98*
Illegal behaviour			
- in shops	68.6	26.7	2.74*
- in queues	62.9	26.7	2.35*
- at work	62.9	26.7	2.35*
- speculation	37.1	20.0	1.19
- in general	57.1	26.7	1.98*
Privileges			
- shops for miners	62.9	26.7	2.35*
- low prices	54.3	26.7	1.80*
- coupons	51.4	26.7	1.62
Behaviour of an intermediary			
- in shops	62.9	26.7	2.35*
- refusal to help	31.4	6.7	1.88*
- unreliability	37.1	6.7	2.20*
- demand for recompense	31.4	13.3	1.34
- unnecessary effort	34.3	6.7	2.04*
Social relationships			
- service in shops	54.3	20.0	2.24*
- aggression	45.7	20.0	1.72*
- privileged in queues	45.7	20.0	1.72*
Relation between prices and incomes	74.3	26.7	3.15*
Hard currency shops	57.1	26.7	1.98*

* indicates statistically significant differences.

most often mentioned as a reason for resignation by teachers (33%), most seldom by workers (10%). Helplessness was most commonly reported by workers (37%) but never mentioned by clerks. Unavailability of alternative strategies and effort larger than possible payoff were most often quoted by clerks (32%). The ability to adapt to deprivation was highest among the private sector respondents and lowest among teachers (Wosinski, 1988).

For some people, passivity seems to be associated with the perception of shortages as a social injustice (Pietras & Wosinski, 1988). In general, those consumers who declare themselves to be passive in the situation of shortages are more prone to perceive particular situations resulting from shortages as unjust (see Table 3).

Consumer Behaviour When Faced With Shortage: Alternative Strategies

Alternative strategies available for a customer are, of course, specific to given economic and social conditions. Here I will refer to strategies typical for Polish conditions, but it would be interesting to compare conditions offered to consumers in other countries experiencing various economic shortages.

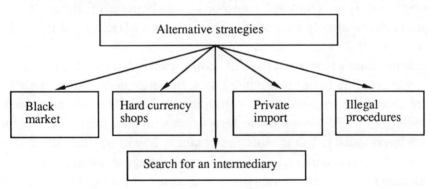

Figure 2: Alternative strategies.

Consumers in Poland can choose between five strategies (see Figure 2). Firstly, consumers may buy a product on the black market. It does not necessarily mean an illegal contract. In Poland there are special "flea markets," where one can buy all kinds of things. It may happen that these things have been stolen or illegally acquired from state warehouses, but these markets are usually places where people sell their own goods, quite often bought earlier on with the intention of resale.

Another strategy, also costly, is connected with the existence of hard currency shops, where one may buy practically all kinds of imported products. To do so one must have foreign currency. It is illegal to buy foreign currency from other people but legally one can procure special bank coupons, the price of which is much higher than the official rates of exchange. Again, this alternative is limited to people who are in a favourable financial situation, work abroad, or get financial aid from family members living outside Poland.

As many Poles have relatives abroad, there is another possibility to acquire the needed products, viz., by "private import." During the period of severe economic problems in Poland in 1982-83, this channel, in addition to some anonymous help from abroad, was one of the most important sources of several basic goods, especially as, in contrast to the two former strategies, it was relatively cheap. However, this strategy is very seldom or never used by people for whom the psychological costs connected with asking for such help appear to be much higher than the costs of dissatisfaction caused by the non-fulfilment of particular needs.

It will always happen in situations of shortage that some goods are distributed illegally as a result of criminal behaviour of some employees who steal from factories, transports, warehouses, or shops. These products are usually sold on the black market or "from hand to hand." Although this type of distribution seems to be rather marginal, every year there are a number of trials of people involved in such traffic.

According to our preliminary data, the strategies mentioned above are chosen by around 10% of consumers as being the only ones used, while another 10% use them in association with the strategy "search for an intermediary." One must remember, however, that there are psychological and moral barriers against admitting the use of some of the strategies mentioned above. The actual number of users may be much higher.

It is interesting to note that subjects' opinions about what other people do when they need to obtain a certain product, differ from the description of their own behaviour. In our study of different professional groups we found that as regards the black market, our respondents believed other people to apply this strategy more often than they did themselves (see Table 4), and they also expressed the opinion that other people more often used the help of an intermediary. On the other hand, respondents believed that the options of acquiring goods from hard currency shops and by private import was a privilege used more often by themselves than by others.

Table 4: The Most Often Used Alternative Strategies (in Percentages)

Strategy	Workers	Medical doctors	Clerks	Teachers	Private sector	Average
	$n = 30$	$n = 29$	$n = 28$	$n = 24$	$n = 22$	$n = 133$
Black market	3.3	3.4	7.1	0	13.6	5.0
Hard currency shops	9.9	20.7	28.5	12.5	18.6	18.0
Private import	16.5	10.3	10.7	16.6	22.7	15.3
Advertisements	3.3	0	0	16.6	22.4	9.6
Institutional intermediary	6.6	0	0	29.1	9.1	8.9
Intermediary	26.4	24.1	17.8	45.8	59.2	34.6

This disparity between the image of what other people do in the situation of shortage and one's own behaviour in analogous conditions did not have the same character for all groups of subjects. PEWEX (the name of the hard-currency shops) was most often used by clerks, the black market and private import by private sector respondents. Intermediaries were mostly used by private sector respondents and by teachers (differences to other groups are significant). Teachers thought that more than 70% of others used intermediaries for obtaining necessary goods.

Search for Intermediaries

"Search for an intermediary" means that a person who needs a product but is not able to buy it simply by visiting a relevant shop or using other strategies, begins searching for an institution or a person among relatives, friends, acquaintances, or even among non-acquaintances, who are able to assist in the procurement of the product.

Previous mention has been made of the special coupons which enable consumers to shop in hard currency shops. But these are available only on the basis of many different rules of rationing. To apply for such coupons also means searching for an intermediary who, in this case, is an institution. The people involved in these resource distribution decisions officially represent an institution. This administrative distribution seems to be much more of a management instrument used by authorities in their contracts with employees, than an active strategy used by consumers themselves. Nevertheless, parallel to other strategies, those who see any chance of obtaining needed products via this channel try to use it, including attempts to influence people responsible for the decisions. This channel is especially enticing since the price of the product is much lower than it would be if obtained by means of other strategies. Recently, under the pressure from people who do not have the possibility to use such privileges, there is a tendency to wind up this form of distribution.

Help from other people may consist of supplying relevant information about the availability of the product, of arranging contacts with a "second-step" intermediary being able to "organize" what is needed, or of delivery of the product itself.

The first step in searching for a private intermediary is devoted to the selection of people who could be of help. The second step is to

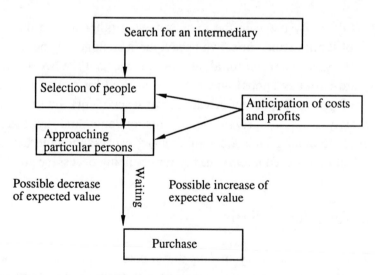

Figure 3: Search for an intermediary.

approach one or more of the selected potential intermediaries (see Figure 3). The selection is based on an estimate of those attributes which make the potential intermediary useful for this particular task. It is also based on the estimation of costs and profits associated with getting in contact with the particular person.

The largest part of these costs is psychological in character. They concern the emotions evoked by the inquiry and further contact with the person in question, the emotional (and behavioural) costs resulting from a possible refusal, and the feeling of dependency that arises. Furthermore, the costs of anticipated recompense must be taken into consideration. The size of these costs are very much dependent on the psychological distance between a potential intermediary and the person seeking to establish a contact, as well as on the intermediary's location in the social hierarchy. It is much easier to ask for help from a good friend than from somebody we know, but do not like. It is emotionally quite a different situation to ask for help from one's boss than from one's subordinate. Quite often asking a particular person for help in such matters goes against one's own moral norms or the norms of the other person; in both cases, emotional consequences may be severe.

It is not without importance that the formation of a contract with a particular intermediary is usually followed by an obligation to provide a reciprocal service in the future. Anticipation of such expectations from potential partners leads to predictions of the forthcoming demands. If they are estimated to be too high, the person is eliminated from the list of potential intermediaries. Sometimes such anticipations are so obvious that the whole inquiry starts with the offer of the supplicant's own services in the future. Information about the supplicant's ability to serve as a resource person whenever a particular need should arise on the side of a partner in the contract, seems to be an important factor influencing the partner's decision to help. Hence, the type of strategy described here can obviously be regarded as an exchange of services. The outcomes of such an exchange are both economic (one receives a particular product and pays for it by cash) and psychological (one pays the emotional price of approaching other people, of becoming dependent on them, and of being obliged to recompense them in the future).

However, a contract between a consumer and a particular intermediary may result not only in psychological costs but also in psychological profits (see Figure 4). The basic profit, of course, stems from the satisfaction of a need (one acquires a needed product). There are also some rewards stemming from the interaction itself, especially if there emerges a positive emotional relationship between the partners to the contract, or at least a positive attitude on the side of a consumer. Additional rewards can come from the social relationship which might develop during the process of mediation. It provides a chance to talk to people, to meet them, to do something for them, etc.

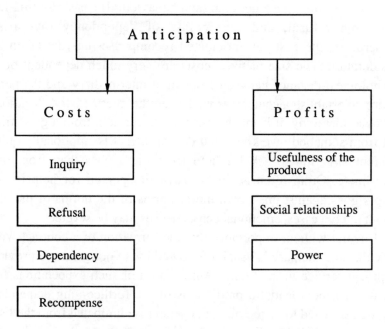

Figure 4: Costs and profits anticipated by a customer during searching for an intermediary.

The contact with a particular intermediary may end with a refusal or a promise on the side of the intermediary. In the latter case, the waiting time that is necessary will be stated more or less precisely. Waiting means a delay in the satisfaction of a need. As a consequence, the need may increase or decrease. For example, if one needs a vacuum-cleaner and must use a broom in the meantime, the need for the desired hardware will become greater and greater. Another person may find a near-substitute, which means that the satisfaction from getting the desired product may not be so high.

The strategy described here means that purchase "costs" include not only the financial costs of the product, but also the psychological costs mentioned above. An additional cost is connected with the necessity of showing gratitude to an intermediary. Whenever a need has increased during the waiting time, this appreciation may be quite spontaneous. It can be more difficult if the need has decreased or the intermediary makes it clear that very high appreciation is required. Post-purchase evaluation thus includes not only an evaluation of the product in the context of a need (its usefulness) but also an evaluation of the intermediary (the effective utility of his/her services). An important part of the post-purchase assessment is the evaluation of the dependency resulting from the contract, including the necessity of recompense (see Figure 5).

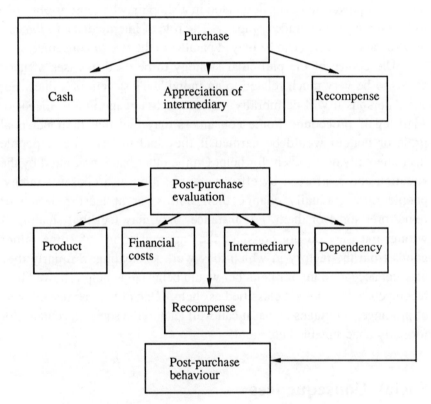

Figure 5: Purchase in the situation when the strategy "search for intermediary" is applied.

Individual Consequences

An important consequence of the repeated "search for an intermediary" is that the capacity to serve as an intermediary becomes an attribute which increases the social status of an individual within a given group. Although intermediaries are often "used" by others instrumentally, they still have the feeling of being useful, important, etc. At the same time they make other people dependent on them which gives a subjective feeling of power, in some cases even real power since to some extent those who apply for help can be ordered around. Czarniawska-Joerges (1987) uses the term "horizontal power," which means "the influence, prestige, and privileges resulting from being a member of a specific network"(p. 8). This kind of power is not equal to "vertical power," which is dependent on the individual's position in the organizational hierarchy. As regards horizontal power, to be a salesperson in a shop may be more useful than to be a manager in a trade company. The role of intermediary becomes a new social role which can be played parallel to the role of consumer.

The choice of the particular strategy to be used in cases of need seems to be very much related to an individual's system of values. For some persons it will be morally impossible to engage in any illegal or "half-legal" procedure. Some consumers may feel that their personal pride or honour would be harmed if they had to "use" other people instrumentally or ask them for help. On the other hand, pressured by the situation and reinforced by effective application of a chosen strategy, people may gradually change their norms, or at least redefine or reinterpret some of them. For instance, they may feel that stealing is wrong, but they do not consider the "appropriation" of some minor goods from the factory in which they work as stealing. Similarly they may not accept asking for help, but would believe that help followed by a recompense does not get classified as "help." One of the greatest dangers of prolonged shortages is that it can well lead to the social acceptance of formerly unacceptable behaviour.

Social Consequences

Consumer behaviour in times of shortage brings about several short-term as well as long-term consequences of social importance. First of all, through learning, strategies used by consumers may be perceived to be the most appropriate forms of consumer behaviour. It means that consumers will have a tendency to repeat behaviour which was effective in satisfying their needs. It may happen that a consumer, instead of searching the market, will immediately use one of the alternative strategies. If a strategy based on an intermediary was the most effective one (and we may assume that it is often successful judging by its frequency: it is applied by 50% of interviewed persons), "organizing" things becomes a sort of social habit, replacing "normal" patterns of buyer behaviour. This effect is reflected even in the vocabulary of children, who instead of asking "please, buy it for me, daddy" say "please, organize it for me, daddy."

Strategies based on intermediaries require broad social contacts and, when used very often, establish a specific network of social relationships. For some people it may be the only way of starting a relationship with representatives of certain social groups. For instance, if a university professor has a neighbour working in a store, he may ask him for help in getting a particular product. Recompense in this case might require inviting the neighbour for coffee and a political chat, even if in any other situation they would be most unlikely to meet socially. In other words, to some people their potential ability to serve as an intermediary opens up an avenue of new social contacts. As their ability becomes a desired trait, the structure of the particular social environment slowly changes.

It has already been mentioned that in a situation of shortages a specific system of distribution develops, a system which guarantees the subjective well-being of only some members of society. Any distribution of resources may be a source of perceived injustice in relationships between individuals and between groups (Syroit, 1984, 1985). The possibility of choosing certain strategies which are unavailable to other people gives certain people quicker or better access to the goods they need. Such a situation may be perceived by others as injustice, with all the associated cognitive, emotional, and behavioural consequences. Therefore shortages may lead not only to the development of new social relationships but also to conflicts between different social groups.

Economic Consequences

Finally, consumer behaviour in situations of shortage have certain consequences for the economy itself. The value of the product becomes much higher than is indicated by its official price. All psychological and objective costs connected with the effort needed for the employment of alternative strategies should be added to this value. Some products which have great usefulness but a low price, will acquire a high value because of difficulties in getting hold of them. In contracts based on the exchange of services, people are eager to pay a high psychological price for this particular type of product.

Another consequence can be described as the development of an informal distribution system. Whereas the established system distributes only certain products or components, the rest is distributed by these informal channels. As this distribution system satisfies also some psychological needs, there is a tendency to maintain the status quo rather than to make efforts directed at changing the situation. In the same vein, we may expect resistance to any proposed change of the conditions. On the one hand, there are people who suffer because of the non-availability of several products and because of the procedures used for their distribution. On the other, there are people, for whom such distribution does indeed satisfy both economic and psychological needs.

It is not without importance that consumer behaviour in the situation of shortages leads to artificially-extended shortages. In the anticipation that some products could be used as a recompense for the assistance of intermediaries or that they may be needed in the future even if it is not necessary to have them now, hoarding of goods is commonplace.

A great amount of energy and time is spent on the search for intermediaries and contacts with them, on playing the role of an intermediary, and for recompense. These are consequences which obviously have economic implications, especially as many of these actions take place during working hours.

Concluding Remarks

The model of consumer behaviour (for the overall model, see Figure 6) introduced in this paper can be called empirical in the sense that it is based on observations of everyday life and on exploratory but systematic studies of the phenomena. The model is general in the sense that if shortage occurs, the behaviour of any consumer can be fitted into this model. On the other hand, it still has only a hypothetical character as the links between the particular elements of the model still require testing in

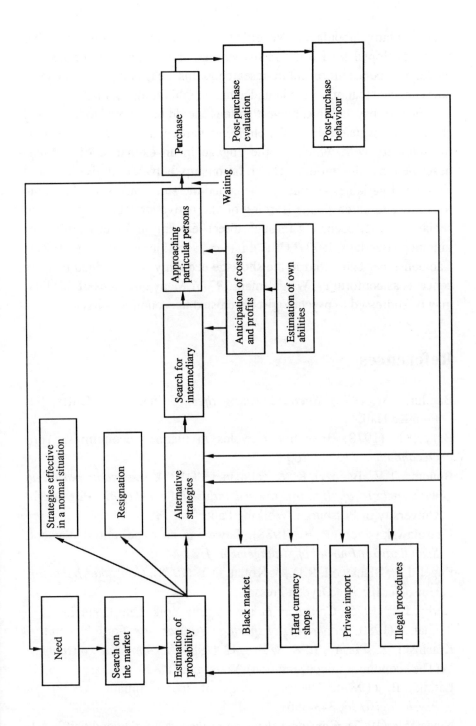

Figure 6: Overall model of consumer behaviour in the situation of shortages.

a representative population. Nevertheless, in conjunction with some other ideas developed by Kornai in his studies of shortage economies, the model may be useful for future research in this area, as it points out some new elements that may help in understanding this complex matter.

Further psychological investigations should be devoted to individual characteristics determining the choice of particular strategies as well as the intensity with which people engage in an exchange of services described by the model. The relationship between individual and situational variables (including the economic situation) is another topic for further research. Is the learning of alternative strategies a process of social learning, occurring through direct learning, indirect learning, or imitation (Bandura, 1977)? Or is it rather a social impact (Latané, 1981)? Can consumer behaviour in the shortage economy be explained by such concepts as conformity (Wrightsman, 1977)? Many questions of this kind may be addressed to psychologists interested in economic behaviour.

References

Bandura, A. (1977). *Social learning theory*. Englewood Cliffs, NJ: Prentice Hall.

Bauer, T. (1978). Investment cycles in planned economies. *Acta Oeconomica, 21,* 243-260.

Bonoma, T.V., Bagozzi, R., & Zaltman, G. (1975). *The dyadic paradigm with specific application toward industrial marketing*. Pittsburgh: University of Pittsburgh. Working Paper No. 138.

Czarniawska-Joerges, B. (1988). Power as an experiential concept. *Scandinavian Journal of Management, 4,* 31-44.

Engel, J.F., Blackwell, R.D., & Kollat, D.T. (1978). *Consumer behavior*. Hinsdale, IL: The Dryden Press.

Kerby, J.K. (1975). *Consumer behavior*. New York: Dun-Donnelley.

Kornai, J. (1980). *Economics of shortage*. Amsterdam: North Holland.

Krasinski, Z., Piasny, J., & Szulce, H. (1984). *Ekonomika konsumpcji* (The economics of consumption). Warszawa: PWE.

Latané, B. (1981). The psychology of social impact. *American Psychologist, 36,* 343-356.

Nicosia, F. (1967). *Consumer decision processes*. Englewood Cliffs, NJ: Prentice Hall.

Nove, A. (1983). *The economics of feasible socialism*. London: George Allen and Unwin.

Pietras, M., & Wosinski, M. (1988). *Shortage economy and consumers' experience of injustice*. Paper presented at the Conference on Social Justice, Leiden, August 1-3.

Sévon, G. (1988). Rationalization of action through value development. In: S. Maital (Ed.), *Applied behavioural economics*, Vol. 1, pp. 412-419. Brighton: Wheatsheaf.

Syroit, J.E. (1984). *Interpersonal injustice. A psychological analysis illustrated with empirical research*. Tilburg: University of Tilburg. Doctoral thesis.

Syroit, J.E. (1985). *Interpersonal and intergroup injustice: Some theoretical considerations*. Paper presented to the Colloquium of the European Association of Experimental Social Psychology, Katowice, September 25-30.

Tomaszewski, T. (1963). *Wstęp do psychologii* (Introduction to psychology). Warsaw: PWN.

Uusitalo, L. (Ed.) (1983). *Consumer behaviour and environmental quality*. Aldershot: Gower.

Verhallen, T.M.M. (1984). *Scarcity: Unavailability and behavioral costs*. Tilburg: University of Tilburg. Doctoral thesis.

Wärneryd, K.E. (1987). *Social influence on economic behavior*. Brussels: European Institute for Advanced Studies in Management. Working Paper 87-6.

Wosinski, M. (1988). Social comparison and experience of injustice. *Journal of Economic Psychology, 9,* 359-367.

Wosinski, M. (1988). Profession and consumer behaviour in the situation of shortages. In: P. Vanden Abeele (Ed.), *Psychology in micro & macro economics*, Volume III. Papers presented at the 13th Annual Colloquium of IAREP, Leuven/Brussels, September 28 - October 1.

Wosinski, M., & Wosinska, W. (1985). Preferences for parity or equity and the experience of injustice caused by the relative decrease of salary. In: H. Brandstätter & E. Kirchler (Eds.), *Economic psychology*, pp. 347-358. Linz: Trauner.

Wrightsman, L.S. (1977). *Social psychology* (2nd brief ed.). Monterey, CA: Brooks/Cole.

Part V

New Views on Economic Analysis

Steven R. Hursh, Thomas G. Raslear,
Richard Bauman, and Harold Black

The Quantitative Analysis of Economic Behavior With Laboratory Animals

Abstract

Studies of animal behavior in the laboratory provide an extensive data set on economic behavior under controlled and replicable conditions. In the studies reported, the food consumption of rodents and non-human primates was studied under a wide variety of conditions of work effort, commodity value, and substitute availability. The results conformed to a single underlying demand function that assumed that demand elasticity was linear in price. Price was defined as a cost-benefit ratio that included consideration of both the effort of the work and the value of the commodity purchased. The parameters of the elasticity equation appeared related to the amount and temporal proximity of a substitute food.

These data from non-human subjects have limitations for predicting human economic behavior. However, these data provide clear evidence that the basic principles of consumer demand theory can be observed in a primitive system. This suggests that the theory is "biological" in the sense that it does not depend on the "cultural" mechanisms of either verbal behavior or money.

The views of the authors do not purport to reflect the position of the Department of the Army of the Department of Defense, (para 4-3, AR 360-5). In conducting the research described in this report, the investigator(s) adhere to the "Guide for the Care and Use of Laboratory Animals," as promulgated by the Committee on Care and Use of Laboratory Animals of the Institute of Laboratory Animal Resources, National Research Council.

Authors' addresses: Steven R. Hursh, Thomas G. Raslear, and Richard Bauman, Department of Medical Neurosciences, Walter Reed Army Institute of Research, Washington, D.C. 20307-5100, USA; Harold Black, The Johns Hopkins University, Applied Physics Laboratory, Johns Hapkins Road, Laurel, MD 20707, USA.

393

Introduction

Recently, a number of investigators have applied consumer demand theory to analyze the behavior of non-human species working under laboratory conditions (see Hursh, 1980, 1984; Lea, 1978; Rachlin, Green, Kagel, & Battalio, 1976). According to the theory, the consumption of most goods will decrease with increases in price (see Figure 1). Any application of this approach to consumption by laboratory animals requires a definition of price in the absence of a medium of exchange (money). The typical animal experiment involves daily observations of performance, usually pressing a lever or push-button mounted on the wall of the cage, which produces some desirable consequence such as presentation of a pellet of food or a drink of water. The performance is called an "operant response" since it "operates" on the environment and the consequence that maintains the performance is called a "reinforcer" since it "strengthens" the performance. Price has been defined as the number of responses emitted per reinforcer.

In the experiments discussed here, the apparatus arranged that following a set number of responses a food reinforcer was presented, a procedure called a fixed-ratio (FR) schedule because it insures a constant ratio of responses to food presentations. For example, a fixed-ratio 10 (FR 10) schedule arranges for a food reinforcer to be delivered after every tenth response. This has been considered a "price" of 10. Hursh (1980) and Collier, Johnson, Hill, and Kaufman (1986) have suggested that a more fundamental definition of price is probably a cost-benefit ratio that considers both the amount of work performed and the amount and value of the commodity consumed. This ratio is called a "unit price" since it specifies the amount of effort expended per unit of the commodity.

In the first study reported here, the unit price concept was tested. Four factors that each alter unit price were manipulated: responses per reinforcer (FR schedule), force requirement of each lever press response, food pellets per reinforcer, and probability of reinforcement. We define unit price as:

$$(1) \qquad \text{Unit price} = \frac{\text{Responses x Lever weight}}{\text{Pellets x Probability}}$$

Consumption is defined as the total amount of food consumed per day which in this study was:

(2)   Consumption = FRs Completed x Pellets x Probability

The function relating consumption to unit price (Figure 1) is the demand curve and usually is a monotonically decreasing function of unit price. If consumption is a unitary function of the cost-benefit ratio, then variations of unit price by the four factors listed above should generate consumptions that fall along a single demand curve.

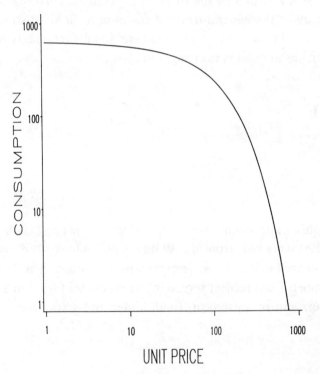

Figure 1: The function relating consumption to unit price.

The function relating response output (expenditure) to unit price is determined by the slope of the demand curve in logarithmic coordinates. The demand curve in Figure 1 is typical of those found for food when a broad range of prices is arranged in a closed laboratory environment (Hursh, 1980, 1984). The slope or elasticity of demand is initially small and increases with price. The response output function producing this demand curve is an inverted U-shaped function with a peak in the vicinity of FR 100. In Experiment I we varied the effort of the response. When effort is a factor in determining the demand curve, the appropriate measure of expenditure is total work (responses x effort) as a function of unit price. If all factors contributing to unit price in this study are equivalent in effect, then work output will be a unitary function of unit price.

Based on the results of the first experiment we assumed that demand elasticity was linear in price and derived a general demand equation. In the second experiment reported below, we varied the availability of substitutable food as a way to alter the shape of the demand curve itself. We tested the ability of the general demand equation to fit six distinct demand curves obtained under a range of conditions and the rationality of the parameter estimates in relation to changes in elasticity.

Experiment I

Method

Subjects

The subjects of this experiment were male albino Sprague-Dawley derived rats, 90-120 days old, from the Walter Reed colony. The rats were individually housed in hanging wire cages which also served as their experimental chamber. Each subject served in the experiment for 7 to 14 days earning their entire ration of food under the experimental procedure.

Apparatus

Behavioral measurements were conducted in six modified hanging wire cages. Each cage was 24.1 cm long, 20.3 cm wide, and 18.4 cm deep. A response lever, water bottle, and food magazine were mounted on the front of each cage. The lever required .265 N to operate in the low effort condition and .530 N to operate in the high effort condition (see Procedure section). Food pellet dispensers were mounted above each cage. These delivered 45 mg food pellets according to the schedule requirements described below. Response sensing, pellet deliveries, and data recording were carried out by a computer located outside the experimental chamber. A 12 hr:12 hr light-dark cycle was maintained in the rooms (lights on at 0600 hrs).

Procedure

Food pellet dispensers delivered food pellets whenever a specified number of responses was made on the associated lever, called a fixed-ratio schedule (FR). The main variables of the experiment were the size of the FR schedule, the number of pellets delivered as a consequence of completing each FR, the probability that at the completion of the FR a reinforcer would occur, and the weight of the lever determining the effort involved in each response of the FR schedule. The food pellets produced by completion of the FR schedules were the only source of food available to the rats during the experiment (a closed economy, Hursh, 1980, 1984).

After a one-week adaptation period, the rats were placed in the experimental cages where they remained until the end of the experiment. The number of responses required to obtain a reinforcer (FR) was changed each day over the seven day period of each experimental condition according to the following sequence of FR values: 1, 1, 15, 45, 90, 180, 360. Data from the first FR 1 in any condition were not used so as to allow for individual differences in bar press acquisition. Eight conditions were studied representing all combinations of the variables: pellets per reinforcer (1 or 2), probability of reinforcement (1.0 or 0.5), and lever force (0.265 N or 0.530 N). Each of the eight groups defined by all combinations of these three variables was studied under the series of FR values listed above. The condition that arranged one pellet per reinforcer with a 1.0 probability using a low response effort of .265 N was considered the control group. For each of the seven other conditions, at least six subjects were studied. For each of these groups, another group of at least six control subjects was studied for comparison. Thus, we collected standard data throughout the course of the experiment to control for all time related changes in the environment (e.g., seasonal variations in temperature or humidity). In all, 108 subjects were studied, including 59 controls, each providing a six-valued demand curve.

Data Analysis

From the perspective of consumer demand theory (Watson & Holman, 1977), the four independent variables of this experiment all contribute to the definition of unit price. If consumption conforms to a single demand function relative to unit price, then all eight demand curves obtained from the eight conditions should coincide. Performance was measured as total work output (Responses per day x Effort per response) and also should conform to a single function when plotted in relation to unit price. The slope of the function will depend on the slope of the demand curve: at low prices, consumption decreases gradually with increases in price and work output increases to defend consumption; at higher prices, consumption decreases rapidly with increases in price and work output decreases (see Hursh, 1978, 1980, 1984).

Results

For each group, median daily food consumption was plotted as a function of unit price, as defined above, on the left panel of Figure 2. These unit price demand curves converged suggesting a single underlying demand function. The greatest variance among groups occurred at the highest prices. The differences appear large in log units but span the range from one to ten pellets a day, which is small in absolute terms.

The response output function was converted to the unit price representation by first calculating total "work output," the product of responses per day times the effort factor (1 or 2). Work output was then plotted as a function of unit price, shown in the right panel of Figure 2. These curves also converged across conditions suggesting a unitary, underlying work output function.

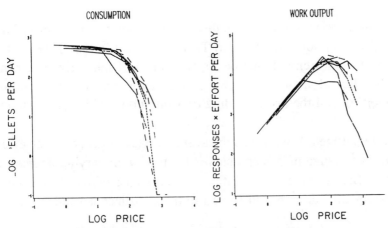

CONSUMPTION   WORK OUTPUT

Figure 2: **Median daily food consumption and work output as a function of unit price.**

Discussion

The results of this series of demand curve determinations confirmed the value of the unit price concept, effort expended per unit of food value earned, as the underlying dimension of price that determines consumption of food in a closed economy (Hursh, 1980). For any given cost-benefit ratio, or unit price, consumption of food was constant. Across increases in the ratio, consumption declined according to a single demand function. Furthermore, the adequacy of this approach was further confirmed in terms of work output, defined as the product of total responses and effort per response, which also converged to a single function when plotted in terms of unit price.

Experiment II

In Experiment I we tested the idea that the basic unit of price was a cost-benefit ratio that included consideration of amount and effort of work required and amount and probability of payoff. The results appeared to conform to a single underlying demand curve when plotted in terms of unit price as defined in Equation 1. The mathematical form of that function was not defined, however.

A general equation that fits the data from Experiment I, accounting for over 96% of the variance, assumes that demand elasticity was a linear increasing function of price. With this starting assumption we derived the "Total Consumption" equations in Table 1. Shown in that table are the equation for elasticity (Equation 3), two forms of the derived demand equation (Equations 4 and 5), the equation for total response output (Equation 6), and the price yielding maximum output, P_{max} (Equation 7).

In Experiment II we varied the availability of substitutes in an effort to examine a range of demand curves for food with varying degrees of elasticity. Based on these observations, we tested the ability of the general demand equation described in Table 1 to fit six distinct demand curves.

Table 1: Total Consumption Equations

Variables:
  Q = Total Consumption (Food Pellets per Day)
  P = Price (Responses per Pellet)
  E = Elasticity

Fitted Parameters
  I: Initial Consumption
  b: Beginning Slope
  a: Acceleration in Slope with Price

Assume **Elasticity (E)** is linear in price:

$$(3) \qquad -E \triangleq \frac{d(\log Q)}{d(\log P)} = b - aP$$

From this we derived the equation for **Total Consumption (Q)**:

$$(4) \qquad Q = [IP^b][e^{-aP}]$$

$$(5) \qquad \log Q = \log I + b(\log P) - aP$$

the equation for **Total Response Output (R)**:

$$(6) \qquad R \triangleq PQ \, [IP^{1+b}][e^{-aP}]$$

and the equation for **Price Yielding Maximum Output (P_{max})**:

$$(7) \qquad P_{max} = \frac{(1+b)}{a}$$

Three monkeys lived in their test apparatus and earned their food by pressing push panels. As in the first experiment, the requirement for each food pellet was a fixed-ratio ("price") ranging from 10 presses per pellet to 372 presses per pellet. Six demand curves were determined across a range of conditions that provided varying amounts of additional food at low cost after the test session – a substitutable supply. We tested the ability of the general equation to describe demand across all six conditions of the experiment with parameters that bore some rational relationship to the observed changes in elasticity.

Method

Subjects

Three rhesus monkeys (**Macaca mulatta**) served in each phase of the experiment. The subjects received no other food than that scheduled by the experimental procedures, except a multivitamin tablet three times a week.

Apparatus

During the experiments, the subjects were housed in cages equiped with four response push panels arranged in two horizontal rows of two. Each panel could be illuminated to indicate appropriate times to work. An automatic food dispenser could deliver precision food pellets (750 mg banana flavored diet) into a hopper located to the left of the push panels. Above the food hopper was a water delivery tube that could deliver 1 ml squirts of water.

Procedure

The upper two panels were used to provide water and their function was not part of this experiment. The lower two push panels provided food pellets. When the left panel was illuminated, a single press illuminated the right panel; a fixed number of responses on the right panel delivered a single food pellet into the hopper and extinguished the lower right panel. Another press on the left panel would again illuminate the right panel for execution of another fixed number of responses. This fixed-ratio (FR) of responses was the "price" paid for the food and ranged in value from 10 to 372 responses per pellet.

A demand curve was determined by first observing the baseline level of responding with the FR set at 10 responses and then increasing the FR each day by 20 % up to the maximum price of 372 in 21 steps. In the first phase of the experiment, the subject had 12 hours to work from 0600 hrs to 1800 hrs. After the work period, free pellets could be delivered to the subjects in addition to those earned in the work session, as described below. In the second phase of the experiment, the subjects had four one-hour work periods distributed between 0600 and 1800 hours. After each one-hour work period, food could be delivered in addition to that earned in the session.

Phase 1

As a way to alter the elasticity of demand and explore the nature of the demand relationship, we determined demand for food under three conditions of extra food. The baseline condition provided the subject only a single free pellet at 1800 hrs. In the one-third free condition, the subjects automatically received at 1800 hrs one-third of the amount of food previously earned at FR 10, the lowest price. In the two-thirds free condition the subjects automatically received two-thirds of the baseline amount of food at 1800 hrs. Under each condition of free food we observed the level of consumption under the same series of 21 prices from FR 10 to FR 372.

Phase 2

In this phase, the subjects worked for food in four one-hour periods each day. In the baseline condition, no free food was available. In the 20 min free condition, the subjects were given 20 min after the last work period at 1800 hrs to earn as much food as desired at a price of one response per pellet (FR1). In the 5 min free condition, the subjects were given 5 min after each of the four work periods to earn food under FR 1. This last condition with four "free meals" was designed to maximize substitution

402

of the low price food for high price food by reducing the maximum time between work and free food from 12 hours to 1 hour. This should greatly increase the elasticity of demand for food earned during the work periods.

Results

Phase 1

Figure 3 summarizes the results of Phase 1 with varying amounts of free food delivered at the end of the 12 hour work day. Each point is the median consumption or response output by the three monkeys at that price.

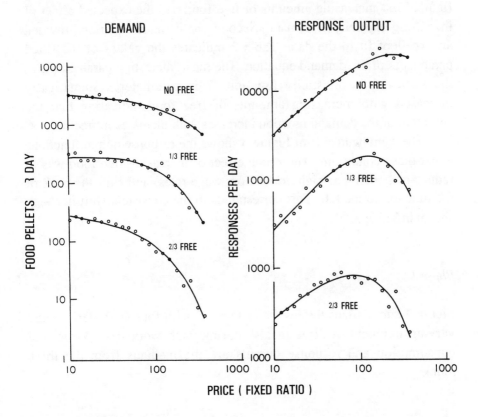

Figure 3: Demand and response output functions in Experiment II, Phase 1.

403

Table 2: Fitted Parameters of the Demand Equation, Experiment II, Phase 1

Condition	Parameters			P_{max}
	I	*b*	$a(10^{-3})$	
No free	407	−0.079	3.71	248
1/3 free	207	+0.167	9.14	128
2/3 free	412	−0.132	10.16	85

The lines through the points are the best fits provided by Equations 5 and 6 using the parameters shown in Table 2. The left three panels show demand curves for food as a function of increasing price with no free, 1/3 baseline free, and 2/3 baseline free. Two points are clear from this figure. First increasing amounts of free food had the expected effect of increasing elasticity of demand. Second, the demand equation provided an excellent fit to the data. Table 2 indicates the values of the fitted parameters of the demand equation. The most interesting parameter is *a*, the slope of the elasticity function. This parameter systematically increased with increasing amounts of free food indicating that the curvature of the demand function increases with increases in free rations.

The right hand side of Figure 3 shows the response output functions under these conditions. The prime effect of increasing free food was to reduce responding at high prices (low wage rates) and shift the peak of the function to the left. This corresponds to the consistent shift in P_{max} shown in Table 2.

Phase 2

Figure 4 summarizes the results of Phase 2 with four work periods and varying numbers of "free meals" during each work day. Again, the consumption and response outputs are the medians from the three monkeys.

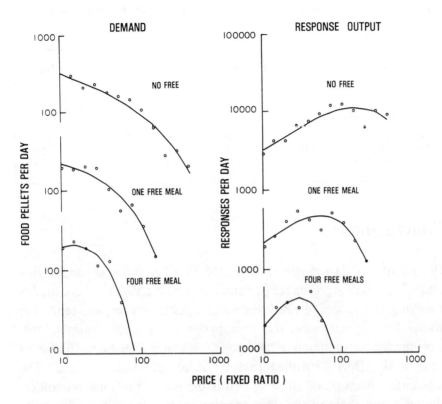

Figure 4: Demand and response output functions in Experiment II, Phase 2.

The fitted lines in Figure 4 are the best fits of Equations 4 and 5 using the parameters shown in Table 3. The left side of the figure shows that increasing numbers of free meals dramatically increased elasticity of demand and the right side of the figure indicates that response output was greatly reduced by the provision of four "free meals" compared to no free food. As in the previous phase, the demand equation and the equation for response output both provided excellent fits to the data.

Table 3 indicates the parameter estimates for this phase. Again, the most interesting effect was a consistent increase in the slope of the elasticity function, *a*. With no free meals the slope was equal to that found in Phase 1. Increasing free food increased parameter *a* twenty fold, indicating that moving the free food closer in time to work periods further increased the curvature of the demand curve.

405

Table 3:   Fitted Parameters of the Demand Equation, Experiment II, Phase 2

Conditions	Parameters			P_{max}
	I	b	$a(10^{-3})$	
No free meals	794	−0.363	3.84	166
One free meal	355	−0.133	15.84	55
Four free meals	48	+0.935	68.15	28

Conclusions

The results of Experiment I indicated that for food, an underlying demand function accounts for performance across a variety of constraints involving differences in FR, lever weight, pellet number, and reinforcer probability. Specifically, the appropriate independent variable that accounts for consumption is "unit price," which is a cost-benefit ratio of total work effort expended to total reinforcer value gained. The appropriate measure of consumption is the product of total reinforcers obtained and their value. The appropriate measure of performance expenditure is total work output, the product of total responses and their effort, which conforms to a single inverted U-shaped function of unit price.

The results of Experiment II indicated that for food, varying amounts of free food can dramatically alter the elasticity of demand and the amount of work output. The proposed demand equation assumed that elasticity was a linear function of price and provided a precise fit to the observed effects. The fitted parameters of the equation, especially the estimate of the slope of the elasticity equation, varied in a rational way with the increases in free food and elastitcity.

These data from non-human subjects have limitations for predicting human economic behaviour. However, these data provide clear evidence that the basic principles of consumer demand theory can be observed in a primitive system. This suggests that the theory is "biological" in the sense that it does not depend on the "cultural" mechanisms of either verbal behavior or money.

References

Collier, G.H., Johnson, D.F., Hill, W.L., & Kaufman, L.W. (1986). The economics of the law of effect. *Journal of the Experimental Analysis of Behavior, 46*, 113-136.

Hursh, S.R. (1978). The economics of daily consumption controlling food- and water-reinforced responding. *Journal of the Experimental Analysis of Behavior, 29*, 475-491.

Hursh, S.R. (1980). Economic concepts for the analysis of behavior. *Journal of the Experimental Analysis of Behavior, 34*, 219-238.

Hursh, S.R. (1984). Behavioral economics. *Journal of the Experimental Analysis of Behavior, 42*, 435-452.

Lea, S.E.G. (1978). The psychology and economics of demand. *Psychological Bulletin, 85*, 441-466.

Rachlin, H., Green, L., Kagel, J., & Battalio, R.C. (1976). Economic demand theory and psychological studies of choice. In G.H. Bower (Ed.), *The Psychology of Learning and Motivation,* Vol. 10, pp. 129-154. New York: Academic Press.

Watson, D.S., & Holman, M.A. (1977). *Price theory and its uses* (4th ed.). Boston: Houghton Mifflin.

Ulrich Witt

Subjectivism in Economics –
A Suggested Reorientation

Abstract

The subjective nature of individual intentions, evaluations, and expectations is a major problem in the attempt to explain observable economic behaviour. "Austrian" and other subjectivist economists have always emphasized its importance in contrast to neoclassical economics where it is played down by means of perfect information assumptions. Important as the problem is, it does not necessitate an aprioristic approach as is argued by proponents of the "Austro-American" school. In fact, as this paper points out, such an approach, if it were to be consistent, would render economics a sterile logic ("praxeology") incapable of explaining any empirically observed economic behaviour.

As a way of coping with the subjectivism problem, a revival of the idea of a psychological foundation for the theory of economic behaviour is therefore suggested. (This idea can already be found in the work of early "Austrian" writers though not as a consistent programmatic vision.) A brief outline is given of how results from psychological research can be utilized in explaining individual economic behaviour without interfering with the subjectivism problem. Some bounds are reached, however, where (objective) novelty is created in the subjective intentions, evaluations, and expectations of the agents. But even here further insights can be gained by adopting the perspective of an evolutionary theory.

The author is grateful to many with whom he was able to discuss earlier drafts of this paper, in particular H. Albert, S. Boehm, B. Caldwell, M. Faber, E. Heuss, J. Irving-Lessmann, I.M. Kirzner, L.M. Lachmann, I. Pellengahr, and D. Schmidtchen. He owes thanks also to the participants of seminars at the Universities of Nuremberg and Heidelberg, the Austrian Colloquium at New York University, the Seminar at the Center for the Study of Market Processes, George Mason University, Fairfax, VA, and the History of Economics Society Congress in Boston 1987, where earlier versions were presented. The usual disclaimer applies.

Author's address: Ulrich Witt, Faculty of Economics, University of Freiburg, Europaplatz 1, D-7800 Freiburg, F.R.G.

Introduction

For a long time, there has existed a minority view in economics that blends methodological individualism with a strong subjectivist interpretation. A prominent example is the so called "Austrian" tradition which can be traced back even to Menger (1871). Another eminent group has emerged in Britain drawing on seminal work by Shackle (1958, 1972).[1] The basic tenet of the subjectivist interpretation can roughly be stated as follows. The key for understanding individual economic behaviour or "action," it is submitted, can be found in the intentions and expectations of the individual agents. These reflect the **subjective** assessment of the prevailing conditions which, of course, is characterized by uncertainty and fallibility. Theories on individual economic behaviour have to take the subjectivity of these views into consideration. The question of how much information on these subjective entities can be obtained by the scientific observer and how reliable a theory of economic behaviour and economic interactions built on such information would be, is highly controversial. This is the very core of the subjectivism problem.

In its emphasis of this problem the subjectivist tradition clearly differs from the individualistic position taken in prevailing neoclassical economics. There the subjective imponderabilities (potentially disturbing any observable behavioural regularity) are simply assumed away: Perfect information or, more recently, rational expectation models hypothesize a one-to-one relationship between "objective" conditions and the individual agents' perception of these. The aim of these assumptions is obvious. If valid, they would allow the scientific (outside) observer, who perceives an agent's situation, to make definite conclusions on the basis of his perception, if not about the agent's intentions and evaluations (preferences), then at least about her/his perceiving the situation. Indeed, this seems to be the prerequisite for the allegedly telling neoclassical model of the optimizing individual choosing the most preferred element from an "objectifiable" set of opportunities.

The only exception – within the neoclassical approach – that admits subjective factors is models of behaviour under uncertainty which incorporate subjective probabilities. The "seed" of objective knowledge, which these models presuppose by the assumption of **correct prior** information, ensures however that subjective influences are quickly neutralized in the process of Bayesian learning. A unique optimum (as it is presupposed to be known by the theorist) is eventually arrived at. Such a construction invites two serious criticisms. First, the very idea is derived from a normative approach that led to Bayesian learning being regarded as optimal behaviour. Its relevance for **actually observed** learning and decision behaviour is therefore highly doubtful (cf., e.g., Slovic, Fischhoff, & Lichtenstein, 1977). Second, if the assumption of correct prior knowledge is abandoned the whole manoeuvre breaks down as Hey (1981) has nicely shown.

Although it is generally agreed upon that the over-simplified, fallacious one-to-one correspondence between the individuals' subjective views and the outside scientific observer's ideas about them is inadequate, the subjectivists' camp is far from reaching agreement when it debates the precise implications of subjectivism with respect to explaining individual economic behaviour. Unfortunately, the attempt to find a clear answer to this question has been hampered by a methodological controversy. It resulted from the radical subjectivist position taken by Mises. He argued (1949, pp. 11-71) that economic behaviour is exclusively made up of conscious, purposive action which by necessity must be "rational," in the sense of adopting the most appropriate means for chosen ends. By **defining** all other kinds of human behaviour as being outside the scope of economics (to be left to psychology), Mises arrived at the conclusion that economics must be a matter of pure logic, of associating means and ends. Hence, the statements in economics or "praxeology," must be as apriorily true as those of logic or mathematics.

For reasons given in the next section this paper rejects Mises' aprioristic position and his unnecessarily narrow definition of economics, both of which are still influential among "Austro-American" writers (Caldwell, 1982, p. 118) who followed Mises, such as, e.g., Kirzner (1976a) and Rothbard (1976). An alternative approach is suggested in the remainder of the paper which favours an empirical theory of economic behaviour including all decision making, conscious as well as unreflected, consistent as well as inconsistent, as long as it is characterized by regularity (cf., Albert, 1985). At the same time an attempt is made to move the "bounds of unknowledge" (Shackle, 1983) with respect to the subjective sphere by erecting psychologically founded hypotheses about subjective perceptions and intentions. Such an approach, it is claimed in the third section, can be seen as a return to common psychologizing practices in the older, **pre**-Austro-American literature.

The fourth section considers the basic subjectivistic objection that might be raised against such an approach: the contention that, due to omnipresent unpredictable changes in individual expectations, there can be no stable empirical regularities in economic behaviour. As will be shown for a wide range of economic behaviour, this assertion is not justified. However, as discussed in the fifth section, bounds still exist and the suggested approach may help in determining where and why in the theory of individual economic behaviour the subjectivist concern sets a limit to positive analysis. Finally, the last section offers some tentative conclusions.

The Limitations of Apriorism

The radical, praxeological approach suggested by Mises in order to cope with the subjectivism problem has caused ongoing methodological confusion. However, as long as Mises' definition of economics as "praxeology" is accepted, the analysis of economic "action" – the association of means and ends – can indeed pass as a matter of pure logic. Given a complete specification of the intentions and values of an agent and the means available to her/him, it may well be possible to reconstruct "through pure ratiocination" (Mises, 1949, p. 39) the action that is to be chosen **for the agent to qualify as rational** in the sense of Mises. No resort to empirical evidence would be required in this respect. But, of course, this is not to say whether or not some particular agent in fact **is** rational (and, hence, her/his behaviour is an object of Misesian economics). The latter question cannot be answered without reference to experience, which is to say that it cannot be true a priori. Similarly, intentions, values, and perceived means-ends-relations cannot be taken as given for some particular agent or group of agents. How does an apriorist arrive at the necessary specification of these subjective entities? Mises apparently had in mind that the specific hypotheses on individual intentions, values, and means-ends-perceptions could come from introspection (Mises, 1957, Ch. 14). Such a route may certainly be fruitful (heuristically). But again, whether or not the results which the observer gets from hypothetical self-exploration, placing himself

412

fictitiously in the role of some individual, have any relevance for understanding that individual's economic behaviour is something that has to be determined by experience. Hence, introspection cannot lead to truth a priori as clearly spelled out by Mises himself (1957, p. 311). Adopting the method of introspection thus implicitly adds at least one empirical hypothesis: that of a reliable parallel between the understanding an observer attains by introspection and the understanding underlying the observed individual's action (cf., also the short review of these problems in Boehm, 1982).

Thus, unfortunately, praxeology does not contribute any insight into empirically observable economic behaviour unless the respective empirical hypotheses are somehow added, in which case the purely aprioristic character would, of course, be lost. This meagre result is clearly at odds with the rather ambitious goals which many "Austrian" economists try to pursue. Indeed, many essential points in the "Austrian" research programme cannot satisfactorily be dealt with without recourse to empirical hypotheses on individual preferences, perceptions, and decision making such as those just mentioned. The following examples may serve as a motivation for the reorientation suggested in the present paper.

Firstly, "Austrian" economics emphasizes the time dimension of economic activities, a point often referred to as a decisive difference to static approaches taken in neoclassical theory (Kirzner, 1976b; O'Driscoll & Rizzo, 1984; see also Faber, 1986). What makes the time aspect non-trivial in the context of the theory of individual behaviour is the fact that people need time to process the information they receive under specific institutional conditions. The way in which an aprioristic approach can deal with this issue is rather vague, however (see Mises, 1949, Ch. 10), since it provides no insight into **how** time is actually used, what the time patterns of individual behaviour changes look like, and what might induce them. Hypotheses which cover these questions are required, in particular, in the context of market process theory to obtain more than the mere statement that time is needed for the agents to coordinate their economic activities, perhaps unintentionally. Richer, more detailed hypotheses on the actual dynamics of the market process are not feasible without the introduction of a theory of individual information processing, learning, and information diffusion (see, e.g., Witt, 1986; Witt & Perske, 1982, for exploratory studies).

Secondly and relatedly, even the statement that economic agents are more or less alert so that new opportunities will at some time or other be detected, exploited, and thereby arbitraged away – the central tenet in Kirzner's influential theory of the market process (Kirzner, 1973, 1979) – is **not** an a priorily true statement. It is a truism (one of the really well-confirmed empirical hypotheses) and it is difficult to see why theory should be restricted to this. A more profound theoretical basis could indicate which factors possibly affect the incentive to be alert, to search for new opportunities, or the time it takes for competition to erode the "alertness"-rent.

It is a curious fact that although alertness and entrepreneurship are key notions in Mises' and Kirzner's contributions, no attempt is made by them to form a theory that could tell what makes one individual alert and enterprising and another not so, i.e., what, in this respect, constitutes the differences between individuals. Such a theory, elaborating on what makes people more or less intensively and persistently look for something they do not yet know, would be highly desirable in Austrian economics. For a situation in which (opportunity) costs are borne without knowing the future benefits is obviously at odds with the neoclassical optimization approach to economic behaviour. The latter requires a knowledge of those alternatives that are to be evaluated. Thus, Austrian economists would here have a good opportunity to demonstrate that they have the more powerful hypotheses on economic behaviour.

A key could be found in a theory of dynamic aspiration levels and, reinterpretable in terms of that theory, in achievement motivation theory. This is a notion well-known from an approach, somewhat misleadingly called behavioural, which has been introduced to economics by Simon and others. As shown elsewhere (Witt, forthcoming, Ch. 4) a complex network of personality factors on the one hand and interactions between internal and external processes on the other hand can be identified on this basis as influencing the individual search for new, unknown alternatives. Hence, "alertness," in this view, is a label under which such diverse personality factors as creativity, daring, persistence, competence, etc., coexist with complicated adaptation processes and factors shaped by individual life experience. Debatable as these conjectures may be, they at least indicate that alertness as well as its manifestation in economic processes are issues on which more detailed, empirical hypotheses can be formulated.

Thirdly, if an attempt would be made to reinterpret Mises' praxeological approach on the basis of a methodology of understanding (Verstehen) in the sense of Max Weber, as Lachmann (1951, 1966) seems to propose (against Mises' own reservations, see the lucid discussion in Vanberg, 1975, Ch. 4) this would amount to abandoning apriorism, as Weber's methodology does not claim truth independent of experience. Unfortunately, however, such a reinterpretation would not yield a very convincing theory of individual economic behaviour. The reason is Mises' narrow conception of economics (as well as that of Lachmann, 1977b) which excludes any spontaneous, unreflected, and not logically consistent behaviour from the domain of economics. Modern research on human thinking, information processing, and decision behaviour indicates that in this case only few of the everyday economic activities would remain in the domain of economics. Many of these activities are based on modes of thinking and acting which deviate significantly from what appears to be the standards of logic and consistency. The latter are the product of some two or three thousand years of selective cultural training and investment in human rationality. Spontaneous, usually less consistent, ways of thinking, which prevail unless they are consciously and skilfully suppressed, have evolved through millions of years of natural selection. Their adaptive value should therefore not be underestimated. In order to be able to apply the methodology of understanding to economic activities, the rules which obviously govern the actual mental processes underlying them would have to be recognized.

Here is not the place to review the relevant theoretical and empirical results. Much research has been done on this topic and many of the key features are quite well understood.[2] In many respects this research has confirmed the critical position which Simon (1955, 1967) has taken with his theory of bounded rationality (see March, 1978, for a survey). Integrating the results from this research might be a way to make progress towards solving the problem about which "Austrian" economics has been so much concerned: that of how people acquire and use knowledge and, on this basis, carry on the economic process (for the classical statement, see Hayek, 1937).

Fourthly, and with regard to the subjectivism problem perhaps most importantly, a discussion of the basic psychic processes, restraints, and personality factors provides an opportunity to develop the notion of subjective value beyond the mere statement of its subjectivity. As is well-known, this notion played the crucial role in the "subjectivist revolution" a century ago in which the Austrian school was established (Streissler, 1972). Since those times, however, hardly any headway has been made. This markedly contrasts with the progress in biological research and behavioural and cognitive psychology where an impressive body of insights into human needs, desires, valuations, or – if one prefers – individual preferences have been gained during that time: how they come about; in which way they change; how preferences can be measured; how subjective cognition of means-ends-relations affects revealed preferences; and which role is played by "framing" effects, to mention just a few of the results. Again, this cannot be elaborated upon here in detail (cf. Witt, forthcoming, Ch. 3, on this). But it is easy to recognize that subjectivist economics would be ready to adopt many of those results, presumably more adequately so than neoclassical economics with its fixation on essentially static utility maximization. The prerequisite would be, of course, to abandon the self-imposed restriction to narrow, sterile apriorism.

Reviving the Idea of Psychological Foundation

In order to obtain a powerful, empirical theory of individual economic behaviour and economic processes, a foundation built upon the results of empirical research in neighbouring disciplines is thus advocated here. Although in clear contrast to the stated disinterest (Kirzner, 1979; Lachmann, 1977b; Mises, 1957, Ch. 12) in such an extension of the "Austro-American" line, the idea is by no means alien to the "Austrian" tradition.

For instance, at a time when psychology was still in its infancy, Menger (1871, p. 94) called his exposition of the concept of marginal utility a "demonstration of a domain of psychology that is as difficult as thus far untreated" (my translation, U.W.). His reflections on the relationships between needs and wants originating in human drives (1871, pp. 32-45) are in a similar vein. As Kauder (1965) has carefully shown, Menger took no great interest in marginalism (although he acknowledged the effect of a variation of the quantity of a good on individual satisfaction). The expression "utility" (Nutzen) is never used in

Menger (1871) – no thought of adopting flat utilitarism à la Bentham. Instead he chooses the more complex notion of "**perceived** usefulness" (**erkannte** Nützlichkeit, p. 84, emphasis by Menger) of something, a notion that clearly addresses the cognitive problem involved here. A similar psychologically oriented realism is expressed in Menger's awareness of uncertainty, expectations, subjective foresight, and fallibility of knowledge, see, e.g., Menger (1871), pp. 21-26. In fact, Menger's disciples characterized his contribution as "founder of the Austrian school of economics, discoverer of the psycho-economic law of marginal utility" (Hayek, 1934, Footnote 37).

Admittedly, however, these psychologically inspired, empirically oriented notions are in some places confused with the entirely different idea of "exact" economic laws for which, apparently, a priori truth is claimed. It seems that Mises, arguably seeing himself as the legitimate successor of the founding triumvir, Menger, Böhm-Bawerk, and Wieser (Craver, 1986), has carried further only this latter idea ignoring all empirically oriented intentions. Hayek, in contrast, has obviously preferred to take the opposite position. This can be seen not only from his own attempt to contribute to the psychological foundation with his extensive discussion of the relationships between the physical and mental spheres in Hayek (1952), but also from his sophisticated pleading for a methodology in economics and the social sciences in general which is based on experience and fallibility, see Hayek (1967a). The present paper likewise favours a revival of the psychological orientation. Some qualifications must, however, be added in order to avoid misconceptions with respect to this proposal.

Firstly, psychology is no longer in its infancy. Faced with a large, ever growing body of research results it would be naive to try to invent what an economist might deem an appropriate psychological foundation. Communication between the two disciplines is necessary, but, unfortunately, present psychological theories are diverse and specialized. The human individual's performance is investigated under a mass of particular aspects without much concern for coherence. Economics, in contrast, is interested in a comprehensive view of the individual, since it is on this unit that economists want to base their inquiry into the realm of interaction and coordination. Thus, constructing the suggested foundation requires a considerable effort at defining the theoretical demands and the appropriate level of abstraction. Sufficiently simplified questions will have to be formulated so that the otherwise amorphous material can be organized and the economist's demands be met. It would not come as a surprise, if these efforts also make a demand for adaptations in psychological theory. At present, the communication between the two disciplines of economics and psychology seems far from even approximating what is necessary.

Secondly, it is not alleged that the well-known concerns within the subjectivists' camp with respect to the existence of stable empirical regularities in individual economic behaviour could be eliminated altogether by merely imposing "behaviourism" or an "information processing view." In view of the subjectivism problem the persistence of such regularities and, correspondingly, predictability cannot be taken for granted. In the next section it will be argued, however, that the range where this indeed prevents fruitful theorizing, i.e., the "bounds of unknowledge," can be somewhat extended on the basis of the insights generated by the suggested foundation.

Where Regularities in Economic Behaviour Can Be Expected

In order to bring out the point consider two different cases: one in which individual economic behaviour is the result of contemplation or cognitive control, and another where it is not. For brevity, the two cases will be referred to as higher and lower level behaviour. It may be claimed then that, at the lower level, behavioural regularities can be expected to be quite stable and predictable. They follow from response patterns which are inherited or acquired through extended conditioning. (For economic behaviour in general, the same idea has been suggested by Heiner, 1983.) As mentioned, Mises (1949) simply excluded it by definition from the realm of "human action." However, as shown elsewhere (Witt, forthcoming, Ch. 3), this kind of behaviour appears to be of considerable significance for observable economic activities. Buchanan (1982, p. 15), who introduces a similar distinction, chooses to label this level the domain "where men are indeed like rats." This is somewhat misleading, because what must be acknowledged here is not so much a direct manifestation of uncontemplated stimulus-response-patterns (the standard topic of experiments with pigeons, rats, and other animals in behaviourism) within the economic domain. Rather, it is a more indirect, long-term process, launched by the inherited human capacity to adapt via conditioning-learning, which shapes what is believed in economic theory to underlie contemplated economic behaviour: individual preferences, habits, and aspiration levels. Thus, at least on this basic level, hypotheses about systematic properties of behaviour can be fruitfully developed and used for explaining certain aspects of, e.g., learning and adapting to the market process or personal dispositions fostering "alertness."

But this is of course not the whole story. As far as the higher level of behaviour is concerned, it must be admitted that even if, some day, it were possible to explain **how** man processes information and how thinking and decision making are "produced" on the basis of the physiological equipment of the human brain, the problem of **what** information an individual processes this way with regard to, say, economic decisions will remain open. And, unfortunately, explanations of economic decisions or, more generally, the cognitively controlled and contemplated parts of behaviour (in which economics is mainly interested) do crucially depend on what information is activated in the various phases of thinking. This information may be collected over a lifetime and may be selectively associated when required. This may happen in a way specific to the current (historical) context and the subjective state of mind. The complexity of this process of combining information may in non-routine situations be very high and a heuristical use of the methodology of understanding may then be a good device to cope with the problem.

The true challenge occurs, however, when, in the individual cognitive process **new** insights, opinions, or expectations on means-ends-relations emerge. The very definition of novelty suggests that the decision which an individual will take can neither be inferred from a previously observed stimulus-response relation nor from information on the supposed state of her/his mind. Under these, the radical subjectivistic tenet that changes in human preferences, intentions, and expectations, and thus future economic decisions, are unpredictable – clearly expressed by Lachmann (1976b), and accentuated even more by Shackle (1958, 1972) – is confirmed rather than opposed in the approach taken here. Consequently, what deserves particular scrutiny when an attempt is made to narrow down the bounds of the unpredictable with respect to cognitively controlled behaviour is the question of novelty.

In the individualistic perspective, novelty can be defined as the occurrence of a previously unexperienced idea that leads to an action which, at least in the given context, has not been chosen before. Using this definition an important distinction can be made (see Figure 1). On the one hand, there are genuine novelties which have not previously been experienced by anybody **including the scientific observer**. On the other hand, something may be a novelty in the sense defined above for some particular individual whereas it is already well-known to others, e.g., a researcher observing the diffusion of an innovation in a certain region or population. For convenience let the two kinds be called objective and subjective novelties, respectively.

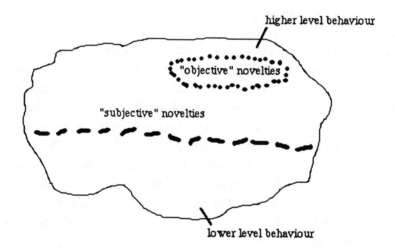

Figure 1: Expository scheme of levels of economic behaviour.

Concerning the **subjective** economic novelties or innovations, the prospects for explaining the associated (cognitively controlled and contemplated) individual behaviour are not bad. In fact, it is known from social psychology, social learning theory (Bandura, 1977), and diffusion research (Rogers, 1983) that much of intentional, considered behaviour is moulded by the information offered by an individual's environment. Moreover, the way in which novelties are communicated and individually conceived is often systematically shaped by the particularities of the social exchange system into which the individual is integrated. Furthermore, there is often a social "model" of behaviour or even of a particular action to be taken, which makes purposeful behaviour predictable because the means and ends offered by the "model" are in fact assumed by the individual.

This kind of research indicates that many differences in individual opinions, purposes, and expectations can be attributed to group-specific (subcultural) interaction and self-reinforcement. Differing among groups, subjective information tends to conform within groups. For example, the same incoming information may be interpreted and evaluated differently from one firm to another, but possibly not so within a given firm. Similarly, with respect to identical new information there may be significant variance, e.g., in interpretation and evaluation among speculating agents on the one hand and administrating agents on the other. Within the respective groups, however, individual differences may be comparatively small. This may, as envisaged by Vaughn (1982), be due to deliberately created rules which govern behaviour, but it may also be the result of similar patterns of spontaneous cognitive reaction. Such patterns can come about by socialization effects and by the striving for conformity with group standards.

Likewise, one and the same offer may be taken up in similar fashion by consumers of similar status, age, education, or local residence but very differently by consumers who vary in these respects. Again, this is not the place to discuss the details. However, there is reason to believe that as far as subjective novelties are concerned, quite reliable hypotheses about subjective information and its impact on an individual's behaviour can be developed by investigating the relevant institutional settings along these lines. In fact, this is what has already begun in disciplines like marketing and organizational research with considerable practical success. Even though it is not usually possible to predict the particular reaction a given person will display with respect to an innovation which is invading her/his environment, the range of likely reactions can be specified quite narrowly. Such a result can be stated in terms of pattern predictions and explanations (cf. Hayek, 1967a).

As seen from a subjectivist's perspective, hypotheses like these are of course conditional ones, conditional on the assumption that one has not left the domain of subjective novelty, i.e., that no genuine novelty emerges in the individual cognitive processes. Unfortunately, this is a possibility that can never be excluded. An agent may come to associate subjective information in such a way that a new idea is created which induces him to deviate from "models," rules, group standards, or norms.

So, even if the distinction introduced above has been successful in shifting the bounds of unknowledge, these bounds are inevitably reached when turning to the domain of **objective** novelty. All the same, the suggested foundation can be fruitful even here, at the heart of subjectivism, as the next section will show.

The Definite Bounds: Reflecting on the Yet Unknown

The information content of objective novelties is unknown by definition. Hence, it cannot be positively anticipated. This is not only a basic tenet of Austrian economics. It is also an elementary fact that any evolutionary theory has to tackle, if it is defined as a dynamic theory that explains the performance of some system in irreversible time including, most importantly, the emergence and dissemination of novelties or "innovations" (for the basic notions and criteria of an evolutionary theory and a survey on relevant contributions in economics, see Witt, forthcoming, Chs. 1 and 2). In view of the crucial role which novelties play in modern economies and the irreversible, historical nature of many economic processes, there can hardly be any doubt that an evolutionary theory would be appropriate for economics. Thus, in affinity with the "Austrian" approach (but in contrast to the neoclassical one which has been inspired by the determinism of classical mechanics) the perspective of an evolutionary theory may be suggested for dealing with the problem of objective novelty and its conceptional implications. As the following considerations show, such a perspective can effectively be backed up by the empirical theory of economic behaviour that has been advocated above.

There is, **firstly**, the obvious fact that novelties result from human intelligence and creativity or, more precisely, from the capacity for associative thinking. Unfortunately, associative thinking is not only a comparatively little developed, and difficult, research topic. More importantly, on grounds of principle, it cannot be expected to yield results which would allow the anticipation of objectively novel ideas. This is how the previous section ended. But, equipped with the insight that this is a basic premise in evolutionary theories, we can now try to proceed the way evolutionary theories usually do.

A result that is helpful here is that of Hayek (1967a). That is, a meaningful, empirically testable theory of objective novelties is deemed possible, if, instead of predicting what will occur, the hypotheses state what will **not** occur, i.e., what, according to the theory, must be ruled out. In the present context we know that the way in which people deal with objective novelties, once they have noticed them, must be in accordance with regular patterns of information processing. Quite reliable hypotheses are available on how people experiment with, get used to, and digest novelties. Thus, at least all time patterns of realizing and adopting new alternatives which do not conform to those hypotheses can be ruled out on the basis of Hayek's device. One of the most trivial implications is that perceptional and cognitive bottle-necks prevent all the consequences of innovations from being immediately grasped. Due to a kind of familiarity fallacy this is often overlooked if an objective novelty appears to be the long sought solution to a well-defined problem.

Secondly, as mentioned in the criticism of apriorism, it is hardly possible to explain the **motivation** for searching for yet unknown alternative actions without elaborating a more detailed, richer model of behaviour. Despite the fact that, by definition, the properties of an objective novelty cannot fully be prespecified, the neoclassical theory of "innovations," as presented in models of R&D-races (see, e.g., Kamien & Schwartz, 1982; Reinganum, 1984), assumes that outcomes are known in advance. The notion of optimization demands some form of correct knowledge, a fact which simply makes it inapplicable in the present context. As has been indicated above, a good alternative to start out from, is a satisficing model (March & Simon, 1958, pp. 47-52).

Its basic hypotheses can roughly be put as follows: (a) as long as the outcome of the best **known** alternative action does not satisfy the current individual level of aspiration, a search goes on for as yet neither known nor experienced, better alternatives including the testing of their consequences (note that the hypothesis allows the inclusion of a source of motivation which is well-known from everyday experience but has no place in neoclassical economics: the motivation to act as a result of dissatisfaction, frustration, or anger); (b) the greater the discrepancy the more intensive the search effort; (c) a favourable search outcome tends to increase the aspiration level – and, hence, does not necessarily eliminate the motivation to search for further improvements – whereas a persistently unfavourable outcome tends to decrease aspiration level and search motivation. (For a discussion of the rather complex internal dynamics of the aspiration level formation and adaptation, see Witt, forthcoming, Ch. 3).

An important implication of these hypotheses is that an individual's search for new alternatives appears to be influenced by the environment: The environment's reaction to the individual's attempt at replacing a customary action by a not previously experienced one determines whether or not the innovative action turns out to have satisfactory results or not. (Besides this there may also be direct effects on the development of one's aspiration level by such environmental factors as "models," preaching, indoctrination, etc.). Thus, even though it cannot be anticipated what the individual might come up with in case of objective novelty, at least the model hints at the possibility that the environment reacts favourably or unfavourably simply because a certain individual behaviour is new, whatever its precise implications might be.

In order to understand such a reaction pattern consider the situation of an individual potentially affected by another agent's attempt to introduce a previously unexperienced activity. Since the full implications of the innovation cannot be anticipated, the individual has to be aware of potentially harmful effects on her/his own future plans and performance. The individual may therefore try to restrain the other agent from pursuing the innovative action, e.g., by moral proscriptions, threat or aggressive behaviour aimed at deteriorating the result the innovative agent will obtain from his innovation. If the number of people who react this way is large enough, this might indeed bring about a discouraging environmental effect on individual innovativeness. A lonely admonisher would, however, have little effect.

If the latter situation prevails, a better strategy for the affected individual may be to put up with innovativeness. In stationary economies lacking the threat of ongoing innovativeness, most of the potential troubles are well-known from hearsay or own experience. The accumulation of inventories, tools, land, and other material assets from the revenue can serve as a provision against more or less clearly anticipatable risk – a self-insurance phenomenon – or, in the terminology of Mises (1949, Ch. 6), a problem of class probability. In the non-stationary, innovative environment, in contrast, the consequences of yet unknown innovations created by others may be most threatening. Accumulation of wealth still provides some security. Since, however, it can never be excluded that future innovations will depreciate that very form of wealth which has been chosen, this kind of self-insurance is less effective. Using revenues for investment in active search for one's own innovative (re)action becomes an attractive substitute which may work even when the other form of self-insurance breaks down.

Furthermore, the highly uncertain future may call for adopting a more flexible way of decision making. A reasonable provision in the latter respect is, for instance, a rolling decision procedure, the decisions at each stage left open to take account of the novelties yet to be revealed. (As Shackle, 1972, pp. 77-79, has pointed out, a cursory outside observer of a sequence of actions chosen by an individual under this procedure might find it hard to identify any consistency of action.) If more and more agents turn to this strategy the uncertainty is, of course, increased for all – a self-reinforcing tendency towards innovativeness and flexibility.

Thus, in considering the environmental effects one is not only led to acknowledge the possibility of a stereotypic reaction fostering or suppressing individual innovativeness as such, but also the apparent frequency-dependency of alternative modes of reacting (a phenomenon that can again be dealt with independently of the unknown information content of the respective novelties). In fact, from ethnological and historical research it is known that societies can persist in phases of economic stagnation over hundreds of years lacking almost any innovative activities and then turn to a phase of intensive innovativeness, rapid development, and economic expansion (and vice versa). The existence of such alternative states with respect to individual interaction and the transition between them is a phenomenon repeatedly addressed by Hayek (e.g., 1967b) as the problem of a spontaneously emerging order, in the present context an order encouraging or discouraging innovativeness.

A discussion of these interactive features, recently more formally expressed in "critical mass" and "bifurcation" models (see Schelling, 1978; Weidlich & Haag, 1983; and an application to the present context in Witt, 1985) is beyond the scope of the present paper. But even without this the considerations allow for an important insight. If it is indeed likely that the environment's expected reaction influences the individual agent's inclination to try something really new (that cannot be theoretically anticipated), then, depending on the prevailing order in innovation oriented reaction patterns, the human potential for innovativeness may become more or less momentous and, accordingly, the bounds of theoretical unknowledge resulting from the yet unknown more or less relevant. The "Kaleidic Society" (Shackle, 1972) is just the one extreme as it can be observed in the leading present-day industrial countries. Lacking the ability to determine theoretically the direction in which individual economic activities will turn in this case, a closer analysis of the interactive features might at least contribute to a better understanding of how the transition to this extreme could happen, what the prerequisites for maintaining it are, and, possibly, what forces speed up or slow down Shackle's Kaleidics.

Conclusions

The subjective nature of individual intentions, evaluations, and expectations is a major problem in attempts to explain observable economic behaviour. "Austrian" and other subjectivist economists as, e.g., Shackle, have always emphasized its importance. This is in contrast to neoclassical economics where it is played down by means of perfect information assumptions. Important as the problem is, it does not necessitate an aprioristic approach as has been and still is argued by Mises and some proponents of the "Austro-American" school. In fact, as pointed out in the second section of the present paper, in such an approach, if it is to be consistent, economics would be rendered a sterile logic ("praxeology") hardly capable of explaining any empirically observed economic behaviour.

In order to cope with the subjectivism problem, a revival of the idea of a psychological foundation of the theory of economic behaviour has therefore been suggested in the third section. This idea can be found in the work of earlier "Austrian" writers though certainly not as a consistent programmatic vision. The fourth section gave a brief outline of the way in which results from research into human behaviour conducted in neighbouring disciplines could be used to make progress in the explanation of individual economic behaviour without interfering with the subjectivism problem. However, there are bounds to this research strategy, too. As explained in the fifth section, a psychologically founded theory of economic behaviour faces limitations where (objective) novelty is created in the subjective intentions, evaluations, and expectations of individual agents. But since novelty, its emergence and dissemination, is a topic of evolutionary theories in general, even here, by adopting an evolutionary perspective, the suggested basic outlook can provide further insights.

Notes

1. Cf. Lachmann (1976a). There are various strands of subjectivist as well as of "Austrian" economics. For a recent survey, see Shand (1981). Attempts to reconsider subjectivism in economics are contained in the volume edited by Wiseman (1983). Contemporary "Austrian" economists can perhaps best be identified by their contributions to volumes such as those edited by Dolan (1976), Faber (1986), Hayek (1971), Kirzner (1982), Rizzo (1979), Streissler, Haberler, Lutz, & Machlup (1969) but see the discussion on that question by Lachmann (1977a).

2. These include attentional processes (Anderson, 1980, pp. 21-59); memory activation and operation (Norman, 1976, pp. 83-129); the role of decision heuristics and "framing" effects which cause formally equivalent decision problems to be seen differently, depending on the particular context in which they appear (Slovic, Fischhoff, & Lichtenstein 1977; Tversky & Kahneman, 1981); and many other relevant aspects of human cognition and evaluation (see, e.g., the volume edited by Wallsten, 1980).

References

Albert, H. (1985). *Treatise on critical reason.* Princeton: Princeton University Press.

Anderson, J.R. (1980). *Cognitive psychology and its implications.* San Fransisco: W.H. Freeman.

Bandura, A. (1977). *Social learning theory.* Englewood Cliffs, NJ: Prentice Hall.

Boehm, S. (1982). The ambiguous notion of subjectivism: Comment on Lachmann. In I.M. Kirzner (Ed.), *Method, process, and Austrian economics: Essays in honor of Ludwig von Mises,* pp. 41-52. Lexington, MA: Heath.

Buchanan, J.M. (1982). The domain of subjective economics: Between predictive science and moral philosophy. In: I.M. Kirzner (Ed.), *Method, process, and Austrian economics: Essays in honor of Ludwig von Mises*, pp. 7-20. Lexington, MA: Heath.

Caldwell, B.J. (1982). *Beyond positivism: Economic methodology in the twentieth century*. London: Allen und Unwin.

Craver, E. (1986). The emigration of the Austrian economists. *History of Political Economy, 18,* 1-32.

Dolan, E.G. (Ed.) (1976). *The foundations of modern Austrian economics*. Kansas City: Sheed & Ward.

Faber, M. (Ed.) (1986). *Studies in Austrian capital theory, investment, and time*. Berlin: Springer.

Hayek, F.A. (1934). Introduction. In: F.A. Hayek (Ed.), *Collected Works of Carl Menger*. London: London School of Economics and Political Science. Series of Reprints of Scarce Tracts in Economics and Political Science, Vol. 17.

Hayek, F.A. (1937). Economics and knowledge. *Economica, 4,* 33-54.

Hayek, F.A. (1952). *The sensory order - An inquiry into the foundations of theoretical psychology*. London: Routledge & Kegan Paul.

Hayek, F.A. (1967a). The theory of complex phenomena. In: F.A. Hayek, *Studies in philosophy, politics and economics*, pp. 22-42. London: Routledge & Kegan Paul.

Hayek; F.A. (1967b). Notes on the evolution of systems of rules of conduct. In: F.A. Hayek, *Studies in philosophy, politics and economics*, pp. 66-81. London: Routledge & Kegan Paul.

Hayek, F.A. (Ed.) (1971). *Toward liberty: Essays in honor of Ludwig von Mises*. (2 vols). Menlo Park, CA: Institute for Human Studies.

Heiner, R.A. (1983). The origin of predictable behavior. *American Economic Review, 73,* 560-595.

Hey, J.D. (1981). Are optimal search rules reasonable? And vice versa? *Journal of Economic Behavior and Organization, 2,* 47-70.

Kamien, M.I., & Schwartz, N.L. (1982). *Market structure and innovation*. Cambridge: Cambridge University Press.

Kauder, E. (1965). *A history of marginal utility theory*. Chicago: Chicago University Press.

Kirzner, I.M. (1973). *Competition and entrepreneurship*. Chicago: Chicago University Press.

Kirzner, I.M. (1976a). On the method of Austrian economics. In: E.G. Dolan (Ed.), *The foundation of Austrian economics*, pp. 40-51. Kansas City: Sheed & Ward.

Kirzner, I.M. (1976b). Equilibrium versus market processes. In: E.G. Dolan (Ed.) *The foundation of Austrian economics*, pp. 115-125. Kansas City: Sheed & Ward.

Kirzner, I.M. (1979). Hayek, knowledge, and market processes. In: I.M. Kirzner, *Perception, opportunity, and profit – Studies in the theory of entrepreneurship*, pp. 13-33. Chicago: Chicago University Press.

Kirzner, I.M. (Ed.) (1982). *Method, process, and Austrian economics: Essays in honor of Ludwig von Mises*. Lexington, MA: Heath.

Lachmann, L.M. (1951). The science of human action. *Economica, 18*, 412-427.

Lachmann, L.M. (1966). Die geistesgeschichtliche Bedeutung der österreichischen Schule in der Volkswirtschaft. *Zeitschrift für Nationalökonomie, 26*, 152-167.

Lachmann, L.M. (1976a). From Mises to Shackle: An essay on Austrian economics and the kaleidic society. *Journal of Economic Literature, 14*, 54-62.

Lachmann, L.M. (1976b). On the central concept of Austrian economics: Market process. In: E.G. Dolan (Ed.), *The foundations of modern Austrian economics*, pp. 126-132. Kansas City: Sheed & Ward.

Lachmann, L.M. (1977a). Austrian economics in the present crisis of economic thought. In: L.M. Lachmann, *Capital, expectations, and the market process*, pp. 25-41. Kansas City: Sheed Andrews & McMeel.

Lachmann, L.M. (1977b). Economics as a social science. In: L.M. Lachmann, *Capital, expectations, and the market process*, pp. 166-180. Kansas City: Sheed Andrews & McMeel.

March, J.G. (1978). Bounded rationality, ambiguity, and the engineering of choice. *Bell Journal of Economics, 9*, 587-608.

March, J.G., & Simon, H.A. (1958). Organizations. New York: Wiley.

Menger, C. (1871). *Grundsätze der Volkswirtschaftslehre*. Wien: Braumüller.

Mises, L.v. (1949). *Human action – A treatise on economics*. London: W. Hodge.

Mises, L.v. (1957). *Theory and history*. New Haven, CT: Yale University Press.

Norman, D.A. (1976). *Memory and attention – An introduction to human information processing.* New York: Wiley.

O'Driscoll, G., & Rizzo, M. (1984). *The economics of time and ignorance.* London: Basic Blackwell.

Reinganum, J.F. (1984). Practical implications of game theoretic models of R & D. *American Economic Review, 74* (Papers and Proceedings), 61-66.

Rizzo, M.J. (Ed.) (1979). *Time, uncertainty, and disequilibrium.* Lexington, MA: Lexington Books.

Rogers, E.M. (1983). *Diffusion of innovations,*3rd ed. New York: Free Press.

Rothbard, M.N. (1976). Praxeology: The methodology of Austrian economics. In: E.G. Dolan (Ed.), *The foundation of Austrian economics,* pp. 19-39. Kansas City: Sheed & Ward.

Schelling, T.C. (1978). *Micromotives and macrobehavior.* New York: Norton.

Shackle, G.L.S. (1958). *Time in economics.* Amsterdam: North-Holland.

Shackle, G.L.S. (1972). *Epistemics and economics.* Cambridge: Cambridge University Press.

Shackle, G.L.S. (1983). The bounds of unknowledge. In: J. Wiseman (Ed.), *Beyond positive economics?,* pp. 28-37. London: MacMillan.

Shand, A.H. (1981). *Subjectivist economics – The new Austrian school.* Oxford: Short Run Press.

Simon, H.A. (1955). A behavioral model of rational choice. *Quarterly Journal of Economics, 69,* 99-118.

Simon, H.A. (1955). Theories of decision-making in economics and behavioral science. In: *Surveys of economic theory,* Vol. III, pp. 1-28. London: MacMillan.

Slovic, P., Fischhoff, B., & Lichtenstein, S. (1977). Behavioral decision theory. *Annual Review of Psychology, 28,* 1-39.

Streissler, E., Haberler, G., Lutz, F.A., & Machlup, F. (Eds.) (1969). *Roads to freedom: Essays in honour of Friedrich A. von Hayek.* London: Routledge & Kegan Paul.

Streissler, E. (1972). To what extent was the Austrian school marginalist? *History of Political Economy, 4,* 426-441.

Tversky, A., & Kahneman, D. (1981). The framing of decisions and the psychology of choice. *Science, 211,* 453-458.

Vanberg, V. (1975). *Die zwei Soziologien – Individualismus and Kollektivismus in der Sozialtheorie.* Tübingen: Mohr (Siebeck).

Vaughn, K.I. (1982). Subjectivism, predictability, and creativity: Comment on Buchanan. In: I.M. Kirzner (Ed.), *Method, process, and Austrian economics: Essays in honor of Ludwig von Mises,* pp. 21-29. Lexington, MA: Heath.

Wallsten, T. (Ed.) (1980). *Cognitive processes in choice and decision behavior.* New York: Academic Press.

Weidlich, W., & Haag, G. (1983). *Concepts and models of a quantitative sociology.* Berlin: Springer.

Wiseman, J. (Ed.) (1983). *Beyond positive economics?* London: MacMillan.

Witt, U. (1985). Coordination of individual economic activities as an evolving process of self-organization. *Economie Appliquée, 38,* 569-595.

Witt, U. (1986). How can complex economic behavior be investigated – The example of the ignorant monopolist revisited. *Behavioral Science, 31,* 73-188.

Witt, U. (forthcoming). *Individualistic foundations of evolutionary economics.* Cambridge: Cambridge University Press.

Witt, U., & Perske, J. (1982). *SMS – A program package for simulation and gaming of stochastic market processes and learning behavior.* Berlin: Springer.

THEORY AND DECISION LIBRARY

SERIES A: PHILOSOPHY AND METHODOLOGY OF THE SOCIAL
SCIENCES

Already published:

Conscience: An Interdisciplinary View
Edited by Gerhard Zecha and Paul Weingartner
ISBN 90–277–2452–0

Cognitive Strategies in Stochastic Thinking
by Roland W. Scholz
ISBN 90–277–2454–7

Comparing Voting Systems
by Hannu Nurmi
ISBN 90–277–2600–0

Evolutionary Theory in Social Science
Edited by Michael Schmid and Franz M. Wuketits
ISBN 90–277–2612–4

The Metaphysics of Liberty
by Frank Forman
ISBN 0–7923–0080–7

Principia Economica
by Georges Bernard
ISBN 0–7923–0186–2

Towards a Strategic Management and Decision Technology
by John W. Sutherland
ISBN 0–7923–0245–1

Social Decision Methodology for Technological Projects
Edited by Charles Vlek and George Cvetkovich
ISBN 0–7923–0371–7

Reductionism and Systems Theory in the Life Sciences
Edited by Paul Hoyningen-Huene and Franz M. Wuketits